# Transitional Justice in Poland

# Transitional Justice in Poland

## Memory and the Politics of the Past

Frances Millard

BLOOMSBURY ACADEMIC
LONDON • NEW YORK • OXFORD • NEW DELHI • SYDNEY

BLOOMSBURY ACADEMIC
Bloomsbury Publishing Plc
50 Bedford Square, London, WC1B 3DP, UK
1385 Broadway, New York, NY 10018, USA
29 Earlsfort Terrace, Dublin 2, Ireland

BLOOMSBURY, BLOOMSBURY ACADEMIC and the Diana logo
are trademarks of Bloomsbury Publishing Plc

First published in Great Britain 2021
This paperback edition published in 2022

Series design by Adriana Brioso

A catalogue record for this book is available from the British Library.

A catalog record for this book is available from the Library of Congress.

ISBN:  HB:    978-0-7556-0133-2
       PB:    978-0-7556-3661-7
       ePDF:  978-0-7556-0135-6
       eBook: 978-0-7556-0134-9

Typeset by Integra Software Services Pvt. Ltd.,

To find out more about our authors and books visit www.bloomsbury.com
and sign up for our newsletters

To Alan Ball

# Contents

# List of tables

# Foreword

This book examines the range of policies and institutions active in Poland's 'coming to terms with the past' in the post-communist era. The restorative or retributive methods by which countries deal with a dictatorial or authoritarian history are collectively known as mechanisms of transitional justice. In Poland this proved a long process – far lengthier than anyone might have imagined after the fall of communism in 1989. Key areas of policy proved divisive, contentious and difficult to reconcile.

We offer a detailed history from the perspectives of law and politics. The first chapter examines the changing nature of the concept of transitional justice itself and examines how it unfurled in the post-communist context of Central and Eastern Europe. It reviews the areas of particular concern in the region, namely the perpetrators of past crimes which had enjoyed *de facto* political immunity; rehabilitation and compensation for those unjustly prosecuted, the restitution of property illegally seized by the communist regime; the vetting and lustration of office seekers and office-holders to assess whether and how far they had collaborated with the old regime; and providing access to their files for those invigilated or surveilled. The chapter then assesses some of the theoretical perspectives used to illuminate the practice of transitional justice.

Chapter 2 offers an overview of the politics of transitional justice in Poland after 1989. This is a chronological discussion, organized by successive governments rather than themes, to reveal the main political fault lines of Polish politics. Lustration remained a key dividing line between Left and Right, as right-wing governments aimed to extend lustration and took a wider view of 'collaboration' with the communists. Thus there are two chapters on lustration, with one each on rehabilitation and compensation, criminal prosecutions, and the restitution of property. Chapters 8 and 9 shift the perspective from policy areas to two key institutions of transitional justice, the Institute of National Remembrance and the Constitutional Tribunal, affecting policy through its adjudication processes.

The year 2015, with Law and Justice in power and the Social Democrats outside parliament altogether, saw a paradigm shift, foreshadowed in the short-lived governments of 2002–7. Law and Justice was the least forgiving of all political parties. Its view of the requirements of justice was very broad, extending to the rewriting of history to provide justice for the victims of communism and the shaping of the national character to undo the unpatriotic elements instilled by communism. For PiS dealing with the past required wholesale decommunization, purging the country of all vestiges of its elites and ideology. This shift brought an end to transitional justice and a move to a project of wholesale social engineering based on a new nationalist conservatism.

Chapter 10 reviews the key policy areas of this project, aiming to provide a thorough cleansing of the deep state and to bring true justice at last. The notion that communist influence persisted in the elites and structures of the state was a risible pretext to mask the pursuit of power. New laws reshaped the structures of the state, including the Constitutional Tribunal, the judiciary, the civil service and the Institute of National Remembrance. Laws on the media increased state control of newspapers and broadcasting. Jarosław Kaczyński and PiS rejected key tenets of liberal democracy, including the rule of law and respect for pluralist diversity. The European Union proved impotent in the face of this anti-democratic onslaught. It should not need stressing that the rhetoric of justice rang hollow.

1

# Approaches to the study of transitional justice

## Introduction

East Central Europe provides a distinctive arena for the study of transitional justice, and Poland is a particularly interesting case. Like other communist countries Poland was dominated by the Communist Party, with a single ideology of socialism and a planned economy. The collapse of communism in Central Europe was (with the partial exception of Romania) peaceful, spearheaded by the negotiated 'exit from communism' in Poland and Hungary in the early months of 1989. Unlike its counterparts, Poland had a strong opposition movement, the Solidarity trade union, penetrating deep into society and providing a strong negotiating partner for the communists. The Catholic Church, which had proved impossible to suppress, provided an alternative moral compass. Although industry was largely in state hands, a land-owning peasantry farmed the land.

This chapter examines the nature of transitional justice and some key theoretical approaches and explanatory frameworks used by scholars to analyse and understand it. It looks at the features distinguishing the countries of Central and Eastern Europe (CEE) in relation to the scope and mechanisms mobilized to remedy the injustices of the previous regime. This provides the basis for the subsequent in-depth analysis of the Polish case. Although it has been suggested that transitional justice is 'under-theorized',[1] it is hard to see how a single theory could encompass different historical periods, different regions, and the different scope and requisites of modern transitional justice practice. Yet there is no dearth of conceptual clarity and insights to be gained from the various approaches and emphases.

## Seeking Historical Justice

New regimes define themselves in terms of the past as well as the future. All new democracies face the question of how to put the formerly repressive, authoritarian regime behind them. How does society come to terms with its past? How should it punish wrongdoers and acknowledge the victims of oppression? After the end of communism in Europe, scholarly focus centred on democratization in a context of 'multiple transitions' to democratic capitalism.[2] Because the rule of law was the essential underpinning of democracy, institution-building was at the core, with emphasis on the need for new constitutions defining and protecting the rights and liberties of citizens vis-á-vis the state and new state structures securing the separation of powers. The past was the starting point of the future, but the new democratic future could expunge the past. 'Liberating the future from the past' would mean a 'past-free future' very different from the future which would have emerged out of the 'old' past.[3]

Ridding the systems of the vestiges of communism, 'de-communization' was often seen as analogous to the denazification processes following the Second World War.[4] But decommunization made CEE distinctive because of the breadth and depth of the project, namely the need to eliminate the communist parties' pervasive penetration of the state, the economy and society. The new elites sought to generate a multi-faceted transformation of the one-party polity to democracy, the planned economy to capitalism and the society of subjects to an open, pluralist society of active citizens. New structures were necessary but so too were changes of personnel: governments inherited political, economic and social institutions whose senior officials had been appointed with Communist Party approval (the *nomenklatura* system) and who were – nominally at least – infused with communist ideology.

The 'transition paradigm' was dominant, if contentious.[5] However, quite quickly CEE was also deemed a relevant arena for approaches based on the concept of 'transitional justice', which clearly overlap but do not wholly coincide with the democracy-building project or decommunization. The aim of the new democratic regimes was not only to alter the system for the future; it also needed to right the wrongs of the past, providing justice for the innocent victims of the authoritarian system.

## What is transitional justice?

The concept of transitional justice is not straightforward. Firstly, it may refer to a particular concept of justice needed for the interim period of change between one regime and another – a justice that was itself 'transitional'. As a student of communism this is what I assumed when I first came across the concept. When the Bolsheviks took power in Russia in 1917, they could not use the 'old' legal system because they rejected the concept of bourgeois law and the institutional separation of powers; during the period of 'war communism' they dissolved the courts and set up people's courts to be guided by 'revolutionary legal consciousness'.[6] Later the legal system was reconstructed on the new ideological basis of 'socialist legality', with judges and legal personnel subject to the dictates of the Communist Party,[7] whose 'leading role' was eventually given constitutional status. After the imposition of communist power in Eastern Europe, the Soviet model of justice was adopted wholesale.

In the 1990s the problem of transitional justice came to the fore in the context of the collapse of authoritarian regimes. The problem arises because the legal order is a mechanism for maintaining predictability and stability, so law is by nature conservative; it defends and upholds the status quo. At the outset of a putative 'transition' to democracy the rule of law is absent or qualified, but the goal of new elites is a state in which the rule of law is the foundation stone for liberal democracy. The new democratic system necessitates radical change in the law as well as mechanisms to ensure the impartiality and independence of judges. Hence, a special kind of 'justice for the transition' seemed a legitimate concern; the problem of law was an essential problem of regime change. Transitional justice was 'a concept of justice, intervening in a period of political change … ; in extraordinary periods of political upheaval, law maintains order even as it enables transformation.'[8] Law plays a constitutive role in times of change, though existing law (prior law) shapes the possibilities available.

However, the term transitional justice has also been used to refer simply to 'justice meted out during the transition', marked by special concern to address the legacies of human rights abuses. In other words, it can refer to justice 'during the transition', rather than a modification of the concept of justice itself. In 1992 the Conference of the Charter 77 Foundation used the term 'Justice in Times of Transition' (transitional justice has no easy equivalent in the Slavic languages), a term that then mutated into the more succinct 'transitional justice'. One result of the conference was the three-volume collection generated by the Rule of Law Initiative of the United States Institute of Peace. Its approach is encapsulated in the subtitle of this major compendium, *Transitional Justice*: 'how emerging democracies reckon with former regimes'.[9] It focused on the policies adopted for this 'reckoning' in twenty countries in six areas: commissions of inquiry, public access to the files of the former secret police, purges and screening practices, trials and (or) amnesty, statutes of limitations, and compensation and rehabilitation.

This approach also embraced some nuanced differences. There could indeed be a distinctive form of justice, often 'dictated not only by strict principles of justice, but also by the need to balance ethical and legal concerns with the hard realities of politics',[10] especially when the military continued to wield *de facto* power. However, others questioned the notion of a different concept of justice; the viability and credibility of new democracies depended on dealing with 'past injustices through means and procedures … consistent with presently valid standards of justice, such as the rule of law and equality before the law'.[11] Nor was 'transitional justice' necessarily qualitatively different from the problems of change in 'ordinary' societies, which also cope periodically with shocks and value shifts.[12] This latter view was hotly contested by Wojciech Sadurski, who saw transitional justice as *sui generis* in post-communist societies.[13]

The body of scholarship is now very large.[14] As it evolved, the concept of transitional justice became more multi-layered and entailed a more complex and broader approach going beyond the strictly legal focus.[15] This gave rise to a third approach: increasingly transitional justice came to be seen as a concern with 'how societies emerge from violent conflict'.[16] Louis Bickford observed that the influence of the human rights movement on the development of the field made it 'self-consciously victim-centric',[17] but it did not only seek 'recognition for victims (but also the) promotion of possibilities for peace, reconciliation and democracy'.[18] Arthur argues that transitional justice was distinctive not in its concern for the victims of injustice under the old regime but in this wider brief, the normative aim of securing democracy.[19]

The focus on divided societies, riven with bitter conflict and memories of recent atrocities, understandably made reconciliation a key issue of transitional justice in countries like Rwanda or Bosnia, where the integration of ex-combatants and the healing of deep divisions were a key element of social reconstruction. International tribunals and courts were part of this process but so too were international non-governmental organizations for peace-building or conflict resolution. Issues such as poverty and gender equality were fed into the mix.[20] Resources provided by the international community proved significant in impoverished countries such as East Timor and Sierra Leone. The Post-Conflict Justice (PCJ) Dataset deals with 'how post-conflict countries address the wrongdoings committed in association with previous armed conflict'.[21] Yet outside parts of the former Yugoslavia post-communism in Europe was different. It did not entail a recent struggle followed by compromise between 'violently conflicting parties'.[22] The international community did not participate directly, as in Rwanda and Bosnia.[23]

This is why in this study we confine ourselves to the first two approaches noted above, excluding wider issues of the creation of a just society. We are dealing with what Hanson calls an 'orthodox case', where 'a fundamental political transition takes place and the new regime employs transitional justice to deal with rights violations committed under a prior regime'.[24] We will argue that there was a distinctive 'justice of the transition' but only in a very limited sense. In most instances, the 'normal' practices of the rule of law applied.

'Transitional justice' remains useful as a shorthand umbrella term to embrace policies dealing with the human rights abuses of the past and with the implications of the past for the new democratic politics. Of course, reckoning with the past also raises questions about how to identify the 'end' of 'transition'. For our purposes the 'end' of democratic transition did not signal an end to the process of dealing with the past, so transitional justice (in either conception of the term) has a longer lifespan than democratic transition itself.

## Transitional justice in Central and Eastern Europe

Our enquiry is limited to Poland in the context of the so-called Eastern bloc of the USSR. Here transitional justice became a central concern, while in much of the former Soviet Union there was little that could be described as 'transitional justice'. The democratic project was not entrenched and indeed went into reverse in many post-Soviet states, including Russia itself. We will make some references to the Baltic states, but the context of our discussion is the European communist regimes within the 'bloc'.

In CEE, the experience of mass repression, purges and murder had largely ended with the death of Stalin in 1953, though individual countries bore the scars of social resistance: protest in East Germany and Czechoslovakia in 1953, the Hungarian revolution of 1956, the Prague Spring of 1968, protest on the Baltic coast in Poland in 1970 and the imposition of martial law in Poland in 1981. But mass murder, large-scale disappearances or the abduction of children did not constitute features of late communism in CEE. In CEE the population largely maintained its passive acquiescence and accommodation with the regime, despite the institutional denial of everyday democratic rights.

Moreover, there was no institutional threat to the new democratic order. The military, which featured so visibly in parts of Latin America, was not accustomed to a political role even in Poland, which had seen General Wojciech Jaruzelski in charge after 1981. This means that a 'key problem' of transitional justice, that of finding a balance between the demands of justice and politics,[25] seemed peripheral in much of CEE. The velvet nature of the 1989 revolutions meant that they were not protracted; with few exceptions social mobilization against the old regime was limited until the roller coaster began to move in Poland and Hungary, and – with the exception of Yugoslavia, outside the 'Soviet bloc' – only in Romania was violence a (short-lived) feature of the 'revolution'. All elites, old and new, were formally committed to establishing a democratic system. There was no 'dragon living on the patio'[26]; no institutions remained 'on the authoritarian side'.[27]

It is of course undeniable that serious rights' violations occurred under communism in CEE. Although rights were nominally guaranteed by the Constitution, these rights could not manifest 'bourgeois individualism'; they could only be exercised if they were consistent with the 'interests of working people'. Mechanisms such as censorship defined the limits of free expression, internal registration procedures controlled individual mobility, and when state interests were perceived to be at stake the compliant judiciary ensured that 'socialist legality' denied due process and equality before the law. Throughout CEE post-communist governments won power by denouncing the abuses of the old system. The first free elections were 'founding elections'[28]; they were essentially referenda on changing the existing system and the promise of a new order. Therefore, the new governments' legitimacy and political capital would be much diminished if, once in power, condemnation of the old regime were not concretized in appropriate legal measures.[29]

This is not to assume that 'justice' could not be subordinated to other values. Bronwyn Leebaw noted that 'transitional justice institutions were historically seen as a threat to national reconciliation' because by their nature they divided society, opening old wounds and focusing on the past.[30] Dealing with the legacies of repression in a period of dynamic change could seem a potentially destabilizing process for democratization.[31] Moreover, some measure of impunity might be the best way to create the political conditions under which the rule of law is 'eventually attainable'.[32] Adam Michnik and Vaclav Havel, who both suffered imprisonment and maltreatment at the hands of communist authorities in Poland and Czechoslovakia respectively, referred to the 'difficult boundary' between justice and revenge. Michnik said, 'We can only offer absolution on our own behalf; to offer absolution on behalf of others is not within our power. We can try to convince people to forgive, but if they want justice, they have the right to demand it.'[33] He argued that where civil society has been fractured by a tyrannical regime and must be reconstructed, a measure of tolerance would achieve more for human rights in the long run than an insistence on punishment, risking further political instability and divisiveness.

On the other hand, reconciliation may hinder establishing the locus of responsibility and undermine the moral commitment to ongoing remembrance.[34] Moreover, the rhetoric of reconciliation could be seen as 'catering to apologists' for the old regime.[35] Nor is it clear whether pardons and amnesties promote reconciliation.[36] The opponents of a reconciliatory approach saw dealing with the wrongdoers of the past as a prerequisite for a new moral and social order and – possibly – a legal requirement. Calhoun argues, 'If states have certain obligations to prosecute violations of human rights, then this obligation is inherited by successor regimes ... International law stipulates that regime changes and name changes do not alter a state's identity and responsibilities ....a government must assume political responsibility for the actions – just or unjust – of its predecessor.'[37] This is not altogether clear for new regimes, separated from the old by what Peter Digeser calls 'moral firebreaks'.[38] Nonetheless, new regimes certainly have legal obligations to compensate victims of past human rights' abuses[39] and they may – and often do – assume responsibility for trying to repair the injuries done by their predecessors.

## The requisites of transitional justice

Transitional justice may be selective. The aims, scope and tools of transitional justice all require choices to be made, although there seem to be several underlying requirements. Finding the truth or the 'knowledge phase'[40] is essential both as an end in itself and because the nature of the past must be understood in order for its injustices to be remedied. Truth-telling 'clears the fog of secrecy … and lays bare the institutional mechanisms that permitted cruel abuses of power'.[41] There are several dimensions to 'truth telling': revealing the actions of culpable individuals but also 'setting the historical record straight'. Cohen claims that in CEE there was less need to 'find the truth': 'Most people at the time knew what had happened … ; no one really believed the official lies.' The desire – for some at least – was to convert the private knowledge held by citizens into official and public acknowledgement.[42]

It is true that people knew of the privileges of the high ranks of the *nomenklatura*. They knew that the Communist Party controlled the state institutions, that the media served as a propaganda organ of the regime and that the security services maintained a network of informers. They knew that the official histories were tendentious. Yet neither the inner workings of the elite nor the scope and scale of informers were known by the population at large. The truth about specific individuals does not fall into this category of 'already known'.

There was clearly a need to understand how the system had interacted with society. The two sides of the transitional justice coin are the old regime's perpetrators of wrongdoing and its victims. In this context the '"functionaries" of the regime (were) … reconstituted as responsible and potentially culpable agents'.[43] But in CEE the functionaries of the regime were not separate from society, they were embedded in it. In addition, those who had cooperated with the security services as part of the widespread network of covert informers were complicit in wrongdoing and morally culpable in their own right. They too were 'part of' society.

Moreover, much 'private knowledge' about the system was highly suspect. Society maintained a reservoir of inaccurate 'knowledge', fed by rumour and gossip but also in response to the tendentious writing of official history. Since the communist regimes controlled the writing of history for political ends – that is, reframing it in terms of class conflict, the 'stages' of socio-economic development, the benevolence of the USSR, the heroic struggle of the proletariat – perceptions of history had also become an object of political struggle. In Poland history played a particularly significant role in shaping perceptions of the present. Andrzej Walicki observed that in Poland 'everything has a historical dimension … We are living, as it were, with the entire burden of our history'.[44] Koczanowicz noted that 'the construction of the past' can be used as 'a tool to define the structure of the political field ....any struggle for the past is in fact a struggle for the future'.[45] 'Official reports can become histories that obscure and render marginal other accounts and narratives of past violations.'[46] Control over the narratives of the past entails control over the construction of narratives for an imagined future.

The aim of 'truth' is inextricably linked with the aim of justice: Achieving accountability for past state crimes has always preoccupied the human rights movement.[47] 'In formal human rights terms, the driving rationale to investigate and generate knowledge is to identify those responsible and bring them to account.'[48] The human rights community maintains the legal accountability of (i) those who directly carried out or ordered human rights violations, (ii) those whose actions were categorized as gross violations and prohibited by international law, such as genocide and 'crimes against humanity' and (iii) actions that were also illegal by the state's own law at the time. It therefore distinguishes such actions from the routine deeds of an immoral system that would be 'unfair or impossible to prosecute'.[49] But what are the mechanisms of moral accountability for those who lied to and informed on their friends and colleagues?

If truth and justice are overriding and interlinked aims, it is not necessarily the case that truth leads to justice. Yet there are other putative benefits to the processes of dealing with the past for the new polity and society itself. Ignoring violations of the rule of law undermines the very rule of law whose value underpins the new regime. In addition, we have already alluded to arguments about democratic legitimacy. Ignoring rights' violators could seriously undermine the legitimacy of a democratically elected government and generate widespread feelings of cynicism towards the new regime.

Moreover, the security of a new democracy depends on mechanisms to safeguard the democratic process from threats of subversion or sabotage by old elites. After the fall of communism the pervasive retention of *nomenklatura* elements throughout the state apparatus – not just the military and security services – was essential because alternative personnel were not available overnight. But any bureaucracy has the power to delay or obstruct the implementation of government policies. The (sometimes separate) deterrence argument claims that mechanisms of accountability will weaken potential support for any future repetition of the same abuses.

Expiation is another dimension of transitional justice linked to a concept of the moral renewal of society. Cohen argues that 'the enormity of what happened in the old regime requires ... radical responses ... Some kind of ritual cleansing is needed ... to remove impure elements or ways of thinking so that they will lose their power'.[50] For Pogany the policies of transitional justice 'serve as moral signposts for societies which have not yet fully come to terms with their past. In highlighting certain events as particularly egregious they play a part in the construction of moral sensibilities; they represent a highly visible part of a broader educative process'.[51]

## Mechanisms of transitional justice

The mechanisms that serve these ends are varied. Although there are common themes throughout CEE, the 'packages' diverged considerably and varied over time. In no country of the former 'Eastern bloc' was 'forgetting' or official amnesty the chosen option, even where reconciliatory strategies were sought. The criminal and civil laws were both relevant, but there were extra-judicial mechanisms too. Kritz's seminal volume identified prosecution and amnesty, purges and screening, compensation and rehabilitation, commissions of enquiry, and public access to secret police files as the major arenas of transitional justice.[52] Our categories are somewhat different, but the basic content is the same.

## Prosecution

Criminal prosecution of the perpetrators of past crimes is often the first mechanism to be considered by new regimes. Prosecution, Huntington writes, was seen as 'necessary to assert the supremacy of democratic values and norms and to encourage the public to believe in them'.[53] Jakovska and Moran saw criminal prosecution as effective both for confronting the past and for rehabilitating victims.[54] It entails identifying those with individual or collective responsibility; assembling the evidence; organizing a civilian trial conducted by standard legal procedures and the implementation of suitable punishment (but not the death penalty, since all of CEE aspired to membership of the Council of Europe, with its prohibition of capital punishment). Prosecution was the dominant normative model, with 'the Nuremberg version most often cited'.[55] In practice, the prosecution of individuals was widespread but limited: it was not always clear just who was responsible for past crimes, it was difficult to assemble evidence so long after the fact, and the violators enjoyed new rights' protection.[56]

The trials conducted in CEE included those of East Germany's party leader Erich Honecker and Stasi head Erich Mielke, East German Berlin Wall border guards, Bulgarian communist party leader Todor Zhivkov and Prague party leader Miroslav Štěpán. In Poland the process also began later, since the first post-communist coalition government included many of the communist officials later charged. Eventually trials in Poland included the top leadership, including General Wojciech Jaruzelski and former interior minister General Czesław Kiszczak. The process was often protracted: Only in 2016 did the first successful prosecutions take place in Romania.[57]

## Rehabilitation and compensation

Communist regimes saw the wilful distortion of the judicial process to mete out punishment to opponents of the regime. Rehabilitation of the wrongly convicted is the least expensive form of redress, with high symbolic value. However, the law still has a role: it must expunge the record and restore the victim's rights. 'Political prisoners can be rehabilitated by simple public declarations. Victims' names can be cleared by searching the police and secret service files to find the falsely accused, the arbitrarily arrested, the tortured, and then publicly reminding people of what was done to them.'[58]

In CEE the agenda included compensation for those who had suffered physical injury, unjustified deprivation of liberty or loss of career. In Czechoslovakia the 1990 Law on Judicial Rehabilitation cleared the names of 200,000 political prisoners and adjusted their pension rights. Later, former political prisoners received a lump sum with additional payment for each month served. Less generous, Hungary offered former political prisoners a small sum in compensation for the injustices they suffered. The 1992 law on Voiding Convictions annulled convictions for conspiracy, illegal border crossing, 'abusing the freedom of association', incitement and insurrection. Romania by contrast lagged well behind in the compensation and late rehabilitation of its political prisoners.[59] In Poland opposition to the regime was more extensive than elsewhere and so too was the process of rehabilitation. Compensation measures included veterans of the anti-Nazi struggle during the Second World War, as well as the anti-communist opposition to the communist takeover, and protesters in Poznań in 1957 and on the Baltic coast in 1970, as well as many illegally engaged in Solidarity during martial law in 1982. They were gradually extended to embrace virtually all those who had suffered death, injury, detention or other hardship for political reasons.

## Restitution

The seizure of private property in the nationalization and collectivisation programmes of Stalinist regimes made restitution another important dimension of the search for post-communist justice. Not only individuals but institutions too had been dispossessed. Restitution could be natural, the return of property to owners or heirs or granting them similar property or it could entail financial compensation. In Poland the Catholic Church was the most important institution to feature in restitution programmes. The reversal of the formal dominance of atheism and the universal restrictions on church activities under the old regime was common throughout the region, and there was considerable sympathy for demands for the restoration of Church property. There were more difficulties with the restoration of Jewish communal property.

The countries of CEE took varied stances on the restitution of property, depending on the strength of domestic political support; constitutional provisions regarding non-discrimination, existing property rights or duties under international treaties; the potential impact of restitution on privatization or other economic policies; and the strength of pressure from foreign claimants and their sponsors. Hungary passed a limited compensation law in 1991. Its Constitutional Court stated that the state 'has no duty to provide … compensation and no one has a subjective right to it … compensation depends exclusively on the decision of the sovereign state'.[60] In Czechoslovakia the restitution of confiscated property was also enabled by the Rehabilitation Law, so that the rightful owners were considered owners of their properties without interruption. The Czechs offered restitution in kind but only to citizens dispossessed between 1948 and 1990. They too began the restitution of property in 1991.[61] The Czech programme of voucher privatization was also seen as a measure of restitution because the 'industrial wealth that was distributed through vouchers represented fruits of the people's labor [*sic*] that had been denied them for decades'.[62] However, land was not restored to the churches until 2012 and that issue remained controversial. In 2019 the Czech Supreme Court dismissed new laws taxing the compensation churches received from the state for property seized during the communist era.

In Poland by contrast restitution of the property of the Catholic Church was on the reform agenda from the outset. The Solidarity trade union was also a beneficiary of restitution. There were special arrangements for the city of Warsaw and for those dispossessed by changes in Poland's eastern boundary. However, successive Polish governments promised but failed to legislate on individual property restitution. With minor exceptions remedies were only available in the civil courts.

## Vetting and lustration

The most important and most frequently used political instrument in CEE was the personnel vetting process, including lustration. The 'weeding' of the bureaucracy is the main element of vetting processes, whereby those deemed unqualified or unreliable can be prevented by administrative or quasi-judicial means from working in the new institutions. Lustration is somewhat narrower, referring primarily to determining whether a proposed appointee to a government post or candidate for election worked for or collaborated with the communist security services. Bronwyn Leebaw calls these 'purge laws';[63] for Roman David they are 'personnel systems'.[64]

Lustration was an administrative process. It did not posit the criminal responsibility of its targets; after all, neither working for state security nor cooperating with its agencies was an illegal act. But as Los noted, 'Even if the justice discourse does not necessarily call for punishment, and lustration measures are not penal in character, the underlying notion is one of retribution ..... Punishment vindicates justice, and its lack signifies an unfairness to those who have practiced self-restraint and forfeited opportunities for illegitimate advancement.'[65] In Poland vetting and lustration were often conflated, as we shall see. Lustration itself came relatively late and proved unusually protracted.

Lustration measures were universal, if not immediate. The German Unification Treaty provided for extensive lustration, disqualifying for fifteen years tens of thousands of government officials, central and local government politicians, judges and anyone whose job required security clearance. Monika Nalepa described Czechoslovakia (the Czech Republic) and Lithuania as the region's 'eager lustrants'.[66] In Poland the eager lustrants did not at first dominate parliament, but their persistence ensured that lustration never left the political agenda.

## Investigative commissions and access to files

Truth-telling is more complex. Aside from Germany and Romania, post-communist countries did not establish the 'truth commissions' common elsewhere; rather, they opted for procedures to open secret police files alongside truth-seeking institutions such as the Czech Institute for the Study of Totalitarian Regimes or the Polish and Slovak Institutes of National Remembrance.[67] Truth-telling and the opening of the files constituted 'a distinct form of justice'[68] since they did not entail the state imposing punishment on violators. However, most of these institutions had a criminal investigative brief. For example, the Totalitarian Consequences Documentation Centre (TSDC) in Latvia prepared documentation 'for the prosecution of criminal acts' and Poland's IPN had 'the duty to prosecute war crimes and crimes against peace and humanity'. These bodies also had the essential truth-seeking remit for purposes of lustration and for the compensation and rehabilitation of victims.

Initially access to security service files for processes of lustration or other forms of vetting was (in theory) narrowly controlled. Opening the files to members of the public came late to most countries, partly as a consequence of unauthorized 'unofficial disclosure campaigns' to identify secret agents, mostly by non-state actors ('wild lustration').[69] In their pursuit of 'vigilante justice' the wild lustrators sought to compel state institutions and officials to accelerate procedures like lustration, access to secret files and the reform of the intelligence services.[70]

Finding the 'truth' also had implications for rewriting history, as these new institutions had educational and research (history-writing) functions. Strictly speaking, questions of how to correct historical bias are not an issue of transitional justice. However, history – and memory – affected debates about justice. In some cases, incompatible or disputed versions of historical truth were fundamental to cases before the courts and before parliament. Many have pointed out that struggles over the past formed an element of current political strife well into the twenty-first century. A party could gain not only from stressing its own role in opposing the communist regime but also from allegations (or evidence) that a rival party was rife with former agents or informers.[71] Equally important were attempts to control the writing of the new history.

## Explanations of post-communist transitional justice

Scholars have offered various (often related) explanations for the course of transitional justice in CEE. Some focused on a particular dimension of the regimes' 'coming to terms with the past', such as criminal prosecution[72] or lustration.[73] However, these explanations cannot automatically be extrapolated to the body of transitional justice measures.

### Historical approaches

Historical approaches provided the first group of explanations, focusing solely on the decision to prosecute past crimes. Samuel Huntington identified transition type (the 'mode of exit' from communism) as the key factor here. 'Officials of strong authoritarian regimes that voluntarily ended themselves were not prosecuted; officials of weak authoritarian regimes that collapsed were punished if they were promptly prosecuted by the new democratic government.'[74]

Huntington was criticized on a number of grounds, including his emphasis on prosecution and his categorization of the 'mode of exit'. He did not, for example, regard Czechoslovakia (as most do) as a case of regime collapse or elite 'replacement'. Huntington seemed to view strength as evidenced by negotiated change, while regimes that collapsed were thereby 'weak'. However, this post-facto concept of a strong or weak regime is highly debatable. Moreover, Huntington believed that a new government had to act 'promptly': 'In new democratic regimes, justice comes quickly or it does not come at all.'[75] This suggests that in regimes with 'negotiated' modes of exit justice would 'not come at all'. Yet there were many cases where prosecution was delayed, including in Poland, where 'bringing communist criminals to justice' was a recurring theme well into the twenty-first century.

The nature of the former regime was also the focus of John Moran's early study of criminal prosecutions. Countries emerging from more repressive regimes were 'more likely' to prosecute because their citizens had had no opportunity to voice dissent or to leave the country. In contrast, the possibility of 'exit' or 'voice' under the old regime meant that steam could be released as in a pressure cooker, and so the new system saw fewer calls for punishment. Without such release the former torturers faced 'explosive situations in the post transition period'.[76] So the more liberal the communist regime, the more lenient the citizenry; the more a regime silenced dissent or refused the possibility of exit, the more inclined was the population to seek retribution and hold former communist officials accountable. Aside from the questionable assumption that demands for justice came primarily from the people, rather than from new elites, there is no linear link between degrees of communist repression and popular attitudes.

Nadya Nedelsky also stressed historical factors as shaping subsequent attitudes to old elites. However, she argued that theories emphasizing the 'mode of exit' could not explain different attitudes to lustration in the Czech Republic and Slovakia, countries with a shared past and shared mode of exit. A more influential factor was the level of the preceding regime's legitimacy, indicated during the communist period by levels of societal co-optation, opposition or internal exile, and during the post-communist period by levels of elite re-legitimization and public interest in 'decommunization'.[77] She defined legitimacy as 'the extent to which people view a regime as acting in accordance with acceptable standards and principles of governance'. 'Lower levels of regime repression in Slovakia both reflected and produced a higher level of regime legitimacy than existed in the Czech lands.' Greater regime legitimacy in Slovakia 'contributed to a lesser interest in transitional justice there'.[78]

Because legitimacy reduced repression, affecting future attitudes to the communist past, legitimacy is the key explanatory factor. Unlike many, Nedelsky downplays the importance of religious dissidence in Slovakia.[79] There were certainly differences in the communist experience in Czechoslovakia. But legitimacy is hard to get a handle on, and in 1990 Slovaks voted out the communists with the same fervour as did Czechs. Lustration and other mechanisms of transitional justice took longer in Slovakia, but they did surface in the end.

Jaskovska and Moran revisited Moran's 'pressure cooker' analogy in 2006, arguing that it still provided the best point of departure for identifying the determinants of post-communist transitional justice. They went further by suggesting not only that communist-era exit and/or voice provide release valves in post-communism, but also that additional escape valves existed when the previous communist regime enjoyed high political legitimacy, when nationalism replaced communism as the dominant form of political legitimacy, or when the torturers themselves disappeared through death or exile. Unless one of these valves relieved the pressure, the country would arrive at a point at which criminal, civil or political adjudications would be realized. Thus the process need not be speedy. They admitted that an 'untainted, non-communist leadership plays an important role in this process', and 'the presence of a large communist party' seems influential in 'increasing the likelihood of post-communist retribution'.[80]

The notion that new regimes were responding to popular pressure (or lack thereof) retained its salience in most historically based explanations. Yet it is hard to find 'explosive situations' in CEE, where even the execution of Nicolae Ceausescu in Romania arose not from popular anger but from elite expediency. Indeed, it has been suggested that throughout the region the public were not much engaged in issues of the past. 'Popular indifference' arose because of 'the relatively "soft" nature of political repression' during the final decades of the communist regimes and the reduced number of victims in the 1980s, preoccupation with economic crisis and the 'new values' affirmed by politicians.[81] Since economic transition was primary, 'retribution for the past was difficult, had low priority, and quickly led to an impasse'.[82] In several countries, including Poland – after 1985 a 'lenient' communist regime – the issue of prosecutions did not disappear. Society remained divided, and while for some forgiveness may have figured, forgetting certainly did not.

**Political explanations**

Gradually political explanations began to supplement or replace historical arguments. Although the power relations of key actors were implicit in Huntington's argument that wholesale removal of the old elite created more scope for transitional justice, Helga Welsh made this dimension explicit. Welsh argued that while the extent of repression and the impact of different modes of transition remained important, increasingly the 'weight of the past' was replaced by the 'politics of the present', when the electoral strength of former communists became key: when they were weaker, decommunization efforts became easier.[83] Calhoun agreed that 'during the transition and the months immediately following, the balance of power among political forces is a valuable predictor of policy choices. Opposition forces will exact retribution if they can; a mobilized population will demand it'.[84]

Again, these generalizations cannot explain why 'retribution' featured in Czechoslovakia but not in Hungary. After the 1990 elections Opposition governments had large parliamentary majorities, facing weak communists (Czechoslovakia) or ex-communists (Hungary). It is hard to credit the Hungarian population with any gratitude to the communists for the negotiated 'mode of exit'. This makes more sense in Poland: communists shared power in a coalition government for some months after semi-competitive elections in June 1989, and the ex-communists in parliament endorsed radical democratizing and pro-market legislation. Yet after the first free election in 1991 the new Polish parliament was dominated by opposition forces, but not all 'decommunizing efforts' became easier.

Still, Welsh offered crucial insights into the dynamics of transitional justice. Although 'the tendency to forgive and forget is enhanced by the passage of time', troubling issues do resurface: 'The issues of dealing with the past never cease to be instrumental in the struggle for political power.'[85] They could also be used by different post-communist politicians against their rivals. 'Justice' could become an instrument of power politics. This division was particularly important in Poland.

Kieran Williams, Aleks Szczerbiak and Brigid Fowler built on Welsh's insights to explain why, despite calls for action from opposition elements in Poland, Hungary and Czechoslovakia, lustration policies differed greatly in their content and their timing. They identified five sources of 'demand' for lustration: Firstly, specific incidents triggered fears about the continuing influence of communist security services. Secondly, disillusionment with broader post-communist outcomes led some elites to attribute failures to continuing communist influence. Thirdly, lustration gave the post-communist right a weapon against both ex-communists and other parties of the former opposition. Fourthly, dissatisfaction with earlier efforts at lustration gave it continuing salience, especially when combined with the final factor, perceived public demand. None of these had much to do with the nature of the communist regime or the mode of exit from it. 'Equally, none need necessarily fade in potency over time .... Indeed, demands for lustration as a means of tackling post-communist ills, or in reaction to unsatisfactory earlier lustration efforts, may ... increase in strength over time as frustration rises.'[86] Whether policies were enacted obviously depended on access to political power and the ability to assemble a pro-lustration coalition in the legislature.

Williams had noted in earlier work that lustration in Czechoslovakia owed less to concerns for historical justice than to fears for the security of the new democratic regime.[87] Szczerbiak concluded that the chief motives for lustration in Poland were a desire for openness in public life together with the need to protect national security and prevent the so-called wild lustration.[88] However, motives may not be shared by all members of a coalition, motives may be mixed and they may also change over time. All these are dimensions to be investigated.

Lavinia Stan combined historical and political arguments to explain attitudes to the past. She concluded that opponents of the previous regime provided the impetus to lustration and file access, while former communists generally opposed them. The outcome of their struggle depended on the composition, orientation and strength of the opposition, both before and after 1989; whether repression or co-optation was the old regime's dominant method of ensuring societal compliance; and the extent of pre-communist experience with political pluralism. Where communist elites remained entrenched for longer, lustration came later and was more limited than in countries with more powerful opposition forces. Stan does not explain how the pre-communist experience affected the nature of opposition under the communists, but it is hard to deny that opposition elites were shaped by their experience of communist rule.[89]

## Rational choice

While elite self-interest forms part of the political explanation for many authors, Monika Nalepa rests her analysis of the nature and timing of lustration on the calculations and self-interested behaviour of new parties and elites. Rational choice approaches can indeed be helpful, though Nalepa's conclusions are not always convincing, at least in relation to Poland. Her starting point is a series of questions: Why did the communists allow free elections, since they could have anticipated defeat?[90] Why did opposition parties keep the promises of amnesty made at roundtables, that is, why did they eschew retribution and refrain from transitional justice measures? Why did post-communists themselves opt to implement lustration? And finally, what factors led to a resurgence of demands for lustration? We will investigate these issues later, but a few points are in order here.

In Poland the communists did not 'allow' free elections. The 1989 election was semi-competitive, deliberately designed so that the communists would retain power. The communists underestimated Solidarity's appeal, and they made elementary tactical mistakes, including providing a freely elected Senate. There is certainly no evidence of a 'deal over amnesty' at the Polish Round Table. Solidarity is often deemed to have 'won' at the Round Table,[91] but both sides believed the communists would continue to govern Poland after the election. Issues of the 'past' could not be negotiated because the limits of Soviet tolerance remained unclear; 'it was hard even to dream of the end of communism.'[92] No one in the Solidarity camp envisaged the possibility that Solidarity could take power immediately. Although it has been claimed that following Solidarity's election victory senior communists planned to seek guarantees against 'persecution', the evidence offered is very thin.[93] Certainly many party members were fearful of Solidarity, but there is no evidence that the Party sought or received such assurances – and why would it?

Nor is it the case that the liberal opposition (in coalition with the communists in 1989–90) refrained from transitional justice measures. In fact, many policies (though not lustration) were put in place during the first post-communist government under Tadeusz Mazowiecki. Nalepa claims that former dissidents delayed lustration because 'they feared the "skeletons in their own closets," i.e. secret police and informers among their own ranks'[94]; thus 'the opposition's preferences over transitional justice were shaped by its beliefs about its degree of infiltration.'[95] There is no evidence for this view. The practical constraints of the international context, the demands of coalition and the liberal values of the erstwhile oppositionists are far more important than fears of revelations about their opposition activities.

Moreover, why revealing these 'skeletons' should be thought so damaging is not clear. That the secret police had infiltrated Solidarity was widely known in general terms; despite some surprising revelations, the extent of collaboration revealed was never such as to seriously damage the Solidarity liberals of the first government. There were many genuine arguments against lustration, as we shall see. It is misleading to argue that the 'promises of amnesty' [*sic*] were finally broken 'with the rise of political elites who had not been infiltrated by the secret police'.[96] The parliamentary coalition that passed the first lustration law in 1997 was a mixture of centre–right elements, supported by a successor party, the Polish Peasant Party (PSL). Subsequently liberal elements of the new party Civic Platform (*Platforma Obywatelska*, PO) supported legislation from Jarosław Kaczyński's Law and Justice Party (*Prawo i Sprawiedliwość*, PiS). The argument that things changed because 'non-collaborating parties came to power'[97] cannot be substantiated.

Nalepa concluded that when former communists anticipated losing power, as in Hungary in 1994 and Poland in 1997, they sought to prevent the harsher legislation favoured by hard-line anti-communists. They behaved rationally by initiating less punitive versions of transitional justice than proposed by their anti-communist rivals. For the former communists, shifting to support lustration was not the result of the desire for an honest re-examination of the past but a pre-emptive strategy designed to protect their political careers from more radical policies.

In fact, the proposals embodied in Poland's 1997 law were very similar to those proposed by parties of the former opposition in 1992 (these details will be discussed later). The ex-communist SLD remained unenthusiastic about lustration, it is true; the past was hardly an electoral asset for them. But there were rational grounds for voting against the legislation, not on 'anti-lustration' grounds but because of serious gaps and flaws in the draft.

So rational choice arguments have some purchase, but they cannot stand alone. We share Lavinia Stan's view: to reduce complex phenomena to 'a manipulating tool used in the cut-throat battles waged by power-thirsty political parties or to relegate it to the grey zone of illusory and unattainable myths ignores the Eastern Europeans' need to know the truth about the communist regime, to confront their own personal history, and to obtain justice and absolution.'[98]

## Conclusion

We have seen that notions of 'transitional justice' have evolved to become ever more complex and wider in scope. A very wide brief does not seem pertinent for Central Europe, so we restrict ourselves to analysing the measures taken to 'come to terms with the communist past' and to redress its human rights' abuses. This will also entail an investigation of (1) whether there was a particular, distinctive quality of justice in these measures and (2) how far the measures reflected a coherent, consistent policy to deal with past wrongs.

Clearly actors' experience of the communist regime varied – not just along the communist vs Solidarity fault-line but among (ex)communists and within Solidarity. These experiences shaped actors' understanding and expectations. While general historical factors such as the level of repression or (lack of) regime legitimacy affected the capacity of opposition forces to emerge and take on the role of a counter-elite, they cannot explain the subsequent behaviour of either the successors or the new elites.

The balance of political forces in parliament is critical to the passage of legislation, and the shifting political configuration in Poland was crucially important to changing views of the past and how to 'deal with' it. Nationalists proved advocates of harsher transitional justice measures than did liberals or social democrats. While electoral advantage remained a pertinent factor, narrowly constructed concepts of self-interest ignore the ideological and ethical dimensions of 'interest'. The first two Solidarity governments (1989–91) were dominated by liberals who eschewed vengeful acts of transitional justice. The right-wing Olszewski government (1991–June 1992) tried and failed to extend its scope to lustration. Suchocka's Solidarity coalition (July 1992–September 1993) deliberately avoided matters of ideological disagreement.

Contingent events are also vital in times of structural flux. Accusations in 1992 that Lech Wałęsa was a 'collaborator' and 'traitor' generated a lasting divide among Solidarity's right-wing politicians. The first social democratic government (1993–7) was forced to confront lustration after shocking allegations that its own prime minister passed secret information to Soviet and Russian intelligence. The subsequent broad-based Solidarity government of Solidarity Election Action (1997–2001), dominated by right-wing anti-communist forces, kept transitional justice issues high on its agenda, with new institutions and wider scope for lustration and individual access to files.

After a hiatus under a second social democratic government (2001–5), Jarosław Kaczyński, a consistent proponent of hard-line measures since 1989, brought in new lustration measures with the support of Civic Platform (PO). These measures were – in part – overturned by the Constitutional Court. Indeed, throughout the period the impact of earlier decisions was reflected in the activities of judicial institutions creating a dynamic parallel to the current political process. Decisions by the courts – including the Constitutional Court – often altered the trajectory envisaged by the politicians. The multiplicity of actors, changing political configurations, and the changing scope of concern, make it unsurprising that there is no single 'theory' to explain transitional justice.

2

# The politics of transitional justice in Poland 1989–2015

## Introduction

This chapter sketches the background and provides an overview of the arenas of transitional justice in Poland after 1989. Although there were areas of consensus, a series of disjointed policy zigzags matched the shifting composition of parliament and government. Two interim governments followed the semi-competitive 'Round Table' election – Tadeusz Mazowiecki's Grand Coalition and the liberal minority government of Jan Krzysztof Bielecki. Fully democratic elections came in October 1991. From then up to 2005, the electoral balance shifted back and forth between Solidarity parties and social democrats (ex-communists). Policies of transitional justice followed suit. After 2005, two Solidarity parties of the right dominated the political scene. Policies shifted from the more moderate policies of Civic Platform (PO) to the radical policies of Law and Justice (PiS).

When PiS gained a parliamentary majority in 2015, a new period of change ensued. Transitional justice gave way to social engineering, beginning with the structures of government. This period will be reviewed in a separate chapter. PiS's new 'measures of transitional justice' had little to do with justice. Notions of justice provided the rhetorical cloak for its programme of full-scale political and social transformation. Justice required the cleansing of the political system, purging all elements and networks surviving from the communist regime. PiS's victory in the 2019 election gave it the political capacity and legitimacy to continue this project.

## The fall of communism

The collapse of communism in Poland began on 6 February 1989, with Round Table negotiations between the ruling PZPR (communist party) and the main opposition, the free Solidarity trade union. On 24 August Solidarity intellectual Tadeusz Mazowiecki became the region's first non-communist prime minister since the Second World War. His government embraced Solidarity, the PZPR and two smaller 'old-regime parties', the Peasants and the Democrats. It took key decisions transforming Poland from communism to a democratic polity with a market economy.

After the suppression of Solidarity by martial law in December 1981, coercion, imprisonments and harassment punctuated the remaining years of the decade. The murder of Father Jerzy Popiełuszko by functionaries of the regime in October 1984 reinforced public distrust, despite the trial and sentencing of the perpetrators.[1] At the same time General Wojciech Jaruzelski's regime embarked on a strategy of controlled participation and political innovation. His new 'social contract' was also intended to enlist popular support for economic reform. Jaruzelski failed on all counts.

The bankruptcy of the regime's efforts to control a recalcitrant society and a troubled economy by various measures of coercion and reform culminated in the unprecedented undertaking of negotiations between the regime and (still illegal) Solidarity. The Round Table provided the mechanism by which the regime crumbled, and it established the political and ideological dispositions of the first non-communist government.

Negotiations began in an atmosphere of anxious uncertainty. Internal opposition to negotiations was strong within both the PZPR and Solidarity. It was a risky strategy for Solidarity,[2] which feared being sucked into a position of responsibility without power, becoming an effective pawn of the communists.[3] Solidarity's leader Lech Wałęsa faced charges of betrayal from internal critics and other radical opposition groupings.

At the Round Table Politburo member Janusz Reykowski argued that negotiations could be effective only if conflicts over the past were put to one side. This view was accepted after 'heated debate'.[4] Lech Wałęsa made a similar point: 'We must speak about the future. Our evaluations of the past – of the last 48 years – differ, but our task is to save the country.'[5] In fact, the past was not absent: Solidarity demanded its own revival and the re-legalization of other associations banned under martial law, as well as the reinstatement of workers dismissed for union activism and protest after 1981, and compensation for losses and imprisonment (the government rejected the principle of compensation).[6] But evaluating the past was put on hold during the Round Table.

The Round Table took four major decisions: (1) the re-legalization of Solidarity; (2) semi-free elections for the lower house, the *Sejm*, with 65 per cent of seats guaranteed to the communists and their existing coalition partners and 35 per cent to be freely contested; (3) wholly free elections for the new Senate; and (4) a new executive presidency. The first formal act of rehabilitative justice was a direct consequence of the Round Table agreement. In May 1989 the communist *Sejm* passed the so-called abolition law.[7] It aimed to aid the 'normalization of social life and to permit citizens who had infringed the legal order for political reasons to play a full part in political life' by expunging certain offences committed between 31 January 1980 and 29 May 1989. Communist power was set to continue, leavened by the presence of genuine opposition deputies in parliament.

The outcome of the purported 'non-confrontational elections' in June surprised both sides: Solidarity won all contested seats in the *Sejm* (35 per cent) and all but one seat in the Senate (99 per cent). The campaign revealed strategic errors and miscalculations by the party's negotiators.[8] Above all, the communist leaders had assumed that their traditionally subservient junior partners would remain irrelevant ciphers. It did not take long for the Peasant Party (ZSL) and the Democratic Party (SD) to assert themselves. This placed the communists' majority in doubt and with it the forming of the government and the election of the president, a post generally understood to be reserved for Wojciech Jaruzelski.

The new parliament elected Jaruzelski president by a margin of a single vote, but there was no majority for his prime ministerial nominee. After fraught negotiations, all sides accepted the candidacy of Solidarity's Tadeusz Mazowiecki. Mazowiecki's Grand Coalition lasted from September 1989 until July 1990, when he removed most communist ministers, leaving Solidarity effectively in charge. During his brief tenure, until January 1991, after losing on the first ballot of the presidential election, Mazowiecki initiated fundamental changes inaugurating the process of Poland's transformation. All parties in the so-called contract *Sejm* supported the principles of democratic reform. In January 1990, when the Communist Party dissolved itself, the triumph of its pro-reform wing was sealed. The PZPR's successor was a new party, Social Democracy of the Kingdom of Poland (SdRP), committed to multi-party democracy and the market economy. Later it became the Alliance of the Democratic Left (*Sojusz Lewicy Demokratycznej*, SLD).

Parliament rapidly agreed a new series of constitutional amendments designed to embody democratic principles. From 29 December 1989 the Polish Republic was restored, a 'democratic state based on the rule of law, realising the principles of social justice'. By March 1990 'socialism' and the Communist Party had disappeared from the Constitution, along with reference to Poland's alliance with the Soviet Union. Local authorities became autonomous organs of 'self-government' rather than agents of central government. Instead of strict limits on the private sector, economic activity was guaranteed freedom of action without regard to type of ownership. Individual civil liberties were no longer automatically limited by the superior rights of the collective or subject to arbitrary political interference.

Economic crisis and the burden of high levels of foreign debt placed the economy centre stage for Mazowiecki's government. Within a fortnight the government presented a draft programme intended to 'transform the Polish economy into a market economy'.[9] The package of economic reforms constituting the 'big bang' or 'shock therapy' was ready by the end of 1989.

## Mazowiecki and transitional justice

Economic hardship was the major source of society's gradual disillusion with Mazowiecki's government, but issues of 'decommunization' provided another focus for growing opposition within the Solidarity camp. In his bid for the presidency in 1990 (Jaruzelski's resignation making the election possible) Lech Wałęsa stressed 'decommunization' and the 'acceleration' of reform. Dissatisfied elements within Solidarity saw Mazowiecki's approach as weak, indecisive and pandering to elements of the old regime.

Mazowiecki had eloquently laid out the stall for his premiership in the *Sejm* in September 1989, promising a radical reform programme, a pluralist democratic polity based on the rule of law and the promise of a new beginning.[10] He began with a reminder of the nature of his government: 'This will be a coalition government based on far-reaching reform ... (which) can be realised only by a government open to the cooperation of all forces represented in parliament and based on new political principles ... We need to re-establish the mechanisms of normal political life.' The most frequently cited passage in Mazowiecki's exposé reads as follows:

> My government bears no responsibility for the situation it has inherited, though these conditions will continue to influence the circumstances in which we have to act. We will mark off the past with a thick line (*gruba linia*). We will be responsible only for what we ourselves do now to rescue Poland from its current crisis. ....
> (T)his road will lead us to normality. We must replace the principle of struggle ... with the principle of partnership. Otherwise we cannot move from a totalitarian system to democracy.[11]

Mazowiecki's tone was certainly conciliatory – a partnership of equal citizens, a government of 'all Poles, regardless of their attitudes and convictions', a lack of thirst for revenge, mutual respect in international relations. However, to read the speech as signalling that the past should be *forgotten* is a misrepresentation of both the ideology and the actions of the new government. Yet within months Mazowiecki's opponents had rewritten the thick line (*gruba linia*) as a thick full stop (*gruba kreska*) to suggest that the new government effectively sought to ignore issues of the past.

The putative absence of 'decommunization' was a central criticism of Mazowiecki in the presidential election, when Solidarity split. Jarosław Kaczyński created a broad alliance based on support for Wałęsa, decommunization, the 'acceleration' of privatization and the removal of the *nomenklatura*. From the outset Kaczyński had taken a radical view. He favoured breaking the Round Table agreement, forming a Solidarity government and moving rapidly towards full democracy and wholly free elections.[12] He had negotiated with the peasants and democrats for a Solidarity-led, non-communist coalition.[13] For him the Grand Coalition was a 'horrendous super-blunder';[14] and the 'thick full stop' (*gruba kreska* [sic]) meant that 'we cannot change the political set-up (*układ*)'.[15]

The notion that Mazowiecki pursued a policy of 'forgetting the past'[16] also pervaded scholarly studies, with claims that the new prime minister gave victims wronged by the old regime 'no voice'.[17] Mazowiecki chose the 'Spanish model',[18] adopting 'a principled forgetting in service to a new beginning'.[19] Some maintained that Solidarity had effectively promised amnesty as early as the Round Table.[20] At the least the opposition promised the communists a 'soft landing'.[21] Andrzej Walicki also saw the 'Spanish model' as the template. He rightly emphasized the political context of the Round Table and the mutual respect of both sides for the agreement; he viewed the thick line as an affirmation that 'in conditions of political freedom ... past loyalties would not be regarded as reasons for discrimination', reassuring members of the PZPR and helping them to accept their political defeat.[22] It is big jump, however, from mutual respect to a 'do nothing' or 'Spanish' approach to the past.

There are two main reasons for rejecting the view that Mazowiecki sought the 'Spanish road'. Firstly, we found no evidence that a promise of amnesty was the price of Solidarity's agreement with the communists (see Chapter 1). Indeed, given the circumstances – the limited aims of the Round Table, the PZPR's belief in its own invincibility and the shock of both sides at the election results in June – the capacity of Solidarity to grant amnesty was simply inconceivable. Only in July 1990 did the political dominance of Solidarity become a realistic vision.

Moreover, the very fact of coalition government, with communist ministers holding key 'power ministries' of the interior and defence, was a major limitation on the power of the prime minister. The Soviet Union still cast its shadow over the new government. Poland still belonged to the Warsaw Pact, with Soviet troops stationed on its territory. Mazowiecki was constrained by the requirements of coalition and the international situation and preoccupied above all with economic issues.

Secondly, there was considerable activity, in government and in the new 'contract *Sejm*'. Solidarity controlled the Senate, while the *Sejm* was made up (roughly) as follows: 38 per cent PZPR ((ex)communist); 35 per cent Solidarity; 17 per cent Peasant (ZSL); 6 per cent Democrat (SD) and 5 per cent Catholic. Deputies mustered large majorities for issues of transitional justice. During Mazowiecki's tenure institutional reform took place and steps were taken in the pursuit of criminal prosecutions, rehabilitation, restitution and personnel.

### Criminal investigations

On 17 August 1989 (just before the instauration of Mazowiecki's government) the *Sejm* established a commission to examine security-service involvement in political murders during the 1980s. The Rokita Commission[23] investigated, among others, a list provided by the Helsinki Committee of ninety-three persons whose deaths suggested the involvement of the security services. It did not deal with four cases, including the death of the young student Grzegorz Przemyk in 1983 and the murder of Father Jerzy Popiełusko in 1984, because the procuracy had already renewed its own investigations.

The commission worked until September 1991. It exposed the methods used to subvert the judiciary (widely known to Western scholars[24]): failure to investigate and to secure evidence, the distortion of evidence, the manipulation and exclusion of witnesses, intimidation, assumptions about guilt and innocence, provocation, intimidation, and the use of violence. It concluded that 'functionaries of the security administration and the militia possessed effective immunity. All state institutions were geared to rejecting responsibility …. In all the cases we examined, the hypothesis that an officer was responsible was excluded from consideration … This model of irresponsibility was systemic, with the status of an unwritten but universally accepted principle of the system'.[25]

The commission recommended the initiation of proceedings against officials in 122 unexplained deaths. It named some 170 officials considered unsuitable for further employment by the state. It is true that some ex-communists called for a 'Spanish solution' (while acknowledging that individuals who committed criminal acts should be brought to justice) – and even some Solidarity ministers like Jacek Kuroń agreed – setting the past aside for the sake of building a strong future.[26] The election was imminent and the report received little media attention (it was not published until 2005).

But the members of the commission certainly took these issues seriously. They urged that after free elections an investigative commission with full powers should consider the period of martial law, preparations for which 'contravened the constitution', and should bring charges against 'all who permitted (*dopuściły się*) criminal acts by the standards of then–then existing law'.[27]

The Rokita committee found it difficult to get access to certain documents. Communist archives had already emerged as a sphere of concern. Early in 1990 student demonstrators found evidence that documents were being shredded and demanded the safeguarding of the files of the communist party and the interior ministry. Solidarity deputies asked the government to guarantee the security of the archives.

In response (ex-communist) Minister Kiszczak issued an order to halt the destruction of files, and the 'Michnik Commission' undertook a general evaluation of security-service archives, albeit without access to individual files.[28] The director of the Modern History Archive sat with two other historians and the editor of *Gazeta Wyborcza*, Adam Michnik. They compiled a short report, confirming the destruction of many files. In December 1989 Mazowiecki placed political 'advisers' as his eyes and ears in the interior and defence ministries.[29] However, the removal and destruction of documents left a long-lasting bitter political taste. The condition and veracity of the files later became a central element of subsequent controversies.

The investigation of former functionaries led to several early trials, if few speedy resolutions: many cases dragged on for years, well into the new century. These were cases seared into the public consciousness, the murders of Grzegorz Przemyk and Father Popiełuszko most deeply of all. In both cases the communists had sought to placate the public by bringing alleged perpetrators to trial; in both cases they failed. The feeling that those truly responsible remained at large was widespread.

Przemyk, son of the opposition poet Barbara Sadowska, was nineteen when he was arrested in May 1983, ostensibly for not carrying his identity document. Two days later he was dead – savagely beaten by militiamen. Przemyk's funeral constituted the most significant mass gathering since the imposition of martial law in December 1981.[30]

Intense public reaction to Popiełuszko's murder in October 1984 threw the communist leadership into turmoil and led to decisive action: Colonel Adam Pietruszka was sentenced to twenty-five years for incitement to murder, and the three perpetrators received twenty-five years, fifteen years and fourteen years. But charges against the head of the security services, Władysław Ciastoń, were dropped; he was transferred to a diplomatic post. The 'trial was skilfully stage-managed ... to demonstrate that the conspiracy did not reach into the higher echelons of the security agency'.[31]

In October 1990 Ciastoń and Zenon Płatek were charged with masterminding Popiełuszko's murder. Płatek had headed the infamous IV Department which dealt with the Catholic Church. Later the procuracy also brought charges over deaths resulting from the use of live ammunition during a demonstration in Lubin in August 1982.

### Personnel policy

In May 1990 the government reorganized the interior ministry, and the Bureau of State Protection (UOP) replaced the Security Service (SB). Solidarity Senator Krzysztof

Kozłowski found that when he arrived in March as undersecretary in the ministry, 'the generals there ... believed that they had nothing to reproach themselves with; they did not intend to make concessions or to resign, just to continue to serve faithfully.'[32] However, the ensuing shake-up was considerable. Some 14,000 people took advantage of early retirement provisions, including virtually the entire upper echelon. The remaining lower ranks would be 'verified' by Central and district Qualification Commissions, whose mandate was to exclude from UOP and the police all who had previously violated the law or basic human rights[33] (though some right-wing politicians rejected verification in principle).

The commissions consisted of government representatives, senators, deputies (including former communists), lawyers and representatives from Police Headquarters and from Solidarity's police union. Of 24,000 former SB functionaries, about 14,500 presented themselves for verification. Of these some 3,500 were rejected, while about 10,000 were deemed suitable for further service,[34] albeit with much criticism that the commissions were over-lenient. Some 'verified' candidates later became the subject of political controversy, like Gromosław Czempiński and Wiktor Fonfara, who assumed senior positions in UOP. However, Kozłowski, the first director of UOP, remained convinced that 'those who were not criminals, even though educated and shaped by a different political reality, should have been given the chance to show that ... they could carry out their functions honestly and professionally.'[35]

The 'verification' of procurators was less demanding. Prosecutors submitted a description of their qualifications and activities; on that basis the minister of justice decided whether a procurator would be reappointed. The minister defended the 'simplicity and inexpensive nature' of this system. Only 359 of 3,278 procurators were not reappointed, with 48 restored on appeal – that is, about 10 per cent were dismissed.[36]

Controversy surrounding the judiciary was initially rather muted. Some judges were deemed to have acquitted themselves quite well during martial law. (This assessment was later questioned.) Many discredited judges resigned in 1989–90 or took early retirement. Some were removed after October 1991, when parliament passed a law permitting the removal of judges 'who had compromised judicial independence'[37] (they were not reinstated when the Constitutional Tribunal invalidated the law as too broad[38]).

### Rehabilitation of the wrongfully convicted

Mazowiecki's government also addressed the issue of rehabilitation. The Ministry of Justice began working in October 1989. A year later it had reviewed 800 of 5,000 cases under consideration.[39] In January 1991 the *Sejm* passed legislation extending privileges for 'combatants and certain persons subject to wartime and post-war repression'.[40] The Senate initiated the Rehabilitation Act in February,[41] the first law to take a retrospective view of the wrongs of the communist past: verdicts issued between 1944 and 1956 could be invalidated if the accused had been sentenced for activity linked to 'the independence of the Polish state'.

### Restitution

Finally, Mazowiecki's government began the restoration of property seized illegally from the Catholic Church. This issue formed part of the redefinition of the relationship between Church and state by the former regime just before the June 1989 elections. The Property Commission (*Komisja Majątkowa*), which functioned from 1989 to 2011, was based on the law specifying the 'State's Attitude to the Catholic Church'.[42] It provided further evidence of the seriousness of the then-communist reformers.

In sum, it is hard to argue that the years 1989–90 were a period of inaction or conscious forgetfulness. Much of what happened in subsequent years built on the foundation laid in this first period of transformative politics. Given the extraordinary demands of the democracy and capitalism-building project in every conceivable sphere, a great deal was achieved in 'righting the wrongs of the past'.

The exception – and it is a major one – was the area of lustration, the purging of office-holders. Mazowiecki was determined to make the communists share responsibility for the transformation. He opposed 'total lustration' (removing all former communist officials) as irresponsible, risking political conflict just when economic reforms were causing profound social dislocation.[43] Later, lustration returned, with a focus on public office-holders who had cooperated ('collaborated') with the old regime. Though the form eventually chosen in 1997 was a minimalist one, often regarded as 'soft' or reconciliatory,[44] lustration remained politically divisive. The first, botched attempt to introduce lustration in 1992 left the issue on hold for a time, but it boiled up again and again.

# The Olszewski government

Mazowiecki resigned after his defeat in the first round of the presidential election though he remained prime minister until January 1991. Lech Wałęsa easily won the presidency.[45] Although Wałęsa had campaigned on a platform of 'decommunization', the government of Jan Krzysztof Bielecki (January–December 1991) concentrated on economic policy, still on its liberal trajectory, and foreign policy, including Europe and the fissiparous USSR. Much of the work described above continued, but there were – not surprisingly – no initiatives from the government.

The past resurfaced as a political issue only after the first democratic parliamentary elections in October 1991.[46] But the new *Sejm* – despite a depleted ex-communist presence – was highly fragmented and inchoate. After several fruitless attempts, former Solidarity defence lawyer Jan Olszewski (1930–2019) formed a minority right-wing coalition in December. It lacked cohesion and controlled only about one-quarter of deputies in the *Sejm* (with little party discipline). Parliament approved the Olszewski government largely in the absence of a palatable alternative.

Right-wing groupings immediately took initiatives designed to widen the scope of transitional justice and put paid to any notion of 'forgetting'. On 1 February 1992 the *Sejm* declared martial law illegal, calling for members of the martial-law council to appear before the Tribunal of State, and establishing an Extraordinary Commission to investigate.[47] This debate over martial law[48] revealed profound divisions between the Centre-Left and the Solidarity Right.

All agreed that the subject was painful, sensitive and emotionally fraught. The Right, including the governing parties, was determined to unveil the past, aiming to reveal the communist 'junta' as a fundamental betrayer of the nation. The *Sejm* debate was bitter and intense; this was the occasion of Leszek Moczulski's famous description of the PZPR as 'paid traitors and flunkeys of Russia' (*płatni zdrajcy, pachołki Rosji*).

The Alliance of the Democratic Left (SLD) did not oppose an investigation, though some speakers used the concepts of 'lesser evil' and 'higher necessity' that later formed the basis of Jaruzelski's own defence of martial law. Speakers from the liberal Democratic Union stressed the need to respect the rule of law, including upholding the statute of limitations.

By spring 1992 Olszewski's government was paralysed and divided. Relations with President Wałęsa had deteriorated, stemming in part from Wałęsa's support for key military officers of the former *nomenklatura*, seen as evidence that he was 'soft on communism'. It was, however, the 'lustration affair' which triggered the fall of the government on 5 June.

On 28 May the *Sejm* unexpectedly passed a 'lustration resolution', initiated by Janusz Korwin-Mikke, leader of the tiny ultra-liberal Union of Political Realism. The resolution required Interior Minister Macierewicz to identify current public functionaries who had cooperated with the security service between 1945 and 1990.[49]

On 4 June Macierewicz delivered secret lists to the leaders of the *Sejm*'s parliamentary groupings. The first identified sixty-four persons whose names had been drawn from the archival records of the interior ministry. The second list of two persons 'of particular significance for the state's security' – President Wałęsa himself and Marshal of the Sejm Wiesław Chrzanowski – was circulated to a more restricted circle.

The lists did not stay secret for long. The revelation that they included the president and other former dissidents whose suffering under the communist regime was widely known raised concerns about their accuracy. The inability of the accused to defend themselves without access to the archives or any mode of due process was a central criticism.

The vote of no confidence submitted by the opposition passed easily. The defence and interior ministers were immediately dismissed from their posts to prevent 'destabilisation'. On 19 June the Constitutional Tribunal declared the lustration resolution to be incompatible with the Constitution's democratic and human rights principles, as well as in violation of laws governing state secrecy and the protection of an individual's reputation. The *Sejm*'s investigative commission accused Macierewicz and Olszewski of personal responsibility for acts of 'political provocation ... aimed at compromising and paralysing the highest organs of state'.[50]

Olszewski was unrepentant. He saw himself as motivated by the highest of national ideals, the safeguarding of Poland's sovereignty and independence. In a televised address he stated that 'former collaborators ... could threaten the security of a free Poland ... it was no accident that a sudden proposal to bring down the government came precisely when we could finally break our links with communism'.[51]

Arguments about lustration continued to dominate Polish political life. Several new right-wing parties formed, with lustration as a central plank. The Solidarity trade union congress supported Olszewski, condemning the 'brutal intervention of the President and post-communist forces, verging on a *coup d'etat*'.[52]

These divisions within Solidarity had major repercussions. The hostility of Olszewski's supporters to Wałęsa created a new fault line in Polish politics in the elections of 1993 and beyond. For the moment, however, a new heterogeneous coalition under Hanna Suchocka of the Democratic Union governed from July 1992, falling on a vote of confidence in May 1993.[53] Preoccupied with constitutional reform, labour relations and the state of the economy, and committed to avoiding controversial ideological issues, Suchocka's government undertook no new initiatives in the sphere of transitional justice, though parliamentary parties supported new lustration efforts. In September 1992 the *Sejm* referred six lustration bills to committee. Although the bills fell with the dissolution of parliament, most of the arguments expressed in the *Sejm*'s debate, and many of the specific provisions of these proposals, would resurface in later years.

Suchocka's government was undone by labour unrest and internal coalition tensions. President Wałęsa immediately called early elections. The first period of Solidarity governance came to an end with the victory in September 1993 of the ex-communists, the SLD. The SLD found a ready ally in the refurbished Polish Peasant Party (PSL), heir to the peasant party of communist days.

## The SLD–PSL coalition 1993–7

The new parliament was very different from its predecessor, with the smallest Solidarity parties now absent. New electoral thresholds punished the divided right-wing parties and gave a seat premium to the SLD and the PSL. The successor parties were anxious to confirm their democratic credentials and entrench their electoral legitimacy. They had no interest in keeping issues of the past on the political agenda. Nor did the government wish to present itself as another variant of the old communist–peasant alliance. PSL leader Waldemar Pawlak became prime minister – not SLD leader Aleksander Kwaśniewski. Kwaśniewski led the parliamentary party, positioning himself for the 1995 presidential election. In the *Sejm* Kwaśniewski apologized in the name of the SLD to 'all … who had experienced the injustices and wickedness of the authorities and the system before 1989'; though the past could not be forgotten, it should be left to historians, journalists and individual conscience.[54]

Despite the coalition's large majority in the *Sejm*, new presidential powers in the Little Constitution enabled President Wałęsa to challenge the government over policy and personnel. As the presidential election drew near, Wałęsa openly attacked Pawlak, charging him with lethargy, paralysis, incompetence and encroachment on presidential powers.[55] Wałęsa had no formal power to dismiss the prime minister; yet, almost single handedly he forced Pawlak out of office. The Social Democrat Józef Oleksy became the coalition's second prime minister in March 1995. As the presidential campaign gathered momentum, Wałęsa heated the atmosphere with skilful use of anti-communist and Solidarity-nostalgia themes.

In 1994 the *Sejm*'s Constitutional Accountability Commission resumed its hearings on martial law. That year the *Sejm* amended the 1991 combatants' law after the Constitutional Tribunal determined that former employees of the security services could claim combatant status if they provided evidence of involvement in pro-independence organizations.[56] Subsequently the government accepted further refinements of this law, including the extension of entitlements to those who took 'part in the struggle for freedom and sovereignty' on the Baltic coast in December 1970.[57]

## Lustration

In mid-1994 the new *Sejm* began to debate lustration. The SLD wanted only background checks on officials for criminal activities. The Democratic Union, now the Freedom Union (*Unia Wolności*), 'reluctantly' tabled a bill providing that secret police files be opened to the public: it was time to 'close the chapter'; the leaks known as 'wild lustration' were damaging innocent people. But the government had other priorities; the *Sejm* abandoned lustration for two more years.

Wałęsa was the witting or unwitting instrument of the return of lustration following Kwaśniewski's presidential victory. On 19 December 1995, the outgoing Interior Minister Andrzej Milczanowski – a Wałęsa nominee under the powers of the Little Constitution – accused Prime Minister Oleksy of collaboration with Soviet and Russian intelligence. Charging Wałęsa with attempted blackmail,[58] Oleksy called the allegations a 'filthy provocation'. Oleksy resigned under pressure, and Włodzimierz Cimoszewicz succeeded him as prime minister.

President Kwaśniewski, while standing formally aloof from the 'Oleksy Affair', seized the initiative to restore lustration to the political agenda. The Oleksy affair finally convinced the SLD that some form of lustration was needed. Kwaśniewski sought a Commission of Public Trust to oversee the archives and to determine whether candidates and high-ranking state officials had collaborated. Individuals would have access to their own files. This approach did not find favour. By February 1996 five draft bills lay in parliament.

The Lustration Law of April 1997[59] was effectively an opposition version, passed with the support of PSL deputies, who defied government policy, but it remained 'soft' – semi-reconciliatory[60] or 'confession-based'.[61] It provided that senior officials, elected office-holders and candidates submit an affidavit stating whether they had worked in or cooperated with state security organs between 1944 and 1990. Penalties did not apply to the fact of 'collaboration' but to mendaciously denying it. Those who made false statements were banned from public office for ten years. However, implementation of lustration was delayed because the new lustration court failed to recruit judges.

## Criminal trials

In March 1996, just as Cimoszewicz took over, the spotlight shifted to the courts. Proceedings opened against Wojciech Jaruzelski, who was indicted over deaths occurring during workers' protests in December 1970. That year Czesław Kiszczak was acquitted of authorizing the use of live ammunition against striking miners following the declaration of martial law in 1981. In October the *Sejm* suspended the Commission investigating martial law. Many saw this as an attempt by the SLD, which dominated the Commission, to forestall, obstruct or prevent justice. Having gathered documents from all key institutions, received oral and written testimony from numerous witnesses, and mobilized the expertise of archivists, lawyers and historians, the Commission (with minority dissent) found the *Sejm*'s martial-law resolution wanting.[62]

Its case was persuasive: because it was not a state institution, members of the Military Council could not be brought before the Tribunal of State; nor indeed had it introduced or orchestrated the implementation of martial law. Moreover, some of the accused had not occupied 'high state office'. The charges were vague, with no specific accusations of wrongdoing against the individuals named. Members of the Council of State, also charged, included one member who voted against martial law, one who abstained and one who was absent. Moreover, the Council of State was constitutionally entitled to issue the decree, and it had genuine internal and external security conditions for doing so. This was the most controversial claim – we will examine it in detail in Chapter 3.

Failure to implement lustration, the prosecution of Jaruzelski (and others), issues concerning access to files and the question of martial law provided grist for the mill of the new Solidarity government. Solidarity Election Action (AWS), reuniting many elements of the ex-Solidarity parties and the trade union, won the 1997 election and formed a coalition with the Freedom Union (UW). This new-found unity did not last – by the end of the parliament the UW had left the coalition and AWS had burst into fragments. However, the election set transitional justice on a new course.

## Transitional justice 1997–2015

September 1997 marked the beginning of right-wing political dominance, broken between 2001 and 2005 when the SLD governed. Under Jerzy Buzek AWS extended policies in all areas of transitional justice, most notably lustration, increasing the role of the Institute of National Remembrance (IPN), which became a central actor in key arenas of transitional justice.

Although AWS policies met some reversals under the SLD, these did not last; the SLD was soon engulfed in internal turmoil. Its government fell apart, the party itself imploded under the weight of corruption allegations, and the SLD began an inexorable decline. In 2005 Jarosław Kaczyński's Law and Justice (PiS) won, but its radical initiatives largely failed; a series of chaotic and ineffective coalition governments brought a premature end to PiS's efforts in 2007.

Civic Platform's election victory in 2007 brought eight years of welcome stability. This period saw new legislation altering the structure of the IPN and further amending file access in accordance with judgments of the Constitutional Tribunal (TK). Indeed, decisions of the TK and the Supreme Court proved central to successive developments.

### Lustration

Lustration remained high on the agenda after 1997. President Kwaśniewski could not muster support for his policies, including the exclusion of intelligence and counter-intelligence officers from lustration, as the SLD had long advocated, and a more precise concept of 'collaboration' (*współpraca*). The Right preferred a loose view of collaboration, the inclusion of all security agencies and a wider definition of posts requiring lustration.

Revising the 1997 law had acquired some urgency because of rumours circulating about Interior Minister Janusz Tomaszewski's alleged collaboration (he was dismissed and was vindicated only in February 2001). The *Sejm* adopted Senate proposals in June 1998.[63]

The Warsaw Appellate Court would now adjudicate lustration affidavits. Some 27,000 persons were required to file affidavits: the president, parliamentarians, ministers and their deputies, as well as directors of state offices, senior officials appointed by the president or parliament, all judges, procurators and lawyers, and those holding key positions in the media.

Lustration became inextricably linked to questions of access to security service files. The 1998 law on the Institute of National Remembrance[64] provided for the transfer of ministerial archives to the IPN. However, only individuals deemed to have been 'harmed' or 'damaged' (*pokrzywdony*) by the security services could gain access to their files. Both the revised lustration law and the new law on the IPN proved intensely contentious over subsequent years.

The 1998 version established the office of Public Interest Commissioner (*Rzecznik Interesu Publicznego*) to analyse the veracity of lustration affidavits and to request the Court for a formal lustration process. The first RPI (1999–2004) was Bogusław Nizieński, whose avowed right-wing views, his profound anti-communism and his enthusiasm for the job made him a controversial figure. The second – and last – commissioner (2005–7) was Włodzimierz Olszewski.

Although the lustration law provided no penalties for admitting collaboration, former Prime Minister Hanna Suchocka, now minister of justice, began to dismiss regional procurators who acknowledged their cooperation with the security services. She also issued an 'appeal' to court chairs to remove judges who admitted collaboration. Włodzimierz Olszewski, then head of the National Judicial Council, expressed his 'opposition and anxiety' at the use of such extra-legal means.[65]

Lustration proceeded slowly. During his tenure Nizieński investigated about 70 per cent of the affidavits filed. In this period the Court issued 100 final judgments, with sixty-three people found guilty of lying and twenty-four not guilty. It also dealt with requests for 'self-lustration' by those who wished to defend themselves against allegations of collaboration. For example, former Speaker of the *Sejm* Wiesław Chrzanowski, whose name appeared on the notorious Macierewicz list of 1992, was vindicated by the Court in 2000.

## Compensation for past wrongs

After 1997 the scope of compensation for past wrongs increased considerably. The IPN became a major instrument of compensatory mechanisms, as people needed documentary evidence. The IPN confirmed imprisonment in the period 1944–56 for political or religious activity 'linked to the struggle for sovereignty and independence' and dealt with requests for documents showing imprisonment for political activity after 1956. It provided evidence for claims under the 1998 pensions law, which attributed pension contributions for periods as combatants or victims of repression, and for those imprisoned for political reasons or who had worked before 1989 for organizations deemed illegal under the-then law.

## SLD governments 2001–5

Following its stunning victory the SLD returned to power in a new coalition with the Peasant Party and the small Labour Union (UP). Faced with mounting economic difficulties, the government limited certain entitlements and suspended the indexation of the 'veterans' pension supplement'.[66] The Constitutional Tribunal found the reversal of indexation unconstitutional, though it accepted the constitutional validity of a reduction in energy and transport subsidies.[67]

The government changed lustration in ways advocated by the SLD since the early days of the debate. The 2002 law[68] excluded those who had cooperated with intelligence/counter-intelligence and with Poland's border defences. It accepted Kwaśniewski's view of collaboration: cooperation must have been 'genuine, harmful, and conscious'. Rulings of the Constitutional Tribunal eroded these clauses but left intact the need for 'genuine' collaboration.

The work of the Public Interest Commissioner was slowed by these amendments, as well as by judgments of the Constitutional Tribunal, the Supreme Court and the European Court of Human Rights. However, the SLD – beset by coalition tensions, internal divisions and increasing public distrust over allegations of deep-seated corruption, resulting in Prime Minister Miller's resignation – did not pursue further legislation.

Yet lustration remained salient, with new accusations surfacing daily. In January 2005 the journalist Bronisław Wildstein, critical of the slow pace of IPN procedures, published a list of over 200,000 names culled from the IPN. The Wildstein List was simply an indiscriminate listing of the names of those on whom files existed, but for many that was enough. Wildstein's critics pointed yet again to the turmoil created for individuals on the list – including some well-known names already awarded 'victim' status by the IPN. The Data Protection Registrar advised the Procurator that IPN Chair Leon Kieres (2000–5) had committed an offence by failing to safeguard information and to prevent unauthorized access.[69] Wildstein was lauded by Jarosław Kaczyński, whose new party Law and Justice (PiS) won a narrow victory in the September 2005 parliamentary election.

By 2005 the Polish political landscape had shifted once again. The most important development was the collapse of the governing party, the SLD. Just as AWS had fallen apart after 1997, so the SLD split after 2002. Voters abandoned the SLD in droves. After the elections two main post-Solidarity parties dominated the political scene, Law and Justice (PiS) in government and Civic Platform (PO) in opposition. PiS, the main beneficiary of the new anti-liberal consensus, became the largest party in parliament and captured the presidency.

## Law and Justice

In 2005 the overarching theme of PiS's approach was its rejection of the chosen path of post-communist transformation and the need for a new constitutional settlement based on moral revolution and patriotic renewal of Solidarity's core ideals and values. This was the project for a new 'Fourth Republic' to replace the corrupt, degenerate system arising from the Round Table. The Fourth Republic would achieve moral cleansing through deep lustration, anti-corruption measures and reaffirmation of Catholic values; it would heal society with a social contract, including fundamental changes in social and economic policy; a new Constitution would repair the state. It would bring to an end the enduring negative legacy of the Round Table.

The Round Table 'contract' lay at the heart of Jarosław Kaczyński's analysis. By pursuing the 'erroneous path' of continuity, the Round Table had generated the conditions for the emergence of a system of control and exploitation (the *układ*) based on a web of interlocking informal networks of powerful interest groups, lobbies and personal coteries allied with state security services and organized crime, pursuing wealth and power through crime, corruption, cronyism and logrolling[70] – all facilitated by the failure of successive governments to pursue a genuine strategy of decommunization. Rooting out the *układ* meant dismantling the structures and removing the personnel that made it possible. Only those with clean hands and a clean past could serve the state – hence the need for new institutions such as a Truth and Justice Commission, Anti-Corruption Bureau and a greater role for the Institute of National Remembrance (IPN).

### Changes under the PiS governments

Governments between 2005 and the premature election of 2007 were volatile and unpredictable. Minority government was followed by coalitions with two radical parties, the League of Polish Families (*Liga Polskich Rodzin*, LPR) and Self-Defence (*Samo-Obrona*, SO). The nationalist LPR eagerly endorsed PiS's worldview, and SO was compliant, if not enthusiastic. PiS was largely thwarted in its efforts to introduce its new radical programme, but this period served as a dress rehearsal for its return to power in 2015.

The new lustration law (2006)[71] was amended before the ink was dry. The revised law,[72] in effect from March 2007, replaced the Public Interest Representative with a Lustration Department within the IPN, designed to identify 'suspicious' affidavits for further investigation. It massively extended lustration to fifty-three categories of people born before 1 August 1972, all those 'fulfilling a public function', including teachers, academics and journalists – some 700,000 persons in all.

Widespread protest greeted the law. Former Foreign Minister Bronisław Geremek, now a member of the European Parliament, said that 'the demand for another lustration declaration under threat of deprivation of my seat is contrary to the principles of the democratic law-based state and disrespectful to the decision of 121,805 electors'.[73] Protests also came from sections of the academic community, including former Prime Minister Cimoszewicz, now lecturing in Białystok, and journalists, including a sizeable contingent from *Gazeta Wyborcza*.[74]

The law proved short-lived. In May 2007 the Constitutional Tribunal rejected some thirty-nine provisions as unconstitutional.[75] Among other things, it rejected the inclusion of journalists (save for the heads of the Polish Press Agency, Polish Radio and Polish Television), academics, directors of private schools, heads of media firms, tax advisers, banking and stock exchange officials, and directors of sporting associations.

It refused to see the communist Censor and the Bureau of Religious Affairs as 'organs of state security'. It rejected the proposed IPN publication of a catalogue of agents and lists of alleged collaborators, while only the highest state office-holders would have their files made public.

Meanwhile the Institute of National Remembrance reopened the question of martial law and finally in 2007 charged its 'authors' – Jaruzelski, Kiszczak and Stanislaw Kania, the communist party's (PZPR) former first secretary (and eight others). The trial began in earnest in September 2008. The accused were charged with inciting the members of the Council of State to violate the constitution by declaring martial law and with having 'directed an armed criminal organisation for the purpose of imposing martial law on 13 December 1981', thereby violating the basic freedoms of Polish citizens. All the accused were elderly and in ill health. Indeed, Jaruzelski, now diagnosed with cancer, was excluded from the trial in 2011 along with three co-defendants. Two others died before the trial ended. Jaruzelski himself died in May 2014 at the age of ninety.

PiS also extended the scope of compensation for past wrongs right up to 1989. Of particular importance were the 2007 changes to the 1991 law on unjust judicial verdicts between 1944 and 1956. They envisaged compensation for all verdicts by the courts and decisions of the security services for acts undertaken in the pursuit of 'independence'.[76] This now included internment and the judgments of civil and military courts after 13 December 1981 (the introduction of martial law), with the possibility of financial compensation for damaged health and harm done after 1956.

PiS's unstable governments came to a premature end in October 2007 with a vote of no confidence and the calling of early elections, won by its main rival Civic Platform. However, the brief period between 2005 and 2007 was eventful, with the extension of the role of the IPN, some high-profile lustration cases, renewed charges against communist leaders for 'communist crimes', disputes over historical interpretations of the past and an attack on the judiciary itself. Several government officials lost their posts, notably the Minister of Finance Zyta Gilowska, accused of collaboration with the security services (Gilowska returned to Jarosław Kaczyński's government after her vindication by the Lustration Court).

## The government of Civic Platform 2007–15

Under Civic Platform (PO), the moderate wing of the Polish Right, few dramatic changes occurred in the sphere of transitional justice. PO had generally supported lustration, albeit with reservations. Over the next few years the lustration process became routine. Only a small proportion of affidavits denying cooperation with the security services were referred to the courts.

However, PO viewed the IPN Chair, Janusz Kurtyka, as linked too closely to PiS and its executive as too politicized, having been chosen in 2007 from nominees of the-then governing coalition. So society expected 'the de-politicization of the Institute of National Remembrance'.[77] The new law changed the chair's appointment and dismissal (in fact, Kurtyka perished in the Smolensk air disaster of April 2010) and required professional qualifications for members of the new governing Council.[78] Now the

IPN could no longer determine whether and to whom documents could be released; persons could gain access to their own files.

Throughout this period the issue of 'communist crimes' continued to unfold in the courts. In 2011 the Constitutional Tribunal declared martial law illegal. The 'martial law' trial continued, with Kiszczak found guilty in 2012. In June 2013 the appeal court suspended the trial on health grounds, but in July 2014 it granted the IPN's request for a new medical examination. By 2014 Kiszczak had effectively been on trial for almost twenty years – including four trials relating to the deaths of striking miners after martial law. Kiszczak died in 2015.

The IPN reopened the most celebrated cases of the post-Stalin era, including the murders of Przemyk and Popiełuszko. After the law on the IPN replaced the concept of Stalinist crimes with that of 'communist crimes' in 1998, what had been 'murder' was reclassified as a 'communist crime' because it had been committed by a state functionary. However, in December 2009 the Appellate Court freed Ireneusz Kościuk, found guilty of the fatal beating of Przemyk, because the statute of limitations had expired. This was confirmed by the Supreme Court in 2010. Charges brought against former officials for irregularities in the investigation of Przemyk's death also fell. By the end of 2012 all investigations into that case had been discontinued.

Civic Platform continued to extend compensation for past wrongs. In 2009 eligibility was extended to the families of those who had died 'as a result of participation in mass gatherings, demonstrations and strikes' between 1956 and 1989.[79] In 2015 the list of 'repressed persons' came to include persons called for military service between 1 November 1982 and 28 February 1983 (during martial law) because of their actions on behalf of Polish independence (i.e., because they supported Solidarity).[80]

This law effectively marked the end of transitional justice in Poland. The main issues had been dealt with, tinkered with and readjusted for twenty-six years. The transition to democracy had long been completed. After PiS came to power in 2015 the discourse of transitional justice continued, but the PiS project became a wider programme of social engineering, with a vision of a different society, a different culture and a different politics. PiS won again in 2019.

# Conclusion

The period after 1997 saw the development of themes that had already emerged after 1989 – identifying the main constituents of transitional justice. Lustration, former crimes, access to communist archives, and compensation and restitution were the subject of debate – and action – from 1989 onwards. However, when right-wing parties took office, they took a different view from the liberal approach of the first non-communist governments. Lustration became harsher, compensation was extended to greater numbers and communist wrongdoers were pursued relentlessly through the courts.

The SLD supported charges against those who had committed unpunished crimes under communism as an essential ingredient of transitional justice. Yet it broadly opposed the trials of communist leaders, seeing – with some justification – the pursuit of the former leadership as a search for vengeance. Right-wing politicians cheered as

IPN procurators appealed virtually every judgment that went against them. Although the courts did take cognisance of the health of defendants, the IPN wreaked havoc on their lives, exacting punishment when the courts did not. There is an obvious case for historians to reveal the injustices of the past – and these injustices were many, often with devastating consequences for the victims of repression. Yet areas such as martial law remained contentious, and many agreed with Jaruzelski that he had chosen the lesser evil. For all the energy and resources expended, justice was not obviously served by the IPN.

It took nearly twenty years to resolve the issue of personal and public access to the files of the security services. Here too the politicization of the process was apparent. Even after 1998 the initial emphasis on 'victims' and the effective discretion of the IPN, as well as the IPN's publication of putative evidence against accused persons made the whole process deeply dissatisfying. Accusations based on deductions about the alleged identity of informers still surfaced in national and local politics in 2015. Data protection issues were ignored. Journalists' access 'for research' seemed particularly problematic.

Lustration was the most highly charged and most deeply political issue of transitional justice in Poland. The putative failure of the Mazowiecki government to 'deal with the past' set in train an issue that persisted for decades. Yet for all the sound and fury, it is hard to regard lustration as a successful policy, even by the lights of its strongest adherents. Despite the undoubted sincerity of its most ardent proponents, lustration was so palpably politicized as to seem to many simply an instrument of the political game, far from the cleansing, truth-seeking process claimed for it.

3

# Reparations through rehabilitation and compensation

## Introduction

This chapter reviews developments in the 'rehabilitation' of the unjustly punished and oppressed. The term rehabilitation was inherited from the Soviet Union. It did not refer to the perpetrators of injustice nor to rehabilitative prison regimes, nor was it linked to ideas of restorative justice bringing together victims and offenders. It was a form of the legal exoneration of individuals, arising with the release of prisoners following Stalin's death in 1953 and restoring them to a state of acquittal (often posthumous). Many prisoners had not had trials at all, but later usage centred on wrongful, often politically motivated convictions by a court of law. In the Polish case the emphasis first centred on Stalinist oppression (1944–56), then extended gradually to opposition protesters in Poznań in 1956 and on the Baltic coast in 1970, and then, from 2007, the activists of underground Solidarity and other opponents of the communist regime in the 1980s. To understand fully the intense divisions that surrounded these concerns, we also need a diversion into the complex web of Poland's wartime history.

The first stage of rehabilitation expunged the unjust record and restored the victim's rights and reputation. The second stage provided recompense. 'Rehabilitated' victims often received financial resources to make amends for past harm, physical and mental, arising from wrongful imprisonment, harassment or abuse by the security services. Compensation could also relate to lost opportunities, material damages and loss of earnings. In Poland a raft of legislation dealt with rehabilitation and compensation (we ignore the legal distinction between damages and compensation). Justice for Poland's anti-communist opposition occupied the *Sejm* from 1989 onwards. Poland was distinctive in the seriousness and scope of efforts to deal with this element of rehabilitative justice.[1]

In the 'contract *Sejm*' (1989–91) the SLD and Solidarity cooperated effectively, with consensus on the need to redress the communist regime's most blatant violations of law and human rights. Following the inauguration of fully democratic elections, when Left and Right alternated in power, governments pursued changes aligned to their own historical assessments of wrongs committed under the communists. After 2005 the SLD's influence disappeared, and new legislation reflected the perspectives of different elements of the Polish Right. The pool of veterans and the unjustly sentenced grew steadily and came to embrace virtually all who had suffered death, injury, detention or other hardship for political reasons.

# Workers' rights

Workers' rights were centre stage at the Round Table in 1989. Solidarity demanded recognition as a legal trade union. It also sought the reappointment of workers dismissed for union activism and protest after 1980 and demanded compensation for losses and imprisonment. Future Prime Minister Tadeusz Mazowiecki tried to secure compensation for martial law offences, but the government side rejected it.[2] The Round Table did agree to reinstate workers dismissed for trade union activity – some 50,000 workers had been dismissed in the period 1981–3. This agreement was embodied in May 1989 in the law on the 'rights of certain persons to renew their employment contracts'.[3]

Those whose employment had been terminated because of 'unlawful' union activity would be reemployed by their former workplace. The important proviso for job reinstatement was 'unless circumstances rendered this impossible'. Amendments to the law by the 'contract *Sejm*' in September also gave reinstatement rights to those who lost jobs after August 1980 because of their political and religious convictions or 'local government activity'. Years of unemployment counted for both workers' entitlements and social benefits.[4]

Re-employment was not straightforward, as the 'shock therapy' introduced by the Mazowiecki government proved – at the outset at least – more shock than therapy. Often reinstatement was deemed 'not possible'. Many state enterprises reduced production and put workers on short time. Uncertainty increased as unemployment rose rapidly: 400,000 by the spring and nearly 1.2 million by the end of 1990. Many workers took advantage of arrangements facilitating early retirement. This in turn created problems in assessing continuity of employment, since pensions were linked to a worker's average earnings.

The time frame was narrow. The Supreme Court ruled that the law did not apply to those punished for trade union activity before 1980.[5] Certain technical issues also took some time to resolve – such as the consequences of an 'unjust' prison sentence for distributing leaflets[6] or the status of missing wages, holiday leave not taken, and enterprise loans made to workers. In the latter case the Supreme Court used 'special circumstances' to reject the lower court's finding that the statute of limitations applied because 'disregarding the legitimate claims of a person injured by the unjust sentencing and repression of the martial law period violates the interests of the Polish Republic'.[7] The Constitutional Court, however, rejected Solidarity's challenge to the system of distributing free shares to workers as part of the privatization process.[8] It found that failing to provide the right to shares for those whose employment contracts had been unlawfully terminated was within the prerogative of the legislature, which had made special provisions for those unjustly dismissed.

# The rehabilitation of individuals

The first formal act of individual rehabilitative justice was also a direct consequence of the Round Table agreement. The Law of 29 May 1989 on 'forgiving and forgetting' certain offences (a so-called abolition law,[9] *ustawa abolicyjna* or act of oblivion)[10] provided for the expunging from the record of sentences for offences committed between 31 August 1980 and 29 May 1989 during strikes, demonstrations and other politically motivated actions, like producing underground publications or collecting funds for prohibited organizations. The law's legal fiction – that the offences never happened – applied to both sides of the political divide, those engaged in opposition activities and those, mostly public functionaries, opposing their protests.

The Constitutional Tribunal affirmed the narrowness of the law's remit. It could not, for example, include acts of serious brutality or later events such as beating a demonstrator after arrest.[11] In 1991 the *Sejm* made explicit the exclusion of serious crimes from the abolition law.[12] The Supreme Court found that a group of Solidarity members were not guilty of 'serious offences' and acted 'out of higher necessity',[13] but two militiamen were excluded from the act and could be tried for their maltreatment of a Catholic priest.[14]

The expunging of verdicts was swift. Within the month provincial courts began to hear these cases – the provincial court in Gdańsk dealt with former Solidarity activists on 23 June 1989 and that in Koszalin wiped clean the records of four martial law offenders on 30 June.[15] We do not know how many took advantage of the law. Records of the Institute of National Remembrance and its comprehensive website 13grudnia81.pl[16] suggested that the courts were not flooded with applications for exoneration. The most notorious cases concerned security service officers who claimed 'political motivation' for their harsh dealings with the opposition.

In October 1989 the Ministry of Justice had begun working on historic rehabilitations. Within a year it had reviewed 800 of the 5,000 cases under consideration.[17] In 1990 the Supreme Court carried out 271 'extraordinary revisions' of rehabilitation cases, mostly of individuals sentenced between 1944 and 1956. By the beginning of 1991 over 1,200 requests were pending at the Ministry of Justice.[18] As a result, the *Sejm* sought to simplify and expedite rehabilitation procedures and to offer compensation. The principle of compensation was not new: supplements to pensions and priority in health and social services for veterans and prisoners of German concentration camps had been in force since 1982.

The task of identifying wronged persons and awarding compensation for their suffering might seem straightforward. It does not appear to form the stuff of passions. This was not the case. Time and again the *Sejm* returned to issues of rehabilitation and compensation. As so often in Poland, the past was present in the present, but it was not the same past for all.

## The historical sources of persistent division

Inter-war-period Poland was a multi-national state, with large numbers of Jews, Lithuanians, Belorussians and Ukrainians. As a result of the Nazi-Soviet Pact of 1939 the USSR occupied its eastern lands, which fell to the Germans after the Nazi invasion of the Soviet Union in 1941. Occupying powers, partisan forces, local self-defence groupings and nationalists of varying colours made this part of Central Europe a particularly bloody battlefield. With the acquiescence of the Western powers at Teheran and Yalta, the USSR retained most of Poland's eastern borderlands, incorporating them into the Soviet republics of Lithuania, Belorussia and the Ukraine. After the war Stalin's insistence on 'repatriation' and forcible population exchanges reduced the numbers of Poles in the USSR's new territories and Belorussians, Lithuanians and Ukrainians in Poland.

During the Second World War the Home Army (*Armia Krajowa, AK*) had unified most Polish resistance groups to become the largest, most effective underground movement in Europe. The smaller communist resistance – the People's Guard (*Gwardia Ludowa, GL*) and later the *Armia Ludowa* (People's Army) – remained aloof. While the Home Army, loyal to the London government-in-exile, sought to restore Poland within its inter-war eastern boundary, the Polish communists acquiesced in Soviet aims to redraw Poland's boundaries along ethnic lines. At the same time Ukrainian and Belorussian nationalist forces sought national independence.

The first Soviet occupation of the region (1939–41) saw the mass deportation of Poles to Siberia and Kazakhstan, inadvertently facilitating Ukrainian nationalist forces after German occupation (1941–3). By 1942, sizeable Polish partisan units had formed in the east to challenge the Germans. In 1943 Ukrainian nationalists began murdering Polish civilians to help 'resolve' the Polish question in Ukraine. The Poles fought back. Ukrainian partisans and peasants 'killed at least 40,000 Polish civilians … in the spring and summer of 1943. Polish partisans of all political stripes attacked the UPA, assassinated prominent Ukrainian civilians, and burned Ukrainian villages'.[19] They 'cleansed' the Ukrainian population from Kowal, Włodzimierz and Lubomel in 1943–4. By the middle of 1944 many Poles still believed they could retake the former eastern borderlands. That summer approximately 150 villages, home to 15,000 Ukrainians, were razed in so-called retaliatory measures.[20] In all, the victims of these massacres totalled over 80,000 Poles and over 20,000 Ukrainians.[21]

As the Red Army and the Polish First Army (Berling's army)[22] pushed eastward, forces of the Soviet security services, the NKVD, secured political control, supporting the small band of Polish communists who established the Polish Committee of National Liberation ('the Lublin Committee') as Poland's provisional government (22 July 1944). The Soviets made use of Home Army (AK) units to fight the Germans but then demanded their subordination to the Polish First Army. Following the AK's major losses during the failed Warsaw Uprising (August–September 1944), resentment at Soviet failure to aid the uprising dashed the hopes of the provisional government for a 'patriotic upsurge'.[23] The AK's refusal to subordinate itself led to increased repression, with mass arrests and deportations following the dissolution of its units by (effectively) the NKVD.

An armed anti-communist resistance took shape. In November 1944 elements of the AK endorsed armed struggle and came together in the National Military Union (*Narodowe Zjednoczenie Wojskowe*), with others active in Freedom and Independence (*Wolność i Niezawisłość*, WiN) after the Home Army's dissolution in January 1945. The National Armed Forces (*Narodowe Siły Zbrojne*) brought together the military wing of the nationalist radical camp the ONR (*Obóz Narodowo Radykalny*) and other nationalist groupings. Violence begat violence in a bloodbath of reciprocity, escalating as the government sought to root out and destroy anti-government guerrillas engaged in assassinations and military attacks on security forces as well as on prisons, detention centres and security headquarters. In eastern areas the 'scale of activities certainly approached that of a civil war'.[24]

The new communist government faced armed action by anti-communists and Ukrainian nationalists, peasant resistance to collectivization, and generalized hostility among the population. Expulsions of minority populations to the USSR and the resettlement in 1947 of the remaining Ukrainians in the western territories gained from Germany (*Akcja Wisła*) were savage and ruthless.[25] It seems certain that without the backing of the USSR the Polish communist regime could not have survived.

There is no doubting the brutality directed against the anti-communist resistance by the Red Army, the NKVD and Polish security forces – arrests, internment, torture, kidnap, false promises of amnesty, imprisonment on false charges, murder, deportation – including the show-trial in Moscow of General Okulicki and prominent leaders of the AK: the Trial of the Sixteen (June 1945). Although most resistance was crushed by 1947, relentless propaganda against the Home Army continued for much of the post-war period. As late as 1950, resistance hero General August Emil Fieldorf was arrested, tortured, tried and finally executed in April 1953 for ordering the AK to 'liquidate Soviet partisans'. For years the regime made no distinction between the anti-Nazi resistance fighters of the AK and the 'accursed soldiers' (*Żołnierze Wyklęci*) who had taken up arms against the communist takeover of Poland.

After 1989 the Left readily acknowledged the injustices wreaked upon the Home Army by the communist regime. Accepting the central role of the AK in the anti-Nazi resistance movement formed part of a new historical consensus. However, the Left opposed attempts to reject the wartime contribution of those who had fought with the Red Army and in the communist anti-Nazi resistance or endorse the accolades awarded to the anti-communist resistance. The stark portrayal amongst sections of the Polish Right of a struggle between the anti-communist forces of Good and the communist forces of Evil underpinned much of the historical debate over the combatants' law and the rehabilitation law.

For one side the anti-communist struggle was an effort by terrorists and reactionaries to overthrow the legitimate government. This was the official position of communist historiography, still shared by sections of the Left. For the other side the anti-communist struggle was a heroic, patriotic effort to rid the country of an illegitimate government backed by a foreign power. This was the view adopted by the Right. Investigators of the Institute of National Remembrance, for example, applauded the anti-communist resistance and condemned the-then government's attempts to combat it: 'Henryk Flame's NSZ group ... was the largest and most active armed anti-communist formation in Cieszyn Silesia and the western part of Little Poland ....Its main aim was the struggle with the communist system by attacks on militia checkpoints and outposts of the security services, killing their employees.' The annihilation of these (NSZ) forces in Operation Lawina (September 1946) was 'a communist crime and a crime against humanity ... by officers of the Ministry of Public Security'.[26]

No one doubts the savagery of Polish Stalinism. The general view amongst historians is that the anti-communist resistance was also brutal, often attacking villages thought to be pro-communist, and resorting to arson and murder of the civilian population.

The National Armed Forces (NSZ) was the heir of the fascistic, anti-semitic ONR with a virulent nationalist, anti-democratic, anti-minority core.[27] The attitude of the NSZ to the Jews remains an unsettled question, though its radical element was anti-Semitic.[28] It has also been accused of collaboration with the Germans, putting anti-communism ahead of the anti-Nazi struggle.[29]

The catalogue of atrocities on both sides is a long one. For all its emphasis on communist crimes, even the IPN acknowledged the 'crimes against humanity' perpetrated against the Belorussian minority by Romuald Rajs and his NSZ unit.[30] Not surprisingly, a bitter divide separated those attacking[31] or lauding[32] celebrations of the 'accursed soldiers' of the anti-communist resistance.[33]

# Rehabilitation

## The New Rehabilitation Laws

### The Law on combatants and repressed persons

In 1990 the 'contract *Sejm*' discussed three draft bills concerning 'combatants (veterans) and repressed persons'. The legislative rapporteur reported members' 'shock' at the depth of the conflict among veterans' organizations and the conflicts, contradictions, and 'dramatic tension' of the committee's hearings.[34] Solidarity's Minister of Labour Jacek Kuroń found 'matters so painful, so bound up with the wrongs inflicted, that it is difficult to discuss them'.[35] In January 1991 the *Sejm* overwhelmingly passed the 'law on combatants and certain persons subject to wartime and post-war repression'.[36] One month later, it passed the 'law on the invalidation of convictions of persons repressed for actions in support of the independent existence of the Polish state'.[37]

The new combatants' law recognized the 'suffering of Polish citizens' for political, ethnic and religious reasons under the Third Reich, the-then Soviet Union and the Polish communist apparatus of repression. These citizens were owed 'the deep respect of their compatriots and a duty of care'. The list of combatants, combatant-equivalents and repressed persons was very long; it embraced Poland's national struggles, the whole of the anti-Nazi resistance, victims of Soviet and Nazi occupation, as well as political opponents of the communist regime up to 1956.

Combatants had taken part in wars, armed actions and national uprisings in military formations or organizations fighting for Poland's sovereignty and independence in the Polish Army, allied armies and underground resistance; organizations for Polish independence in 1918 and within Poland's pre-war boundaries before September 1939 up to the end of 1956; and those who had fought against the Ukrainian Insurrectionary Army or groups of the Wehrwolf.

Combatant equivalents were those with civil functions in national organizations, wartime underground organizations between 1939 and 1945 and civilian underground independence organizations between 1945 and 1956; teachers in the underground education system; those fighting on Polish merchant vessels during the Second World War; those who fought for 'Polishness' and Polish freedom after 1914 and in risings in Silesia, Great Poland, Gdańsk, Lubuskie Province, Pomerania, Kashubia, Warmia-Mazuria and other occupied areas; and those killed or injured in the rising in Poznań in 1956.

Finally, imprisonment or internment in Soviet or Nazi labour camps or concentration camps also counted as periods of combat. Those incarcerated in the Soviet Gulag or in prisons or camps run by the NKVD in Poland or held in Polish prisons (1944–56) by court decision or without trial for political or religious reasons linked to the 'struggle for sovereignty and independence' also gained combatant status.

'Repressed persons' were those detained for political, ethnic, racial or religious reasons in Nazi prisons or camps; in ghettos; in Soviet camps or prisons or places of deportation; in Polish prisons sentenced by special or military courts between 1944 and 1956 or detained without trial for activity linked to the independence struggle.

The list of entitlements was also long: veterans and repressed persons received (among others) pension supplements, provision for early retirement; health and social care privileges; and reduced energy and transport costs. The law explicitly excluded Nazi collaborators, those who worked for Soviet security services and those who had worked for Polish security services, including military intelligence, military judges and prosecutors, as well as the civil judiciary and the procuracy (Art. 21). Article 21 remained controversial after the *Sejm* failed to reject Senate changes by the two-thirds majority then required. The *Sejm*'s original version (bitterly contested) had rejected the implication of collective guilt, requiring evidence of wrongdoing by individuals against those 'persecuted for their political or religious activities in the struggle for sovereignty and independence'. The Solidarity Senate took the view that no persons who had worked in the military and judicial structures of the communist state could be regarded as combatants, no matter the valour of their wartime records.

### The rehabilitation law

The invalidation or 'rehabilitation law' was similar in tone to the combatants' law. It laid out judicial procedures for the nullification of decisions issued by military, security and judicial organs between 1 January 1944 and 31 December 1956 regarding actions taken in connection with the independence struggle – including resisting the collectivization of agriculture. The *Sejm* agreed that the situation up to 1956 was distinctive – this was the period of the most intense struggle for independence and that of the greatest repression – and needed separate regulation; after 1956 the struggle for human rights predominated over the struggle for independence.[38] Nullification applied unless the actions that had been committed were such that 'the 'cost was grossly disproportionate to the benefit gained or sought or if the means used were grossly incommensurate with the ends' (Art. 1(3)). The invalidation of a sentence was equivalent to a not-guilty verdict. Once granted, it provided the basis for compensation from the State Treasury, for the person repressed or if deceased, to his or her immediate family.

## The evolution of the combatants' law

The *Sejm* was deluged with claims from those demanding the extension of the law to further categories; those wishing to extend the time frame up to 1989; and those protesting their exclusion from or deprivation of veteran status (between August 1992 and October 1994, some 9,300 persons lost existing entitlements, often because they, like many from the wartime resistance, had later worked for state organs). These cases also reached the courts, which issued strong procedural guidance.[39] Formal protests led to Supreme Court guidance (7 May 1992),[40] noting that the law provided no opportunity for individuals employed in military intelligence, the security services, the procuracy or the courts to challenge their exclusion. This issue continued to fester.

In 1993 Hanna Suchocka's government extended the category of repressed persons to include those who had been 'repressed for their actions on behalf of Polish independence' by Soviet security or judicial institutions with the consent of the Polish provisional government after Soviet troops had entered Polish territory.[41] This issue had also been debated in 1991, when the *Sejm* regarded decisions by Soviet officials – and compensation for their actions – as a matter of international law and treaty.

After Suchocka lost a vote of confidence, early elections returned the successor parties to power. The Alliance of the Democratic Left (SLD) joined in coalition with its erstwhile satellite, now the Polish Peasant Party (PSL). In the new parliament (1993–7) reform proposals were put on hold after a challenge by the Ombudsman to the Constitutional Tribunal (TK) and because of mounting conflict between President Wałęsa and the new coalition.

The TK agreed with the Ombudsman that the combatants' law should have excluded only those who had worked in sections of the security apparatus directly engaged in repression.[42] It defined the repressive apparatus as the Security Department (UB), Security Service (SB) and Military Intelligence (IW) but not the whole of the police and judiciary. Indeed, the latter included many who had served the public good: maintaining order, combatting crime, protecting the security of citizens. However, it took another two years before parliament responded to the TK's concerns. Many post-Solidarity groupings still agreed with the president that the security services should be conceived as an integrated whole, whether or not a particular element was itself engaged in repression.

Few were satisfied with the combatants' law, including the veterans themselves. Pressure for amendment led to successive changes – three times in 1997 alone. In January qualifying persons with no pension or other income gained a special supplement.[43] Then entitlements were extended to those who took 'active part in the struggle' on the Baltic coast in December 1970.[44] The law of 25 April 1997[45] finally met the objections of the Constitutional Court by barring from combatant status only those who had worked in the repressive apparatuses or directly engaged in repression. Combatant status could be claimed by those who had worked in a repressive apparatus or engaged in functions involving repression if they provided evidence that they had functioned as 'agents' of pro-independence organizations. At the same time, those who had joined the Soviet-orchestrated paramilitary 'destruction batallions' (*Niszczycielskich Batalionach/Istriebitielnych Batalionach*) in the struggle against Ukrainian nationalism in 1944–5[46] were added to the category of combatant. The new Constitution of October 1997 confirmed the 'special protection of veterans of the struggle for independence, especially invalids' (Art. 19).

Although the social democratic view on collective guilt had largely prevailed, some grievous decisions continued to arouse the anger of the Left. The best example was the annulment in 1996 of the death sentences passed on NSZ commanders Romuald Rajs and Kazimierz Chmielowski and in consequence the compensation obtained by their heirs.[47] The court found that although their actions entailed the loss of human life, these actions could not be seen as disproportionate to the end sought, namely Poland's independence. They acted out of 'higher necessity which forced them to commit actions not always unambiguously ethical' [*sic*].[48]

The *Sejm* elected in autumn 1997 was determined to make further changes, and Jerzy Buzek's new right-wing AWS government proved receptive. Deputies presented five draft bills, and the Senate made further proposals. In 1998 the time limits for filing for combatant status were extended.[49] In 1999 the law extended entitlements to those who had sheltered Jews during the war. It excluded from combatant status functionaries of the Polish Workers' Party (PPR) and the Polish United Workers' Party who had been responsible for the supervision (*nadzór*) of the repressive apparatus.[50] President Kwaśniewski failed to convince the Constitutional Tribunal that this provision was unconstitutional.[51]

The Institute of National Remembrance (IPN) gained a key role in identifying the organizations to which the law would apply.[52] After Jacek Taylor became head of the National Veterans' Bureau in 1998, a further 50,000 veterans of left-wing organizations lost their entitlement to combatant status.[53] It was 'little wonder', commented Jan Turski, director of the Bureau after 2001, that it 'was widely perceived as the 'national bureau of decommunization'.[54]

Not surprisingly, then, the centre–left coalition elected in 2001 supported changes in the combatants' law – the 2001–5 *Sejm* saw twelve draft bills proposing amendments and another forty bills relevant to combatant benefits. Economic difficulties halted the expansion of entitlements, with indexation of the 'veterans' supplement' suspended.[55] In 2004 the TK found part of that law unconstitutional and it reversed the law's provisions for indexation of pensions, but it accepted reductions in energy and transport subsidies.[56]

The TK argued that the Constitution, providing for the 'special protection of veterans of the independence struggle' (Art. 19), had a 'systemic significance such that the care of veterans is an essential constitutional value'. This means that it can only be limited in circumstances defined by the constitution itself, including a threat to democracy or public order or conflict with the rights of others (Art. 31). The situation of veterans is different from that of other social beneficiaries. 'The dignity and honour of veterans of the independence struggle demand that the legislator respect the promises embodied in Art. 19 .... (These) privileges constitute a constitutional departure from the principle of equality because of the exceptional constitutional value ascribed to the struggle for independence.' However, suspending indexation did not violate the prohibition of limiting acquired rights because this prohibition was not absolute. The legislator had a legitimate concern with budgetary issues, so changing energy and transport subsidies for beneficiaries was acceptable, especially since the entitlements were not of the 'essence' of combatant service but also provided for other groups.

When Jan Turski became director of the Veterans' Bureau, he tried to heal the historic political divide between left and right among veterans and political parties. Turski greatly influenced a draft bill which sought to remedy some perceived injustices, notably by more precisely defining the categories excluded from combatant status and by rejecting the notion of collective guilt implicit in the exclusion of those who later worked in the repressive structures of the regime (a theme of the debate in 1990, partly dealt with in 1997). Instead, exclusion required proof that an individual had engaged in repressive actions.

The opposition of sections of the veterans' movement and their supportive deputies, coupled with ever-present worries about the financial implications, led to the bill's narrow defeat, as the whole of the opposition and – unexpectedly – most of the peasant coalition partner mobilized against it. Turski's compromise – aiming 'to soften divisions among veterans and avoiding the enactment of yet another version of Polish history'[57] – came to nothing.

Left-wing deputies rapidly returned to their previous theme with another bill. Combatant status was denied to those guilty of 'repression or other forms of human rights violations against individuals or groups classified as a crime by the law in force at the time of committal' (this was the formulation of the 1998 Law on the IPN).[58] It added militiamen who had fought against Ukrainian nationalists to the list of combatants (hitherto only those who had fought as soldiers were included). This bill, along with other drafts which sought to grant combatant status to 'those soldiers and civilians who worked to detect and deactivate landmines as part of the military operation to clear the country' (from the Senate)[59] and to exclude (the handful of) Spanish Civil War veterans who had retained combatant status because they had never worked in state institutions (from Law and Justice, PiS),[60] fell with the elections of 2005.

Between 2005 and 2007 PiS was dominant, but the parliamentary term was cut short. The Veterans' Bureau, now under PiS's control, entered the fray. Since the cost of entitlements was high, major revisions were needed to the combatants' law, or better still, a new law altogether.[61] The number of combatants would be reduced, with the law extended to a group of beneficiaries with a 'more precise nomenclature'; the law would become a 'normative act constituting an element of the state's politics of history' and it would be 'cleansed of provisions enabling persons who had engaged in suppressing the independence aspirations of the Polish Nation to retain combatant privileges'. The government responded enthusiastically to these proposals, but they simply ran out of time. Only one law passed in that short *Sejm* – unanimously in 2007 – altering the system for allocating aid to veterans and repressed persons.

After Civic Platform won the elections of 2007 PiS deputies returned to their project, with a draft bill 'on the rights of combatants, participants in civil struggle 1914–1945, activists opposing communist dictatorship, and certain victims of totalitarian repression'.[62] The new government did not support these changes, and the draft was badly worded and imprecise – particularly those clauses removing combatant status from existing beneficiaries.[63]

At the same time Left-wing deputies tried again to gain recognition of wrongs committed by the anti-communist resistance after 1945. Their bill restored earlier attempts to enable compensation by extending repressed-person status to 'those taken from their parents as children for purposes of extermination or forcible denationalization' and 'those who died or suffered damage to health as a result of the actions of (anti-communist) formations'.[64] This bill disappeared into the miasma of the *Sejm*'s committee system. In 2011 doughty social democrat deputy Eugeniusz Czykwin tried again, resubmitting the 2008 draft.[65] Czykwin, a Belorussian himself, was particularly exercised by the atrocities committed by the anti-communist NSZ forces in the villages of eastern Polesia. Granting the participants combatant status while ignoring their victims' status as genuinely 'repressed persons' was a grave injustice.[66]

The *Sejm* proved unresponsive to these concerns. Moreover, in 2011 it established a new national holiday, 1 March, the National Remembrance of the 'Accursed Soldiers'.[67] This law rubbed salt in the wounds of the Polish Left and reinforced the enduring divisions between those who had supported the communists and their opponents following the Second World War.

March 2014 saw increased health benefits, a new 'Corpus of Veterans of Struggles for the Independence of the Polish Republic', and a database of combatants and repressed persons.[68] In 2017 members of the Veterans of Struggles gained the right to wear uniforms, with the Ministry of Defence charged with designing a special uniform.[69] PiS returned to its previous attempt to revise the combatants' law by excluding those who 'had not rendered any service to the cause of Polish independence or who had actively harmed the cause' (mostly by fighting in Soviet divisions). Polish citizenship became a requirement for a widow's or combatant's pension. Benefits were increased for soldiers, mostly pacifists serving alternative service, who had been forced to work down coalmines, in quarries, uranium ore mines or construction battalions. In March 2018 President Duda vetoed the so-called demotion law, which stripped communist-era generals, admirals and marshals of their rank, including all members of the Military Council of National Salvation.

## The evolution of the rehabilitation law

The rehabilitation (invalidation) law underwent little revision after 1993, with technical changes in 1995 and 1998, when time limits were defined for acts committed on former Polish territory in the east,[70] and substantive change only in 2007.[71] PiS's 2007 changes enabled persons repressed for 'pro-independence activity' between 1 January 1944 and 31 December 1989 to seek invalidation of their sentences and gain compensation for acts against them, including internment under martial law. Only one compensation claim could be made – no matter how many times a claimant had suffered injustice – and for those convicted after 1956 the law limited compensation to 25,000 PLN. By the end of 2011 an estimated 75,000 oppositionists had received compensation for false arrest or internment. In that year the Constitutional Court declared the limit unconstitutional, requiring assessment of the amount of compensation in each individual case. In 2015 Civic Platform deemed persons called for military service between 1 November 1982 and 28 February 1983 (during martial law) as 'repressed' because of their actions on behalf of Polish independence (in other words because of their support for Solidarity).[72]

## Other laws

Several other laws were also relevant to questions of rehabilitation. Although not pertaining directly to the restoration of rights or compensation for injustices, they sought remedies for persistent suffering or deprivation. Some communist-era legislation, such as the law of May 1974 'on provision for wartime invalids', remained in force. Many benefits' laws – health benefits for invalids and the disabled and other entitlements – were also pertinent. In 1994 parliament passed the law 'on entitlements of soldiers forcibly employed in mines, quarries, construction battalions and uranium extraction'[73] during the Second World War, and in 1996 the law on 'monetary recompense for persons deported to forced labour or settled in labour camps by the Third Reich or the Union of Soviet Socialist Republics'.[74] In 2009 the *Sejm* introduced 'compensation for families of the victims of collective actions for freedom'.[75] Fifty thousand zloties would be available for the immediate families of those who had died during collective actions 'defending freedom, human dignity and civil rights under the totalitarian communist system' from the army, the militia or other organs of the security services – in Poznań in June 1956, in Warsaw in October 1957, at the Baltic coast in December 1970, in Radom in June 1976, under martial law from December 1981 to 22 July 1983, and in protests and strikes between 1983 and 1989.

## Anti-communist activists

In 2015 under Civic Platform the *Sejm* passed the 'law on activists of the anti-communist opposition and persons repressed for political reasons'.[76] This was a further 'rectification of the wrongs done to the anti-communist opposition and those repressed by the communist regime (and it was) both a moral and legal responsibility'.[77] This was not compensation as such and did not fall within the scope of the combatants' law or the invalidation law, though there was some overlap. In part it was a response to judgments of the Constitutional Court (see below). The law provided benefits to alleviate economic or social hardship through monthly or single payments. Of these, the most important was the payment of 400 PLN monthly to those with very low incomes to meet extra costs of disability or illness.

The law was detailed in its coverage of activities under the communist regime, and it is worth reporting in full, though it affected no more than a few thousand people. The wording shows just how difficult it was to define the categories in question. An anti-communist activist was 'a person within organized structures or cooperating with them for at least twelve consecutive months who was threatened with criminal liability for undertaking acts aimed at the regaining of Poland's sovereignty and independence or for political rights in Poland' from 1 June 1956 to 4 June 1989 (31 July 1990 in the 2017 changes). A 'person repressed for political reasons' was one whose actions for independence or political rights had led to their being (a) held in prison or the equivalent on the basis of a court judgment between 1956 and 1989 or held once without sentence for longer than forty-eight hours or many times for a total period exceeding thirty days or (b) held in a place of detention under the martial law decree or (c) served in the army for more than thirty days after conscription for political reasons.

This category also included those whose participation in pro-independence protests had caused death, bodily harm or damage to health lasting longer than seven days. It included activists in the independence movement who had suffered criminal damage as a result of surveillance; who had been deprived of the ability to work in their own field, dismissed from work or expelled from education; whose writings were banned by the Censor for more than one year; or who were the subject of an arrest warrant, accused of or sentenced for pro-independence activities.

Those who worked for the security organs were excluded unless they could prove that they had, 'without the knowledge of their superiors', actively assisted those working for Polish independence or political rights, so long as the IPN held no documents demonstrating their collaboration with the security services. This law thus echoed the controversial exclusions condemned by the social democrats. However, the Left was now powerless, reduced to a small rump after the disastrous election of 2005 and then disappearing from parliament altogether between 2015 and 2019.

### The Brześć Trial

It might seem as though issues of rehabilitative justice had run their course after more than twenty-five years. However, in January 2016 Peasant Party (PSL) deputies submitted a draft bill delving deeper into the reaches of Polish history: it proposed to 'recognise as invalid the sentences of former *Sejm* deputies at the Brześć trial for activity on behalf of a democratic Polish State'.[78]

The Brześć Trial of 1931–2 was indeed notorious. In 1930 deputies from the Centre–Left opposition, including former Prime Minister Wincenty Witos, were incarcerated in the infamous Brest Fortress (now in Belarus), maltreated and accused of plotting to overthrow the government. Ten deputies received relatively short sentences, from one and a half to three years, or they could choose exile. Norman Davies saw it as 'a model of public justice' compared to secret Stalinist-era trials,[79] but this is hardly a good comparison. Still, the resurrection of the trial certainly provides further illustration of Davies's thesis that the past lives in Poland's present.

PSL and SLD deputies had pursued this matter through interpellations since 2005. However, the Procuracy found that there was insufficient documentation to establish legal violations by the courts, while 'analysis of the sentences … does not indicate that the courts engaged in a tendentious evaluation of the evidence ….and historical assessment cannot serve as the basis for cassation'.[80] The draft bill sought 'the full restoration of the honour and human dignity to these Polish citizens repressed for their defence of Polish democracy' because the 'complete amnesty and restoration of all civic rights' granted to the defendants in October 1939 'to erase the dilemmas (*rozterki*) of the past' acknowledged the shortcomings of the judicial process. However, following the 2015 elections and the return to government of Law and Justice (PiS), these views found it difficult to gain a hearing. PiS politicians were amongst the most vocal supporters of the Manichean view of history.

## The Constitutional Tribunal

We noted above the decision of the Constitutional Tribunal (TK) in 1994, agreeing that the combatants' law should exclude only those who worked in sections of the security apparatus directly engaged in repression.[81] The TK also reviewed the legislation in 2003, 2009, 2011 and 2012. In 2003 it found that time limits for filing for combatant status violated the principles of equality before the law and citizens' confidence in the state. Definitions of combatants and repressed persons, however, were a matter solely for parliament.[82] In 2009 the TK rejected the claim of the brother of a wrongly executed man to inherit the right to compensation. The law's provision that only 'the spouse, children, and parents' could inherit was unusual but reasonable; it was not linked to general property or testamentary rights.[83] In effect, it was a measure of transitional justice. In 2012 the Tribunal upheld residency requirements regarding acts committed by Soviet authorities on former Polish territory: as the Polish state had no obligation to provide compensation for acts committed by the Soviet Union, requiring Polish residency as a prerequisite for compensation was reasonable.[84]

These were minor clarifications. However, several decisions affected the shaping of the landmark decision of the Constitutional Tribunal on the legality of martial law later that year. The TK declared that limiting compensation for those repressed after 1956 was unacceptable.[85] Different treatment for persons in a similar position – having been repressed for pro-independence activities – was unconstitutional: it was arbitrary and discriminatory, and it breached the principles of social justice. Furthermore, the right to full compensation for the unlawful deprivation of freedom was protected in the Constitution.

In its decision on martial law in 2011[86] (see Chapter 4), the Constitutional Tribunal conducted a survey of existing rehabilitation legislation and found it wanting. The rehabilitation law envisaged the annulment of actions, ascribed or alleged, linked to activity supporting Polish independence; sentences issued because of such activity; and also resistance to the collectivization of agriculture. Outside its remit were other actions prohibited by the decree on martial law which had no direct connection to the independence struggle or resistance to collectivization. Thus, not all verdicts issued during martial law were subject to the terms of the invalidation law.

Moreover, the Tribunal argued that those who could benefit from the law did not fully enjoy the means to ensure the constitutional rights and freedoms violated by judicial decisions up until 1989: the invalidation law specified the prerequisites for declaring a sentence invalid (notably activity on behalf of Polish independence) and thus required the court to investigate whether the prerequisites had been met; only then could it reach a judgment; it could not invalidate a sentence because of lack of relevant evidence.

Other laws were also flawed: for example, the 2009 law on compensation of families envisaged compensation only in the event of a victim's death, excluding compensation for damage to health. In sum, the Court found that current legislation did not suffice to ensure the erasure of the negative consequences of the (illegal) martial law legislation. The activists' law of 2015 was at least partly a response to this judgment and to that of 2014, when the TK ruled that the invalidation law did not extend to those who had successfully evaded internment, only to those who had been detained. The law, it said, did not seek to remedy all cases of harm but only those entailing deprivation of life or freedom.[87]

## Compensation

With the 2007 laws extending the right to the nullification of sentences and compensation to the 1980s, the judgments of the Constitutional Tribunal rejecting the 2007 limit of compensation to 25,000 PNL and the TK's 2011 judgment declaring martial law illegal, the way was open for thousands of new claims for compensation. At the same time the courts were still dealing with cases arising from the immediate post-war period.[88]

Under martial law cases were heard by civil and military courts. Many civil judges had belonged to Solidarity (*NSZZ Pracowników Wymiaru Sprawiedliwości "Solidarność"*).[89] With some judges already interned, the Ministry of Justice purged the judiciary of its Solidarity element and appointed some 200 new judges. Almost 10,000 persons were interned.[90] Between 13 December 1981 and 21 July 1983 military courts sentenced 5,681 persons on the basis of the martial law decree and the general courts 979.[91] The general courts dealt with continued (illegal) trade union activity, organizing strikes or protests and 'compelling others' to engage in such activity.

Less serious violations went to the *Kolegia* for Misdemeanors (*Kolegia do spraw wykroczeń*). Between 13 December 1981 and 21 July 1983 they issued penalties for violating the martial law decrees to 207,692 persons, of whom 4,273 received short custodial sentences. Another 30,000 were sentenced under the accelerated procedures provided for other offences committed in this period.[92]

Closely linked to martial law were new regulations concerning persons 'evading work'. The Council of State introduced the obligation to work in a decree of 30 December 1981. In January alone the police identified 4,214 'social parasites'. Over just two months, January and February 1982, the police provided the employment organizations with information on some 57,000 persons required to work. The police also tracked persons allegedly evading military service. By the end of February 7,000 parasites had been taken into the army.

Between 1991 and 2013 some 50,000 persons had their sentences annulled.[93] From 1991 to 2008 about 70,000 persons received compensation averaging about 16,000 zloties each. The Constitutional Court's judgments led to more cases, with new plaintiffs, and more appeals, from those who had received the-then maximum 25,000 PNL. A further 6,831 persons received compensation (up to 2013). In 2011 the Ministry of Justice took the initiative, seeking the invalidation of sentences imposed for political reasons – notably death sentences between 1944 and 1956.[94]

After 2015 Procurators of the Main Commission could directly request the courts to invalidate decisions of communist courts. In 2016 alone procurators added 388 cases to the register of pending invalidation reviews. The courts dealt with 132 requests in 2016, of which 59 were completed.[95] The declaration that a judgment was invalid paved the way for compensation under the 1991 law. The IPN assumed a greater role in the area of rehabilitation and compensation for the victims of the old regime.

There is no complete record of the individuals awarded compensation because many preferred to keep their cases private. Newspapers and television provided numerous examples, however. Some cases caused a stir because of the large claims. Antoni

Klusik sought some 375,000 zloties as compensation for 12 months' internment and several short periods of detention. In 2008 the district court awarded Klusik 24,999 PNL. On appeal in 2012 he received 62,000 PNL, 5,000 for each month of internment and 1,000 for each of two documented detentions.[96] Andrzej Sobieraj received 65,000 PNL of a claim of 1.2 million. Antoni Lenkiewicz had received 23,750 PNL in Wrocław, just under the-then maximum. In 2014, claiming 2 million, Lenkiewicz was dissatisfied by the award of (an additional) 4,000 PNL by the district court.[97]

Some cases involving prominent underground activists attracted criticism for the very fact of seeking compensation. 'Legend of the opposition', Zbigniew Romaszewski (1940–2014) was a dissident activist from the mid-1960s onwards. Among other things he was a member of the Workers' Defence Committee (1977) and the founder of the Polish Helsinki Committee (1979). During martial law he set up Radio Solidarity and helped to establish the secret Solidarity executive of the Mazowsze Region. Imprisoned from 1982 to 1984, Romaszewski was an Amnesty International prisoner of conscience. In 1989 he was a member of Solidarity's Round Table delegation. He served in the Senate from 1989 to 2011, with roles as deputy speaker and chair of the Human Rights Committee. After losing in the 2011 election he was elected to the Tribunal of State and received the Order of the White Eagle for distinguished service. With his public standing and comfortable pension, Romaszewski's claim (he received 240,000 PLN) aroused criticism from many Solidarity activists, including Lech Wałęsa.[98]

Another prominent example was provided by the case of Adam Słomka, formerly of the underground Confederation for Independent Poland (KPN) and a three-term deputy. The appeal court rejected his demand for 1 million zloties but increased the original award for his eighteen-month period of imprisonment from 180,000 to 270,000 PNL. Such sums were far from insignificant – almost £50,000 at current exchange rates (2016).

# Conclusion

After a short period of consensus over the nature of Polish Stalinism, the politicization of rehabilitation proceeded apace, with Left and Right viewing the past through very different lenses and playing to different groups of constituents. For the post-Solidarity Right victims of political persecution were heroes of the 'struggle for Polish independence'. This moralization of memory meant division into two camps, the good guys and the bad guys. The Right saw the state as an illegitimate, undemocratic puppet regime of the USSR. No distinction was made between those imprisoned on false charges and those of the anti-communist resistance who committed the crimes of which they were accused. There was no analysis of how a state may legitimately defend itself against armed attacks, arson or the murder of its civilian population. Effectively, agents of the state were traitorous criminals and its opponents were martyrs.

There was recognition in some circles that 1956 was a watershed, after which Poland had full control of its own domestic affairs. Yet the concept of a 'struggle for independence and sovereignty' persisted in both rhetoric and law. When former Solidarity elites were in power, in 1991, 1997 and after 2005, they gradually extended the scope of the rehabilitation laws to embrace virtually all who had suffered negative consequences for their opposition activity.

The Left (i.e. the SLD) had a difficult hand to play. It was conscious of the wrongs committed by the communists, and its leaders did not wish to appear as apologists for the old order. Their message was one of a new leaf: a new party, committed to pluralist democracy, although in common parlance they were 'post-communists'. At the same time there was a reluctance to embrace the blame for the deeds of their Stalinist predecessors. Moreover, many held the view that the old regime had positive achievements to its credit, including industrial development and highly developed health and welfare provision. It was as legitimate to support the ideological principles of the regime as to oppose them, even if those principles were not always reflected in practice. Martial law itself was viewed by the party and its supporters not as an illegal act but as a necessary evil, a legitimate defence of the system.

The enduring nature and depth of anti-communist sentiments meant that attempts to secure a consensus broke down very rapidly. Ironically, it was the SLD that mobilized the arguments for individual rights against the notion of collective guilt embodied in the exclusion from combatant status of anyone who had worked for the military, the security services, the police or the judiciary. It achieved partial success when the Constitutional Tribunal agreed that those working outside the security bureaux should not be excluded if they had not undertaken functions linked to combatting the opposition. Such exclusion was incompatible with the principle of equality before the law. However, the SLD was not powerful enough, even in government, to introduce the requirement of evidence of wrongdoing by specific individuals to substantiate their exclusion as 'combatants'.

Moreover, when it rejected the legality of martial law in 2011 (see Chapter 4), the Constitutional Tribunal paved the way for a huge increase in claims for compensation by those punished for violating martial law decrees. Although martial law sentences had been invalidated by early legislation, the fact that the decrees no longer counted as constituting the law of the time made a key difference. Following that decision, the *Sejm* sought to fill gaps identified by the TK in the rehabilitation legislation – including the law on 'activists of the anti-communist opposition and persons repressed for political reasons' in 2015.

It is certainly impressive that in general, so many wartime fighters and victims of Nazi and Soviet and Polish oppression have been restored to honour and respect – and helped materially in important ways. It is regrettable that historical animosities so often trumped national reconciliation, resulting in an effective division between 'good combatants' and 'bad combatants' unworthy of that status. The early promise of a benign narrative proved short lived.

# Dealing with past crimes

The prosecution of past crimes proved difficult in all communist countries. The view that prosecution would come 'quickly or not at all' proved unfounded. Samuel Huntington's argument that a negotiated exit from communism meant that officials would not be prosecuted[1] held true only in the short term. Nor were less repressive regimes more likely to 'forgive and forget'.[2] Poland had a 'negotiated exit' and a less repressive regime, but its trials of senior communists lasted not years but decades.

It is true that Poland's 'mode of exit' ruled out any prosecution of the communist leadership for alleged past crimes during 1989 and 1990. After the Round Table elections communists filled key posts in Mazowiecki's government, and General Wojciech Jaruzelski held the presidency. There was considerable public support for this configuration. In 1989 almost half the respondents (47 per cent) believed that Jaruzelski would be a good president.[3] Twenty years later in 2009, 49 per cent thought it 'not a good choice but appropriate at the time'; only 15 per cent of respondents viewed Jaruzelski's presidency as a 'bad choice'.[4]

In July 1990 the communists left the government, and after the first direct presidential election in December, Solidarity's Lech Wałęsa replaced Jaruzelski. Yet even while dealing with the upper echelons of the communist leadership was in abeyance, we can see the beginnings of a long process of bringing to book former functionaries of the old regime. The issue was already 'out in the open'.

In the 'Contract *Sejm*' (1989–91) the Rokita Commission recommended proceedings against certain persons. In September 1990 the minister of justice ordered an official investigation into the deaths on the Baltic coast in 1970. Władysław Ciastoń, former deputy director of the interior ministry, and Zenon Płatek, former director of Department IV, dealing with the churches' 'anti-state activities', were charged with masterminding Jerzy Popiełuszko's murder in 1984. The Commission Investigating Crimes against the Polish Nation began to investigate officers of the Ministry of Public Security.

The first successful trial was that of Andrzej Augustyn, sentenced in 1991 for shooting a student during a demonstration in 1982. In 1996 twelve former security officers, including the notorious Adam Humer, were convicted of torturing political prisoners in the 1940s. The trial evoked stark reminders of the systematic brutality of the Stalinist regime.

After four years, in August 1994, Ciastoń and Płatek were acquitted, but the appeal court ordered a retrial. In 2000 Płatek's trial was suspended on health grounds. In

December 2002 Ciastoń was acquitted again; the Court found no evidence of his involvement. When Płatek's health was reviewed in 2008, he was still unable to stand trial. He died in June 2009. Later Ciastoń faced other charges in connection with martial law (see below).

Only after the democratic elections of 1991 was the possibility of charging more senior communist leaders seriously mooted and politically feasible. In December 1991 the *Sejm* resolved that members of the Military Council of National Salvation be brought before the Tribunal of State for implementing martial law in December 1981. On 1 February 1992 the *Sejm* declared martial law illegal.[5] During the short 1991–3 parliament two committees examined martial law.

Unusually, the new *Sejm* (1993–7) voted to continue the work of the Committee on Constitutional Responsibility. In 1996 the *Sejm* accepted its recommendation to discontinue proceedings in the matter of martial law. Because the government was dominated by the SLD with a strong presence in the *Sejm*, this was generally seen as a political decision. A majority of the Committee's members broadly accepted Jaruzelski's claim to have acted from 'higher necessity'. While the decision was undoubtedly political, the committee did probe the historical-legal dimension with great thoroughness. Nor did this decision preclude the subsequent trial of Jaruzelski and other senior leaders. Criminal trials became a permanent feature of the judicial landscape.

## The judicial process

Few trials resulted in convictions. The process was protracted, and the age and ill health of many defendants were a key factor, with many trials ended or interrupted by death or incapacity. Many witnesses had died, and faulty memories affected the nature and quality of evidence. The process was extended by uncertainties regarding appropriate jurisdiction, constant appeals and the bringing of new charges.

### The statute of limitations

As elsewhere,[6] the statute of limitations remained an obstacle to prosecution until the Supreme Court reached a partial resolution in 2010. The inexperience of the new legislature clearly told. In 1991 the Constitutional Tribunal (TK) 'signalled' problems with the law on the Institute of National Remembrance (IPN),[7] which gave the Commission on Nazi Crimes additional responsibilities to investigate 'Stalinist crimes'. Stalinist crimes were defined as crimes perpetrated up to 31 December 1956 by the authorities of the communist state or 'inspired or tolerated' by them. The law provided that 'since these are war crimes or crimes against humanity', there was no time bar to prosecution. The TK ruled that this law 'over-stretched the concept of crimes against humanity' and violated the principle of non-retroactivity. Moreover, the definition of Stalinist crimes was imprecise and incompatible with the principle of the 'definability' of a prohibited act. 'Stalinist crime' seemed to embrace any crime committed up to 1956, whatever its nature. The law introduced new, imprecise legal terminology, 'inspiring' and 'tolerating'. Also, Polish law recognized crimes committed by specific individuals, not legal persons ('the authorities').[8]

After 1993 the new parliament amended the Criminal Code to clarify the statute of limitations: it would begin on 1 January 1990 for crimes punishable by deprivation of freedom for longer than three years committed by a public functionary between 1 January 1944 and 31 December 1989. It was extended from 20 to 30 years for crimes, with 10 years for a misdemeanour punishable by a sentence of more than five years' imprisonment, and five years for other misdemeanours.

From 1997 the new Constitution, a fully revised Criminal Code and a new law on the Institute of National Remembrance (IPN) regulated time limits for criminal acts. According to the Constitution there was no statute of limitations for war crimes or crimes against humanity (Art. 43). It maintained the provision of the revised Criminal Code (1995) that 'the statute of limitations for actions connected with offences committed by, or by order of, public officials and which were not prosecuted for political reasons, shall be suspended for the period during which such reasons existed' (Art. 44). In other words, time limits did not run during the (communist) period, when certain crimes were not prosecuted for 'political reasons'. The starting date of 1 January 1990 for the statute of limitations signalled the new political-legal system which could now investigate past injustices.

The amended Criminal Code of 1997[9] redefined some limits. Major changes came with the new Law on the IPN in 1998,[10] which substituted 'communist crimes' for the dubious concept of 'Stalinist crimes'. A 'communist crime' involved 'repression or other human rights' violation. ... constituting an offence in Polish law at the time ... and perpetrated by a state functionary ... from 17 September 1939 to 31 December 1989' (Art. 2). Crimes against humanity included genocide and 'acts prohibited by Polish criminal law at the time that constitute other serious persecution on grounds of belonging to a particular national, political, social, racial or religious group if ... committed by or inspired or tolerated by a public functionary' (Art. 3).

In 2005 new terms for some misdemeanours were added to the Criminal Code.[11] In 2007 the new law on the IPN extended limits to forty years for the 'communist crime' of murder and thirty years for 'other communist crimes', with the start date altered to 1 August 1990.[12] In 2008 the Constitutional Tribunal accepted these changes, since extending the time limit did not 'worsen' the position of the accused, who, when committing an offence, could not foretell whether the time limit would change. However, it also observed an undesirable tendency to extend time limits and warned against over-frequent changes. The decision did not give a free hand to the legislature to extend time limits.[13]

In 2010 however the Supreme Court[14] rejected the arguments of IPN prosecutors that the amended law on the IPN 'definitively resolved' the issue in 2007; the Court found that its provisions must be taken in conjunction with the Criminal Code as revised in 1995 and 1997, including the starting date of 1 January 1990 as the legal beginning of the new system. Applying the 1995 Criminal Code meant that the statute of limitations had *already* expired for certain offences. Once the term had expired, it could not be reversed by later changes.

Hence in the case in question the conviction of Bogdan M. was out of time. He had tried to extract information from Franciszek K. in the early 1980s by physical and psychological abuse, frequently arresting FK for extended, unlawful periods, searching his home without cause, using physical threats and verbal vulgarity. As a communist functionary whose acts violated basic human freedoms, Bogdan M's acts were 'communist crimes' subject to a maximum of three years' imprisonment.[15] For such offences the statute of limitations had run for five years from 1 January 1990 and had therefore expired in 1995. This assessment had immediate consequences for the IPN, which discontinued proceedings in 246 cases.[16] The Supreme Court's judgment did not apply to more serious cases, which the IPN continued to prosecute.

# Leadership trials

The issue of the culpability of communist leaders persisted for thirty years. Wojciech Jaruzelski himself, along with former interior minister General Czesław Kiszczak and others, faced charges until his death in May 2014. These charges were linked to the deaths of workers on the Baltic Coast in December 1970, the declaration of martial law and the deaths of striking miners protesting martial law.

Jaruzelski was the central figure in the trials of the senior communist leadership in Poland. He was a complex figure, a professional soldier and politician *malgré lui*. Born into the gentry in 1923, educated by the Jesuits, exiled as a child to Siberia with his family, enduring forced labour in the coalmines of Kazakhstan, where he suffered the snow-blindness that led to a lifetime of eye problems – his early biography sounds like the formative years of an entrenched oppositionist. Yet Jaruzelski became a convinced communist. By 1943, he was serving in the Soviet-sponsored Polish forces, where he saw active service alongside the Red Army. After the war Jaruzelski graduated from the Polish Higher Infantry School and the General Staff Academy. He joined the communist party in 1947 and rose steadily through the ranks of both party and army, becoming minister of defence in 1968. He became a member of the Central Committee in 1964 and joined the Politburo in 1971 after Gierek's removal as leader. Jaruzelski became prime minister in February 1981 and party leader in October, continuing as minister of defence. He was minister of defence during the Baltic upheavals of 1970, and he was central to the decision to impose martial law in 1981. He later played a key role in the Party's decision to negotiate with Solidarity – leading ultimately to the June 1989 elections and the demise of the communist regime. In July 1989 he was elected president by the Polish Parliament by the margin of a single vote.

## Deaths on the Baltic Coast

After Edward Gierek became communist party leader in December 1970, the Party investigated the 'Baltic events' of that month, when the army and militia moved to quell growing protests in Baltic cities against increases in the price of basic foodstuffs; some forty-three civilians and one soldier died, and more than 1,100 persons were wounded. In 1990, since no *formal* investigation had taken place, the Naval

Procuracy began another investigation. Over a three-year period it discontinued proceedings against twenty political, army and militia leaders – some were long dead while others had died after the investigation had begun. They included the two men condemned by the party's own investigation as ultimately responsible – former Party leader Władysław Gomułka (1905–82) and his right-hand man Zenon Kliszko (1908–89). The investigation of Wojciech Jaruzelski, the-then minister of defence, continued.

Once charges had been prepared, the process hit the first of many technical-legal obstacles in April 1993.[17] According to military law, in such a serious case the court must include a judge of at least the same rank as the accused. In Jaruzelski's case no one met the requirements. To resolve this the justice minister simply transferred the case to the civil procuracy. During the investigation procurators interviewed 4,500 witnesses and gathered thousands of documents. They envisaged that 1,091 witnesses would testify at the forthcoming trial.

Charges were presented to the Gdańsk Provincial Court on 7 April 1995. They were brought against twelve persons[18] under Articles 16 (the preparation of an offence)[19] and 148 (murder) of the Criminal Code and – for Jaruzelski and Kazimierz Świtała – violating the constitutional duty of the government to ensure public order and security.[20]

Jaruzelski was accused of causing twenty-nine deaths and the wounding of 105 persons in Gdańsk, Gdynia and Szczecin. It was alleged that

> as Minister of Defence …, directing the actions of the Polish Army to suppress the protesters. …. he issued a command at the instigation of … Władysław Gomułka and in contravention of Art. 32 (7) of the Constitution, for military units to use live ammunition against the demonstrations, while understanding and accepting that this could result in the deaths of an unspecified number of persons.

Jaruzelski's co-defendants were similarly charged with culpability for these deaths. Świtała had been minister of the interior; Stanisław Kociołek, deputy prime minister; Tadeusz Tuczapski, deputy defence minister; and Józef Kamiński, commander of the military district. The army officers were charged with issuing orders to fire on workers at shipyards in Gdańsk and Gdynia.

Still the trial did not begin, with confusion over the correct jurisdiction. After three months the court sought additional materials from the procurator. His successful appeal against this request brought the case back to the provincial court, which in turn decided to return it to the military court (*Sąd Marynarki Wojennej*); once again the provincial court was reversed on appeal.

At last, on 28 March 1996 seven defendants, including Jaruzelski, presented themselves to the court in Gdańsk. Still the charges were not read. Because four defendants were absent for medical reasons, the court dealt only with procedural matters, as it did in several subsequent hearings. Two were particularly important. Jaruzelski's lawyers had resigned on grounds of their own ill health and petitioned to move the trial to Warsaw, where they could still act in his defence. The second was a formal request to suspend proceedings against Jaruzelski, Świtała and

Kociołek because as ministerial office holders in 1970, the Tribunal of State was the appropriate forum for them.

On 25 April the court discontinued proceedings against Jaruzelski and Świtała because violating the Constitution did not fall within its jurisdiction. Kociołek had not been charged with violating the Constitution and his case continued, alongside the remaining officers. The court was reversed on appeal. Jaruzelski and Świtała would be tried in the provincial court.

With jurisdiction established, the case rapidly foundered on the ill health of the defendants. In July 1996 Jaruzelski was excluded from the trial – with kidney disease, spinal and eye problems, and bouts of depression. Over the next few months five hearings were postponed. In March 1997 the court determined that four other defendants should be dealt with in separate proceedings, to be renewed when their health permitted. Periodically the court required medical examinations to establish whether the condition of the accused had changed. In February 1998 doctors advised that Jaruzelski and Kamiński were unfit to travel; they could be tried, but not in Gdańsk. Kubalica and Świtała could not be tried at all.

On 15 June 1998 the trial of the remaining seven defendants[21] began at last. The ill health of defendants continued to generate interruptions in scheduled hearings. At the end of 1999 the Supreme Court transferred the entire case to Warsaw; it argued that justice could not be served by piecemeal, interrupted proceedings.[22]

That decision made little difference. The trial remained beset with procedural difficulties. Much of the court's time was taken up with reading out documents from the archives. Jaruzelski was the first defendant to testify – on 18 October 2001. Over the years successive defendants were excluded, designated for separate proceedings (health permitting) or removed altogether by incapacity or death. In July 2011 the trial began all over again following the death of a lay judge. Jaruzelski was again excluded, following a diagnosis of cancer. By 2012 only Kociołek and army officers Fałdasz and Wiekiera remained on trial.

After almost eighteen years, in April 2013, Stanisław Kociołek was acquitted. The officers were guilty of 'assault with lethal consequences'; they received suspended sentences of four years, halved by amnesty. The procurator contested the court's 'internally contradictory judgment'.[23] When the appellate court rejected his appeal against Kociołek's acquittal, he appealed to the Supreme Court. In April 2015 the Supreme Court ordered a retrial. Kociołek died in October.

### December 1970: Substantive matters

When Jaruzelski died in May 2014, proceedings against him were discontinued, so there was no verdict in his case. However, several points are worth extracting from the verdicts on the two officers. The first is the legalistic approach taken by the court. Unlike the Soviet Constitution, the Polish Constitution did not enshrine the 'leading role of the Party' (that was added in 1977). This meant that the decision taken on 15 November 1970 by Party Secretary Gomułka to issue live ammunition to soldiers and militia was – according to the Warsaw court – an 'illegal and criminal decision'.

Jaruzelski's defence, however, was based on the absence of the rule of law in communist Poland; he stressed the political reality of Communist Party supremacy and the *de facto* subordination of state institutions. Throughout the years until his death he steadfastly maintained the position expressed in his speech to the new Central Committee in 1971: 'For the ministers of defence and the interior the decisions taken (by Gomułka, fm) possessed both actual and formal-legal force. I cannot imagine, comrades, that either then or today or tomorrow the leaders of our people's army could fail to implement decisions of the party-state leadership, especially when justified by a threat to the socialist social order.'[24]

Many commentators shared the procurator's view that Jaruzelski should have questioned the decision to issue live ammunition.[25] Given the context, however, his silence is not surprising. More senior officials, including the prime minister and the chairman of the Council of State, were also present at the meeting of 15 November, and none demurred. Jaruzelski's response was based on a lifetime of loyalty and subordination to the Party. The Party was in charge, and state institutions – including the defence ministry – were instruments of the Party. The 1971 Report to the Politburo noted that the ministers of defence and the interior attended the meeting in order to 'receive the decision for implementation.'[26] Nor was Jaruzelski involved in the direction of troops. A special unit took charge, with Politburo member Zenon Kliszko seen as the key political decision-maker. When Jaruzelski testified in 2001, he maintained that the indictment was groundless, with crucial gaps and errors. Jaruzelski claimed (not without reason) that the procurator's case was tendentious, selective and wrong on key points of law and fact. He noted that he had not been involved in the decision-making process or the deployment of troops. 'During the tragic events of December 1970, I did not violate the constitution, I did not issue an order to use firearms, I did not commit any crime.'[27]

There is little doubt that the-then communist leadership feared that violence might spread from the Baltic to other cities.[28] Rumours spread regarding the presence of fascist extremists and 'marginalised hooligan elements'. However, Jaruzelski's responsibility was not proven. Ultimately the Court made an historical judgment, not a legal one. In its rationale the Court noted that 'after the burning … of the Central Committee headquarters of the provincial PZPR and the Municipal Headquarters of the Militia, the protection of important or strategic state buildings was necessary. On the other hand, there was *no need* to send fully armed army divisions to the Tri-City area.'[29] This was at best a highly contentious judgment and begged the question of Jaruzelski's role.

# Martial law trials

## Wujek

The first trials linked to martial law (13 December 1981–22 July 1983) centred on the brutal 'pacification' of the Wujek coal mine, where nine striking miners were killed on 16 December after a special ZOMO platoon (Motorized Reserves of the Citizens' Militia) fired on them. In 1993 Czesław Kiszczak, then-minister of the interior, was charged along with local ZOMO commander Kazimierz Wilczyński, platoon commander Romuald Cieślak and twenty members of the platoon. Because of his poor health Kiszczak's case (and later that of Wilczyński) was tried separately. In 1997 the defendants were acquitted, but procedural irregularities led to a retrial in 2001, with the same verdict. The appeal court found similar procedural faults and 'improper evaluation of evidence'. In a third trial fifteen remaining defendants were convicted in September 2004. With amnesty Cieślak – found to have fired the first shot – received six years, with the others sentenced from two and a half to three years in prison. After failing to establish who had sent the platoon to Wujek, the court acquitted the former deputy police chief in Katowice. In April 2009 the Supreme Court confirmed the verdicts.

Kiszczak himself was tried five times for the deaths at Wujek. The first trial in 1994, when he was accused of sending a coded telegram authorizing the use of live ammunition, resulted in acquittal in 1996. At the second, completed in 2004, Kiszczak was convicted of contributing to the miners' deaths. The court sentenced him to four years, halved by the amnesty and suspended. Again the appellate court ordered a retrial, which began in 2006. In July 2008 the court declared Kiszczak's 'unintentional guilt' (*winę nieumyślną*), inadvertently contributing to the miners' deaths, but it discontinued proceedings because the statute of limitations had expired. The appellate court disagreed, and Kiszczak's fourth trial began in February 2010 despite his deteriorating health. Kiszczak was acquitted on 26 April 2011. This verdict too was overturned on appeal, and a retrial was ordered.

The Appellate Court agreed with the objections expressed by the procurator. The court had over-emphasized testimony that Kiszczak was ignorant of the coded telegram. As interior minister, Kiszczak must have realized that the use of weapons could lead to a 'very dangerous situation'. However, the fifth trial was delayed by further medical assessments. In June 2012 the judge suspended proceedings. The appellate court agreed that Kiszczak's mental state had deteriorated and he was unfit to stand trial. The trial was postponed indefinitely (*odroczony beterminowo*).

## The decision to implement martial law

In 1991 the *Sejm* had resolved that martial law was illegal, but attempts to bring communist leaders before the Tribunal of State ceased when the *Sejm* suspended proceedings in 1996. Ten years later IPN procurators renewed the investigation. In April 2007 they filed charges against the 'authors of martial law': Wojciech Jaruzelski, Czesław Kiszczak, Florian Siwicki and Tadeusz Tuczapski (and others). All had been members of the Council of State and the Military Committee of National Salvation. The court sought more information from the IPN and bizarrely demanded testimony from (among others) Margaret Thatcher and Mikhail Gorbachev. The charges were read in September 2008 after the appellate court found these requests 'unreasonable'.

## Issues in the martial law decisions

The legality of martial law remained an issue for many years, with contradictory legal judgments from the Supreme Court and the Constitutional Tribunal and controversy among lawyers, scholars and politicians. The procedural and substantive arguments that formed the basis of claims of illegality are roughly as follows. The first claim was that the decree was illegal because of procedural failure, since it was issued by the Council of State, not by the *Sejm* (which was sitting at the time). The 1952 Constitution provided that 'when the *Sejm* is not sitting, the Council of State issues decrees with the force of law'.[30]

The second claim was that constitutionally martial law could not come into force until publication in the *Journal of Laws* because acts enter into force on the day of their publication. The decrees were passed on 12 December and published in an issue of the *Journal of Laws* falsely dated 14 December, with the *Journal* available on 17 December at the earliest. In this way the decrees violated the principle that law may not operate retroactively.

The 1952 Constitution dealt very briefly with the subject of martial law. The Constitution did not explicitly incorporate the interwar concept of the 'exceptional state' (*stan wyjątkowy*), which its authors saw as a bourgeois tool of the ruling class against the workers' movement and thus wholly irrelevant to the new political reality.[31] It conceived two types of special circumstances. The first was a state of war (*stan wojny*) declared in the event of an armed attack on the country. The second was martial law (*stan wojenny*): Article 33(2) provided that 'the Council of State may introduce martial law in a part or the whole of Polish territory if considerations of the protection or security of the state demand it'.

No laws regulating martial law were introduced after the promulgation of the Constitution. This is why in 1981 the Council of State first issued its resolution in the matter of introducing martial law with regard to the security of the state[32] and then three decrees on martial law,[33] 'special proceedings for crimes committed during martial law'[34] and the assigning of certain crimes to military courts during martial law.[35] However, this constitutional lacuna was crucial: if the *resolution* was given constitutional validity by Article 33(2), which envisaged no role for the *Sejm*, the claim that the *decrees* violated Article 31 because the *Sejm* was in session was a strong one.

The second claim of procedural irregularity – that of delayed publication in the *Journal of Laws* – is linked to: (1) amendments to the martial law decree after its approval by the Council of State, (2) the wording of the decrees and (3) the role of the International Covenant on Civil and Political Rights, to which Poland was a signatory. The first relates to the extra-constitutional modification of the original decree on martial law before its publication. After representatives of the Catholic hierarchy met with the deputy chair of the Council of State, they 'made some corrections, removing certain provisions restricting the activities of the Church'.[36] One cannot be sure whether publication was delayed by these modifications to the decree, but the changes clearly had no basis in law.[37]

The wording of the decrees gave rise to allegations of procedural irregularity because the final article of each decree contained two contradictory phrases: Article 61 of the decree on martial law provided that 'the decree comes into effect from the date of publication with force (*z mocą*) from the day it was passed'. The other decrees came 'into effect from the date of publication with force from the introduction of martial law'. Clearly the decrees were intended to take immediate effect; the declaration of martial law was widely publicized through the media. Jaruzelski's speech announcing martial law was repeatedly broadcast on television and radio. The confused wording obscured this intention, creating a basis for the argument that the acts applied from their publication on 17 December and thus could not apply retroactively from the 13th to the 16th.

The 1952 Constitution did not prohibit retroactive legislation. However, the International Covenant did so. Whether the Covenant should apply – it had never been incorporated into Polish law, and neither judicial practice nor doctrine of the People's Republic accepted the direct application of international law – was disputed. This debate surfaced only after 1989.

Finally, questions surrounded the Law on the Specific Regulation of Law under Martial Law, which the *Sejm* passed on 25 January 1982.[38] This short law acknowledged

> the introduction by the Council of State on the basis of Art. 33 §2 of the Constitution of the Polish People's Republic of the resolution of 12 December 1981 on martial law having regard to the threat to the fundamental interests of the nation and the state and with the aim of countering the disintegration of socio-economic life and ensuring the effective functioning of the organs of state, and also for creating the conditions for the effective defence of the sovereignty and independence of the Polish People's Republic, and having regard to the fact that for the effective restoration of social peace and the rebuilding of the country's economy it was essential to introduce extraordinary legal measures not envisaged in existing laws

and it confirmed with immediate effect the four decrees of the Council of State of 12 December 1981 with validity from 12 December 1981. Since the *Sejm* was the highest constitutional authority, it might appear incontrovertible that it had endorsed all the actions of the Council, including its procedural irregularities.[39] This was not however the dominant view, and we shall see that it was not shared by the Constitutional Tribunal.

Although procedural issues were central from the point of view of law, substantive issues also surrounded the martial law case. These hinged largely on the justification for martial law. This is an important debate, no doubt. Historians, political scientists, lawyers and participants continued to offer very different perspectives.[40] The central claim for the prosecution was that there was no justification for martial law, whether because of an external threat of intervention or an internal threat to public safety and public order. The counter-argument was that the Constitution empowered the Council of State to judge the necessity of martial law, regardless of whether its judgment was sound.

Jaruzelski offered a two-fold justification: Firstly, given the political and economic crisis, domestic instability raised the prospect of 'civil war'. Indeed, the martial law decree referred to 'the threat to the vital interests of the state and the nation'; the 'decline in social discipline' and the need to 'create conditions for the effective protection of peace, harmony and public order'; and the 'security of the state'.[41] Secondly, martial law was necessary to forestall the greater evil, that of armed Soviet intervention. This argument was (understandably) not made at the time, but it became central to Jaruzelski's case.

Soviet anxiety was manifest from Solidarity's earliest days; Soviet intervention was considered a genuine threat by Solidarity, by the Polish leadership and by the United States. The Brezhnev Doctrine, justifying intervention to 'protect socialism', was well known to all concerned. Indeed, plans for a Warsaw Pact invasion in December 1980 were well advanced.[42]

By autumn 1981 Jaruzelski was the central figure in the Polish leadership – he had become prime minister in February and Party leader in October. With Stanisław Kania he had engaged in numerous discussions with Soviet leaders, as well as with the drawing up of plans for martial law. It is clear that the Polish authorities felt beleaguered, facing economic and social deterioration, the strengthening of radical voices within Solidarity, the anxieties of their own activists and relentless pressure from the USSR. As the situation in Poland deteriorated, the Warsaw Pact launched its largest ever military exercises on the eve of the Solidarity Congress in September 1981. For eight days Poland's allies mobilized in the Baltic republics and along the Polish coast.

By this time, however, the Soviet position had moved in favour of a 'Polish solution'. The weight of academic opinion suggests that despite pressure on Poland from its socialist neighbours since Solidarity's birth in August 1980 – including threats of armed intervention – there was no prospect of external intervention in December 1981.[43] However, Poland's leaders may well have feared a Soviet invasion. They 'may have genuinely believed that an invasion would occur if a solution "from within" Poland did not materialize. Indeed, Soviet leaders themselves may have wanted to create that impression ... because they believed it would induce the Polish authorities to take action'.[44] Matthew Ouimet quotes General Gribkov: 'It became necessary to extend the duration of the exercise (in September 1981,fm) to show the Polish leadership and the Polish people that we were prepared to defend Poland from counterrevolution ... although we were not.'[45] Moreover, according to Ouimet, some Soviet leaders remained convinced that 'only the threat of invasion would guarantee a favourable resolution of the crisis'.[46]

Everything suggested that Jaruzelski was reluctant to introduce martial law. However, Soviet General Viktor Anoshkin's notebook seemed to confirm previous suggestions by some Soviet leaders that Jaruzelski believed that Poland needed help to introduce martial law: he had made repeated requests for Soviet military assistance with his proposed crackdown, and the Soviets had refused.[47] The apparent revelation that Jaruzelski had requested Soviet military assistance changed many views on his position. Yet it leaves unanswered the question posed by Jaruzelski himself – if he believed that martial law would fail without Soviet military assistance, why did he proceed to implement it (successfully) without such assurances?[48]

## Martial law in the courts

It took some time before the courts passed judgment on these issues. The first major ruling concerned judges who had issued sentences in the early days of martial law. The chair of the Supreme Court's Disciplinary Court rejected the IPN's request to waive their immunity. The IPN appealed. After the chair requested clarification from the full bench, in 2007 the Supreme Court issued a resolution to guide the courts.

The Supreme Court dealt with the argument that now-retired judge Zdzisław B. had sentenced Eugeniusz R. and Henryk B. for actions on 13 December 1981 that were not at that time unlawful. Since the martial law decrees could not apply until the date of their publication, the judge should not have applied them. The Court concluded that the prohibition on retroactivity did not apply because the 1952 Constitution contained no such prohibition; because the Polish People's Republic was not a democratic, law-based state; and because no mechanism existed for ensuring the consonance of domestic law with international law.[49] Therefore despite its ambiguity, the decree on martial law – providing legal force from 'its publication, with legal force from the day of passage' – could not be regarded as unconstitutional. Since judges did not enjoy a power of judicial review, they had no grounds to refuse to apply the law.

This utterly convincing view of martial law did not endure. The following year trials of the senior leadership for martial law began. The central defendants, including Jaruzelski, Siwicki and Kiszczak, stood accused of the 'communist crime' of 'directing an armed criminal organisation' for the purpose of violating the human rights of Polish citizens and of inciting members of the Council of State to exceed their constitutional powers by issuing decrees while the *Sejm* was in session.[50] Former party leader Stanisław Kania was accused of helping to plan 'the illegal introduction of martial law'. Other members of the Council of State – Eugenia Kempara, Krystyna Marszałek-Młyńczyk (she died in 2007 before the case opened) and Emil Kołodziej – were charged with voting for the (putatively illegal) martial law decree. Tadeusz Skóra, former deputy minister of justice, was charged with inciting members of the Council of State to violate the Constitution.

These are strange charges: accusing government officials who already controlled the state institutions of coercion of 'directing an armed criminal organisation' and 'deliberately setting out to issue illegal decrees' seems to defy common sense. Of course, martial law by its nature entails the limitation or suspension of human rights; that is precisely why it is an extraordinary measure in any legal system.

Over the next two years five defendants were excluded from the trial. Tuczapski, former deputy minister of defence, died in 2009. Skóra was excluded because the IPN forgot [*sic*] to apply to waive his judicial immunity. Jaruzelski and former Defence Minister Siwicki were too ill to stand trial. Kołodziej's case was excluded temporarily on health grounds; his case was heard separately.

In October 2011 Kołodziej became the first person to be convicted in connection with the martial law decrees. However, proceedings were discontinued because according to the Supreme Court's resolution of 2010, the statute of limitations applied. In January 2012 the court issued its verdict in the case of the three remaining defendants. As with Kołodziej, it acknowledged Kempara's guilt, but discontinued her case because of the time limit. Kiszczak received a suspended sentence of four years, reduced to two because of amnesty provisions. Kania was acquitted (he was not a member of the leadership after October 1981 and had steadfastly advocated a political solution).

In 2013 the Warsaw Appeal Court rejected the IPN's appeal against Kania's acquittal and temporarily suspended Kiszczak's appeal on health grounds. Kania's case was closed in April when the Supreme Court rejected the IPN's request for cassation. Kiszczak's appeal continued, though the Wujek case had already been suspended indefinitely. In December 2014 the court ordered that Kiszczak be taken by ambulance to Gdańsk for psychological, psychiatric, geriatric and neurological examination. He was found seriously mentally impaired and unfit for trial. In April 2015 the appellate court ruled that the appeal could be renewed, since Kiszczak's health 'would make it difficult' but not impossible to continue proceedings. In June 2015 the appellate court upheld Kiszczak's conviction. He died on 5 November.

# The Constitutional Tribunal

The Constitutional Court (TK) heard two major martial law cases. The first, in 2010, concerned the culpability of judges applying the martial law decrees. The second, in 2011, concerned the decrees themselves. Both cases arose from petitions of the Ombudsman. In the first he argued that the law on the courts (2001) did not prohibit the waiving of immunity for judges who had applied the martial law decrees because the decrees violated the principles of non-retroactivity and 'no crime and no penalty without law'. This was directly at odds with the view of the Supreme Court.

In a tortuous decision the Tribunal – with six dissenting views – largely agreed with the Ombudsman. The Supreme Court (SN) had based its resolution on Article 80, which the TK now declared to be unconstitutional. It provided that 'if a request to permit a judge to be charged with criminal responsibility does not accord with formal legal procedures ... or if a request is *obviously unjustified*' (italics mine), the chair of the disciplinary court should reject it.[51] The TK ruled that the resolution contravened the constitutional principle that Poland is a democratic, law-based state.[52] Although the TK had no competence to verify judicial decisions, it claimed jurisdiction here because Article 80 assumed 'new normative content' as a result of the 2010 resolution and 'the subject of constitutional control is (not the resolution but) the content that those provisions acquired in the course of their application'. The TK argued that because the resolution 'bound not only courts of lower instance, including appellate courts, but also other state organs', this could result in a '*chilling effect*', discouraging investigative organs from bringing to account judges who had reached verdicts on the basis of the retroactive provisions of the martial law decree.

All six dissenting judges[53] – despite differing views on the merits of the Supreme Court's resolution – saw the judgment as inappropriate and inadmissible: in effect, despite its denials, the TK was judging the resolution. Since acts of judicial oversight are not subject to constitutional control by the TK, the Tribunal had exceeded its competence and encroached upon the jurisdiction of the Supreme Court.

Following the Supreme Court Resolution, the IPN had suspended its investigation of judges. The TK's judgment was now taken as a green light for renewed attempts to waive the immunity of the 'most zealous' judges for 'illegal sentencing' during martial law. At the time of the resolution the IPN had submitted thirty-two requests to waive immunity – with potentially many more now pending.[54] However, death, the statute of limitations and the reluctance of judicial disciplinary panels meant that there were no further trials of the martial law judges.

The second case involved the decrees themselves. In December 2008 the Ombudsman had asked the Constitutional Tribunal to find a series of decrees linked to martial law illegal, as well as the law of 25 January 1982 because the Supreme Court's 2007 judgment was 'inconsistent and essentially incorrect'. The Court had considered the issue of retroactivity but not the illegality of the decree on martial law, issued by the Council of State while the *Sejm* was in session. The impact of the martial law decrees continued to be felt by individuals who had been unjustly sentenced; yet, they had no legal redress. The Ombudsman sought to 'facilitate the moral and legal compensation' of those who had suffered repression under martial law and to 'satisfy the needs of historical justice'.[55]

The TK finally addressed these questions in 2011.[56] This was another strange judgment. Instead of a holistic approach, the TK declined to rule on several elements of the martial law package, including the crucial question of whether the law of January 1982 validated the decrees. The Court relied heavily on the law on the TK,[57] specifying that the Tribunal discontinues proceedings if a judgment is unnecessary or inadmissible or if a law is no longer in force – *unless* judgment of a repealed law is 'necessary to protect constitutional rights and freedoms'.

The TK did not judge the resolution introducing martial law because it was not a 'provision of law issued by the central state organs'; because it was an implementing measure only; because it had been repealed in 1983; and because the Ombudsman had not provided examples of its continuing impact on human rights. Nor did the Tribunal rule on the transfer of certain offences to the criminal courts; this was 'superfluous' because that decree had lost force with the new law on martial law of 2002. It did not judge the constitutionality of the law of January 1982 sanctioning martial law because its provisions had ceased to apply. 'The decree on martial law and the law on introducing martial law are separate legal acts. They cannot be reviewed together. They were different in nature and were issued on different bases.' One might argue that when a law validated a decree, the two are not at all different in nature but are inextricably linked. This is particularly important because of the TK's finding that the decree on martial law was unconstitutional.

In key respects the TK argued that the Ombudsman was correct. It found two decrees of 12 December 1981 – on martial law and on the procedures for crimes and misdemeanours under martial law – incompatible with the Constitution and the International Covenant of Civic and Political Rights. The underpinning of its arguments was the application of Article 39(3) of the law on the Constitutional Tribunal, namely that judgment of an expired law could occur if 'necessary to protect constitutional rights and freedoms'. It found that the consequences of an expired law could, and in this case did, persist long into the future.

The Court agreed that the Council of State was empowered to issue decrees only when the *Sejm* was not in session; the contested decrees were therefore unconstitutional because the *Sejm* was sitting. Moreover, the decrees violated the principle of non-retroactivity embodied in the International Covenant: because they were published on 18 December but backdated to 13 December, 'they were not part of the Polish legal system' for five days.

The two elements are separate of course. The decrees clearly violated the procedural norms of the Constitution. Indeed, the *Sejm* enacted the 1982 law precisely because of the flaws in the original martial law decrees. By arguing that the decree was unconstitutional without considering the superior status of the law validating it, the TK flaunted both logic and common sense by denying the *Sejm* the capacity to confirm the principle and practice of martial law.

The TK's justification for applying the International Covenant was similarly weak. It ignored the Supreme Court's conclusion that Poland lacked mechanisms for incorporating international law into domestic law. Instead it noted that communist ministers had 'assured the UN' that the Covenant's provisions were part of Polish law, claiming that Polish law embodied civic and political rights 'to an even greater degree' than did the Covenant. It is hard to believe that the TK took typical communist rhetoric at face value.

The Tribunal went further, however, claiming that the decrees also violated basic constitutional principles relating to the functioning of state organs. The Council of State would have had *no right* to issue the decrees *even if* the *Sejm* had not been in session: 'As an act infringing the contents of the Constitution of the PRL, the Council of State was not empowered to issue the decree on martial law (because) that act suspended or limited the basic rights of citizens defined in the 1952 Constitution and other laws and international agreements.' This argument makes no sense. Martial law always entails the suspension of or limitation of some basic civil liberties as a means of protecting the state itself.

Although the Tribunal claimed to have applied the principles of the 1952 Constitution, this stance is difficult to sustain. That Constitution made the *Sejm* the supreme legislative power, subject – as all other institutions – to the 'leading role' of the Party (from 1977). In 1981–2 the highest authorities of the state – the Council of State and the *Sejm* – agreed that the relevant circumstances existed for martial law.

The Constitutional Tribunal ignored all previous scholarship on the limitations of freedom and the political use of the Constitution in an authoritarian regime. It ignored its own strictures, failing to apply the prohibition on retroactivity to its own deliberations. The TK's failure to link the martial law decrees to the 1982 law validating them appears little more than legal sophistry. According to the chair of the TK from 2008 to 2010, the Tribunal should not have ruled on martial law. It should have refused judgment of an expired law.[58]

## The martial law trial

In the martial law trial the Warsaw Court followed the findings of the Constitutional Tribunal, with some embellishment. At its conclusion in January 2012 three defendants remained: former First Secretary Kania, former Interior Minister Kiszczak and former member of the Council of State Kempara. The court acquitted Kania. It agreed that Kempara had exceeded her authority but applied the statute of limitations. Kiszczak was found guilty. He received a sentence of four years, reduced to two by the amnesty law and suspended for five years because of his poor health.

The court agreed that an 'armed criminal conspiracy' had functioned in 1981 and 1982. 'At least as early as March 1981' senior figures within the leadership secretly agreed to resolve the Solidarity crisis 'by illegally introducing martial law'. They were fully aware that using the powers of the Council of State to issue decrees while the *Sejm* was in session would be illegal. They also knew that applying martial law would entail the 'deprivation of freedom through internment (and) ... other crimes against freedom, as well as crimes against the inviolability of the person, the freedom of correspondence and the labour rights of Polish citizens'. Jaruzelski as Party leader and Kiszczak at the interior ministry assumed 'full control of the entire apparatus of the state and the party'. The members of the group did not need to form separate structures for their criminal association; they used the existing structures of the state for this end. This understanding among a group of the 'highest leaders of the ... Army constituted a criminal association of an armed nature'.[59]

Although the Council of State was empowered to declare martial law, it did so after first issuing a decree establishing the principles of martial law. Since the decree was illegal because the *Sejm* was in session, there was no legal basis for the declaration of martial law. Moreover, the declaration and the decrees violated the principle on non-retroactivity, since they were implemented before publication on 17 December.

The court took a similar position on issues of substance. The defence of 'higher necessity'[60] did not apply because there was ample evidence that 'when martial law was introduced, there was no immediate threat of armed intervention by Warsaw Pact forces'. The 'illegal introduction of martial law' was not undertaken to prevent intervention from outside forces; it was simply an attempt to maintain the existing regime and safeguard individual leaders.

The verdict is unconvincing, both its venture into 'objective' history and its embracing of the IPN's eccentric charges. The notion that legitimate political authorities using the institutions of the state could constitute an 'armed conspiracy' to defend an existing regime is peculiar to say the least. And it is simply preposterous to claim that 'plans for the illegal introduction of martial law' had existed since March 1981. Why should one suppose that the authorities planned to introduce martial law illegally when they had the necessary power to introduce it legally? If the decision were illegal, the timing made it so, not the planning. The judge turned the procedural question of whether the decree establishing martial law was illegally issued by the Council of State into the imputation of motive, such that the procedural illegality was deemed to have been 'planned' from the start by members of the 'armed conspiracy'. And since martial law by its nature entails the suppression of civil rights in national emergencies (but see the TK view above), knowledge that rights would be violated is not an argument for its illegality either.

The IPN did not cease its pursuit of convictions. From 2008 it had prepared new charges against Florian Siwicki, on trial as a martial law conspirator, and Władysław

Ciastoń, already acquitted in the Popiełuszko case. In November 2012 Siwicki was deemed too ill to continue (he died in March 2013). The trial of Ciastoń and General Józef Sasin was finally scheduled for August 2013. According to the IPN, military training held at the turn of 1982/3 was a pretext for depriving several hundred opposition members of their freedom, isolating them from the workplace and subjecting them to cruel treatment: using training exercises for political repression constituted 'communist crimes' and 'crimes against humanity'. The view of the district court that the statute of limitations had expired was not shared by the appeal court: although the crimes could not be categorized as 'crimes against humanity', as 'communist crimes' they could be prosecuted until 1 August 2020. The trial began in March 2015. Ciastoń and Sasin were sentenced to two years' imprisonment (subject to appeal) in February 2018.

# Conclusion

After twenty-six years these mighty labours bore negligible fruit: aside from some early trials of former secret police officers, by 2018 only Kiszczak, Ciastoń and Sasin had been found guilty. Most defendants in the martial law trials were dead or incapacitated by the time of the judgments of the Constitutional Court in 2011 and the Warsaw Circuit Court in 2012. Despite the currency of historical explanations of transitional justice under post-communism, no assessment of the legitimacy of the regime, the 'softness' of approaches to society or popular mobilization can explain the ways of dealing with 'communist crimes' in Poland.

It is certainly true that history was crucial to understanding how these processes unfolded. Electoral politics remained polarized between Solidarity and the (ex) communists until about 2005, when the centre-left was weakened and discredited, and periods of right-wing government followed. Only for the brief period of the Mazowiecki government was there formal cooperation between the former communist camp and Solidarity. Bringing criminal charges against the co-architects of the Round Table was unthinkable in 1989 and 1990, when Jaruzelski was president, Kiszczak interior minister, and Siwicki minister of defence.

Diametrically opposed perceptions of the past remained a fundamental element of Polish politics. However, the IPN became the institutional embodiment of one historical interpretation and a retributive approach to dealing with past injustice. As itself an element of the judicial system it was deeply political, yet politically unconstrained in its relentless pursuit of alleged wrong-doers.

The question of 'transitional justice' appears rather moot. Lower courts proved inadequate to the complexity of these cases, and virtually all judgments were appealed, whether by prosecutors or defendants. There is no convincing evidence of political manipulation or 'the intimidation of judges, prosecutors and witnesses',[61] as some have claimed.[62]

The Constitutional Tribunal rarely claimed the necessity of special transitional measures. It claimed by and large to be applying the legal principles of the time when the crimes were committed, but the application of legal rules to a system not governed by the rule of law often made its arguments illogical, tendentious and unconvincing, while its ventures into historical analysis were simplistic and inappropriate. No one was satisfied. No one believed that the endless trials and retrials brought justice – whether because the defendants 'escaped' through illness or death or inadequate sentences or because the drawn-out trials of ill and aged men seemed more like persecution than the pursuit of justice. In neither instance could one argue that the search for retribution strengthened and enhanced the rule of law.

# The restitution of property

If the trials of those alleged to have committed past crimes centres on the perpetrators, then issues of restoring rights or making reparations focus on the victims. Rehabilitation, compensation and restitution all entail redress of loss – both material and moral. Here we focus on the restitution of property. Although since the Middle Ages there have been many theories of property rights, there is no recognized right to restitution of property, whether in international law or in general principles of justice.[1] Restitution, widespread throughout Central and Eastern Europe, was a political choice.

Individuals may receive redress of past grievances but so too may collective entities.[2] The latter took precedence in Poland. The restoration of assets to individual owners (known as 'reprivatization') was not a priority for the new democratic politicians, whose immediate focus was on two pillars of the anti-communist opposition, trades unions and the Catholic Church. Restitution to other religious bodies, including Jewish communal property, soon followed.

The scope for individual restitution was less than elsewhere in the region, not least because the peasants had maintained their private landholdings. Although successive governments promised individual property restitution, they failed to deliver. An exception came for those dispossessed by Poland's eastern boundary changes, the 'people from beyond the Bug'. Some distinctive features also characterized restitution in the capital, Warsaw. Despite the specific nature of their case, no general provision was made for individual Jewish properties seized by the Nazis or through subsequent communist expropriation. Restitution proved difficult, protracted and incomplete.

## The restitution of collective property

### The trades unions

The Round Table agreement of 1989 made the Solidarity trade union legal again, along with other organizations banned under martial law. In October 1990 the 'contract Sejm' passed the law on 'the return of property lost by trades unions and social organizations as a result of the introduction of martial law'.[3] This was a basic measure of social justice. It was also intended to permit Solidarity to resume its place in public life.

The law related primarily to the confiscation and transfer of Solidarity assets to the pro-government OPZZ, the All-Polish Alliance of Trades Unions (*Ogólnopolskie Porozumienie Związków Zawodowych*) during martial law. Solidarity's claims were mostly against the OPZZ, but if restoration proved impossible, the State Treasury would meet the obligation. Amendments added in 1996 and in subsequent years[4] took account of Constitutional Court judgments, especially regarding the mechanisms and calculation of compensation, and to increase the role of the State Treasury.

In 1992 the Court found parts of the law unconstitutional: the return of resources used to provide services to union members (including Solidarity members who had joined the OPZZ) contravened the constitutional principle of social justice.[5] In 1994 both Solidarity and the OPZZ complained to the International Labour Organization – Solidarity because of delays in the restoration of its property and the OPZZ on the grounds that the large sums required as compensation impeded its activities.

Property claims were settled by the Social Claims Commission (*Społeczna Komisja Rewindykacyjna*) under the minister of labour. It functioned as a three-person bench, selected from among twenty members, at least half possessing legal qualifications. If the SKR could not broker agreement of the parties, it would decide by majority verdict, with a right of appeal to the administrative courts. By 1998 about 3,000 requests had been made for restitution, about 10 per cent of which were resolved by agreement of the parties.

Evidence of union funds could be difficult to establish, since trade union property had been destroyed in the early days of martial law; many documents had perished; and both the SKR and the courts were reluctant to depend on witness testimony. The OPZZ questioned both the principle and the time period to which indexation should apply. The courts dealt largely with technical matters of compensation[6] but also some spurious claims of substance. The Supreme Administrative Court dismissed the OPZZ's argument that Solidarity unions could not receive funds and property since they had not enjoyed legal continuity, having been abolished in 1982.[7] It also dismissed a Solidarity claim that had already been met in full, before the restitution law came into effect.[8]

Delays, often due to the protracted nature of the appeal process, meant mounting costs of interest payments and index-linking, with a substantial burden on the State Treasury: 82 million PNL and counting in 1998[9] and about 250 million in 2001.[10] Appeals against decisions of the SKR came not only from the unions but also from provincial governors, effectively acting as agents of the Treasury.[11] The restoration issue returned to the Constitutional Tribunal (TK) in 2006.

In 2001 after successive appeals the Polish Union of Journalists (SDP) regained (among others) its former headquarters in Warsaw. During martial law many journalists were interned, the SDP was dissolved and its property transferred to the pro-government journalists' organization, currently known as the Association of Journalists of the Polish Republic, SDPRP. In 2003 the SDPRP challenged the constitutionality of the law.

Both the charges and the TK's decision were complex.[12] The Tribunal found the claims imprecise and badly articulated. The SDPRP's main argument, however, was that property relations between trades unions and social organizations were not administrative matters and should not be settled through administrative processes. In an unusual, albeit implicit reference to the requirements of transitional justice, the TK argued that 'the extraordinary nature of the institution of the return of property to social organizations ... justified the adoption of various extraordinary legal means (*nadzwyczajnych środków prawnych*)', and the restoration was lawful.

Despite the lengthy and costly nature of the restoration process in some cases – a few continuing as late as 2013 – Solidarity largely received the resources of which it had been deprived. There was no public controversy in this sphere; clearly, trade unions could not function without funds. The state assumed much of the cost of restoration, leaving both Solidarity and the OPZZ in good financial shape.

## Religious bodies

In the 2011 census 98 per cent of those professing religious faith were Roman Catholics. From the stateless nineteenth century onwards the Catholic Church had been a potent national symbol. For the avowedly atheist communist regime the Church was an unwelcome competitor for the loyalties of the population. Despite attempts to undermine it, the Church remained strong and deeply entrenched, with an upsurge in Church attendance following the election of the Polish Pope John Paul II and the papal visit of June 1979. Under martial law religious gatherings were the only lawful form of public assembly and thus a major outlet for popular frustration and despair.

Other faiths included the Polish Autocephalous Orthodox Church, which had been established in 1924 to accommodate Orthodox Christians who lived primarily in Belarusian and Ukrainian territories that had been part of the Russian Empire, where only the Russian Orthodox Church was permitted. In 2011, 0.46 per cent of believers professed Orthodoxy – about 156,000 believers. There were Baptists (0.02 per cent in 2011), Lutherans (0.21 per cent) and Jehovah's Witnesses (0.4 per cent). About 2,000 Muslims of Tatar descent live in northeastern Poland.

All communist regimes confiscated the property of religious organizations and strictly controlled their functions. In March 1950 when the *Sejm* dispossessed the Catholic Church, priests largely kept their own small farms, and the revenues from the nationalized lands were allocated through a new Church Fund (*Fundusz Kościelny*) for ecclesiastical and charitable purposes. The state nationalized some 337,000 acres as part of its attempt to 'destroy the economic basis of the Church and thus break its resistance'.[13]

# The Roman Catholic Church

The Catholic Church was dealt with quickly during the crucial months of 1989 – even before the fall of communism. The Church received generous, relatively unlimited restitution in the Law on the Relation of the State to the Catholic Church adopted in May.[14] The law aimed in part to secure the Church's support for the Round Table, with its presumption of continuing communist rule. In this it failed, but the benefits to the Church remained. Indeed, the 'easy adoption of restitution of church property was especially glaring in comparison with the stalemate on other issues of restitution, which remained unresolved despite continuous debate and dozens of failed legislative attempts'.[15]

The law regulated matters of Church property and provided the legal basis for the Property Commission (*Komisja Majątkowa*, KM). Amendments in 1991 permitted the transfer to the Church of state-owned properties originally used for religious purposes, mostly in former German areas.[16] This law gave the Church Fund a statutory basis; among other provisions the Fund would pay the insurance contributions of nuns, missionaries and some clergy (all registered religious organizations benefitted from the Fund). In 1993 the Property Commission was enshrined in the new Polish-Vatican Concordat.

Although envisaged to last for two years, the Property Commission sat from 1991 to February 2011. Its work came to an end under the amended law on state–Church relations.[17] Formally, the commission was abolished because its task was virtually complete. Abolition would also 'signal state neutrality' in matters of conviction.[18] However, the KM had become the focus of much unwelcome media attention.

### The Property Commission

Six representatives of the KM came from the Interior Ministry and six from the Secretariat of the Episcopate. Individual cases were reviewed by a panel of four, two from each side. The aim was to seek agreement, but if no agreement could be reached, the panel or sometimes the full KM issued its decision, against which there was no appeal. Where land could not be restored, an equivalent was offered from state or local government holdings or monetary compensation was awarded. In 2001 the government and Episcopate agreed new procedures. Until then a parish would receive as many hectares as it had lost. The Church argued that this did not take account of the fact that the land was now worth far more than at the time of its seizure. After 2002 the Commission restored land by value, not by area, further fuelling local controversies.[19]

The Commission received 3,063 requests. It confirmed 1,486 agreements and 990 decisions returning property, whether the original or an alternative. It rejected 666 cases, and in 136 cases the Commission did not agree a decision. The KM returned about 66,000 hectares and some 490 buildings and it awarded compensation of about 144 million PNL.[20] In 2011, 216 cases remained to be resolved (by the courts). The Supreme Administrative Court (1991[21]) and the Constitutional Court (1992)[22] affirmed the distinctive status of the KM. It was neither a judicial nor an administrative body of the state but rather a 'type of mediating institution'. These rulings made the KM difficult to challenge.

Perhaps because it was hastily drafted, the 1989 law on church–state relations did not include a starting date for claims, so the Catholic Church could and did claim for property taken before 1939, as far back as the nineteenth century or even earlier. In its 1992 judgment the TK found that only in two instances could the Church claim restitution of property lost in the nineteenth century: first in cases of former Uniate property,[23] and second when buildings used for religious purposes still existed and could be restored to these purposes, including educational and charitable work.

## Criticism and challenge

Under the SLD government (1993–7) deputies made several attempts to amend the 1989 law, limiting the right to restitution to the post-1944 period, introducing a right of appeal and including the newly established local governments as participants in the process.[24] These efforts foundered, largely because of the opposition of the junior coalition partner, the Polish Peasant Party. Much later, in 2009, the provincial governor was made a participant in the Commission's proceedings.

Critics of the KM emphasized its secrecy, lack of transparency and insensitivity to local issues. Controversy abounded, especially when the property sought was currently being used for public purposes such as schools or hospitals; when land offered as an alternative to the original undermined local development plans; or when restored property was immediately sold to developers for huge profits. Some obviously outrageous claims failed – such as the Franciscans' demand for the National Museum in Gdańsk, housed in a former monastery not held by the Church for some 400 years. In Krakow, historically a major centre for many monastic orders, the Church made gains even when few nuns and monks remained. Among others, the Commission awarded land, buildings or monetary compensation to the Archdiocese of Krakow, the Franciscans, the Cistercians, the Augustinians, the Felician Sisters and the Albertine Sisters.

The first test of the Commission's rulings came in 1996, when the Supreme Court rejected the National Teachers' Union's claims for compensation from the State Treasury for loss of its user rights. The KM had returned the land in question to the Servants of Jesus, basing compensation to the union for its investment in the property on expert assessments which the union strongly contested. Its decision explicitly noted that it did not deprive the applicant of the right to make further claims 'in accordance with generally applicable provisions of law'. However, the Supreme Court determined that since the State Treasury no longer owned the property, the union could make no claim against it.[25] The union appealed to the European Court of Human Rights, but there was long delay before its judgment in 2004.

The ECHR argued that the teachers' union had incurred considerable expenditure in respect of the property, given that it had been using and maintaining it for twenty-five years. 'In the Court's view, and bearing in mind what was at stake …, to restrict further access to a court in respect of claims concerning outlays for maintenance and renovation … must be considered disproportionate.' It found that denying claimants any way to pursue their rights before a court of law violated the right to a fair trial guaranteed by the Convention.[26]

The ECHR's verdict had no practical effect for other cases. Individuals and organizations did not gain the procedural means to challenge decisions of the Property Commission. In 2007 the Supreme Court found that in negotiating an agreement for a period of usage rights, the KM had exceeded its powers, since it had ignored the rights of those who had earlier purchased the land in question.[27] However, the accountability of the Commission remained an issue.

Political pressures increased, as newspapers aired some flagrant abuses and a long-awaited legal challenge in the Constitutional Tribunal seemed imminent. The media endorsed criticism that the KM's decisions were generally taken without consultation with local government or property administrators. Journalists also claimed that valuations offered by the Church's experts were not corroborated. In 2006 the president of Krakow requested the procuracy to investigate whether the Commission had exceeded its powers when it took 407 allotments from the city as an alternative to land claimed by the Church.

Land values were a perennial source of conflict. In 2008 the KM granted the Sisters of Elizabeth 47 hectares in Warsaw for their losses in Poznan. The Church's expert valued the land at 30 million PNL, while the local authority assessed its value as 240 million. The Anti-Corruption Agency (CBA) advised the Procuracy of potential offences in eleven decisions. The CBA concluded that – in accord with previous court decisions – members of the Property Commission were not liable for its decisions because although paid by the state, they could not be regarded as its employees. They could in theory be charged with corruption, but corruption was difficult to prove.[28]

The KM was largely, if not wholly, insensitive to public concerns. In 2008 it unexpectedly reversed a decision to award land used by the army as a substitute for restitution claimed by the Jesuits. After consulting the army, the KM agreed that the Ministry of Defence could offer an alternative property. This was the first time that interested parties had been invited to participate in the Commission's deliberations.[29]

In 2009 a group of SLD deputies challenged the law in the Constitutional Court on the grounds that there was no opportunity to appeal, especially where local authorities had not been consulted. The government responded promptly, announcing that because of 'negative press articles' and local government claims of lack of consultation, the KM had revised its procedures.[30] Firstly, in each case the provincial governor (*wojewoda*) would play a role, partly as a mediator but also to oppose the immediate sale to third parties of land listed as a possible substitute for land lost by the Church. Secondly, participants would be able to present their views at all stages of the proceedings and to receive access to all estimated values and calculations. In uncontested cases the KM could issue a decision without the participants, but they would be informed in advance. Finally, expert valuers should be appointed where the value ascribed to property was disputed. These changes did not save the Commission. The situation became ever more fraught as corruption allegations intensified.

When the Constitutional Tribunal finally issued its verdict in 2011,[31] it ruled on only one issue. The challenge to six other regulations was discontinued because the law had already ceased to apply. The TK rejected the argument that the Court should investigate outdated regulations because they remained significant for the protection of rights and freedoms (the clause used by the TK in its examination of the martial law decree). However, the Tribunal found the criteria for determining what state and communal property could be used as compensation to be vague, hence unconstitutional. This arose because of the new constitutional position of the commune (*gmina*) after 1997. When the Property Commission offered substitute restitution, it came mainly from *gmina* property. The Tribunal's judgment paved the way for *gminas* affected by the decisions of the KM to gain compensation directly from the beneficiaries if the Church had received substitute property at their expense.[32]

Controversy did not cease with the demise of the Commission. In February 2012 *Gazeta Wyborcza* located an unpublished government report in the court papers of corruption proceedings.[33] It painted a damning picture of major losses to the Treasury and an 'unparalleled shambles' of maladministration in the KM. Records, such as they were, were held manually. There was no register of documents. Records were missing or incomplete, misfiled, or not filed at all. Although charged with protecting the public interest, the government's representatives had failed to do so. They had not assessed the valuations presented to them by the Church's agents nor investigated whether the land they were allocating was currently in state hands. There were no written records of votes taken and the justifications of decisions were 'sloppily written'. Members were selected with no criteria of competence and no provision was made for potential conflicts of interest. No government audits took place during the twenty-two years of the Commission's operation.

### Allegations of corruption and criminality

Its quasi-administrative status made it difficult to challenge the KM in the civil courts. However, corruption allegations were subject to prosecution. The authorities had already begun to investigate the activities of Marek P., a lawyer and former officer of the security services who was the Church's most successful intermediary and general wheeler-dealer in matters of restitution. After 2008 several regional procuracies launched investigations into allegations of bribery and misrepresentation, especially in erroneous land valuations. In June 2010 the first charges were laid in Warsaw against seven persons, including Marek P., members of the Property Commission and the commission's stenographer, in respect of restoration to the Sisters of Elizabeth. The procuracy halted proceedings because 'no crime had been detected'.[34]

The matter did not end there. A new investigation was launched in 2012 at the request of the Sisters themselves. They claimed deliberate undervaluation of the restored land, for which moreover they had not been paid, after the purchaser quickly resold it for some 80 million PNL (the original valuation was about 30 million). When this investigation was also discontinued, the court accused the procuracy of a flawed, incompetent and incomplete investigation.[35] A fresh trial of Marek P. began in January 2015.[36]

After bouncing between courts Marek P.'s first trial began in Krakow in June 2013, along with the KM's former deputy chair, the priest Mieczysław Piesiur and lawyer Krzysztof Wąsowski, with other members of the Property Commission and its stenographer. Corruption, bribery and other improprieties were said to have cost the state some 33 million PNL.[37] The Church acknowledged that the investigation of Marek P had proved 'most damaging to the reputation of the Commission'.[38]

These investigations continued well into the middle of the decade. In 2014 the Anti-Corruption Agency was still investigating the role of Marek P., Piesiur and Wąsowski, and three valuation experts, with putative inflation of the value of land claimed by the church and under-valuation of land proposed in exchange. Other allegations related to the allocation of land which had already been sold or for which the Church had already received compensation.[39] In 2015 a family of business people from Silesia were acquitted of money laundering from the purchase of restored Church property.[40]

The civil courts were also busy with matters arising from the KM's activities well after its demise. At the end of 2012 some 120 cases were pending. Some were unfinished business – claims not yet dealt with. Others arose from dissatisfaction with the Commission's decisions. The Church's spokesman Krzysztof Wąsowski (he who was later charged with corruption) commented that 'from the Church's perspective I can say that we are not happy with the work of the Property Commission ....(which) has not satisfied the Church's claims for the property it lost. The Church lost a great deal more'.[41] There were also pending claims for additional compensation – such as that of the Sisters of Elizabeth for 13 million PNL.[42] Local government authorities also made claims for compensation, but their claims were largely frozen or dismissed.[43]

The Ombudsman remained anxious because the current law conflicted with constitutional guarantees of property rights. Indeed, the extent to which the decisions of the KM came under the administrative courts had remained an issue unresolved by the Supreme Administrative Court (NSA) since 2008. The NSA had waited for the decision of the TK, but as we noted above, the TK largely avoided judgment. The situation was further complicated by the abolition of the KM, since it now ceased to be a party to proceedings, and the law had not named a successor organ. The Ombudsman argued that the interested parties – including local government – were deprived of the right to resolve property disputes by an 'impartial and independent court'.[44]

The Property Commission was a distinctive body, a quasi-mediating body specific to the cause of transitional justice and itself 'transitional'. The unparalleled success of the Church's claims for restoration suggests that there was little 'mediation'. The corrupt nature of the restoration process made it hard to argue that the KM served the cause of justice.

## Other religious bodies

All religious bodies gained the same rights as the Catholic Church and a similar model of decision-making. Their claims were neither as extensive nor as controversial as those of the Catholic Church. The first law, in July 1991, dealt with relations with Polish Orthodoxy. Its legal status and property were regulated by presidential decree in 1938 and the law of 1939 on the regulation of the property of the Orthodox Church. The outbreak of war meant that this law was not implemented. After the war these lands became in effect the property of the State Treasury.

Laws also provided for restitution to the Lutherans in May 1994 and the Methodists in June 1995. In 1997 Poland legislated the return of communal Jewish property. Ultimately the claims of virtually all religious minorities were acknowledged, including Evangelical Christians, Anglicans, Baptists, Seventh Day Adventists and the Moslem Religious Community. From September 2000 the Inter-Church Regulatory Commission dealt with claims from these smaller groups.

The process was especially complex for the small religious organizations. The deletion of the names of former owners from title deeds and the frequent absence of former owners' names in earlier court decisions often made it difficult to demonstrate ownership. The destruction of documents, especially during wartime, and flaws in the communist legal system were countered by a presumption in favour of the religious bodies. Their restitution commissions continued to function after the abolition of the Property Commission in 2011.

## Polish Orthodoxy

The Polish Autocephalous Orthodox Church (PAOC) had suffered badly from 'Operation Vistula' (*Akcja Wisła*), the mass deportations in 1946–7 of Ukrainians, Belorussians and Lemko-Rusyns from the southeastern provinces of Poland to former German land, the so-called Recovered Territories in the west – in order, it was said, to undermine Ukrainian terrorist organizations. In the Lemko region virtually all Polish Orthodox churches were destroyed. Nine parishes and one monastery remained in Chełm and southern Podlasie. Some Church land was confiscated by the state, and some places of worship were taken over by the Catholic Church.

After 1989 the Polish Orthodox Church set out to revive its structures in the east, where a small Orthodox population remained. As a result of the 1991 law it regained part of its lands and most of its cemeteries. The process was quite lengthy, and it was not trouble free. Churches which had been taken over by the Catholic Church were not returned. Indeed, under the 1989 law they had become the legal property of the Catholic Church. There were Orthodox-Catholic disputes and disputes between Orthodox and Uniates.

Up until March 2015 the regulating commission for the Orthodox Church received 566 claims for restitution. Of these 345 resulted in agreements or decisions, returning property or awarding compensation. Seventy-two cases were discontinued or rejected. The commission returned undeveloped land of 5,171.9 hectares in area; developed land totalling 39.4 hectares; housing and commercial property amounting to 1,749.6 m$^2$; and thirteen cemeteries amounting to 5.4 hectares. It also received the total sum of 18,030,988 PNL in compensation.[45]

The Uniates lacked their own property commission because their claims were subsumed under those of the Catholic Church. When the communists banned the Uniates, the State took over their land and transferred the use of their churches, some to Roman Catholics and some to the Orthodox Church. The Catholic Church received title to these under the 'principle of the status quo' of the 1989 law on the Catholic Church – making the decision about which rite would be used exclusively an internal Catholic matter.

The 1991 law gave the Polish Orthodox Church legal title to property in use when the law came into force, except for property that had previously belonged to the Uniates. A separate law was to regulate this. The Orthodox Church maintained the right to use the property, with ownership remaining with the Treasury until the new law was passed. The loudest repercussions came in the case of twenty-four former Uniate places of worship used by the Orthodox.

The Orthodox Church claimed discrimination. The Constitutional Tribunal argued that the law was constitutional. It did not discriminate because separate legislation was foreseen, if not enacted. Moreover, since the Church had not previously owned the real estate under dispute, it could not be stated that it was deprived of protection.[46]

The Church protested that one judge, a Senator in 1991, had participated in the law-making process. At the European Court of Human Rights it argued that legal uncertainty regarding the status of its places of worship infringed its right to peaceful practice of its religious rites. In 2008 the ECHR postponed its deliberations after the government agreed to negotiate afresh. The government proposed to pass the separate law envisaged in 1991 and to create an expert group, including Catholics, Uniates and Orthodox to seek compromise solutions to disputed property.[47] The law of December 2009 regulating 'certain property remaining under the control of the Polish Autocephalous Orthodox Church'[48] provided that the Uniates would gain title to one church in southeastern Poland, while the Orthodox would gain the remaining contested places of worship. In specified cases the state would provide compensation. A Church emissary reported to the ECHR that the law 'satisfied all claims'.[49]

## The Jewish communities

Before the Second World War Poland had Europe's largest Jewish population – some 3.5 million. Although the number of Jews in Poland was now small (the 2011 census did not register them), the restoration of Jewish property proved difficult and protracted. Before the Holocaust thousands of Jewish communal properties had served Poland's Jews. The 1997 law on the restoration of these properties[50] identified nine Jewish religious communities with legal status and the right to property which they owned on 1 September 1939. The government was essaying a balance between 'the demands of (world) Jewish organizations and fear of an anti-Semitic backlash but achieving neither'.[51] Initial negotiations with the World Jewish Restitution Organization (WJRO) foundered on questions of how much property should be returned, with the Polish government arguing that restitution should relate to the religious needs of the current Jewish community. The WJRO regarded this as unjust, and it questioned whether the small community in Poland could represent the Jewish past. The WJRO argued that this law 'legitimizes, facilitates, and sustains the great Nazi plunder of Jewish property'.[52]

The law came into effect in May 1997, providing a 2002 deadline for restitution applications – a problem because of the large number of properties and the small size of the current Polish Jewish community. The Foundation for the Preservation of Jewish Heritage in Poland (FPJHP) was established jointly between the Polish Jewish community and the WJRO in late 2001. They agreed that the Polish Jewish community would file claims in certain geographic areas, and the FPJHP would do so in others. Many properties were 'heritage properties', notably cemeteries, whose maintenance represented a potential cost of considerable magnitude. To meet these expenses the Foundation and the community agreed to sell properties not needed by the community.

The Polish Jewish community filed nearly 2,000 applications by the deadline and the FPJHP about 3,500 claims.[53] By the end of 2006 the commission had concluded 1,143 cases, of which 316 were settled by agreement with 336 properties restored. Some observers complained about the slow pace and government reluctance to return valuable properties. Agreements between the government and Jewish organizations were often contested by local governments, 'which present(ed) all possible obstacles and arguments against restitution'.[54] However, in cities like Warsaw and Łódź local governments were supportive, and restitution was easier. The law did not address instances where communal properties were now privately owned by third parties, leaving some controversial cases unsettled.

By December 2014 the Commission for Communal Jewish Property had dealt with 5,504 cases and held 6,949 sessions. As many as 2,568 cases were wholly or partly concluded: 1,132 by agreement or positive decision of the Commission, 1,386 were discontinued or rejected. As much as 28 million PNL were awarded in recompense and over 56 million as compensation.[55] Dissatisfaction remained, though one commission member regarded its work as 'more positive than negative'.[56] The issue of restitution to individuals was not resolved (see below).

### Other faiths

Restoration to other religious organizations proceeded largely without incident. The Lutheran Church (*Kościół Ewangelicko-Augsburski*) submitted 1,200 claims. In 438 cases agreement was reached or a decision issued. As many as 522 cases were discontinued, whether by common agreement or rejection. Up to March 2015 the church received land amounting to 402.76 hectares of undeveloped land, 47.2 hectares of developed land and some 2 million PNL in monetary compensation.[57] The Inter-Church Commission received 170 cases, but its work was very slow. By 2015 it had initiated only ninety-one, just over half the claims submitted by the smaller religions. Thirty-two of these concluded with the restitution of property, the award of a substitute property or compensation.

## The restoration of individual private property

A basic tenet of communist regimes was the state ownership of the means of production, through nationalization and the collectivization of agriculture. Unusually, in the Polish case collectivization was never completed and in the political upheavals of 1956 most land was restored to peasant owners. Pogany argued that measures of restitution are the product of 'political and discretionary processes', making choices between categories of former property owners to be included or excluded from restitution or compensation.[58] The peasantry remained politically significant, and no political party supported the restoration of land to large landowners, most of whom had been dispossessed in major land reforms of the inter-war period and under the communists (but see below).

Stanisław Tyszka argued that the principle of individual property restitution – reprivatization – was rejected; since the whole of society suffered under communism, universal remedies were impossible.[59] This is not borne out by opinion surveys. Public support for 'reprivatization' is difficult to gauge because of confused notions of reprivatization and differences as to what should be returned and how. But almost two-thirds supported reprivatization in 1991, dropping to just over half in 1992, when the so-called small privatization was already under way.[60] Support vacillated over the years, with a low reached in 2008, when 44 per cent of respondents opposed it and 34 per cent favoured it.[61] There remained however a consistent majority view that reprivatization should apply to those whose property was unlawfully seized.

Successive governments never grasped this nettle. After 1989 the new government made commitments and deputies proposed draft laws – none enacted – to deal with the restitution of confiscated private property. The first debates on reprivatization came in 1992. Only in 2001 did the *Sejm* pass a bill, proposed by Prime Minister Buzek, which envisaged compensation of 50 per cent of the value of confiscated property. President Kwasniewski vetoed the bill because of its budgetary implications, said to be about US$70 billion.

Under Prime Ministers Marek Belka (Social Democrat), Kazimierz Marcinkiewicz and Jaroslaw Kaczyński (both of Law and Justice), virtually identical versions of a bill, first proposed in 2005 – on compensation for property seized by the State – were submitted but never voted on by the *Sejm*. The bills were patently unsatisfactory: they did not provide for restitution *in rem*, excluded compensation for property seized in Warsaw, offered severely limited compensation and proposed a burdensome claims process. PiS returned to these proposals in 2017.

In 2008, a similar bill was proposed by the government of Donald Tusk (Civic Platform), who had earlier promised reprivatization legislation. It was not even submitted to the *Sejm*. Having failed repeatedly to pass a restitution law, notwithstanding recurring commitments to do so, the government shifted tactics in the spring of 2012. Claiming that such a law was superfluous, Civic Platform insisted that claimants wrongfully deprived of property should pursue their remedy in the Polish courts.

The new PiS government after 2015 paid lip service to reprivatization, but its proposals aroused substantial criticism. In October 2017 it published draft legislation that would effectively bring property restitution to an end. Under the proposals, restitution would cease, and compensation would be capped at 20 per cent of the property's pre-war value. Only Polish citizens would be eligible for compensation, and applications would be restricted to the spouses or direct descendants of pre-war owners applying from within the country. Anyone who had given up their Polish citizenship or served in a foreign military force would be excluded – thus excluding most Holocaust survivors and their families. The proposals were also criticized because pending proceedings would be discontinued and existing claims terminated; because they limited the range of heirs entitled to compensation; and because of the short deadline for submitting a request for compensation.

Of course, from the beginning of the democratic regime remedies had been available in the civil courts. Claimants had to initiate and pursue separate, sequential civil and administrative proceedings. An aggrieved party seeking restitution had first to claim with the appropriate administrative agency and exhaust all administrative procedures. Administrative findings that a property expropriation was null and void were relatively uncommon, as most property in the communist era was confiscated pursuant to lawfully issued laws. Only following an administrative ruling that the property at issue was seized in 'a shocking breach' of pertinent communist nationalization laws could a claimant file for restitution or related compensation in the civil courts.

There is general consensus in law that a decision issued without legal basis is annulled; the state has no right to possess property seized unlawfully, which should be returned to its owner or compensation provided. Clearly, one problem was considerable discretion as to 'shocking breach' of law. Another arose when the state had already disposed of the property, since the rights of a new *bona fide* owner were protected. Claims also became more difficult because of the communalization of state property, the privatization of state assets from 1988, and new and changing statutes on rural and urban development.[62]

Despite cumbersome and costly procedures many private property claimants did succeed in the courts. In 2015 the property restitution information website estimated that claims that reached the courts were settled in all major cities (Warsaw was an exception, with thousands of claims pending, on which see below). It estimated the percentage of accepted applications for restitution as 90 per cent in Gdynia, Lublin and Łódź, and 80 per cent in Katowice, Poznań and Krakow.[63] Overall about 4,000 applications for invalidating nationalization decisions were filed (1989–2012), with three-quarters completed, mostly in favour of the previous owners. In the early 1990s, most such cases ended in restitution *in rem*. From 2001 until 2012 the State Treasury also paid out damages to 402 claimants for illegal seizure of industrial plants.

Former landowners were in a different position because their claims came under land reform measures rather than nationalization laws. A 1945 edict of the ministry of agriculture had served as the basis for determining whether a specific estate was subject to reform. That process was subject to appeal to the administrative courts. In March 2010 the Constitutional Tribunal (TK) ruled that the edict had lost force from 1958 so that cases could no longer be resolved by (cheaper) administrative procedures but only by the civil courts. However, in 2011 the Supreme Administrative Court argued that the TK decision was not binding, since it had not reviewed the merits of the issue. It found that the 1945 edict could still be administratively reviewed in order to 'repair the irregularities of confiscation' after 1944. Increasingly, castles, palaces, country manors and non-arable land were returned to their previous owners.

## Jewish property

The situation of individual Jews was particularly complex – not only because of the Holocaust but because many who escaped from Poland did not return after the war. Generally communist nationalization measures 'legalised and post-facto fixed the status quo of expropriations made by German occupying forces'.[64] Land registries in many areas were destroyed during the war, making ownership difficult to prove.

Former owners whose property had been seized by the Nazis and their collaborators lost title to their property as a result of the 'Post-German and Deserted Properties Decree'. Any property (as of 1 September 1939) not recovered by its owner within ten years of 1945 passed to the state. Not surprisingly, few Jewish property owners were able to recover their property before 1955.[65] Even when this decree lost force, titles to properties apparently continued to accrue to the state. In 1987 the Supreme Court affirmed the presumption that properties not recovered between 1945 and 1955 reverted to the state.[66]

Although approximately 500 individual claims totalling $183 million were settled in the courts between 1997 and 2007, the Polish government estimated that 56,000 potential claims valued at approximately $16.7 billion remained outstanding pending the establishment of a formal claims process. At its annual meeting in Warsaw in

February 2007 the Conference on Jewish Material Claims against Germany (the 'Claims Conference') pressed for urgent passage of a private property restitution law with more lenient filing requirements. Although Donald Tusk committed himself on successive occasions to restitution legislation, it was not forthcoming. In 2012 the government adopted its view that claimants seek redress in the courts – as indeed they could have done all along. Despite protests by the WJRO, representatives of the American Congress and even the British House of Lords, individual proceedings remained the sole method of restitution. The WJRO maintained that 'tens of thousands of Jewish owners and heirs ... continue to be left without what is rightfully theirs, while the government of Poland fails to provide even a semblance of justice'.[67] It may be observed that the PiS government elected in 2015 was notably unresponsive to their case.

### Restitution to the people from beyond the Bug

The 'people from beyond the Bug (*Zabużanie*)' constituted a special case of a different kind. Strictly speaking, they could not enjoy restitution, since their property was in a foreign country. Following the conferences at Yalta and Potsdam through a series of agreements with the authorities of various Soviet republics, Poland assumed the obligation to compensate citizens 'repatriated' from the territories beyond the Bug River. These people lost their land and most of their material possessions.

The Polish government estimated that about 1.2 million persons left now-Soviet territories between 1944 and 1953. The majority were compensated, either by the granting of perpetual use of land or with land belonging to the Polish State. However, in the 1990s some 100,000 *Zabużanie* were still entitled to compensation or additional compensation. The main method was that of offsetting the amount of compensation against land purchase or other liabilities, but this was far easier in theory than in practice. The test case was that of Jerzy Broniowski, which proceeded in the Polish courts and at the European Court of Human Rights.

Broniowski's grandmother had been repatriated to Poland from Lwów (Lviv), now in independent Ukraine, where she owned 400 m² of land and a house. On 19 August 1947 the Polish State Repatriation Office issued a certificate attesting her ownership. Her daughter, Broniowski's mother, inherited the entitlement and obtained partial compensation in 1981, with the right to perpetual use of 467 m² of land near Krakow (later estimated as constituting about 2 per cent of the Broniowski entitlement[68]). Following his mother's death Broniowski inherited her property and her claims. In September 1992 he requested full compensation from the government for the land lost in Lwów. His claim was registered locally but he was informed that it 'could not be satisfied'.

On 12 August 1994 Broniowski filed a complaint with the Supreme Administrative Court (NSA), but the Court found 'no indication of inactivity' on the part of the state authorities: the Krakow District Office and the provincial governor's office had replied to him. In March 1996 Broniowski filed an application alleging a breach of Article 1 of the Protocol to the Convention for the Protection of Human Rights: The State, after having conferred on him an entitlement to compensatory property, had failed to fulfil its legislative duty to regulate the matter in a proper and timely manner. It had also enacted obstructive laws that had rendered the obtaining of property as compensation almost impossible. In March 2002 jurisdiction was transferred to the Grand Chamber of the ECHR.

On 5 July 2002 the Ombudsman applied to the Constitutional Court (TK), requesting that the provisions restricting full compensation be declared unconstitutional. The TK found provisions of several laws invalid and ordered their amendment,[69] though it did not endorse the principle of 'full compensation'. It found that although lacking the status of international treaties, the so-called republican agreements[70] required the Polish authorities to provide a statutory settlement for those Polish citizens who lost their immovable property in connection with the altered borders of the state. This was not just compensation but chiefly 'an ancillary benefit of a social nature to assist in resettlement'. With a distinctive character as a property right of a public–private nature – in a certain sphere 'a specific surrogate of the right to property' – it nevertheless enjoyed the constitutional protection of property rights and the equal protection of the law. The government responded with the Law of 12 December 2003 on offsetting the value of property abandoned beyond the present borders of the Polish State.[71]

The ECHR issued its judgment in August 2004.[72] Far from remedying Broniowski's claim, the 2003 law effectively extinguished it: the law created a difference in treatment between persons who had never received compensation and those, like Broniowski, who had already been awarded a lower amount. Poland had failed to strike a fair balance between the general interest of the community and Broniowski's right to the peaceful enjoyment of his property. Since Poland had reaffirmed its obligation to compensate the Bug River settlers in 1985 and 1997, it had incorporated obligations under international treaties existing prior to the ratification of the Convention for the Protection of Human Rights and Protocol No 1. The rule of law further required that Poland fulfil such promises in good time and in compliance with internal judgments, such as that of its Constitutional Tribunal.

The ECHR considered that Poland should have eliminated dysfunctional provisions from its legal system and rectified extra-legal practices that hindered compensation. In the view of the court, Polish authorities had made it impossible for Broniowski to seek compensation. The state's agencies had thwarted all possibility of offset. They had applied practices that made it unenforceable and unusable, destroying the very essence of his right. The court also found that the state of uncertainty in which Broniowski found himself as a result of years of delay and obstruction was itself incompatible with Protocol No 1. Furthermore, Broniowski's situation was worsened by the fact that his already, in practice, unenforceable entitlement was legally extinguished by the December 2003 legislation.

The ECHR found that because this situation also concerned thousands of other persons, this was not only 'an aggravating factor as regards to the State's responsibility … but also … a threat to the future effectiveness of the Convention machinery'. In September 2005 the ECHR accepted a settlement between Broniowski and the government. Broniowski received the equivalent of 20 per cent of the value of his grandmother's property and €12,000 as compensation for material and non-material harm arising from the inaction of the Polish authorities.

Meanwhile the Constitutional Tribunal had also returned to the issue. It found several elements of the 2003 law unconstitutional.[73] It reaffirmed its view of 2002 that at issue was not 'damages' in the meaning of civil law, such as that for nationalized property. This compensation could not be equated with that for illegal nationalization, since it did not arise from actions of the Polish state but from geopolitical circumstances. It was *sui generis* in nature. Payment was an element of public-law property rights, with an element of property compensation and a social element to assist in resettlement.

Although it upheld the citizenship and settlement requirements, the TK rejected the 'arbitrary and unjustified' proviso that claimants must have resided permanently in Poland from 30 January 2004 (when the law came into force). It recognized that the state could legitimately limit property rights for the public good, but limiting compensation to 15 per cent of the value of the property left behind was a permissible limitation only if the legislature justified it in terms of safeguarding other constitutional rights and values. Moreover, the cap of 50,000 PNL entailed unequal treatment, since some claimants would receive a greater proportion of their claim than others. Finally, as the ECHR also found in the Broniowski case, excluding those who had already received partial compensation amounted to unequal treatment, it was discriminatory and socially unjust – hence invalid.

In 2005 a new law entitled the Bug River claimants to compensation amounting to 20 per cent of their property's original value, in kind or in money from a new Compensation Fund (*Fundusz Rekompensacyjny*).[74] Up to the end of 2012 some 45,719 persons had received payments from the Fund. However, it did not fully resolve the issue, which once again reached the Constitutional Tribunal.

In 2012 the TK reaffirmed that payments were an element of public-law property rights, with a predominant social element and an element of compensation.[75] But the proviso that claimants must have been resident on 1 September 1939 in the-then territory of the Polish Republic was unconstitutional. This date was absent from the 1946 decree which first regulated the issue.

The TK observed that it first appeared in 2003, resulting in a clear denial of property rights and the unequal treatment of several hundred persons who happened to reside elsewhere on that day. But the plaintiff could not claim inequality of treatment with those compensated for property seized by the Polish state. The Polish state had no control of the eastern borderlands; hence, its obligations were weaker here. The essence of the constitutional problem was the assessment of the proportionality of the solution provided in the compensation law of 2005. The TK argued once again that the right to compensation is not equivalent to the right to property and 'need not meet the highest possible standard'. The state must assess the financial consequences – both directly and in its constitutional task of maintaining order and security.

At the same time the residence requirement of 1 September 1939 obviated the social element of the compensation and did not guarantee compensation for all who lost property. Narrowing the sphere of persons entitled to compensation did not meet the requirement of proportionality. However, in order to give the legislator the opportunity to correct the law, the TK postponed the loss of validity of the invalid provision because of the complexity of the issue and its budgetary implications.

From February 2014 the law provided compensation for anyone 'who on 1 September 1939 was a Polish citizen, resident on the former territory of the Polish Republic, but was required to leave or unable to return'.[76] It was hoped that this would finally resolve the problem of compensation for the *Zabużanie*. Yet the procedures remained so complex that applicants were advised to consult professional advisers.

## The case of Warsaw

The 'Bierut Decree' of 1945 had authorized the confiscation of almost all private land in the centre of Warsaw as necessary for the reconstruction of the devastated city. In theory, dispossessed owners had six months to apply for property in another location. In practice, these applications were refused, often without alternative compensation. In the 1990s specialist law firms sprang up to purchase rights to compensation, often for tiny sums. Lawyers then filed compensation claims for millions, especially for valued sites in the city centre.

In June 2015 a new 'small reprivatization'[77] gave the State Treasury and the City of Warsaw first refusal when compensation rights arising from the Bierut decree were offered for sale. This was justified by 'negative social effects', including the eviction of tenants and the loss of school playgrounds. Just as the law was due to come into effect, investigative journalists at *Gazeta Wyborcza* revealed the scale of irregularities in the 'wild reprivatization' of Warsaw properties.[78]

The minister of justice established a special 'verification commission' to investigate these improprieties, with quasi-judicial powers, including the right to ban the disposal of real estate, the right to waive final administrative decisions *ex officio* and the right to assess decisions from the perspective of circumstances which arose after they were issued. Hanna Gronkiewicz-Waltz, then mayor of Warsaw and a member of the opposition party Civic Platform, dismissed several mid-ranking officials from her office; three were later charged with corruption. The scandal later embraced her husband Andrzej, who was investigated after inheriting part of a corruptly acquired tenement from his aunt. Waltz paid the city 1.8 million PNL.[79] The first successful legal challenge to the verification commission came in March 2019.[80]

After PiS won the election of 2015, it renewed its earlier controversial proposals to bring a halt to reprivatization with limited compensation and no restitution in kind. However, in October 2017 Deputy Justice Minister Patryk Jaki, the chair of the Verification Commission, announced that his ministry would be introducing a new comprehensive reprivatization law, at last righting this long-standing wrong. Nothing more was heard after Jaki became a Euro-MEP in 2019.

# Conclusion

Claims for restitution often rest on the sanctity of private property, but all states have mechanisms for taking property for the public good. In largely maintaining the formal requirements for compensation, the communist regime provided a legal cloak for its property seizures in the 1940s. There seems no compelling reason why this property should be returned to its former owners or their heirs at the cost of the current generation – save in cases where legal breaches can be identified. In that sense the Polish lawmakers seem to have got it right, in substance, if not in procedure: inefficient, cumbersome, costly and time-consuming processes placed a great burden on individuals seeking redress. We have stressed the difficulty of establishing a 'shocking breach' of communist law and the transparent injustice of recognizing the 'Post-German and Deserted Properties Decree'.

The *Zabużanie* could not have their property restored to them, so compensation was essential. Although governments accepted the obligation to provide compensation, they proved reluctant, incompetent and obstructive in doing so. The situation of the *Zabużanie* provided a contrast to the treatment of restitution for Solidarity, where the State Treasury assumed most of the restitution obligations.

Indeed, the restitution of property to the Solidarity trade union was the most consensual and least difficult area of restitution in Poland. The settlement reached with the Catholic Church was of quite a different order. Once the mechanism for restitution to the Catholics was established, the rights of religious freedom, equality before the law and non-discrimination meant that similar principles of restitution for other religious bodies had to follow. The restitution of places of worship and sacred sites such as cemeteries seems uncontroversial. It is the size of its pre-communist land holdings, the institutional arrangements for restitution, the extent of restitution and the difficulty of challenging the judgments of the Property Commission that made the Catholic Church distinctive. The Catholic Church was the big restitution-winner. The absence of any public interest brief for government representatives on the Property Commission, the lack of transparency and accountability, and the lack of appeal to the courts were serious flaws, creating new injustices while seeking to remedy old ones.

# Lustration. The first stage 1989–2005

## Introduction

Of all arenas of transitional justice lustration attracted most scholarly attention and proved the most intensely politicized. This chapter deals with lustration up to the parliamentary election of 2005. Up to then, lustration had been strongly contested by the conservative and social democratic wings of Polish politics. Following the triumphant election of 2001, the SLD split and lost its coalition partner. Its minority government staggered on until 2005, when the SLD received only 11.3 per cent of the vote. The decline of the Left paved the way for a resurgence in radical solutions to issues of transitional justice, spearheaded after 2005 by the victorious Law and Justice Party.

Not only was lustration highly politicized. Of all transitional justice measures, lustration affected the largest number of people. Lustration proved remarkably persistent, first surfacing in 1990 but thwarted, first by procedural concerns, then by the fragmentation of the 1991 parliament and the return to power of the SLD in 1993. After allegations of spying against the prime minister in 1995, all parties agreed on the need for legislation, but the content of the 1997 lustration law remained hotly disputed. That law was immediately amended after Solidarity (AWS) won the 1997 election. The SLD government elected in 2001 sought to refine the concept of collaboration, but it came into conflict with the Constitutional Tribunal.

We begin with a general discussion of conceptual arguments about lustration and its role and timing. Then we examine the abortive steps taken in 1991 and 1992 following Poland's first, but indecisive, fully democratic elections. We review the parliamentary debates to extract the broad general arguments that persisted both for and against lustration and to provide a benchmark to assess how views changed over time, particularly among liberals and social democrats. We analyse the first lustration law of 1997, the significant changes made under the AWS government of Jerzy Buzek and further attempts by the government of Leszek Miller after 2001.

## Lustration and its implications

In Central Europe lustration entailed the assessment of individuals to determine their past relationship with the communist system. This is closely akin to vetting. In Chapter 1 we argued that vetting is a wider concept, since vetting may employ non-political criteria such as qualifications or competence for a post. Lustration is essentially a subset of vetting.

We also saw that for some scholars, lustration is effectively synonymous with transitional justice. It was indeed the most complex aspect of transitional justice. It was closely linked to questions of democratization as well as to Poland's national security. These security concerns were enhanced by numerous corruption scandals, including scandals alleging secret links with Russian security services. Lustration was also inextricably entwined with issues surrounding access to files of the security services, since 'informers', 'collaborators' and agents could not otherwise be revealed.

The objects of lustration are two-fold: occupants of senior posts in the communist political system and those in society who cooperated with them as agents or informers. Each may be broadly or narrowly conceived. The broad view embraced all those holding senior positions in the apparatuses of party and state. The narrow view focused on those working in the security apparatus and the judiciary. The broad view was that individuals who had secretly cooperated with organs of the state were morally compromised, even when they had been blackmailed or coerced. The narrow view identified extenuating circumstances.

Lustration was mainly concerned with appointees to public posts or candidates for election. Lustration may be seen as a 'personnel system' (David[1]), a political tactic (Nalepa and Kurski[2]), a means of truth-seeking and historical understanding (Stan and Nadelsky[3]) or a moral necessity for a new democracy (Appel[4]). It was indeed all of these, if not for everyone or at all times. In Poland a visceral anti-communism underlay lustration and fuelled its most ardent proponents, namely activists from the right wing of Polish politics.

Although initially the term lustration was not used, the need to 'verify' office-holders and bureaucrats was accepted and instituted by Tadeusz Mazowiecki's government. Widening this process and revealing the identities of informers were part and parcel of the wide-ranging decommunization programme advocated by Jarosław Kaczyński's Centre Accord (PC) and the Christian nationalists (ZChN) in 1990. This was adopted as an element of Lech Wałęsa's successful presidential campaign. Originally referring to Roman purification rituals, lustration retained this notion of cleansing or purification. After the passage of the Czechoslovak Lustration Law in 1991, the term lustration was widely used throughout the region.

In Poland the extent of lustration and its mechanisms changed over the years, though the fundamental arguments for and against lustration changed little. Their relative weightings shifted, some individuals and parties changed their minds, and obvious failures gave impetus to new positions on scope and methods. Although much attention has been given to Poland's 'late' lustration, the absence of lustration before 1997 can be explained by a series of contingent factors.

Firstly, the government of Tadeusz Mazowiecki was a coalition of Solidarity with the communists/ex-communists, who were neither politically nor ideologically inclined to lustration. Secondly, after the first democratic elections in 1991, the fragmented *Sejm* was incapable of coherent action; indeed, the *Sejm*'s lustration resolution of 1992 led to the fall of Jan Olszewski's minority government. Thirdly, the Social Democrats' electoral victory in 1993 and the exclusion of most Solidarity parties from that parliament delayed lustration until allegations of spying made against Prime Minister Józef Oleksy convinced many doubters that some action was necessary. Oleksy resigned in January 1996. The first Lustration Law came in 1997, six years after the election of the first fully democratic parliament. Given all the circumstances – and the fallout from the 1992 fiasco – that does not seem unduly 'late'.

Moreover, it is important to stress that lustration never left the political agenda. It remained a core aim of right-wing politicians from 1989 onwards. The political configuration is the key: when these pro-lustration Solidarity elites came to power in 1997, they acted to refine and extend the lustration law. The right-wing view of Polish democracy, its quality and its requisites, stemmed not just from the dictates of political expediency but also in large part from personal histories and deep-seated ideological hatreds. Since the communist system was illegitimate and immoral, those who had cooperated with it were its immoral agents.

Lustration was also politically useful – like other forms of personnel displacement, lustration opened up vacancies for party patronage. It is also significant that Poland was not alone in the persistent character of lustration. Many countries came late to lustration, including Slovenia, Latvia and Macedonia, or returned to it, as did Slovakia and Romania.

Horne sees late lustration as lustration 'reframed and implemented in conjunction with and in some cases as a substitute for anti-corruption measures'. It was 'used by governments to address public frustration and inequity associated with the continued privileging of former communist elites'.[5] There is some merit in this argument. However, it cannot really explain 'late' lustration in Poland, since from the beginning of the democratic system lustration had been presented as a key policy for undermining the putative privileges and corruption of former communist elites. We shall see in the next chapter that this was certainly true of Jarosław Kaczyński, who put lustration high on the agenda after finally achieving political office (2005–7) and who sought a wide-ranging decommunization programme after again taking the reins of government in 2015.

Aleks Szczerbiak rightly links arguments about lustration to questions of the quality of Polish democracy.[6] However, he too ignores the consistency with which Kaczyński and his allies argued their case after 1989: democracy *needed* lustration to combat the corrupt cronyism whose origins could be traced back to the Round Table. It is true that the full-blown arguments for a 'moral revolution' and a new 'Fourth Republic' came somewhat later – as Kaczyński refined his earlier position to include a critique of the failures of the first years of post-communism. But he, and many of those who migrated to Law and Justice (PiS) from the defunct Christian National Union (ZChN), had steadfastly argued that decommunization, as well as lustration, was inextricably linked to the democratic project.

Monika Nalepa saw lustration as a tool 'to skew the results of elections and other democratic processes'.[7] However, her view that liberals opposed lustration because they were frightened of the 'skeletons in their closet', while others such as Kaczyński's PC knew from the files that it had no skeletons[8] is not sustainable. The PC certainly believed its members were historically 'clean', but it could not 'know' this; the files remained closed. Nalepa's claim that after the 1992 lustration affair 'nothing would convert (the liberals) into supporters of lustration'[9] fails on several counts. Liberals did embrace lustration, however reluctantly. Her explanation that lustration was late because 'eventually non-collaborating parties came to power' does not apply to either the 1997 law or its amended version in 1998.

Lustration was a multi-faceted vehicle. It was intensely political and one cannot doubt its use as a political tool. It became an important means of delegitimizing the Round Table and an instrument in the struggle for power. It was an ideological battle to control perceptions of the past. It was also a moral reaffirmation, albeit with a specific perspective on the nature of morality. It was truth-seeking, if often with a monomaniacal view of truth.

## The first steps

The first legislative initiative came in May 1991, with proposed amendments to the electoral laws for the first fully democratic elections. These amendments required the interior minister to provide the Electoral Commission with the names of candidates who had worked for or collaborated with the (now defunct) Security Service (SB). The Commission would publish the information, but there was no sanction attached – it was presumed that voters would reject such candidates.[10] The *Sejm* rejected these amendments after Deputy Interior Minister Jan Widacki stated that while the Ministry could certainly advise on former functionaries of the SB, it could not identify informers or collaborators: the concept of 'collaborator' was imprecise – indeed, many who were noted as collaborators had never signed undertakings nor were even aware that they were labelled secret collaborators (*tajni współpracownicy*); moreover, the files included some 3 million names, including falsified files and fabricated informers.[11]

Following the elections of October 1991 the new Prime Minister Jan Olszewski announced 'the beginning of the end of communism' and 'the accountability of those who … had acted against the national interest'.[12] Lustration was clearly on the agenda. The most ardent lustration advocates, the Centre Accord (PC) and the Christian National Union (ZChN), constituted the core of Olszewski's minority coalition government. Minister of the Interior Antoni Macierewicz was charged with drafting the first tranche of 'de-communizing' legislation. The Ministry prepared a lustration bill 'on the conditions for assuming certain positions' in the state administration and local government, the presidential chancellery, the police, the army, the judiciary and the procuracy.[13] Macierewicz himself preferred a system giving senior officials, politicians and members of the judiciary the opportunity to resign before making public their collaboration.[14]

Meanwhile the Olszewski government's relations with President Wałęsa deteriorated rapidly, mainly over issues of defence. The government saw Wałęsa as too close to members of the former officer corps, while Wałęsa did not share the government's fears of a resurgent communist threat. Differences over the new Polish–Russian Treaty in May 1992 led Wałęsa to withdraw his support from the government.

## The lustration resolution

The unexpected intervention of Janusz Korwin-Mikke of the radical liberal Union of Realist Politics (UPR) set in motion the process that would lead to the fall of the Olszewski government, further splits in the post-Solidarity political configuration, and a temporary halt to lustration and decommunization initiatives. On 28 May 1992 Korwin-Mikke tabled a resolution (*uchwała*) obliging the interior minister to provide information on officials and parliamentarians who had collaborated with the Security Services between 1945 and 1992.[15] After some kerfuffle the *Sejm* added the resolution to the order of business and the UPR presented a slightly amended version, adding councillors and the commune (*gmina*) executive to the list of posts covered. Without debate the *Sejm* voted overwhelmingly for the resolution 'requiring the Minister of Internal Affairs to provide by 6 June 1992 complete information on state administrators from the provincial level upwards, senators, and deputies; within two months on judges, procurators and lawyers; and within six months on commune councillors and executive committee members who collaborated with the Security Bureau (UB) and the Security Service (SB) between 1945 and 1990'.[16]

With no formal debate, several deputies used their right to make personal statements (*oświadczenia*) to condemn the resolution. Jacek Taylor protested on behalf of four parliamentary clubs – the Democratic Union (UD), the Congress of Liberal Democrats (KLD), Labour Solidarity (SP) and the Polish Economic Programme (PPG): he argued that the resolution contravened the *Sejm*'s regulations – it did not provide the required justification, nor did the proposer answer deputies' questions. It was illegal because only legislation could authorize the minister to take such action. It did not guarantee citizens' rights, providing no legal procedure for lustration and no right of defence.[17] Some deputies from the liberal parties and the reformed social democrats of the SLD tried to block the resolution by lack of quorum; they were present but did not vote. President Wałęsa himself asked Macierewicz to provide information on the manner of implementing the resolution. Wałęsa sought assurances that an opportunity for individuals to defend themselves would be provided, for 'otherwise, that would be the greatest victory of the old Security Service'.[18]

When Macierewicz provided his two lists of sixty-four persons and two persons respectively, he did not actually fulfil the terms of the *Sejm*'s resolution, which required a list of 'collaborators' with the security services. The interior ministry issued a statement confirming that 'the minister does not feel entitled to identify who was and who was not a collaborator … (but) felt obliged to provide information on materials at the disposition of the ministry'.[19] The lists identified persons recorded in the secret police archive, even though it was widely known that many files had been destroyed and that documentation did not always take the form of individual files on named informers, agents or collaborators.[20] However, the secret lists soon became public. They included prominent figures from the opposition movement, with Speaker of the *Sejm* Wiesław Chrzanowski and President Lech Wałęsa on the second list, distributed to a narrower circle. On 4 June Polish television viewers of the *Sejm*'s proceedings heard Kazimierz Świton declare that Macierewicz's list included the president.[21]

Wałęsa supported the pending vote of confidence, accusing the government of acting outside the law and of providing materials that were clearly fabricated. He referred to the destabilization of the polity and its political parties.[22] The vote passed easily, by 273 votes to 119, with 33 abstentions. The *Sejm* also approved Wałęsa's nominee for prime minister, peasant party leader Waldemar Pawlak (Pawlak proved unable to form a government). Olszewski's fall became part of the mythology of the right.

In its judgment of 19 June 1992 the Constitutional Tribunal vindicated critics of the lustration resolution, declaring it incompatible with the Constitution's commitment to democratic principles and human rights, as well as in violation of laws governing state secrecy and the protection of an individual's reputation. Moreover, only legislation, not a resolution, could authorize the minister of the interior to encroach on the sphere of individual civil liberties. The *Sejm* had also violated its own procedures.[23] The Court noted that the resolution was 'exceptionally obscure'. It failed to define the term 'full information', to identify to whom the information was to be provided, to define the term 'collaborator' (*współpracownik*), to elaborate the criteria for identifying an individual as a 'collaborator' and to specify the legal consequences of providing information. In short, regardless of the methods of implementation, the resolution itself led to the violation of individual rights.

The judgment did not halt the flood of innuendo and half-baked gossip about those on Macierewicz's list. Animated rumours circulated regarding secret agents Bolek (allegedly Wałęsa) and Zapalniczka (allegedly Zdzisław Najder, formerly of Radio Free Europe). It was difficult for individuals to defend themselves. Wałęsa was reduced to pleading for all files connected with him to be made public, while Najder published an affidavit and an Open Letter to the minister of the interior.[24] Both Wałęsa and Speaker Chrzanowski were later exonerated, along with many others – though over the next two decades Wałęsa faced recurring allegations of collaboration. The inability of the accused to defend themselves, denying them access to the archives and providing no mode of due process, was a central criticism upheld by the Constitutional Tribunal.

Ructions on the right – with Olszewski leaving the Centrum to form a new party, Wałęsa condemned as a national traitor and the Confederation for Independent Poland outraged at the presence of its leader Leszek Moczulski on Macierewicz's list – did not bring a halt to lustration efforts. A lustration element was grafted onto the 1993 electoral law. Each candidate had to append a statement that s/he had or had not worked as a functionary of or cooperated with the organs of state security [Art. 81, ¶ 5(4)].[25] There were no sanctions envisaged for falsehood, nor was there any definition of the notion of 'cooperation'. The Constitutional Tribunal ruled in July 1993 (two months before the election) that the submitting of a false declaration, however morally reprehensible, could not serve as the basis for a challenge to the outcome of the election.[26]

The bills debated in the *Sejm* in autumn 1992 did, to varying degrees, take account of the Tribunal's earlier judgment on the *Sejm*'s lustration resolution, including a right to defense and an appeal mechanism. However, the parties took very different views. The two largest parties, the Alliance of the Democratic Left (SLD) and the Democratic Union (UD), had strong reservations about lustration, and so too did the Peasant Party (PSL). There was little hope of a consensus even among the lustration enthusiasts, although requiring an affidavit confirming or denying collaboration with the security services was a common feature.

The mildest form and the narrowest scope of lustration was represented by the Liberal Democrats' (KLD) draft.[27] In that version only judges and procurators faced dismissal for false affidavits. In all other cases false declarations would be made public but no other consequences would follow. This 'public shaming' model did not garner much enthusiasm.

The most radical version came from Kaczyński's Centrum (PC), whose bill (and that of the Christian National Union) included decommunization processes as well as lustration.[28] It provided for the removal from office or loss of the right to practise one's profession of persons who had held a wide variety of posts under the communist regime: in the ministries of the interior and public security (MBP); in a number of military institutions; the Bureau of Religious Affairs; the Bureau of the Censor (GUKPPiW); and all positions in the Communist Party (PZPR) from the commune level upwards, as well as department directors and their equivalents. Krotoszyński rightly calls this a 'decommunizing purge'.[29] The 'lustration' dimension covered those who had collaborated with the security services. All six bills were referred to committee and fell with the dissolution of parliament (Hanna Suchocka's government, itself divided and preoccupied with other matters, fell on a vote of no confidence in May 1993). However, the parliamentary debate held in September 1992 rehearsed most subsequent arguments for and against lustration, albeit some lost force with the passage of time.

## Arguments for lustration

In the debate on six lustration bills submitted by four political parties – the Liberal Democrats (KLD), the Confederation for Independent Poland (KPN), the Christian National Union (ZChN), the Centre Accord (PC) and one each from the Solidarity trade union and the Senate – all right-wing parties and the German Minority supported lustration. The liberal Democratic Union (UD), the Social Democrats (SLD) and the Peasant Party (PSL) broadly opposed it.

After 1995 all parliamentary parties supported lustration in some form, but the Freedom Union (formerly the UD) and the social democrats favoured a narrower scope with different rationales. Both camps emphasized democracy and human rights, but while lustration's strongest advocates stressed the dangers to democracy of the vestiges of the old regime, those less enthusiastic about lustration focused more on the implications for individual rights.[30]

The pro-lustration arguments of the right-wing parties were highly ideological and inter-linked. Virtually all took as their premise the evil, 'criminal' nature of communism and the problematic nature of the Round Table 'contract'.[31] Firstly, lustration was a requisite of democracy. The new system required that only 'democrats of sound moral character' hold key positions in the state. Democracy needed clean hands and clear consciences. This automatically barred from public office persons who had worked for or cooperated with the security services: the security services were organs of repression against the citizenry. Collaborators shared responsibility for the denial of personal liberty and dignity, breaches of civil rights and, for betrayal of the fatherland, violation of Poland's sovereignty, rendering the Polish state subservient to the interests of a foreign power and creating a system based on terror. 'Lustration', said Jan Piątkowski of the Christian National Union, 'is not an act of vengeance but an act of justice pursued exclusively for moral reasons, an act of reckoning with the vestiges of an imposed system of totalitarianism'.[32] Lustration would represent 'the embodiment of justice in public life', said Maciej Srebro. Most parliamentarians distinguished between elected and appointed positions. Collaborators could not be appointed to public office. But 'if voters wish to choose a person regardless of whether s/he was an informer or first secretary of the Party or anything else, their decision is of over-riding importance' (Marek Muszyński of Solidarity).

Secondly, lustration (and, for some, wider programmes of decommunization) would signal a definitive break with the past. The old elites persisted thanks to the Round Table. Lustration would end their influence, marking 'the final break of the independent Polish state with the communist past, and above all with the continuing presence of a network of agents of the foreign power which occupied Poland for 45 years' (Sławomir Siwek, PC). In this regard lustration would also serve to protect society and democracy from a 'planned communist resurgence' and the 'danger that it could succeed in destroying the democratic system' (Tadeusz Wójcik, Peasant Accord).

Lustration would also safeguard economic reform. Those linked to the old system were 'blocking the functioning of new mechanisms' (Bartłomiej Kołodziej, PC) and 'slowing or obstructing reform' (Marek Markiewicz, Solidarity). Moreover, wider security interests were also at stake. There was a genuine risk that Poland would remain in thrall to a foreign power (Sławomir Siwek). The intelligence services must be lustrated, since they 'never served Poland's national interest' but rather that of the Soviet Union (Senator Zbigniew Romaszewski). Moreover, those who had collaborated with the security organs were open to blackmail (Paweł Abramski, KLD; Piotr Wójcik, RdR).

Lustration was necessary to ensure the trust of society, cleanse the atmosphere of public life, provide 'evidence that the state has embarked on the path of true democratic development' (Erhard Bastek, German Minority) and give 'moral satisfaction to millions of Poles' (Wójcik). Opinion polls showed public demand for lustration (Markiewicz, Stefan Pastuszewski, Christian Democracy). (In June 1992 the polling firm OBOP found that 62 per cent of respondents supported lustration, confirmed by a CBOS report in March 1993.)[33]

Finally, lustration would provide the truth, with the 'long hoped-for day when society would come to know the names of the secret collaborators' (Andrzej Tadeusz Mazurkiewicz, KPN). Revealing the truth of the past would enable society to judge its politicians (Stanisław Rakoczy, ZChN). However, truth-seeking was a lesser argument, used by parties such as the KPN, whose draft bill permitted each citizen access to his/her files.

## Arguments against lustration

The arguments against lustration centred mainly on its immediate effects, its human rights' implications and its moral underpinnings, including tolerance, compromise and affirmation of the importance of the Round Table. Nor were pragmatic considerations absent. Many speakers in the 1992 debate stressed the potential destabilizing consequences of the process at a time of considerable economic and social upheaval. 'Poland is on fire, literally and metaphorically', said Andrzej Wielowieyski (UD), 'and this requires maximum effort and concentration on what is most important'. The timing was wrong: lustration should yield to other, more pressing matters, notably the economy (Jacek Taylor, UD; Kazimierz Chełstowski, Party X). Lustration threatened not only destabilization but the spreading of hatred and intolerance (Adam Halber, Koło Poselskie Spolegliwość) and an increase in social tension (Maria Dmochowska, UD; Joseph Oleksy, SLD).

Secondly, the draft bills contained provisions contravening the constitutional principle of the equality of citizens and the International Charter of Human Rights (Andrzej Wielowieyski, UD; Jacek Taylor, UD). Both the Democratic Union (later the Freedom Union, UW) and the social democrats of the Democratic Left (SLD) stressed the protection of individual rights through the rule of law as a keystone of modern liberal democracy. The wrongs done, the serious errors committed and the damage wreaked in the past 'cannot justify the principle of collective guilt' (Wielowieyski, Oleksy, Kowalczyk, PSL; Iwona Śledzińska-Katarasińska, UD; Barbara Blida, SLD). Oleksy said, 'We (of the SLD) have supported all proposals to judge and punish those who broke the law, did harm to others, abused their office and their privileges ....De-communization laws are not needed ... They introduce retrospective law and ... violate the presumption of innocence. They limit the right to choose one's job.'

Thirdly, lustration was no more than a political ploy and a desire for revenge. 'For base aims of political gamesmanship ... (the proponents of lustration) are ready to lead Poland to the edge of the abyss of a new totalitarianism' (Włodzimierz Cimoszewicz, SLD). 'We have no illusions that the aim is the brutal elimination of the Left from political life' (Oleksy, SLD). 'We are dealing more with the aim of making political gains than with the rational resolution of these complex, difficult and many-faceted matters' (Janusz Piechociński, PSL). 'The decommunization bills are truly an act of vengeance' (Wielowiejski, UD). Moreover, lustration was addressing a 'false issue': there is 'no problem with the communist *nomenklatura* in state institutions' nor any sign of a social basis for a communist restoration (Kowalczyk, PSL).

Finally, opposition centred on specific aspects of certain drafts, especially the inclusion of communist party members as subjects for lustration, since many communists had supported Solidarity and many had 'served their country well' (Wielowieyski, Taylor, Oleksy). President Wałęsa and the minister of defence agreed that lustration of the police, the military and the intelligence services would 'weaken the security of the state' (Zofia Kowalczyk, PSL; Andrzej Baraniecki, SLD). Indeed, even some members of the Christian National Union opposed lustration in the military.

For others, lustration was unnecessary; there were simpler means available. Former members of the security services could be prevented from holding public office by amendments to the electoral law and powers for the prime minister to 'extract the necessary information' (Taylor). Or the electoral law could require candidates to provide complete information on their political, social and professional activities (Piechociński). Limited lustration of the highest offices of state could take the form of checking the dossier of a candidate at the interior ministry and publishing relevant facts (Kowalczyk).

Four years later many of these arguments resurfaced in renewed lustration debates, though by then the composition of the *Sejm* was very different. Following the 1993 election the SLD formed a coalition with the Polish Peasant Party (PSL). Of the pro-lustration parties active in the previous *Sejm*, only the Confederation for an Independent Poland (KPN) survived. Already, however, there were signs of a new pragmatic approach on the part of the Democratic Union. As Bronisław Geremek put it, 'The subject of lustration is a proxy matter ... but the skeleton is in the cupboard and we need to finish with it ....; but though I regard lustration as essential, I regard decommunization as undermining the basic democratic order.'[34] Geremek's view was partly realized in 1997, but it would take the triumph of AWS Solidarity in the September 1997 elections to revive the 1992 arguments for more radical lustration.

## The SLD after 1993

Although leading figures in the SLD, including its leader Aleksander (later President) Kwaśniewski,[35] now favoured some form of lustration, their version was very limited. The SLD bill, setting out criteria for the vetting of senior government posts, was initially the only bill referred to committee.[36] Elements of this bill were later incorporated into the new Lustration Law, along with new proposals gaining support after the shock of the Oleksy Affair in 1995–6. The charge that Prime Minister Józef Oleksy was guilty of longstanding, treasonous collaboration with Soviet and Russian spies – and the realization that he had no way to challenge it – led his party's doubters to acknowledge the need for a formal lustration mechanism. Oleksy was forced from office, though no credible evidence emerged to support the allegations.

The Council of Europe also weighed in, with Resolution 1096 on Measures to dismantle the heritage of former communist totalitarian systems, including its Guidelines to ensure that lustration laws and similar measures comply with the requirements of the rule of law.[37] Among other things the guidelines envisaged that lustration

> be limited to positions in which there is good reason to believe that the subject would pose a significant danger to human rights or democracy, that is to say appointed state offices involving significant responsibility ... relating to internal security, or appointed state offices where human rights abuses may be ordered and/or perpetrated, such as law enforcement, security and intelligence services, the judiciary and the prosecutor's office.

Lustration should apply to elective offices only at the request of the candidate, since voters are entitled to elect whomever they wish. It should not apply to private or semi-private organizations. Where disqualification for office was envisaged, it should not exceed five years.

The first Lustration Law (April 1997) was developed by the *Sejm*'s extraordinary committee on lustration on the basis of five drafts, including one from the president (Kwaśniewski also announced the creation of a Commission of Public Confidence to enable those originally accused by Macierewicz to contest the allegations and to oversee a partial opening of the files).[38] The Committee met twelve times from November 1996 to March 1997,[39] with some alterations from the *Sejm* itself at third reading.[40] By now the Freedom Union (*Unia Wolności*, UW, the heir of the UD), the PSL and the SLD were converts to lustration. The UW's view was that because 'the spectre of lustration weighs heavily on political life', the *Sejm* needed to take control to 'ensure the maximum possible guarantees of the rights of those subject to screening processes', while also serving the interests of the state by ensuring that those occupying or standing for high positions are 'not burdened by suspicions of moral turpitude'.[41] This stance reflected the party's longstanding liberal emphasis on individual human rights.

The SLD also accepted the principle of lustration. However, it sought to exclude intelligence and counter-intelligence bodies, for fear of revelations about current operational matters. It may also have feared individual revelations, for although the security services had effectively been prohibited from recruiting party members, this was not true of intelligence/counter-intelligence. The SLD also sought a clearer, narrower view of collaboration. It proposed that collaboration be 'conscious collaboration involving action against the churches ..., the democratic opposition, independent trades union or action damaging the sovereign aspirations of the Polish nation or involving the transmission of such information as to threaten civil and personal rights'. SLD support for the proposed law was conditional upon this amendment[42] so when it was rejected, SLD deputies voted against the law. Amongst all other parties, including the SLD's coalition partner the PSL, support was virtually unanimous.[43]

The law of 11 April 1997 'on revealing employment or service in the security organs of the state or collaboration with the security services 1944-1990 by persons holding public office'[44] represented a type of 'soft' or 'lenient' lustration.[45] Nalepa calls it a 'confession-based truth revelation procedure' in contrast to an 'accusation-based' procedure,[46] but this is problematic, as we shall see: there are accusatory elements in the Polish system, and the lack of penalty applies only to candidates for office, not public functionaries.

Wojciech Sadurski estimated that some 22,000 persons were subject to lustration.[47] The bill defined 'collaboration with the security services' as 'conscious, secret cooperation' as an informer or person assisting in the gathering of information (Art. 4 ¶1). Its remit was quite wide, but narrower than the scope proposed in the 1992 lustration resolution and the KPN draft bill. Public offices subject to lustration included the president, deputies, senators and other persons appointed to senior state positions by the president, *Sejm*, the presidium of the *Sejm*, the Senate or the prime minister, as well as the Head of the Civil Service, directors general in government ministries, national and provincial agencies, and judges and the procurator. They also included members of supervisory bodies and bureaux, programme directors and directors of regional centres and agencies of Polish Television and Polish Radio, the director general of the Polish Press Agency, directors of bureaux, editors-in-chief and directors of regional divisions of the Polish Press Agency, the chair of the Polish Information Agency and its deputy chairs, executive members, and senior members.

The law required that all these office holders and candidates for office born before 20 May 1972 file an affidavit regarding their relationship to the security services. Those standing for election would have their affidavits checked only after being elected, those appointed on accepting the appointment. The affidavit was seen by many firm lustration advocates as a way of dealing with the destruction of files; people did not know whether or not their file had been destroyed so they would reveal their collaboration even where the archives could not confirm this.[48] The law also envisaged so-called auto-lustration: persons holding public office before the law came into effect and who had been publicly accused of working for the security services could submit an affidavit directly to the Lustration Court. This gave redress to those who had been falsely accused.

The Lustration Court would consist of twenty-one judges of appellate and provincial courts, appointed for a four-year term by the Ministry of Justice on the recommendation of the National Judicial Council. The Public Interest Defender and two deputies would also serve for four years; they would be persons of 'exceptional legal competence' possessing judicial qualifications and they would enjoy 'full and free' access to ministerial archives (Art. 17 § 4). If the Lustration Court found an affidavit to be untruthful, the 'lustration liar' would be deemed to lack the moral qualifications essential for public office and would be barred for a period of ten years.

The law passed in April but it had not been implemented by the parliamentary elections in September. It proved impossible to find candidates for the new Lustration Court. Some argued that this was because there was no increase in remuneration (judges needed to move to Warsaw), nor any scope for career progression for members of the Lustration Court. Others argued that judges balked at the political nature of the lustration process, requiring the interpretation of questionable evidence from doctored secret police files, without a clear presumption of innocence and without clear criteria of 'collaboration'. For elements of the Right, the refusal of judges to serve was an indicator of the continuing contamination of the judiciary by its association with the previous regime.[49]

The 1997 election saw a shift of power to the allied Solidarity parties (Solidarity Election Action, AWS) in coalition with the Freedom Union (UW). The SLD had gained votes since the last election, but the return of the right-wing parties, now united in AWS, gave the coalition a comfortable paper majority. However, the coalition did not gain the presidency: Aleksander Kwaśniewski was re-elected president on the first ballot of the presidential election in 2000.

## The government of Jerzy Buzek

The revised Lustration Law of June 1998[50] added lawyers to the list of those subject to lustration, as well as persons appointed to posts by the Speakers of the *Sejm* and Senate.

The Public Interest Defender (RPI) gained increased powers and a six-year term of office and – to assess the veracity of lustration affidavits – full access to the archives of the Bureau of State Protection (UOP), the ministry of the interior (MSW), the ministry of defence (MON), the foreign ministry (MSZ) and the Ministry of Justice (MS). To secure its complement of judges the Warsaw Appellate Court was now to serve as the Lustration Court.

In December 1998 the Lustration Division was created at the Appellate Court in Warsaw. The new Public Interest Defender Bogusław Nizieński began work in January 1999. Lustration was now a reality, but many questions remained unresolved. In judgments of October and November the Constitutional Tribunal by and large accepted the principles and practice of lustration[51] when it dealt with presidential and SLD challenges to the amended law. The Tribunal rejected their contention that the law required public officials to incriminate themselves; it argued that the law attached no penalties to the acknowledgement of collaboration but only to a false affidavit. However, the TK found the provision for the resumption of proceedings at any time in the light of new evidence unacceptable, violating individual liberty by creating 'a state of permanent uncertainty for a lustrated person' incompatible with the requirements of a democratic state (in 1999 parliament amended the law to restrict the renewal of lustration proceedings to ten years[52]).

Most significantly, the Court also agreed that the definition of a collaborator was imprecise. It specified that agreement to collaborate was not enough; action was also necessary, such as actually conveying information to the security services.[53] IPN investigators Sławomir Cenckiewicz and Piotr Gontarczyk would later claim that this definition eliminated from the lustration process the 'decided majority of those for whom there was evidence of collaboration'.[54]

In December 1998 the *Sejm* passed a new law on the Institute of National Remembrance (IPN).[55] This was the government's response to President Kwaśniewski's proposal to guarantee citizens' access to their own files through a Civic Archive.[56] Under the new law the IPN would take control of the ministerial archives (interior, justice, defence and the Bureau of State Protection). One section of the archive would remain secret, reserved for matters affecting state security; only the head of the IPN could grant access to the secret section. Access to the remaining collection was also limited. Only individuals 'harmed' or 'damaged' (*pokrzywdony*) by the security services could gain access to their files (a person not identified as 'harmed' had no means to challenge this judgment). Access could also be given to functionaries of the security services (Art. 35, ¶2) and to scholars for research purposes (Art. 36). Kwaśniewski vetoed the law on grounds that it was discriminatory, but the *Sejm* overrode his veto. It was not until 2005 that the Constitutional Tribunal dealt with various aspects of the right to access one's files (see below).

Extra-legal developments also affected the course of lustration. On 12 April 1999 the main governing party AWS-RS (Solidarity Election Action-Social Movement (*Akcja Wyborcza Solidarności–Ruch Społeczny*)) resolved that persons recommended by the party for public office must resign if the Public Interest Spokesman (RIP) requested the court to initiate lustration proceedings against them. Despite allegations to the contrary, the RIP found Prime Minister Buzek's affidavit to be truthful. However,

RIP Nizieński began proceedings against several other members of the government, leading immediately to the dismissal of Interior Minister Janusz Tomaszewski and Deputy Ministers Robert Mroziewicz and Krzysztof Luks (Tomaszewski was later vindicated, proceedings against Mroziewicz were suspended and Luks was deemed a lustration liar). Moreover, contrary to the spirit of the law, dismissals of self-confessed collaborators also occurred. Hanna Suchocka's justice ministry saw the dismissal of several procurators, while Deputy Minister of the Economy Janusz Kaczurba submitted his resignation after admitting that he had provided economic intelligence to the security services[57] (he later served as economic adviser to President Kwaśniewski).

All candidates in the 2000 presidential election submitted lustration affidavits. Under electoral law these were dealt with by the Appeal Court, not the RIP. Kwaśniewski's case was prolonged, as the Bureau of State Protection claimed publicly that he had been Agent Alek, a *Życie Warszawy* journalist collaborating with the security services. Kwaśniewski was vindicated, in part because he had never worked for *Życie Warszawy*. One candidate, Andrzej Olechowski, former minister of finance and foreign affairs, acknowledged that, like Kaczurba, he had cooperated with economic intelligence, but this did not seem to damage him. Kwaśniewski was re-elected on the first ballot with 53.9 per cent of the vote, but Olechowski, standing as an independent 'citizens' candidate, came second with 17.3 per cent of the vote, soundly defeating Krzaklewski, the Solidarity candidate. He later played an active role in the formation of Civic Platform (*Platforma Obywatelska*).

## Lustration under the SLD

With the institutions of lustration in place and the process under way, the SLD returned to office with a resounding victory in September 2001. Jerzy Buzek's defeat was dramatic: neither the AWS nor its erstwhile coalition partner the UW entered parliament. However, the political scene remained turbulent. New parties, Civic Platform (*Platforma Obywatelska*, PO), Law and Justice (*Prawo i Sprawiedliwość*, PiS), Self-Defence (*Samo-Obrona*, SO) and the League of Polish Families (*Liga Polskich Rodzin*, LPR) gained representation in the *Sejm*. Leszek Miller's SLD-PSL coalition lost its majority when the PSL withdrew from government in 2003, and after a short period of minority government, Miller submitted his resignation in May 2004. The SLD split and began its trajectory of decline. Marek Belka led a shaky caretaker coalition to the end of the parliamentary term in 2005.

After winning the 2000 election, President Kwaśniewski submitted a bill designed 'to correct certain deficiencies observed in the practical application' of the lustration law and to incorporate judgments of the Constitutional Tribunal and the Supreme Court, notably regarding the concept of 'collaboration'.[58] The bill narrowed the definition of collaboration to include only 'secret, conscious, and genuine cooperation with the security services'. As the SLD had long advocated, collaboration did not include providing information to the intelligence services, counter-intelligence or border authorities, and it excluded service in military or police units. The bill abolished the hated '*donos poselski*', whereby a member of parliament could request someone's lustration. It also tightened the process in regard to the Public Interest Defender and strengthened the rights of the accused. For example, the RPI would have three months in which to refer a case to the Lustration Court, while a judgment would not be released publicly, nor the accused deprived of office until the exhaustion of the appeal process. The Lustration Court could no longer suspend proceedings in the face of lack of evidence but must find in favour of the accused. The government supported the president's proposals, but they were vigorously contested by the opposition.

The opposition parties rejected the argument that information provided to intelligence and border services should not constitute 'collaboration'. They repeated the concerns expressed in 1992: these were an 'integral part of the security services … dealing with internal opposition as well as external threats …. and penetrated by the (Soviet) KGB'.[59] They did not serve Poland's national interests but those of the USSR. Moreover, the concept of collaboration had been clearly defined by the Constitutional Tribunal and the Supreme Court, such that further changes would merely muddy the waters.

The Peasant Party (PSL), though still a member of the governing coalition, also rejected the new proposals, notably the exclusion of the intelligence services. The head of the presidential chancellery noted that objections were misguided: informing the intelligence services about (for example) the activities of Radio Free Europe or the Church would fall within the lustration remit because these were not statutory intelligence functions. The courts would determine whether intelligence activities were conducted in the interests of the state.

To try to clarify this issue, the concept of collaboration was amended further at the committee stage. The SLD proposal excluded activity that did not 'harm churches and other religious bodies, the democratic opposition, independent trades unions, the sovereign aspirations of the Polish Nation' and did not threaten 'the rights and freedoms of the individual or the personal goods of other persons'.[60] The *Sejm* rejected this newly defined, awkward version of collaboration when the PSL voted against it with all the opposition parties. The most important argument was that – as Jan Olszewski noted – it would be almost impossible to prove that the 'activity of informers actually caused harm to a particular organisation and that it was their conscious intention to do this'.[61] However, the SLD-dominated Senate restored the new definition of collaboration, and the *Sejm* failed to muster the necessary absolute majority to reverse it. The revised law came into force on 8 March 2002.[62]

Three months later the Constitutional Tribunal found that the Senate had exceeded its rights to amend legislation: the Senate could amend and correct legislation but it was not entitled to give the law an 'entirely different content'. It also found against a new provision enabling proceedings to be halted if the lustrated person resigned from his or her post before a court began to hear evidence. The Court noted that 'the lustration law clearly has a "public-private character" concerned with making public information about specific persons not only because they had worked in or served or collaborated with the security services but because they aspired to public office.' This provision violated the constitutional principle of equality: having seen the evidence the lustrated person received an opportunity to calculate the chances of success, while other persons, such as candidates for election, did not.[63]

The Tribunal's decision thus nullified a crucial change in the concept of collaboration. However, the Senate responded with a new proposal: 'collaboration does not include collecting or transmitting information falling within the mandate of the intelligence services, counter-intelligence, and the security of state borders', nor is it 'simulated (*pozorne*) cooperation or a refusal to provide information despite the formal fulfilment of actions or procedures required by the security services'.[64] It excluded the requirement that collaboration must have harmed the opposition or the Church. It also prevented new rules being applied to current proceedings – so those against Oleksy, Marek Wagner and Jerzy Jaskiernia were suspended because they stood accused of cooperating with the intelligence services.

In the *Sejm* the SLD successfully proposed another amendment, enabling lustrated persons to replace, within fourteen days, an affidavit given earlier under the previous definition of collaboration. This meant that those who had cooperated with the intelligence services, for example, could now declare themselves non-collaborators. Passed with the support of deputies from Self-Defence (SO), the amended lustration law came into force in November 2002.[65] On 13 November 2002 Jaskiernia was cleared by the Appeal Court. That same year in August the establishment of new administrative courts led to the addition of 'a person who is not a judge applying to be an administrative judge' to the list of persons carrying out 'public functions' in the Lustration Law.[66] The introduction of lustration for candidates to the European Parliament, scheduled for 2004, was largely uncontroversial with cross-party support.[67]

In response to a request from the Human Rights Ombudsman the Constitutional Tribunal (TK) returned to lustration with its judgment of March 2003.[68] In this case the Court dealt with the issue of employment in the security services. The Ombudsman maintained that the law infringed the constitutional rights to privacy and dignity of those working in roles unrelated to repression. The TK agreed in part. It noted that although the 'openness of public life in a democratic state' was ensured by the publication of the very fact that someone worked or served in the security services (Annex A of the lustration form), this information was insufficient to clarify the situation of particular individuals. This issue could be resolved, however, by publishing Annex B, specifying the individual's function and the duration of employment. In this way individuals not involved in the processes of repression could clarify the role they had played while working for the security services.

In May at the request of a group of opposition deputies the TK again returned to the question of collaboration.[69] The Court agreed with the petitioners that the exclusion of the intelligence services violated the constitutional principles of the democratic law-based state, equality before the law and the right of citizens to gain information about the activities of organs of the state and persons occupying public office. It found that lack of clarity in the notion of 'intelligence functions' made it impossible for either the person lustrated or the court to assess the nature of this cooperation.

This judgment and the minority position of the SLD after its split in April 2004 gave new hope to the right-wing opposition parties aiming to extend the scope of lustration. A united opposition succeeded in inserting into the law on higher education of 2005[70] a long list of positions in higher education and university administration, which were now defined as 'public functions'. Through opposition incompetence or oversight, however, the occupants of these posts were not added to the list of those required to submit lustration affidavits, so the designation was meaningless. Nonetheless, the opposition was serving notice that lustration was not yet a closed chapter.

## Wild lustration

In the run-up to the September 2005 elections leaks or 'wild lustration' became frequent, as people with access to files released information on alleged collaborators. In January the issue had gained momentum with the internet publication of 'Wildstein's List',[71] some 163,000 names culled by the IPN from its communist-era files and illicitly copied by journalist Bronisław Wildstein, an advocate of 'deep lustration'.[72] Although Wildstein never claimed that this was a list of 'agents', it was widely treated as such. Nizieński, the chief investigator of lustration cases, also made clear his view that hundreds of guilty lustration liars remained in post for lack of evidence.[73] Wildstein's list stoked lustration fervour, with further fallout from successive file revelations, including alleged collaboration and betrayal by some prominent Solidarity dissidents,[74] and by a deluge of applications to the IPN for file access.

As a result of the storm surrounding wild lustration, Civic Platform and Law and Justice proposed minor changes in the law on the IPN to enable redress for those falsely accused. All parties supported these changes, as did the chair of the IPN and the inspector for Data Protection. The law[75] required the chair of the IPN to issue a declaration within fourteen days affirming whether the personal data of the petitioner matched those found in the catalogue of functionaries, collaborators with the security services or candidates for collaboration.

Political turmoil did not abate. The government's position was precarious and early elections seemed a distinct possibility. In June 2005 the themes of corruption and decommunization meshed. In the *Sejm* members of the committee investigating corruption in the oil giant, Orlen gained access to the IPN files of some thirty individuals, including the president, the prime minister and former Prime Minister Buzek, on the grounds that Orlen had 'deep roots in the (old) security services'.[76] Press leaks revived discredited charges of collaboration against the previously vindicated Kwaśniewski and implied that Prime Minister Belka's file also contained compromising material.[77]

# Conclusion

From 1997 to the end of the SLD's tenure, the principles and methods of lustration remained largely unchanged, though the concept of collaboration was tightened in accordance with the judgments of the Constitutional Tribunal. Throughout the first phase of lustration emphasis was on truth-telling in the form of an affidavit. Persons falling under lustration law gradually gained greater protection, including limits on the reopening of proceedings and delay of its negative consequences until final appeals had been exhausted. However, with the decline of the SLD its influence on the course of lustration effectively ceased. As we shall see, the radical lustrators aimed for ever-wider lustration.

# Lustration after the fall of the SLD:
# The return of the Right

After 2001 the political scene changed profoundly with the steady decline of the SLD and the growth of two right-wing post-Solidarity parties, Law and Justice (*Prawo i Sprawiedliwość*, PiS) and Civic Platform (*Platforma Obywatelska*, PO). In 2005 Law and Justice took centre stage, when Lech Kaczyński, twin brother of Jarosław, won the presidency and PiS became the largest party in elections to the *Sejm*. From 2005 to the early elections of 2007 PiS governed first as a minority government, then in a series of fractured, re-forming coalitions with Self-Defence (*Samo-Obrona*, SO) or the League of Polish Families (*Liga Polskich Rodzin*, LPR) or both. As part of a wider decommunization programme PiS launched radical lustration initiatives, including a restructuring of the IPN. Much of this legislation failed at the Constitutional Tribunal. At the same time the Catholic Church became embroiled in a series of wild lustration scandals as clergy 'harmed' (*pokrzywdzony*) by the communist regime gained access to their own files and made public the names of those who had allegedly informed on them.

Civic Platform (PO) governed for eight years after winning in 2007 and 2011, with the Peasant Party (PSL) as its junior coalition partner. Under Civic Platform rulings by the Constitutional Tribunal led to wide public access to the files of the security services. No longer was access restricted to those 'damaged' or 'harmed'. New legislation established opportunities for all individuals to obtain copies of their own files from the IPN. The revised law on the IPN was the main focus of Civic Platform's initiatives. Lustration was shaped more by the courts than the legislature.

In 2015 PiS achieved a stunning electoral success,[1] winning enough seats to govern as a single-party majority government. This enabled Jarosław Kaczyński to return to his wider decommunization strategy, with profound structural changes proposed for the judiciary, including the Constitutional Tribunal. PiS claimed – with justification – that at the end of its parliamentary tenure Civic Platform had attempted to pack the Constitutional Tribunal with its own nominees. This led PiS to a full-scale onslaught on the TK, unhampered by the opposition, the European Union or the Council of Europe's Venice Commission. By the end of 2016 PiS controlled the Constitutional Tribunal, both indirectly through its nominees and directly through executive vetting of Tribunal decisions (see Chapter 10). The 2019 elections strengthened PiS's position in the *Sejm*, though it no longer controlled the Senate.

In the 2005 election campaign lustration was part of Jarosław Kaczyński's proposal for a 'Fourth Republic' to replace the corrupt degeneration of the Third and expunge the disastrous legacy of the Round Table. For Kaczyński the new Fourth Republic would entail moral cleansing through 'deep lustration', anti-corruption measures and reaffirmation of Catholic values. Only those with 'clean hands' and a 'clean past' could serve the state – hence the need to buttress lustration with new institutions such as a Truth and Justice Commission and an Anti-Corruption Bureau and a greater role for the Institute of National Memory (IPN). Besides the Truth Commission (which was never established) PiS favoured opening the files of all public officials and the publication of the names of all 'functionaries and collaborators', as well as 'property lustration' of politicians and their families. The files were now centre stage. Civic Platform also favoured opening the files and making them publicly available.

## PiS in power 2005

At the beginning of the new parliament the Constitutional Tribunal (TK) pronounced on the question of access to the files. In its judgment of October 2005 on the statute of the IPN,[2] the TK condemned the restriction of access to those 'harmed' (*pokrzywdzony*) as unconstitutional. The law breached Article 51 of the Constitution, providing that all persons must have the right of access to documents concerning them, as well as the right to 'demand the correction or deletion of untrue or incomplete information, or information acquired by means contrary to statute'. It also breached the right to legal protection of an individual's 'private and family life, honour and good reputation' (Art. 47). The implications of this decision were profound: effectively, it granted all individuals access to their files in the IPN archives.

The *Sejm* moved quickly, with draft bills from Law and Justice (PiS), Self-Defence (SO), the League of Polish Families (LPR) and Civic Platform (PO). PiS's approach was radical; it represented a basic change in the institutions and processes of lustration, abolishing lustration affidavits and removing the Public Interest Representative.[3] The new lustration law passed in October 2006[4] was based largely on PiS's draft, but it received support from all parties except the SLD. This new mode of lustration did not survive, but it provided PiS with an important lesson in the powers of the Constitutional Tribunal. In this regard it also provided the prelude to PiS's all-out attack on the TK following its return to office in 2015.

The law of 2006 gave all persons the right to apply for an 'official confirmation' (*urzędowe potwierdzenie*) stating whether or not the IPN archives held files pertaining to them. Anyone holding or seeking public office was required to apply for this certificate. The law also provided a vastly extended list of those deemed to be public functionaries, beginning with the president and ending with a 'member of a managerial organ, supervisory body or internal control organ of a Polish sporting association'. It extended lustration to the private sector, including journalists, directors of private schools and lecturers at private universities. The press estimated that the new law would affect some 100,000 persons.[5]

Other key provisions centred on the IPN's role in issuing 'declarations' specifying the details of an individual's relations with the security services. If there were evidence of links to the security services, the declaration would specify the nature of the links indicated in the IPN archive – for example, whether the individual had been regarded as a 'personal source of information' (*osobowe źródło informacji*, OZI), a secret collaborator (*tajny współpracownik*, TW) or an operational contact (*kontakt operacyjny*, KO). It would note the types of documents and the registration records available and the duration of employment or service in the security organs. The declaration would be taken into account 'in evaluating the moral qualifications, especially the blameless character, unblemished, impeccable reputation, and adherence to basic moral principles, that are required of a public official'. This 'evaluation' could form the basis for severing an employment contract, dismissal or disciplinary procedures.

The Register of Declarations would be accessible to the public and available in electronic form. It could not be amended, but a person could append supplementary materials, corrections and explanations to his/her record. A declaration could be challenged by civil action as to the quality of the documentation and its status as a true record. Although the court's decision would be appended to a newly issued declaration and to the register, civil action did not prevent publication and need have no influence on any sanctions imposed.[6]

This law was palpably flawed. It was based on the premise that the files of the security services were accurate. It bypassed the Constitutional Court's definition of collaboration as 'conscious' and 'genuine'. Declarations alleging collaboration would be published before any opportunity to challenge them. Criticism of the law was widespread, including by the president himself, though he did not veto it. Instead, defying convention, President Kaczyński signed the law but submitted his own amendments – in fact a rather different law – almost as soon as the ink was dry. The 2006 version never came into force.

The president argued that the 2006 law made impossible demands on the IPN. Moreover, the catalogue of positions requiring lustration needed further development. Most importantly, however, the existing law gave credence to communist files: it was not right that these unverified files 'could influence the lives and professional careers of many people'. But it was also not right that 'a person who confessed to collaboration with the security services may occupy the most important functions in the state'.[7]

Based on the president's variant, lustration affidavits returned in the law of 2007.[8] They would now be checked by a new Lustration Bureau within the IPN. The list of persons subject to lustration was still wide, embracing forty-three categories of employment. Many were positions in which the occupants' past seemed of little relevance, such as members of the Post Office Council, or jobs like the directors of private schools that were not part of the machinery of the state. The presidential chancellery estimated that 350,000–400,000 people would now be lustrated under the new law.[9] The Lustration Bureau was also charged with preparing catalogues of collaborators based on types of collaboration.

As in previous laws the truth of the affidavit regarding employment or cooperation with the security services was central. The sanction for failing to submit an affidavit on time was loss of the post in question. Those found to have submitted a false declaration would lose their jobs, face a ten-year ban from office and lose the right to stand for election, also for ten years (as before, this exceeded the Council of Europe's suggested maximum of five years). The submission of a false declaration was now a criminal offence, subject to the Code of Criminal Procedure. Lustration liars were also subject to a term of imprisonment from three months to five years.

The 2007 law gave all persons the right of access to copies of documents concerning them, save documents which they had written themselves or which were created as part of their collaboration with the security services or documents whose content indicated that the individual had been viewed as a 'personal source of information' (OZI) by the security services. The law also further limited the rights of former functionaries of the security services. They were not permitted to request closed sessions in proceedings where sensitive information concerning ethnicity, religious convictions, health status or sexual activity might be revealed. They did not have the right to appeal. For them filing a false affidavit was punishable by a longer prison term, six months to eight years.

President Kaczyński's efforts to modify it could not save the law, which was rapidly emasculated by the Constitutional Court. In its complex judgment of 11 May 2007,[10] with nine out of eleven judges submitting separate opinions, the Constitutional Tribunal found parts of the Preamble and the whole or parts of some fifteen articles of the 2007 law incompatible with the Constitution. It dealt with those provisions of the 2006 law retained in 2007 and the appendices, which offered a template for lustration affidavits and a categorization of types of collaboration.[11]

# The judgment of May 2007

The Constitutional Tribunal restated its view that lustration – understood as ' … a mechanism for investigating the links and dependencies of persons occupying the highest offices of state or applying for them or occupying other public positions with a high degree of responsibility and requiring the confidence of society' – was in principle compatible with the Constitution. However, the means used to dismantle 'the legacy of the totalitarian communist regime' must maintain the formal-legal requirements of the democratic law-based state and must be 'directed against dangers threatening basic human rights or the process of democratization'. Lustration cannot 'satisfy the desire for revenge … It must respect such basic freedoms as the right to due process, the right to a fair hearing or the right to defence, and it must apply these to persons who would not respect them were they in power'. Although the law may not enact retrospective penalties, it could punish persons 'for actions which did not constitute crimes when committed but were regarded as offences when judged by the principles acknowledged by civilized countries' (an unusual departure from the principle of 'no crime without law'). The TK laid down the requisites of an acceptable lustration law (see below). In general, its arguments rested on principles of proportionality, social justice, the right to a fair hearing and the need for legislative clarity and precision.

The TK took issue with the scope, procedures and sanctions of the law. It assessed seventy-seven elements of the new law and set aside thirty-nine as unconstitutional. It argued that the catalogue of persons carrying out public functions 'could not include functions and jobs that had no connection with the state authorities nor with state-owned elements of the economy nor the State Treasury'. The TK accepted the lustration of lawyers (*radcy prawni*), bailiffs, notaries; persons at the head of public radio, television and information agencies; and those directing the State Treasury and local government, as well as persons representing state authorities on enterprise boards. It rejected the lustration of chancellors, vice-chancellors and others occupying managerial positions in private institutions of higher education, as well as university academics, directors of private schools, members of executive or advisory boards, persons publishing or distributing radio and television programmes, journalists, tax advisers, those persons in posts subject to the Audit Commission and those in charge of sporting unions or businesses managing professional sport.

The TK also challenged the list of 'organs of the security services' as too encompassing and too imprecise. The 'arbitrariness' of the legislator was demonstrated by the inclusion of the Censor and the Bureau of Religious Affairs, which did not conduct operational activities. Moreover, the Court noted that the provision on collaboration repeated the phrasing of the 1997 law rather than incorporating previous judgments of the TK itself: thus, it was constitutional only insofar as its interpretation required collaboration to be 'conscious and genuine'.[12] The Court found unconstitutional references in the preamble and Appendix 2 to the concept of a 'personal source of information' (OZI) as a category of collaboration. It also rejected the model lustration affidavit as unreasonable, for it explicitly required 'understanding the law of 18 October 2006 as amended' (and with no unified version available, this was a difficult task).

The Court agreed that former functionaries of the security organs suffered unconstitutional discrimination because they were denied the possibility of closed sessions to safeguard personal information and because they enjoyed limited rights of appeal. Moreover, the publication of a publicly accessible register of lustration declarations exceeded the permissible limits of data gathering on citizens. The penalty of permanent disbarment from a post for not filing an affidavit was disproportional and inflexible, hence unconstitutional, while the penalties for candidates for election represented 'excessive interference' in electoral rights.

Although the Tribunal's judgment interrupted the creation of a catalogue of collaborators, the catalogue of functionaries and employees of the security services was not affected. Yet, as Krotoszyński notes, this too must be seen as a form of lustration.[13] Finally, the TK criticized the lack of mechanisms enabling individuals to challenge the list or to expunge incorrect data as provided in the Constitution.

This savaging of the law was widely criticized by Law and Justice and its sympathizers, including the-then Ombudsman Janusz Kochanowski, who deemed it politically biased, inconsistent, incoherent and internally contradictory.[14] The judgment presaged PiS's full-blown attack on the TK after its return to power in 2015.

The May judgment had serious effects. Some unconstitutional provisions were immediately deleted from the law. Certain procedures which were 'in process' at the time of the judgment were suspended or halted. Some provisions were left intact, subject to the proviso that they be interpreted only as specified in the judgment. Other instances of unconstitutionality created unacceptable lacunae in the law which needed to be amended by the legislature. Piotr Radkiewicz argued that by defining the requirements that a lustration law must satisfy, the TK rendered the legislature merely an implementing organ for its judgment. Alternatively, parliament could rethink the lustration process in its entirety.[15]

Parliament did not 'rethink'; it continued to tinker. In May 2007 it extended lustration to the director of the National Centre for Research and Development (*Narodowego Centrum Badań i Rozwoju*)[16] and then to generals and admirals and certain other posts in the military.[17] In June parliament amended the law on the IPN to take account of the TK's judgment that academics and journalists must meet specifically defined criteria for access to the IPN's archives.[18] In September a short amending law[19] offered a revised template for the lustration affidavit. It also provided for the return to their authors of affidavits submitted by those now excluded from lustration by the TK's judgment, which had considerably reduced the posts for which lustration was necessary. It also introduced flexibility in sanctions for the submission of a false affidavit, namely deprivation of the right to hold public office or to stand for election, now to be a period of three to ten years. However, amendments introduced by the Senate – providing for the deprivation of the right to hold non-elected office for those not submitting an affidavit – did not accord with the TK's judgment: The Court had argued that the 'automatic penalty for not submitting an affidavit without regard to the causes' was unconstitutional.

## Lustration and the Roman Catholic Church

Although the Church was excluded from lustration laws, by 2006 the issue of clerical collaboration was fermenting. The revelation in 2002 that the priest Stanisław Skorodecki, a close associate of Cardinal Wyszyński, had informed on Wyszyński during their imprisonment in 1953 was the first major instance of alleged clerical collaboration at the highest levels. However, at the time there was little public reaction, while the Church hierarchy itself pursued a strategy of 'don't know and don't want to know'.[20] Just after Pope John Paul II's death IPN Chair Leon Kieres announced publicly that the Priest Konrad Hejmo, the 'guardian' of Polish pilgrims in Rome, had collaborated with the security services in the 1970s and 1980s. Hejmo denied the allegations, and he had many defenders, including the historian Peter Raina.[21] The list of allegations grew longer – the Pope's friend Mieczysław Maliński, the theologian Professor Michał Czajkowski, the Zakopane Priest Mirosław Drozdek and others.

The Episcopate made its first statement in March 2006. It deplored the climate of sensationalism and over-generalization, but it acknowledged that some in the Church had 'betrayed its trust'. In August the bishops accepted the declaration of the Episcopate 'on the collaboration of some churchmen ... between 1944 and 1989'.[22] Although 'conscious and voluntary cooperation with the enemies of the Church and religion is a sin ... , the "cleansing of memory" should proceed through penance and atonement', leading to forgiveness and unity, and not only to condemnation and conflict. The Church set up its own Historical Commission, with subsequent similar investigative committees in most dioceses.

Many allegations came from the Priest Tadeusz Isakowicz-Zaleski, who had gained access to his file as a person 'harmed' by the communist authorities and who subsequently continued his research at the IPN. Zaleski continued to protest against the Church's 'protection of its communist agents'. The well-known former Priest of Lech

Wałęsa, Henryk Jankowski, also revealed the names of nine clerical informants from his own file, including the Bishop of Wrocław, Wiesław Mering.[23] The list of alleged collaborators was extended to include Archbishop (later Primate) Józef Kowalczyk,[24] Archbishop Józef Życiński[25] and many others.

The year 2007 began with a major scandal as the media accused Archbishop Stanislaw Wielgus, newly appointed to run the Warsaw diocese, of collaboration; his file was published on the internet. Requested by Wielgus to examine his case, the Historical Commission found 'considerable evidence' of collaboration.[26] The archbishop resigned on the day of his inauguration. Clearly Wielgus had cooperated with the security services, but whether he had provided useful information – the test of 'collaboration' after the Supreme Court judgment of 2000[27] – was moot.

The Church's Commission worked for a year. Unconvinced that it would reveal the truth, Isakowicz-Zaleski continued his investigation at the IPN. He published *Priests and the Security Services in the Archdiocese of Krakow*,[28] naming thirty-nine priests, including three bishops, who had collaborated with the secret police between 1944 and 1989. However, when the Historical Commission reported, the bishops declared the matter of lustration in the Church 'closed': it concluded that a dozen or so bishops had been registered as secret collaborators, but it named no names. It maintained that the incomplete and chaotic nature of the files rendered it impossible to judge how far collaboration was 'conscious' or whether it had caused a degree of harm.[29] There were no grounds for claiming that members of the Episcopate had consciously and voluntarily collaborated with the security services of the Polish People's Republic. There would be no further comment on instances of alleged collaboration. However, some in the Church, including Isakowicz-Zaleski, continued to criticize the absence of 'genuine lustration', and revelations of alleged collaboration continued.[30]

## Lustration under Civic Platform

In 2007 following early elections Civic Platform (PO) emerged as the largest party in parliament. It formed a coalition with the Peasant Party (PSL) under PO's leader Donald Tusk. Although Civic Platform was pro-lustration in principle, it was rather uninterested in practice (it had voted for the controversial PiS law). PO's main response to lustration followed a series of controversies surrounding the IPN, not least the reappearance of claims concerning Lech Wałęsa in the 2008 publication, *The Security Service and Lech Wałęsa*.[31] It repeated the claims that Wałęsa had served as an informer in the 1970s and that as president (1991–5) he had received, amended and removed or destroyed incriminating evidence against him. The book was as much a political weapon as a historical document. The young historians were accused of placing too much weight on the files themselves. This fed into wider issues of 'the politics of history' (see below). The saga did not end there. The division between the supporters and opponents of Wałęsa persisted, with periodic accusations of Wałęsa's 'collaboration' and new evidence from the IPN. Jarosław Kaczyński and PiS were firmly in the anti-Wałęsa camp.

The Lustration Law persisted in truncated version after the important judgment of the TK in May 2007. The main structural change was the weakening of the power of the chair of the IPN. It provided a new mechanism for appointment (and removal) and ensured properly qualified members of the new Council (*Rada*) of the IPN. PO hoped that a 'new professionalism' would counter objections of excessive partisanship and a 'tendency for a questionable vision of interpretations of the past'.[32]

Minor legislative alterations followed the Smolensk air disaster. In April 2010 the plane carrying President Kaczyński to ceremonies marking the 70th anniversary of the Katyń massacre of thousands of Polish prisoners of war by the Soviet NKVD crashed on the approach to Smolensk, killing all ninety-six persons aboard. National mourning was punctuated by political controversies questioning the burial of the presidential couple in Wawel Cathedral in Krakow and the siting of a cross in front of the presidential palace. PiS accused the government of dishonouring the memory of Lech Kaczyński.[33] Numerous conspiracy theories purported to explain the air crash itself as a political assassination, probably the result of sabotage, probably by the Russians, with (at the least) an organized cover-up by Donald Tusk's government. In the immediate aftermath this was not enough to deny PO the presidency, when Bronisław Komorowski defeated Jarosław Kaczyński on the second ballot in June. Nor did it prevent Civic Platform from winning the 2011 parliamentary election.

We should note here that for Jarosław Kaczyński the disaster at Smolensk meant not only the loss of his twin but many other close friends and associates, including core members of his party in parliament and allies such as Janusz Kurtyka, head of the IPN and the Human Rights Ombudsman Janusz Kochanowski. There is no doubt that Jarosław was deeply scarred by the death of his brother. Smolensk remained a running sore. Kaczynski's battle for the 'truth' about Smolensk and the glorification of his brother's legacy remained key elements of Law and Justice's programme. After a short hiatus, when he appeared more conciliatory,[34] Jarosław fully embraced the notion of his brother's martyrdom at the hands of Poland's enemies.

Civic Platform's amendments to the law on the IPN introduced provisions providing for a temporary head in the event of the death of the incumbent; it also amended the rules regarding the appointment of deputies.[35] Łukasz Kamiński, director of the IPN's Bureau of Public Education, replaced Kurtyka in accordance with the new procedures. The new Council existed for five years, when PiS once again 'reformed' the IPN.

Kamiński was certainly less controversial than his predecessor, at least until the end of his tenure. He aroused criticism in 2016 when the IPN published two tranches of papers from the home of General Kiszczak, including Lech Wałęsa's alleged Bolek file and letters from prominent individuals, published without removing their personal details.[36] Kamiński argued that these were not private letters but extracts taken from an unpublished work prepared with the cooperation of Kiszczak; moreover, they were documents directed to the Ministry of the Interior and as such belonged in the IPN archive. If he aimed to curry favour with PiS, his efforts failed; Kamiński was not reappointed by the new PiS government.

## The lustration process

When he became head of the IPN, Kamiński noted certain 'obstacles to the organizational efficiency of the IPN'. Given the slow rate at which lustration affidavits were being checked, he suggested that procurators should be given independent access to the archives, rather than the archive department serving as intermediary.[37] The IPN should also permit interested parties to conduct their own search for relevant documents, rather than relying on IPN employees.

By now the lustration process was more or less routine. Table 7.1 shows the work of the Lustration Department of the IPN after 2009. Column 1 shows the number of new affidavits received. In 2010 the IPN received 152,712 new lustration affidavits.[38] In 2011 it registered 141,151 new affidavits, as well as 37,397 declarations from persons who had filed previous affidavits.[39] Numbers are far higher in election years, especially the local elections held every four years – the 2014 and 2015 figures include local, national and European parliamentary elections. Numbers rose in election years but fell over time, as increasing numbers of candidates had previously submitted affidavits and more candidates were exempt, having been born after 1972.

In 2009 the IPN provided former Self-Defence Deputy Zbigniew Nowak with a list of 1,706 persons who had acknowledged working for or cooperation with the security services. By the end of 2013 this number had risen to 2,785. Although reporters found it increasingly difficult to obtain detailed information from the IPN,[40] the IPN's annual reports provided general data. Table 7.1 shows that only a small proportion of affidavits were referred to the regional courts for assessment of their truth. The column 'final court judgments' refers to cases completed – that is, after all appeals had been exhausted, so the figures here are not necessarily related to the annual referrals in the previous column. However, we can conclude from Table 7.1 that the IPN did not unearth many 'lustration liars'.

**Table 7.1** Lustration affidavits 2001–18

| Year | New affidavits received | Affidavits verified | Referred to court | Final court judgments of lustration lying[b] |
|------|------|------|------|------|
| 2009 | *c.* 6,500 | 5,300 | 79 | 13 |
| 2010 | 152,712 | 5,000+ | 68 | 27 |
| 2011 | 141,151 | 7,548 | 87 | 38 |
| 2012 | 8,651 | 7,715 | 136 | 68 |
| 2013 | 2,915 | 10,000 | 211 | 135 |
| 2014 | 68,535 | 9,758 | 175 | 157 |
| 2015 | 70,000+ | 9.460 | 133 | 124 |
| 2016 | 3,618 | na[a] | 144 | 127 |
| 2017 | 34,984 | 11,747 | 151 | 140 |
| 2018 | 41,507 | 12,090 | 229 | 176 |

[a]Not available.
[b]These are cases where all avenues of appeal have been exhausted and the court's decision has legal force.
Source: IPN, 'Informacja o działalności Instytutu Pamięci Narodowej – Komisji Ścigania Zbrodni przeciwko Narodowi Polskiemu', Annual reports to the *Sejm*.

As of the end of December 2018 the Lustration Bureau had accumulated 420,127 lustration affidavits and 23,824 declarations that an affidavit had previously been filed. Of the total on file at the Lustration Bureau, 3,297 affidavits acknowledged employment, service or cooperation with the communist security organs.[41] If we add this number to the 1,005 guilty lustration liars over ten years, we have 4,302 former collaborators seeking public office in this period. Bogusław Nizieński, Public Interest Spokesman (1999–2004), believed that many escaped justice during his tenure, either because of insufficient evidence or because judges were too willing to accept the testimony of secret service functionaries.[42]

Notwithstanding, the enormous cost and effort expended on identifying individuals who had cooperated with the security services hardly seemed commensurate with the outcome.

## The costs of lustration

Moreover, the IPN did huge damage to many individuals. It publicized the names of persons whom it was 'investigating', suggesting their guilt even before initiating proceedings. Accusations of 'lustration lying' were common, and it could take years for an individual to gain vindication. Allegations were sufficient to cause resignation, as we saw in the case of Interior Minister Janusz Tomaszewski; his case was further prolonged because the Public Interest Commissioner appealed against the Court's finding that Tomaszewski's affidavit was truthful. Former Speaker of the Sejm Wiesław Chrzanowski, whose name appeared on the notorious Macierewicz special list of 1992, was vindicated by the Court only in 2000. The case of former Prime Minister Oleksy also began in 1999 and ended only when it was discontinued in 2007. It took sixteen years before diplomat Maciej Kozłowski was finally cleared of allegations of collaboration. Leszek Moczulski, erstwhile leader of the Confederation for Independent Poland (KPN), battled to prove his innocence until 2018, when he withdrew his request for auto-lustration, claiming that he no longer had the strength to continue. The right-wing newspaper *Rzeczpospolita* called this 'the final defeat of lustration'.[43]

In mid-2005 Andrzej Przewoźnik was a serious candidate for chair of the IPN. When *Rzeczpospolita* claimed that Przewoźnik had been an informer, his chances vanished. The decision of the Lustration Court clearing his name came too late. The (false) allegations against *Sejm* deputy Professor Marian Filar (SLD) and Senator Zbigniew Pawlowicz (PO)[44] were loudly trumpeted by the IPN.

Another prominent case was that of renowned communist-era journalist Irena Dziedzic, who had appealed after being branded a 'lustration liar' in 2010. In 2011 the Appellate Court ordered a retrial, when the original Warsaw Court found her affidavit to be truthful. The Appellate Court refused to allow the IPN to appeal in 2013. Some cases just did not go away. That of Lech Wałęsa, former Solidarity leader, Nobel-Prize winner and ex-president resurfaced with alarming regularity.

Justices of the Constitutional Tribunal were not immune. In 2007 a PIS deputy claimed that two justices had cooperated with the intelligence agencies. Marian Grzybowski and Adam Jamróz were removed by the Court's chair from lustration proceedings. No proceedings were initiated against Jamróz, but Grzybowski was charged as a lustration liar; he was finally vindicated in 2013. In 2010 the Appellate Court rejected the IPN's appeal against the lower court's finding that TK Justice Mirosław Wyrzykowski was not a lustration liar.

## The files

The most important legislative change was the amendment of the law on the Institute of National Memory in March 2010.[45] It aimed to 'depoliticize' the IPN and to increase its collegiality[46] (the SLD proposed to end lustration altogether). The law provided full access to the archive; all citizens would be able to see documents affecting them, and they could exclude access by others for a period of fifty years. Those responsible for creating documents could also gain access to them (including reports by functionaries and notes written by 'informers'). Former employees of the security services also gained the right to withhold sensitive personal and financial data. These provisions accommodated some TK criticisms made in its May 2007 judgment, as well as judgments against Poland in the European Court of Human Rights.

In 2007 the Court had ruled in the case of Matyjek v Poland. After exhausting the appeal process against the verdict of lustration-lying in February 2000, Tadeusz Matyjek lost his mandate as a member of parliament and took his case to the ECHR, where he challenged 'the very essence of the lustration proceedings, in particular their allegedly unequal and secret nature, the confidentiality of documents, and the unfair procedures governing access to the case file and the conduct of hearings'.[47] Matyjek won his case, chiefly because his restricted access to the archives hampered his defence (this limit was by now altered by the new law on the IPN). Matyjek's case returned for retrial in November 2012, when he was again found guilty of submitting a false lustration affidavit. On 8 October 2014 the Supreme Court revoked the judgment and sent the case back for retrial. Among its reasons were the court's 'faulty appraisal of the evidence' and failure to make an independent assessment of the facts, which 'had been copied from another judgment'.[48]

The ECHR applied similar logic to the cases of Luboch in 2008,[49] Rasmussen[50] and Jałowiecki in 2009,[51] and Moczulski in 2011.[52] Zbigniew Luboch, a lawyer, had been deemed a lustration liar and lost the right to practise as an advocate. The Court found that Luboch, like Matyjek, had suffered from restricted access to documents, exacerbated by the fact that some relevant documents had been classified as 'top secret'. He could remove neither courtroom notes taken during the hearings nor the notes he took from documents held in the court's secret registry. Moreover, the government did not produce copies of the written reasons in the proceedings before the Court, invoking their classified character. The Court found a breach of Article 6 of the European Convention on Human Rights, specifying the conditions for a fair trial. The Court considered that

> due to the confidentiality of the documents and the limitations on access to the case
> file by the lustrated person, as well as the privileged position of the Commissioner

of the Public Interest in the lustration proceedings, the applicant's ability to prove that the contacts he had had with the communist-era secret services did not amount to "intentional and secret collaboration" within the meaning of the Lustration Act were severely curtailed.

Leszek Moczulski, long-time underground activist and founder of the Confederation for Independent Poland (KPN), was the first person to apply under the new provisions for 'auto-lustration' in March 1999 (see above); this was his opportunity to defend himself against charges of collaboration dating back to 1992, when his name appeared on Macierewicz's list. In November 2001 a panel of three judges determined that Moczulski's lustration declaration had been truthful. However, the Public Interest Commissioner (RIP) appealed against this judgment. In 2002 the Appellate Court sent the case back for reconsideration. On 6 April 2005 the Appellate Court (now acting as the first-instance lustration court) found that Moczulski had lied in his lustration affidavit; he had collaborated with the security services between 1969 and 1977. Moczulski appealed, but in September 2006 he lost the appeal. The ECHR found a breach of Article 6 because – as in the Luboch case – Moczulski's restricted access to documents was exacerbated by the classification of certain documents as state secrets.

Moczulski steadfastly maintained that his file had been falsified by the security services. The IPN continued to maintain that he was a lustration liar. As a result of the ECHR judgment the Supreme Court returned the case to the Warsaw Regional Court to hear the case as court of first instance. Moczulski's second auto-lustration trial began in May 2015. In 2018 the court suspended proceedings after he withdrew his petition for auto-lustration. After twenty years Moczulski had 'had enough'.[53]

Opening the files removed a central criticism of the lustration procedures. Once the files were open, several thousand people sought access to their own files each year. In 2010 the IPN received 4,222 requests for documents and in 2013 3,743, excluding requests for copies from former security-service functionaries. In 2014 there were 3,800 requests from persons for their own files. Almost 2 million people accessed the IPN's internet catalogues.[54] The IPN also added 13,151 persons (12,586 new entries and 565 amended) to its catalogues of secret service functionaries, persons occupying senior party and state posts in the People's Republic, public persons and persons investigated by (*rozpracowywanych*) the security organs.

However, the files were not always what they seemed. Moczulski's own claim that his dossier had been doctored fit with the widespread acknowledgement from the beginning of the 1990s that many files had been falsified or even concocted wholesale – as well as being incomplete. In 2015 a former legal adviser to Solidarity, Piotr Bożek, was cleared of lustration lying on the grounds that the security services had falsified the receipts for his alleged services; his vindication took almost twenty-five years.[55]

False files were not the only problem. The journalist Piotr Pytlakowski recounted his own case (and that of others), explaining how his three-month employment in 1972 as an orderly (*salowy*) in a hospital run by the interior ministry led to his listing as a person working for the security services (he had also been on Wildstein's list). Access to his dossier at the IPN by right-wing journalists led to claims that the job was a 'cover' for Pytlakowski's work as an agent. Pytlowski launched and won a legal battle to clear his name. However, when he appealed to the IPN to remove his file, Kamiński, head of the IPN, conceded that the hospital was 'not an organ of the security services' and that Pytlakowski had not been a functionary of the SB. However, his file could not be expunged because his employment file had been transferred to Bureau C of the Interior Ministry; since Bureau C was an organ of the security services, the IPN had an obligation to preserve it.[56]

## Lustration under PiS

Following PiS's amendment of the law on the IPN, it was widely expected that a new lustration law would be the next step. PiS Deputy Arkadiusz Mularczyk believed that PiS would return to the system envisaged in the short-lived law of 2006, namely the replacement of lustration affidavits by declarations provided by the IPN and a widening of the categories to be lustrated.[57] However, President Duda had already made clear his opposition to the 'declaration model', chiefly because of the 'state of the files' and the lack of judicial process.[58]

The IPN began to release documents from the reserved collection (*zbiór zastrzeżony*) of the archives, scheduled for completion by March 2017. IPN Chair Jarosław Szarek announced that the inventory of all files would be made available on line. Individuals' files would be categorized as files of functionaries, persons investigated by the security services (*rozpracowywanyc*h) and those qualified by the security services as various types of 'personal sources of information' – in effect a list of agents and informers.[59] As the minister of education observed, access to these files would 'give everyone the opportunity to know who collaborated'.[60] The persistent issue of the accuracy of the files was completely ignored.

### The Bolek Affair (cont.)

The Bolek Affair was one aspect of the increasing politicization of the IPN. In 2016 General Kiszczak's wife Maria revealed that she had documents concerning Lech Wałęsa – she hoped to sell them to the IPN. The IPN promptly sent the procuracy to the Kiszczak villa to secure the documentation as rightfully belonging to its national archive. Following the release of the files Wałęsa's defenders accepted the fact of his cooperation with the security services in 1971–6, though disputes remained over the true context of his actions and their significance.

One main issue was the attempt to cast doubt on Wałęsa's subsequent role as the leader of Solidarity. Despite the lack of any evidence for subsequent collaboration,[61] the view that Wałęsa had sold his soul to the security services remained prevalent amongst the right wing and functioned as an important element of the delegitimization of the Round Table. 'In my view', said Krzysztof Wyszkowski, 'his collaboration never ended and endures to this day. An agent who fails to confess that he was an agent remains an agent. This principle has been scientifically proved by the IPN'.[62]

The public, however, remained largely unconcerned. One survey suggested that about two-thirds of respondents regarded the revelations as 'unimportant', while a similar number reported that they had not changed their view of the former Solidarity leader.[63] Between 2008 and 2018 the former president lost significantly in public esteem,[64] but people were not much concerned. For those who cared, Lech Wałęsa remained a polarizing figure, either a traitor or a hero.

## Lustration: The final stages

In fact, lustration was fading from the political agenda. If 'everyone' could learn who had collaborated, the formal process was hardly necessary. 'Lustration is a matter for history', declared Bronisław Wildstein.[65] IPN Chair Jarosław Szarek agreed that as the years passed lustration became less relevant. Given the backlog of unchecked affidavits – some 300,000 – Szarek argued that only affidavits of victorious candidates should be examined. But this was not quite the end. Szarek himself favoured the extension of lustration to persons occupying 'positions of public trust', including scholars and journalists.[66]

PiS did not want to let lustration go. The Ministry of Sport sought the lustration of officials in sporting bodies.[67] Solidarity demanded the lustration of the civil service and local government. 'We estimate that there are as many as 40 thousand persons with a shameful past in the administration', said Robert Barabasz, who led Solidarity employees in the state administration and local government.[68] A group of PiS deputies asked the environment minister for the lustration of hunters, since 'many former functionaries and collaborators ... are members of the Polish Hunting Association and own individual hunting weapons ..., while some are also involved in the Committee for the Defence of Democracy (KOD) and through social media are threatening to use (their weapons) in the event of legislation detrimental to their interests'.[69] Does one laugh or cry at this idiocy?

Journalists were also in the line of fire, fitting well with PiS's concerns about the 'unpatriotic media'. In April 2017 the National Media Council (three of its five members were PiS deputies) approved a resolution submitted by PiS Deputy Joanna Lichocka on the lustration of journalists.[70] The resolution appealed to the boards of public radio and television and the Polish Press Agency not to employ persons who had worked for or collaborated with communist security organs and to check all employees in the IPN archives. Lichocka suggested that if dissolving an employment contract should prove impossible, then these former functionaries, employees and collaborators should not appear in nor exercise any influence on programmes of the public media. She said, 'I don't think the former secret police and their collaborators should shape public opinion in the national media'.[71] The deputy minister of culture agreed that 'journalists and publicists are professionals of particular public trust; the public has the right to know that they are decent people who had nothing to do with such shameful actions as collaboration ... with the oppressive regime'.[72] Critics noted that – given the large-scale personnel changes in the media – the resolution was an 'empty symbol'[73] and 'wholly unnecessary'.[74]

New legislation from the Ministry of Sport (July 2017) provided that 'a person who was an employee, functionary, or soldier of the organs of state security cannot be a member of an internal control organ of a Polish sporting association'; it required a lustration affidavit from prospective members.[75] This (with other amendments) 'highlighted the high ethical and moral demands on those involved in Polish sporting bodies'. However, unlike other lustration measures this bill concerned only those who worked for the security services. It made no mention of informers or 'secret collaborators'.

Despite these demands for the lustration of some remaining categories, the long lustration saga was virtually complete by 2017. The new focus on 'economic lustration' – already apparent in the new law on sporting bodies – ostensibly centred on greater transparency, combatting corruption, countering 'unrevealed lobbying' and greater civic control. In October 2017 a new draft law on 'openness in public life' was issued for consultation. All those carrying out public functions, from national bankers to firefighters, would submit property declarations to be published on line and evaluated by the appropriate agencies, including the Anti-Corruption Bureau (CBA). Any non-governmental organization wishing to take part in legislative consultation would also have to reveal their sources of finance. After extensive criticism of potential invasions of privacy, including that from the Civil Rights Ombudsman,[76] the government backtracked somewhat, providing for the economic lustration of 151 occupational groups but limiting the number of publicly available declarations.[77]

The process of lustration by affidavit entailed punishment only insofar as the submissions were deemed not to be truthful. Revealing 'collaboration' however caused pain and damage to reputation so telling the truth was also a form of punishment. There was never much nuance in discussions of why someone might have cooperated with the security services or limited the manner of their cooperation to *faux* revelations. The element of vengeance was an undercurrent of the actions of those claiming the moral high ground.

This appetite for revenge shone through even more strongly in the so-called 'deubekisation laws'. The law of Act of 23 January 2009 amending the laws on pensions of soldiers and functionaries reduced the pensions of security service functionaries and of members of the Military Council of National Salvation (WRON). Pensions were lowered equally for all persons who served in the state's security services within the meaning of the Lustration Law, regardless of where they worked or their duties (including athletics stars, often nominally employed by the police) and regardless of whether a functionary was positively verified in 1990 – unless they had assisted the Opposition. The Constitutional Tribunal upheld the law (with five dissenting opinions), arguing that the reduction of pensions was considerable but within the scope of legislative freedom. The law did not aim to deprive representatives of the former regime of the social minimum 'nor to humiliate them'.[78] In December 2016 under PiS[79] further draconian cuts were made, restoring collective guilt and 'effectively abolishing social insurance' for some 30,000 people.[80] The constitutional challenge to this law (case P 4/18) was heard in July 2020.

## Conclusion

Over the years since 1992 the practical arguments had largely disappeared, though elements of the Polish Right retained their ideological fervour for lustration. Few feared a 'communist resurgence', even after the electoral success of the SLD in 2001. Arguments about the potential obstruction of capitalist economic reform were a distant memory, if the cronyism and corruption of the old elites remained a leitmotif of PiS's depiction of the economy. The uses of lustration as a political football also declined, especially after the elimination of social democracy from the Polish parliament.

It is true that decommunization and its lustration subset continued to fuel the Law and Justice assault on the Third Republic and the legacy of the Round Table. Yet these were not central to PiS's 2015 election campaign, which stressed welfare issues, scandals within Civic Platform and the migrant crisis – along with the emotive case of Smoleńsk for its core supporters.[81] Having won the election, PiS returned to its broad strategy for the maximum concentration of power (see Chapter 10).

In theory the basic model of lustration brought 'truth' centre stage, since the test of an individual's lustration affidavit was not whether it revealed employment or collaboration with the security services but whether it was truthful. Lustration lying was the punishable offence. In practice the situation was not always so straightforward, since some did lose their jobs after submitting a positive affidavit, while the IPN practice was to pursue all avenues of appeal against court findings that an affidavit was 'truthful', often prolonging the process for many years. The 'problem of the files' did not disappear, even with access granted to all individuals in the 2010 legislation. Assumptions about the veracity of the files were implicit in lustration law.

The politicians of the Polish Right had kept lustration alive long after it ceased to concern the public. I cannot share Szczerbiak's view that 'public opinion ... was always sympathetic to radical approaches towards truth revelation', whatever that radicalism might be.[82] It is true that when asked, large numbers favoured lustration, or removing former communists from senior positions or publishing IPN lists. This did not make the public the motor of lustration. Lustration was never a central election issue. Jarosław Kaczyński almost single handedly kept the issue alive. His passion to remove from public life all those who had been part of or cooperated with the communist regime was both pragmatic and deeply ideological. Purges always open up avenues for patronage or, more kindly perhaps, 'promoting turnover of the political, cultural and business elites'.[83] Institutions like the IPN developed vested interests in their vengeful approach to individuals in the files.

Up until the end of 2016 the Constitutional Tribunal's lustration judgments proved a major bulwark against violations of human rights' principles and the basic tenets of the rule of law. The TK tightened the definition of 'collaboration' and gave greater protection to persons falling under lustration law. When PiS came to power in 2005, it attempted to vary the 'soft' approach to lustration, including the removal of the individual affidavit. But the TK eviscerated the 2006 legislation and prevented the extension of lustration to ever-widening categories, including the private sector. The widespread acceptance of the affidavit as the linchpin of the system was at least in part due to the acknowledged state of the files of the security services, including their incompleteness, their unreliability or even their downright falsity. Initially it was expected that people would reveal their collaboration even where the archives could not confirm this – they did not know whether or not their file had been destroyed. The Constitutional Tribunal placed human rights' considerations at the heart of its deliberations.

After 2015 when PiS returned to power, ever-new categories were suggested for lustration, but much of the heat had leaked from the issue. Kaczyński shifted his focus away from lustration to the structures of the Polish state. By the second decade of the twenty-first century issues of transitional justice were no longer issues of justice or truth or democracy but – insofar as they were still relevant – simple instruments of political power.

# History and memory. The Institute of National Remembrance

The Institute of National Remembrance – the Commission for the Prosecution of Crimes against the Polish Nation (*Instytut Pamięci Narodowej – Komisja Ścigania Zbrodni przeciwko Narodowi Polskiemu*) – became the most important instrument of transitional justice. Commonly known as the IPN, it was created by statute in December 1998[1] as an extended incarnation of the original Commission for Investigating German Crimes in Poland, established in 1945, and its successors: the Central Commission for the Investigation of Nazi Crimes in Poland (1949–84); the Central Commission for Investigating Nazi Crimes in Poland – the Institute of National Remembrance (1985–91); and since 1991 the Central Commission for Investigating Crimes against the Polish Nation – the Institute of National Remembrance.

When Solidarity Election Action (AWS) won the 1997 parliamentary elections, questions of 'dealing with the past' returned centre stage. James Mark notes that in both Poland and Hungary by the mid-1990s parties of the right identified the 'founding sin' of the new system as the negotiated transition, which had failed to remove the communists from the political arena.[2] These parties 'developed unifying programmes based on powerful critiques of the transition process', with historical memory at their centre: 'They recast the liberal-left coalitions as the enemy, the post-Communist left as the successor to movements that had suppressed national resistance, and liberals as their willing collaborators.'[3]

The IPN was the key institution in this project of providing redress for the victims of the communist regime and reshaping collective memory. In accord with the new law Parliament selected an eleven-member committee representing the full spectrum of political parties. The National Judicial Council would oversee the activities of the Institute and present the *Sejm* with candidates for chair of the IPN.

It proved difficult to find a chair, who needed the support of the Committee and three-fifths of *Sejm* deputies. After several months it 'seemed increasingly probable that the Institute would not arise at all'.[4] The impasse was broken in June 2000. The first chair of the IPN was then-Senator Professor Leon Kieres, a lawyer and lecturer at the University of Wrocław. He had been a Solidarity adviser in the 1980s, then chair of the Lower Silesian provincial assembly in the 1990s. He was elected senator in 1997.

The IPN was a peculiar hybrid – it was part of the public administration and enjoyed ministerial status but was (nominally) politically independent. Its chair was practically irremovable, enjoying a protected status comparable only to that of the Polish president.[5] Its headquarters was in Warsaw, with branches in the eleven cities with appellate courts and subsections in a further seven cities. In 2001 the IPN employed about 800 people with a budget of about 83 million PNL. In 2016 it had just over 2,000 employees. In 2017 it received 289 million PLN from the state budget (that year the budget for the whole of the Polish Academy of Sciences was 81.5 million). The budget for 2020 was 423 million PLN.

## Structure and functions of the IPN

Under the 1998 law the three main elements of the IPN were the Main Commission, the Archives and the Bureau of Education, with eleven branches in major cities. The procurators of the Commission would continue to investigate and prosecute Nazi crimes, 'communist crimes', and international crimes against peace, crimes against humanity and war crimes. Initially the IPN played a secondary role in lustration. It provided relevant documents to the Public Interest Spokesman (RIP), whose office evaluated the veracity of lustration affidavits. In 2007 under the government of Law and Justice (PiS) a new Lustration Bureau was added to the structure of the IPN. It replaced the RIP as the body charged with identifying 'suspicious' lustration affidavits for further investigation and referral to the courts. The extension of lustration to new categories increased the investigative role of the IPN.

The Archive was the largest of the IPN's departments. It brought together all key ministerial archives (interior, justice, defence and the Bureau of State Protection); court documents dealing with 'repressed persons'; and documents from the State Archives (*Archiwum Akt Nowych*) concerning the Communist Party (PZPR) and its predecessor, the Polish Workers' Party (PPR), as well as documents of the security services of the occupying powers. This was an enormous task, requiring the reclassification and cataloguing of 90 kilometres (by 2017) of files. The IPN was charged with securing, conserving and analysing these documents. Its security procedures were called into question by the publication of the so-called Wildstein List of names copied from IPN archives by the journalist Bronisław Wildstein in 2005.

The Archive was also charged with making accessible all documents linked to the implementation of the lustration law, the law on the IPN and later also the 'deubekisation' laws of 2009 and 2017, which reduced pensions of former communist bureaucrats and functionaries.[6] One section of the IPN archive remained secret until 2016, reserved for matters affecting state security; until then only the head of the IPN could grant access. Access to the remaining collection was also limited until 2007.

The Bureau of Education publicized information about the documents held and their implications. It also conducted active research. Initially the task of its historians was to promote knowledge of the structures, methods of operation and personnel of the institutions 'responsible for crimes against the Polish Nation'. As its remit widened to include the entire period following the partitions of Poland in the eighteenth century, the IPN became the largest and best-funded historical research institute in the country, publishing hundreds of books and thousands of articles, as well as its own journals such as *Pamięć i Sprawiedliwość* (Memory and Justice, from 2002) and its own Bulletin (*Biuletyn IPN*, from 2001–11 and again from 2017). The Bureau was also linked to many new projects for museums and exhibitions.

## The Archive: Access to files

After 1998 the IPN became a major instrument of the compensatory mechanisms of transitional justice. People needed affidavits or documentary evidence for a variety of reasons. Requests for affidavits or evidentiary materials came from individuals and from the judicial organs. The IPN also responded to requests to confirm imprisonment in the period 1944–56 for 'political or religious activity linked to the struggle for sovereignty and independence'. It also dealt with requests for documents showing imprisonment for political activity after 1956.

In July 2001 the IPN began to accept requests for access to files. For almost a decade only individuals 'harmed' or 'damaged' (*pokrzywdzony*) by the security services could gain access to their own files (a person not identified as 'harmed' had no means to challenge this judgment). A 'harmed' person was one about whom the security services purposefully gathered information. During its first year of effective operation the IPN granted 459 persons the status of '*pokrzywdzony*'. Between July 2001 and the end of 2007, 9,826 persons were deemed '*pokrzywdzony*' and thus able to see their personal files.

Those not granted this status (often because the archive lacked documentation) still had no means of challenging the so-called revelations of wild lustration. The release of the Wildstein List in 2005 created potential injustice for thousands of people who were on the list but were not granted 'damaged' status. Although the IPN was inundated with requests to provide affidavits of non-collaboration, it had no powers to do this. If a name figured on the list, it could do no more than confirm a mistaken identity. The only concession was – ironically – to former security service personnel, who gained the right to see their own personnel files (but not their reports on their targets) after the 2005 Constitutional Court judgment. Although President Kwaśniewski had unsuccessfully vetoed the law on the IPN as discriminatory, it was only in 2005 that the TK deemed the restriction of access to those harmed to be unconstitutional.[7]

In 2007 the revised Lustration Law[8] removed the status of '*pokrzywdzony*'. But Article 30 §2 of the law on the IPN still provided that it would not make available documents whose 'content revealed that the applicant a) was treated by the security services as a secret informer or aided in the operational gaining of information b) obliged him/herself to provide information to an organ of state security or provided such an organ with any assistance whatever in operational actions'. When the TK struck down Article 30 in May 2007, the IPN continued to reject applications. The head of the IPN rejected the argument that since Article 30 §2 had been declared unconstitutional and repealed, it followed that a different provision (Art. 31 §1) with the same content was also unconstitutional. He argued that only when the Constitutional Court expressly declared unconstitutional a given provision of the law was the IPN under the obligation not to apply that provision.

The 2007 lustration law also provided that individuals could request the names of functionaries who had dealt with them and those persons who had provided information about them. They could also request that personal data in their files – health status, sexual preference, ethnicity, religion and so on – should not be made available. Academics and journalists gained full access to the files with further amendments of June 2007; this had been suspended for a few months as a result of the Constitutional Tribunal's decision in May.[9] The IPN remained exempt from the provisions of the data protection laws. Despite the changes in 2010 privacy provisions did not affect access of scholars and journalists to unexpurgated files. They were not restricted in the use of this information.

From 2007 citizens could also gain access to the files of persons holding high offices of state and employees or functionaries of the organs of state security, including personal information. Those who felt injured by any subsequent revelations could take civil action. In the *Sejm* SLD spokespersons had argued that each citizen should have the right to inspect the documents about him or her and to remove inaccurate or incomplete information.

The 2007 law gave all persons the right of access to copies of documents concerning them, save documents written by them or which were created as part of their job with the security services or those whose content indicated that they had been viewed as a 'personal source of information' by the security services. The Law of 2010 (under PO) on the IPN[10] provided full access to the archive: all citizens could apply to see their own files with all documents affecting them and they could exclude access by others for a period of fifty years. Thus those 'responsible for creating documents' could now also gain access to them (these included reports by functionaries and notes written by 'informers').

The lawmakers acted to reduce the problems that had arisen from efforts to construct legal mechanisms to prevent access to their files of former functionaries and 'their human sources of information'. It was difficult for those refused access to defend themselves against charges of collaboration with the security services – a process made even more difficult by the IPN's 'ever-wider and arbitrary' criteria for granting access to documents.[11] The revised law meant that the IPN could no longer determine whether and to whom documents could be released; it must release documents to anyone making such a request for their own files (Art. 30).

These changes were designed to reflect Civic Platform's policy of 'depoliticizing' the IPN and to meet the requirements of another Constitutional Court judgment finding sections of the 2007 legislation unconstitutional. After rejecting Article 30 (see above) the TK now also found that Article 31, similarly providing for the refusal of documents, violated the right to protection of one's private life, the right of access to official documents and collections of data, and the right to demand the correction of incorrect or incomplete information. Applications to the IPN and refusals are enumerated in Table 8.1. These requests did not diminish over time. Although the IPN noted the surprising 47-fold increase in security service functionaries or collaborators seeking copies of documents in 2017 compared with 2016, it did not suggest a reason for this.

**Table 8.1** Requests for access to personal files held by the IPN (number)[a]

| Year | Article 30 requests granted for access to documents (anonymized to May 2010) | | Requests granted for access to/copies of non-anonymized documents | Article 35 requests for names and data pertaining to employees, functionaries and secret collaborators | | |
|---|---|---|---|---|---|---|
| | Applicants receiving access | Applicants refused (Art. 31) | Applicants receiving documents/ copies | Requests realised | Functionaries refused access | Secret collaborators (TW) refused access |
| 2007 | 10,285 | 215 | 1,827 | | 22 | 1,563 |
| 2008 | 15,765 | 949 | 3,323 | 697 | 85 | 1,838 |
| 2009 | 4,497 | 1,133 | 6,345 | 914 | 174 | 2,025 |
| 2010 | 3,462 | 264 | 4,024 | 423 | 213 | 1,282 |
| 2011 | 2,463 | n/a | 2,305 | 262 | 38 | 857 |
| 2012 | 1,901 | n/a | 1,759 | 185 | 25 | 353 |
| 2013 | 2,246 | n/a | 2,129 | 133 | 25 | 469 |
| 2014 | 3,838 | n/a | 2,252 | 161 | n/a | n/a |
| 2015 | 4,000 | n/a | 2,205 | 124 | n/a | n/a |
| 2016 | 6,154 | n/a | 3,298 | 161 | n/a | n/a |
| 2017 | 8,546 | n/a | 7,244 | 8,464 | n/a | n/a |
| 2018 | 6,876 | n/a | 8,250 | 1,182 | n/a | n/a |

[a] The table excludes applications submitted and pending.
Source: compiled from IPN annual reports to the Sejm 2008–16: *Informacja o działalności Instytutu Pamięci Narodowej – Komisja Ścigania Zbrodni przeciwko Narodowi Polskiemu.*

# The Main Commission

The Main Commission for Investigating Crimes against the Polish Nation was the investigative arm of the IPN. Some 100 procurators worked at the centre and in eleven regional counterparts. The procuracy (*prokuratura*), led by the Procurator General (a post occupied by the minister of justice from 1990 to 2010 and again after 2016), is the guardian of the rule of law. The director of the Main Commission was also deputy procurator general. IPN procurators had two key roles. Firstly, they were in direct charge of investigating offences (more rarely, they supervised a police investigation). Secondly, the procuracy took charge of the trial process, bringing charges and supporting them during trial. Here, in practice, the procurator enjoyed little discretion; 'if he or she concludes during the investigation that an offense has occurred, in principle a prosecution must ensue'.[12] The procuracy also had broad authority to appeal both acquittals and convictions.

The procurators of the Main Commission investigated Nazi crimes, communist crimes and war crimes or other crimes against humanity or against peace. Their brief was to investigate only those actions that were crimes at the time they were committed in cases where the perpetrator had not been brought to book. They also investigated the destruction of or damage to documents in the IPN archive. The aims of investigation were not only to charge offenders where possible but also to 'clarify the full circumstances of the crime and, in particular, to identify those persons harmed by it' (Art. 45¶3). This would meet both the needs of domestic law and the international obligation to deal with crimes committed by 'functionaries of totalitarian systems' as well as the IPN's broad objectives of disseminating knowledge about the extent of repression and preserving the memory of victims. This is why the IPN investigated crimes regardless of whether their perpetrators were still living.

Cases relating to the Stalinist period, before 1954, when repression was at its height, proved particularly difficult. The Report of the Mazur Commission, set up in 1956 to investigate Stalinist abuses in the military courts at a time when the 'restoration of socialist legality' was the watchword, provided the IPN a useful starting point with a list of military judges, prosecutors, investigating officers and their victims. However, in many cases indictments were not possible (or were dismissed) because the alleged perpetrators were dead.

The IPN also turned its attention to the phenomenon of 'judicial crimes' perpetrated by procurators and judges, both civil and military. These were violations and distortions of law and procedure committed by judges and procurators in trials of the communist period. This investigation was seen as the corollary of the rehabilitation process: if those convicted had been rehabilitated and their sentences invalidated, as many had been under the terms of the *Sejm*'s 1991 Resolution, then those who caused the original injustice should also be brought to book.

Foreign governments did not always cooperate. For example, on three separate occasions between 1999 and 2008 Poland unsuccessfully sought the extradition of former procurator Helena Wolińska-Brus from the UK; she had left Poland in 1968 with her husband, the eminent economist Włodzimierz Brus, as a consequence of the 'anti-Zionist' campaign then waged by the communist authorities. The Polish indictments charged Wolińska-Brus as an 'accessory to judicial murder', allegedly having fabricated evidence leading to the execution of General Emil Fieldorf in 1953 and the wrongful arrest and imprisonment of twenty-four other anti-Nazi resistance fighters. In 2010 the Swedish authorities similarly refused to extradite another 1968 exile, former judge Stefan Michnik, accused of presiding over a dozen or so problematic trials of former army officers in the Stalinist period.

Lower-level functionaries also faced investigation. At first the IPN focused on officials of the security services and investigating officers, including their responsibility for (among others) false arrest, intimidating witnesses, manufacturing evidence, extracting confessions under duress. These cases included the detention and trial of anti-communist resistance fighters during the Second World War, as well as the post-war activities of 'pro-independence organisations' more generally. Cases relating to the Stalinist period, before 1954, when repression was at its height, proved particularly difficult.

Investigations continued even though the statute of limitations meant that many prosecutions could not proceed, particularly after the Supreme Court decision of 2010, which applied the limit to communist crimes punishable by up to five years' imprisonment. In 2016 the Ombudsman Adam Bodnar failed to persuade the Constitutional Tribunal to reconsider; he argued that suspending proceedings due to the statute of limitations violated basic principles of justice, since 'citizens treated by the former regime in an abusive manner, with characteristics of torture or inhuman treatment, have the right to have these actions judged'.[13] Still, the investigations of the Main Commission would diminish over the course of time. Most of the remaining communist crimes were set to 'expire' in 2020 under the statute of limitations, with only murders remaining until 2030.

The IPN started work in the year 2000. Before that, military or civil procurators had investigated and prosecuted former communist leaders. The prosecutor in the trial of those charged with causing deaths in the Baltic protests in 1970 was Bogdan Szegda of the Gdańsk procuracy. The procuracy in Katowice dealt initially with the 'pacification' of the Wujek mine in 1981 by the paramilitary police ZOMO. The final verdict came in 2007, convicting the remaining thirteen defendants of a 'communist crime'. Earlier, in 2005, a military court had rejected the IPN's attempts to bring charges against the military procurators investigating the Wujek tragedy in the 1980s on the grounds that their investigation did not constitute a 'communist crime'. We saw in Chapter 4 that the IPN also took over the case against General Kiszczak, who was tried four times for Wujek, beginning in 1994. It successfully appealed against his acquittal in April 2011. The retrial demanded by the appellate court did not take place – Kiszczak was deemed unfit to stand trial on grounds of his mental health (he died in November 2015).

The IPN's Main Commission took over cases where retrial had been ordered by the courts and the appellate process, but it also brought new charges. For example, it brought charges of religious discrimination against Kiszczak in 2009. He was found guilty (but amnestied) of dismissing a policeman who had sent his daughter to her first communion in 1985. Notably, the IPN reopened investigations into the declaration of martial law. In April 2007 IPN procurators filed charges in Warsaw against the 'authors of martial law', including Generals Jaruzelski and Kiszczak, when the central defendants stood accused of the 'communist crime' of 'directing an armed criminal organisation' for the purpose of violating the human rights of Polish citizens[14] (see Chapter 4).

The IPN used this notion of an 'armed criminal organisation' within the Interior Ministry to reconsider other high-profile cases, including the murder of Father Jerzy Popiełuszko. By 2016 the IPN was 'still investigating', having gathered 127 volumes or materials, 82 volumes of appendices, and 104 volumes of documents from the police and courts in the case of the repression and murder of Popiełuszko. The IPN believed, but never proved, that senior figures in the party-state hierarchy – in particular the 'armed conspiracy in the Ministry of the Interior' – were responsible for Popełuszko's murder.[15]

The IPN pursued its cases with undoubted tenacity. Yet some of its work appears curious to say the least. From 2008 to 2013 the IPN investigated the death of Poland's wartime leader General Sikorski, killed in a plane crash in 1943; after exhuming his body the IPN concluded that it could neither confirm nor refute the possibility of sabotage. In May 2017 the IPN announced that the assassination attempt on Pope John Paul in May 1981 was not the work of a lone individual but had been orchestrated by Bulgarian intelligence services.[16] In February 2017 it initiated criminal proceedings in cases of the deaths of Polish citizens killed on the electrified border with Czechoslovakia in the years 1961–5 and sought the exhumation of their bodies.

The IPN also continued its dogged pursuit of former President Lech Wałęsa. In 2017 the IPN suspended its investigation of the falsification of documents on Wałęsa taken from the home of General Kiszczak after concluding that the files were in fact accurate (fifty-three documents were deemed genuine, six had falsified signatures).[17] Shortly afterwards the IPN announced that it was investigating Wałęsa for submitting false testimony.[18]

During 2016 the procurators of the Main Commission completed 1,198 investigations, of which 687 concerned communist crimes, 465 concerned Nazi crimes and ten concerned war crimes or other crimes against peace or humanity.[19] The IPN did not maintain a presumption of innocence. Each new case was designated in advance as a Zk (communist crime), Zn (Nazi crime) or other crime (Zi). Despite thousands of investigations charges were few, though there were annual fluctuations. Only seven charges, relating to eight people, were filed in 2016. In 2015 fourteen charge sheets were presented against sixteen people and in 2014 twelve against twenty-eight people. In 2012 twelve people were brought to trial and in 2011 seven. The IPN reports failed to provide data on convictions, but we know that many trials were discontinued, not least because of the death of the accused.

## Lustration and the role of the IPN

Lustration was perennially controversial, as we have seen. The left wing, both post-communist and post-Solidarity, opposed many features of lustration legislation even while accepting lustration in principle. Others from the civil-libertarian wing of the former liberals and the Democratic Union shared these views. Andrzej Romanowski left the UW as a consequence of the new lustration law of 1997. He opposed lustration, in particular 'the division of society on the basis of history' and the 'process which makes culpability absolute'.[20] Romanowski saw the IPN as the 'institutionalization of wild lustration', motivated solely by vengeance.[21] It was an 'institutional monstrosity' born of 'lustration mania'.[22]

However, the IPN did not assume a key role in lustration until after the abolition of the Public Interest Representative and the establishment of the IPN's Lustration Bureau in 2007. Its three departments reflected its major functions: The Department of Lustration Files, Notification and Publication investigated the validity of the lustration affidavits of election candidates and public functionaries. The Department for the Preparation and Supervision of Lustration Proceedings prepared the case against those whose affidavits were found to be inaccurate. The Cataloguing Department prepared and published four catalogues: of functionaries of the security organs under the communist regime (PRL); persons holding high office (*kierownicze stanowiska*) in the party and state apparatuses of the PRL; persons investigated (*rozpracowywanych*) by the communist security services who were not collaborators (published with their agreement); and persons currently carrying out public functions.

The Lustration Bureau got off to a slow start. Partly this was due to confusion over the relevant legislation. The May 2007 judgment of the Constitutional Tribunal (TK) had rejected the widespread extension of lustration in the 2006 law. The IPN registered some 120,000 lustration affidavits but had to return those submitted by persons no longer obliged to undergo lustration. It also proved difficult to recruit procurators, especially in the cities of Poznań, Łódź and Lublin. The amended law of September 2007 introduced a new template for the lustration affidavit, as required by the TK. The new declarations began to arrive at the IPN in large numbers only in March 2008; by the end of that year the Lustration Bureau had received 142,014 affidavits.[23] At the end of 2009 that figure stood at 147, 606, of which 1,736 acknowledged employment in or collaboration with the communist security services.

Gradually the number of new affidavits fell because increasing numbers of candidates and potential office holders were born after the cut-off year of 1972 and because many repeat candidates had already been lustrated. In 2016 the IPN registered only 3,618 new lustration declarations. Between 2009 and 2016 its procurators initiated lustration proceedings in 1,033 cases of suspected false affidavits (excluding seventeen presidential candidates lustrated in separate procedures). Final verdicts were issued in 980 cases. Of these, the courts agreed that 680 (69 per cent) of the affidavits tested in court were untruthful; their authors were 'lustration liars' now banned from holding public office (see Table 8.2).

**Table 8.2** False lustration affidavits 2008–16

| Year | Cases referred for lustration proceedings | Cases reaching final verdicts | Lustration liars | % Liars |
|------|------|------|------|------|
| 2008 | 0 | 0 | 0 | 0 |
| 2009 | 79 | 16 | 4 | 25 |
| 2010 | 68 | 52 | 27 | 52 |
| 2011 | 87 | 70 | 38 | 54 |
| 2012 | 136 | 123 | 68 | 55 |
| 2013 | 211 | 183 | 135 | 74 |
| 2014 | 175 | 210 | 157 | 75 |
| 2015 | 133 | 168 | 124 | 74 |
| 2016 | 144 | 158 | 127 | 80 |
| 2017 | 151 | 176 | 140 | 79 |
| 2018 | 229 | 299 | 176 | 59 |
| Total | 1,413 | 1455 | 996 | 68 |

Source: Compiled from IPN annual reports to the Sejm 2008–16: *Informacja o działalności Instytutu Pamięci Narodowej – Komisja Ścigania Zbrodni przeciwko Narodowi Polskiemu.*

Table 8.2 records the cases submitted by the IPN procurators for lustration proceedings in each year since 2008. However, the cases reaching final verdict in those years are not the same cases. The judicial process was lengthy. Cases inherited from the Public Interest Spokesman continued for many years. Most cases finding untruthful affidavits were appealed by the individual concerned, and the standard practice of the IPN was to appeal cases in which it had failed to convince the court that an affidavit was false. Although the IPN was vindicated in almost 70 per cent of the cases it took to court, the number of lustration proceeding was few in relation to the thousands of affidavits received.

These numbers raised doubts about the resources expended in achieving convictions, as well as the costs to individuals wrongly accused (see Chapters 6 and 7). With unconscious irony the IPN's report for 2014 responded to media criticism of the paucity of lustration proceedings initiated by its procurators: it blamed the time-consuming and difficult process of finding witnesses, notably the 'handlers' of alleged informants in the security services, their unreliability and their efforts to protect their informants.

> Evidentiary material gathered in these matters is derived from archival documentation created mainly by functionaries of the organs of the PRL in the years 1944–1990 – people now of advanced age, often chronically ill, finding it difficult to remember events that took place more than twenty years ago. At various points in the proceedings they often change their testimony ..... Functionaries testifying as witnesses in lustration proceedings ... often claim to have falsified operational documents ..., thus raising doubts as to the validity of the evidence ... Their testimonies are given with a sense of impunity.[24]

Of course, these were precisely the arguments used by the opponents of lustration.

## The Bureau of Education and The righting of history

At the start established historians often proved reluctant to work with the IPN,[25] though there were important exceptions, including the first director of the Bureau of Education Paweł Machcewicz (his disagreements with the PiS government came later). Many younger historians, however, were well disposed to the IPN ethos and welcomed the opportunity to conduct independent research.[26] Andrzej Dudek, for example, joined the education bureau in 2000 as the director of the Department of Scholarly Research. He shared PiS's concerns with the persistence of the old networks of the communist state (the *układ*): since these were 'already entrenched in the economy and the media with no possibility of removing them', he said, the 'only field remaining was the battle for the historical understanding of the younger generation ....I went to the IPN because I believe that there is a chance of a partial change of (the historical) understanding (*świadomość*) of the communist regime, if not of the whole of society, then its elites'.[27]

The concern to reveal the truth about the communist regime certainly found a wide echo, reflecting a central concern of historians throughout the 1990s.[28] The founders of the IPN took a narrower approach. They saw truth and justice as inextricably linked: by revealing the regime's inner workings and its mechanisms of repression, the truth would provide justice for its victims.[29] After a year of activity the IPN's annual report listed 140 scholarly publications and 260 'popularising' articles in journals and newspapers on multifarious aspects of Poland's wartime, post-war and communist history.[30]

Although the leading figures of the IPN steadfastly affirmed their commitment to objectivity and impartiality,[31] and despite much praise for the quality of their output – 'pioneering synthesis, the publication of unknown documents, and ground-breaking monographs'[32] – IPN historians attracted considerable criticism. In the early years this centred largely on the practice of direct extrapolation from documents without reference to their context, selective use of documents, the lack of peer review of their publications and the absence of dialogue with other scholars. Privileged access to the archives for IPN historians was also a source of friction. Moreover, IPN salaries were higher than in academia and the IPN offered better prospects for young employees for upward mobility.[33]

Such criticisms intensified, especially after 2005. Particular attention was given to the uncritical acceptance of the security service files as the key source for the communist period – despite widespread recognition that many individuals' files had materials exaggerating or falsifying their relationship with the communists. Professor Andrzej Romanowski, former editor of the Catholic journal *Tygodnik Powszechny*, observed that these young historians deemed any form of coexistence with the regime 'collaboration' or 'undercover activity'.[34] The historian Peter Raina accused the authors of the IPN report on Father Hejmo of serious methodological failures and false conclusions.[35] We have already referred to the controversial study, *The Security Services and Lech Wałęsa*.[36] Indeed, the dispute over Wałęsa's past seemed unending. In 2013 the book's co-author Sławomir Cenckiewicz published *Wałęsa. The Man from the File*,[37] a loathsome book, dripping with bile. In 2017 Cenckiewicz's online essay detailing 'fourteen myths about Wałęsa'[38] attracted scathing criticism from the respected historian of Solidarity, Andrzej Friszke.[39]

## Historical politics

The IPN was closely associated with PiS's project of 'historical policy' or 'historical politics' (*historia polityczna*) as an element of its critique of the III (post-communist) Republic. After the successful celebrations of the sixtieth anniversary of the Warsaw uprising against the Nazis and the inauguration of the Museum of the Warsaw Uprising in 2004, a number of historians and philosophers endorsed the 'necessity of a conscious and active historical policy … to take its place alongside economic, social, or foreign policy'.[40] The journalist Krzysztof Piławski described the Warsaw Uprising as 'the founding myth of free Poland for the architects of the IV Republic' and the Museum as 'archaic ideological messages … wrapped in post-modern form'.[41] Robert Traba saw it as 'a permanent act of redress for the victims of one of the bloodiest uprisings of the twentieth century' but at the same time 'a manifestation of the organising of cultural memory'.[42]

The problem here is not that of historical revisionism or new interpretations of history. The problem is the 'ideologization' of history and the attempt by the state to impose its own monolithic version on a pluralist society. Anna Wolff-Powęska defined historical politics as 'the conscious action of the political class with the aim of shaping the scope and character of collective historical memory'. She argued that 'years of dictatorship made it difficult to accept the fact that in a socially differentiated, democratic state historical memory is polyphonic, dynamic, accelerated, and commercialized'.[43] Eugeniusz Ponczek similarly stressed that 'historical policy may (though it need not) depend on the suitable manipulation of selected information about the past, including in large part mythologized elements serving political aims'.[44]

According to its supporters 'the sphere of historical policy aims to promote our own (Polish) heritage in our social consciousness and … to represent the values of Polish history and our historical rationales to the outside world'.[45] So on the one hand it was oriented towards national consciousness and on the other to the international arena. Historical policy needed to be promoted by the state 'in the name of justice' in order to build Polish consciousness and identity: 'we need to depict the true heroes who lay in the dustbin of history for seventy years and we must resist the efforts of the last fifteen years to keep them there', said Andrzej Nowak; 'we have to do this in the name of … elementary justice'.[46]

These views often went hand in hand with attacks on the centre-left and liberal governments of the first post-communist period. According to Zdzisław Krasnodębski, 'The ideology of Polish liberalism and the utopia of the open society negated the need for collective memory and state policies on history'.[47] The social consciousness of 'real history' had been infected and distorted by ideology and censorship under the communists. Social memory had to be restored and consciousness purged by the elimination of 'the historical lies manipulated by the (communist) regime'.[48] Moreover, 'active state policies in the sphere of history' were needed because 'a state which consciously eschews such actions becomes the object of the historical policies of others'.[49] The notion that Poland needed to counter false or misleading interpretations of its history fostered by other states was a common theme.[50] PiS's concept of historical policy during its period in government in 2006–7 became an element of domestic politics and a constituent of international politics.[51] The international dimension found particular expression in the deterioration of Polish–German relations. After PiS came to power in 2015 the emphasis shifted markedly to Polish victimhood.

The themes of 'historical politics' or 'history policy' became a driving force for the IPN when Janusz Kurtyka (1960–2010) took over as director in December 2005. During his tenure (he died at Smolensk) the IPN's historians concentrated on both the repressive apparatus and the character of the opposition in the 1970s and 1980s – including publications dealing with Lech Wałęsa, Aleksander Kwaśniewski and Wojciech Jaruzelski. In 2006 the IPN made public the file of Archbishop Stanisława Wielgus. In 2009 the IPN was required to apologize to Adam Michnik for 'violating the dignity of his (late) father' by repeating falsehoods in its history of the events of March 1968. When Jan Żaryn lost his job as director of the education bureau in 2009 for stating publicly that Wałęsa had illegally achieved the status of '*pokrzywdzony*', Żaryn became an adviser to Kurtyka. Kurtyka fully endorsed the mission to shape Polish national consciousness. He emphasized the popularizing of IPN research through public lectures, travelling exhibitions, multi-media presentations, internet portals, brochures and leaflets, teacher training materials, and a strong presence on Facebook.[52]

Andrzej Frisze saw Kurtyka's tenure as a 'time of politicisation and political exclusion'.[53] Dariusz Stola referred to the emergence of a particular type of 'militant historian' engaging in symbolic politics and presenting a polarized black-and-white view of history; this makes for bad history, as 'polarized narratives pay … insufficient attention to support for and adaptation to the regime (willing or not), which evidently dominated; to strategies of evasion rather than resistance; and to mass participation in various institutions of the regime, beginning with the communist party itself'.[54] Andrzej Romanowski saw 'the postulate of creating national pride' as based on 'a huge dose of hypocrisy and deceit' as well as 'a touch of propaganda'.[55] Wiesław Władyka accused the IPN of replacing nuanced history with the 'active construction of stereotypes' and interpretations verging on caricature.[56] Civic Platform's Minister of Culture Bogdan Zdrojewski referred to the dominance of an 'instrumental view of history'.[57]

President Lech Kaczyński (from December 2005) took a keen interest in the politics of history and the memorialization of Poland's past, including – as mayor of Warsaw – his support for the Museum of the Warsaw Uprising and the Museum of the History of Polish Jews. During his presidency two public holidays were added at his initiative, the National Day of Remembrance of the Warsaw Uprising and the controversial National Day of Remembrance of the Accursed Soldiers. President Kaczyński pursued a 'new policy' for recognizing heroes of the independence struggle. He granted the Order of the White Eagle to hierarchs of the Catholic Church, victims of Stalinist repression, participants in the Poznań riots of 1956, and several anti-Wałęsa Solidarity activists, as well as depriving the 'perpetrators of repression' of orders and distinctions awarded by the communist regime.[58] The Accursed Soldiers were formally rehabilitated with IPN support on 15 August 2016.

The Second World War was a constant presence for Poles of all persuasions, and there was broad consensus over the desire to commemorate decisive events of the war. Following its formal rehabilitation many monuments to the Home Army were erected, including the Polish Underground State and Home Army Monument near the *Sejm* in Warsaw, unveiled in 1999. A museum was planned at Westerplatte, site of the German attack on Poland on 1 September 1939 and from the mid-1950s another symbol of the Polish struggle for independence. Civic Platform's Prime Minister Donald Tusk, born in Gdańsk, took a personal interest in the project to create a Westerplatte Museum. In 2008 Tusk set up a working group attached to the Ministry of Culture for the creation of a bigger project, the Second World War Museum, led by Paweł Machcewicz and Janusz Marszalec, formerly of the IPN. The Museum opened amid much controversy in 2017, with the PiS government threatening to close it down altogether for purveying 'the wrong kind of history' (see Chapter 10).

It is not surprising that the 'historical politics' of Law and Justice focused on the Second World War as emblematic of Poland's national, patriotic past. What is striking, however, is the failure to emphasize the more recent anti-communist struggle of

Solidarity.[59] Solidarity and its legacy were divisive, particularly after President Lech Wałęsa played a major role in the demise of the Olszewski government in 1992 and following the first 'revelations' about the Bolek file, allegedly demonstrating Wałęsa's collaboration with the communist authorities. Much of the right saw elements of Solidarity, including Wałęsa, as co-responsible for the Round Table negotiations and the ensuing 'national betrayal'. There was no 'symbolic closure' of the communist period[60] but rather 'a fractured memory regime'.[61] Instead of 'bringing about society's cultural restitution', the Right stressed how the Round Table served the treacherous Solidarity liberals and the communists at the expense of the Polish nation.[62] Kaczyński embarked on a strategy of 'mnemonic warfare'.[63]

By the mid-1990s the Right had recast Solidarity itself, leaving behind Solidarity's liberal ('pink') wing as 'inauthentic' and refashioning 'authentic' Solidarity as the starting point and inspiration for a traditional Catholic revival.[64] Yet rather than promoting Solidarity's achievements in ending Communism, anti-communists looked to the Warsaw Uprising for their narrative of resistance. Indeed, the museum and library of the European Solidarity Centre (*Europejskie Centrum Solidarności*) in Gdańsk opened only under the government of Civic Platform in 2014.

The blurring of history, identity and memory gathered pace after the death of President Kaczyński at Smolensk in April 2010. The cult of Lech Kaczyński gained momentum when PiS returned to power in 2016 and a second commission was set up to investigate the Smolensk crash. The new commission fed the conspiracy theories; indeed, its Chair, Antoni Macierewicz, had long claimed that the plane was brought down not because of poor visibility or mistakes by the pilot but by explosions on board. But the Kaczyński cult had emerged immediately following the disaster, with the holding of mass vigils outside the presidential palace and the burial of the president and his wife in Wawel Cathedral in Krakow. After April 2010 Jarosław Kaczyński always dressed publicly in black. The monthly meetings held in Warsaw were religious observances under Polish law, registered under Poland's new law on assembly as 'cyclical' or recurring until 2020. Held on the tenth day of each month these *miesięcznice*, with a mass followed by prayers 'on the spot from where the president left on his final journey', reinforced the view of Lech the victim and martyr, the president who strived for a truly independent Poland and paid the ultimate price. Kaczyński became a part of the myth of the tragic destiny of the Polish people.[65] Zubrzycki shows how Lech Kaczyński was woven into the thread of Poland's messianic martyrology.[66]

## The spaces of memory

It was not until 2008 that the IPN ventured into the area of commemoration and naming. After 1989 the 'fragmentation and decentralisation of memory production' characterized the politics of Polish space. Democratization and pluralization 'resulted in a greater questioning of the national master narrative at local level ... This reconfiguring of memory (was) ... undertaken by local elites, organisations of civil society and the empowered ethnic minorities which were suppressed under communism'.[67]

Local authorities used their new powers of self-government, especially at municipal level. Indeed, many moved quickly to remove the names of communist heroes or events associated with the communist period. Often streets and squares reverted to their inter-war names. In Warsaw the square named for the Polish Bolshevik Feliks Dzierzhinsky, best known for establishing the Soviet secret police, once again became Bank Square (*Plac Bankowy*), while Paris Commune Square reverted to its former name (Woodrow) Wilson Square. By 1966 most communist-inspired street names had been changed in major cities. Sometimes new names honoured local heroes or recent events; many Solidarity streets appeared along with Pope John Paul II streets. In many towns the issue of local place names returned every few years, especially with changes in the political configuration of local government bodies.

Within the IPN there was widespread support for national legislation governing the naming of public spaces. In 2007 in an intemperate, one-sided and invective-ridden article, 'Time to Clear the House of Rubbish', Piotr Szubarczyk of the Gdańsk IPN argued that hundreds of public spaces continued to honour those whose 'only service was service to Moscow'.[68] He strongly supported new legislation giving the IPN control of naming, since it could not fulfil its education brief 'in a situation where ... there are no streets of the anti-communist independence conspirators but there are streets named for Soviet cowards'. The IPN needed new powers to defeat the 'various post-Soviet interest groups dedicated to nurturing communist relics'.

Janusz Kurtyka, director of the IPN, agreed strongly. The IPN was already attempting to increase its influence in this sphere. In 2007–8 Kurtyka sent local authorities a list of street names which should be changed because of their communist resonance. Kurtyka commented that 'maintaining these names in independent Poland should be treated as anti-educational, glorifying criminal ideologies, and as betrayal of the Fatherland and an incentive to undertake action contrary to the Constitution'.[69]

There was no groundswell of opinion in favour of these changes. When surveys asked about renaming in 2007, a considerable majority (65 per cent) simply did not care whom their street or square was named after. Moreover, when asked whether their locality had streets whose names evoked the communist period or commemorated persons connected with the old regime, only 4 per cent of rural respondents and 9–10 per cent of urban dwellers, depending on the size of city, answered in the affirmative. Almost half of respondents in rural areas (48 per cent) said the question was not relevant: there were no such streets. In the largest cities 43 per cent said there had been such places but they had already been renamed, while 38 per cent said there were none and had never been any. In towns of 20,000–100,000 inhabitants these figures were 48 per cent and 22 per cent, respectively.[70] Nevertheless in December 2007 a group of PiS deputies submitted a draft bill on Sites of National Memory (it did not complete the legislative process).[71] PiS then returned to this issue in 2016 with its new 'decommunization law' (see Chapter 10).

## Structural changes under PiS

In April 2016 PiS's newly amended law on the IPN[72] reversed some major provisions altered under the government of Civic Platform. The Collegium returned, replacing the Council, with five members chosen by the *Sejm*, two by the Senate and two by the president. Higher education was no longer a criterion for a seat on the Collegium.

The method of appointing the IPN chair also changed: the Collegium would nominate candidates and the *Sejm* would decide, with the agreement of the Senate. Kamiński, the (as it proved) outgoing chair, endorsed the proposal to open (most of) the 'secret', reserved collection of the IPN archive. This was a key provision of the law.

Kamiński criticized the weakening of the chair, who would be 'the only state official of this rank not elected by an absolute majority. Moreover, the addition of new structures would risk the emergence of a "bureaucratic leviathan".'[73] *The Legal Gazette* called the new law a 'gangsters' assault' on the IPN, and arguments between the-then director of the IPN and PiS deputy Arkady Mularczyk were an act in the 'theatre of the absurd'.[74]

In June the *Sejm* chose PiS's candidates for the new Council (Kolegium). They included six professors – Andrzej Nowak, Piotr Franaszek, Józef Marecki, Tadeusz Wolsza, Wojciech Polak and Jan Draus – as well as Bronisław Wildstein, Sławomir Cenckiewicz and Krzysztof Wyszkowski. All had longstanding links to PiS. Draus was primarily a local historian; he had already served two terms on the Kolegium (1999–2011). Marecki was a historian of the Catholic Church. Wildstein was he of the Wildstein List. Wyszkowski was a publicist, one of the first openly to accuse Lech Wałęsa of collaboration with the security services in the 1970s, fighting a lengthy case (2005–11) for infringement of Wałęsa's personal rights. Cenckiewicz had spent his career searching for documents relating to Lech Wałęsa, publishing books and articles on Wałęsa's alleged role as 'Bolek' and the workings of the security services. His most recent book (with others) was *Informants (Konfidenci)*.[75] As late as August 2016 Cenckiewicz was still discovering (and publishing on Facebook) 'amazing' documents suggesting a hidden official agenda to protect Wałęsa.[76]

This was a monolithic Council well suited to serving PiS's vision of politics and history. A new, wider role was envisaged for the IPN, with a single interpretation of history designed to reshape the patriotism of the young with a sense of pride in Poland's history and a willingness to stand up and defend it against any effort to question the country's heroic past. Increasingly the government found itself supported by far-right groupings, not least as a result of its own anti-migrant rhetoric and its growing conflict with the European Union. The Independence Day March on 11 November 1917 attracted radical activists from across Europe, complete with anti-Semitic and Islamophobic banners and calls for a 'White Europe'.

# Conclusion

The IPN became an institution of unparalleled importance in the sphere of transitional justice and in wider areas of collective memory and national identity. By 2015 it was already an organizational leviathan, based on the Main Commission, the Archives, the Bureau of National Education, the Lustration Bureau, and the Bureau of Historical Research. As it evolved, it extended its functions: to punish the guilty, offer vindication and homage to the victims of communist repression, reveal historical truth, ensure the integrity of those holding public office, reshape the collective memory and redefine the designations of public space.

It is impossible to offer a definitive assessment of these divisions of the IPN, given the diversity of its activities, the interrelations among its functions and the evolution of its priorities over time. Undoubtedly, it was a curate's egg, good in parts. We have noted the controversies surrounding the IPN's historical research, its prosecutorial methods and its role in lustration. Yet there is no doubt that the preservation of documents and the extensive interviews conducted with both perpetrators and victims constitute an invaluable resource for future historians. It is hard to take issue with the IPN's broad objectives of disseminating knowledge about the nature of communist repression and preserving the memory of its victims.

Some criticisms levied against the IPN were a consequence of the poor quality and imprecision of legislation, as witnessed by the many findings of unconstitutionality in the judgments of the Constitutional Tribunal. Other criticisms stemmed from the ethos of the IPN itself. They included the uncritical acceptance of the security service files as the key source for the communist period. The IPN's publicity of its investigations and its effective rejection of the presumption of innocence, its determination to appeal every case that went against it, and its public condemnation of judicial findings brought hardship, loss of employment and permanent loss of reputation for the innocent as well as the guilty.

Few could have envisaged the evolution of the IPN as the effective instrument of a single political option. IPN officials endorsed the project to reveal past injustices and often criticized Constitutional Court judgments limiting their powers (e.g. IPN historians objected to the TK's requirement that collaboration must be conscious and substantive[77]).

However, PiS's project of 'historical politics' (*historia polityczna*) went beyond the direct concerns of transitional justice. PiS used the language of justice to redefine history as an instrument of state policy, intended not only to govern the writing of history but to shape the collective memory, inculcate patriotism and so mould national identity. The past must be revealed and its legacies conveyed to future generations. IPN historians embraced the notion of a monolithic view of the communist past as relentlessly repressive and its opponents as heroes, whose recognition would yield justice at last. This was a deeply ideological perspective that decried all attempts to present a more nuanced view of the old regime. As Jan Darasz noted, in Poland's culture wars 'history was weaponized'.[78]

As the Left declined as a political force, the composition of the Constitutional Tribunal also changed, giving the TK a more clearly right-wing profile and increasing its amenability to the arguments of the IPN. We shall see in Chapter 9 how PiS's success in gaining control of the Tribunal brought the TK in line with the IPN's perspective, with all new justices expressing open sympathy for PiS's broad political objectives.

Attempts by PiS to extend its control over the judiciary risked a judicial vindictiveness to match the political vindictiveness shown to its political opponents. Still, the IPN did not function as a monopoly. Its attitudes, policies, judgments and interpretations were subject to constant challenge in a (still) pluralist society. With the effective opening of the files in 2010, there was no barrier to access by independent historians and journalists. The rewriting of history – including the recent history of Poland's exit from communism – could not easily be controlled from above. Neither can collective consciousness and identity be shaped from above.

# The Constitutional Tribunal

The Constitutional Tribunal (*Trybunał Konstytucyjny*, TK) enjoyed an uneventful first few years as a key institution of the democratic state, enjoying high prestige and a reputation for competence. With the new Constitution of 1997 the TK gained some powers and continued its practice of creative adjudication.

This chapter puts transitional justice into its structural context. It reviews the functions of the TK and their evolution, from both the legal and political perspectives. As the adjudicator of legal issues and the guardian of the rule of law the Constitutional Tribunal was a critical institution in all areas of transitional justice. In the early years the Tribunal operated with a high degree of consensus. Then, for a brief period after 2005 and again from 2015 the governments of Law and Justice (PiS) attacked the nature and status of the TK, culminating in a full-blown constitutional crisis. This chapter shows how up to 2015 the Tribunal was a key partner in all areas of transitional justice. After 2015 it was a willing instrument of the ruling party.

## The early years 1989–97

The origins of the Constitutional Tribunal lie with General Wojciech Jaruzelski's reform programme of the 1980s, also including the Civil Rights' Ombudsman and the Tribunal of State. The 1985 law on the TK established an independent constitutional court providing judicial review, with a two-thirds majority *Sejm* override. The public remained unconvinced by Jaruzelski's reform efforts, seeing the Court (as all other state institutions) as a pawn of the Communist Party. In its first few years the TK did not adjudicate matters of significance. Nevertheless, it found certain regulations unconstitutional, to the consternation of the government.[1]

After 1989 the TK took its place within the new democratic architecture of the state. Although there was general agreement that the Tribunal should be strengthened, early modifications were piecemeal.[2] The Tribunal acquired the new power to issue resolutions embodying binding interpretations of law,[3] while the president could now seek the Tribunal's view before signing a new law. However, the *Sejm* retained the power to reject TK judgments. Nor did the TK have the power to consider disputes between competing state organs or to assess the conformity of domestic law with international treaties. It could not consider laws passed before 1982 or laws which had not been questioned for five years. (All these restrictions disappeared with the new Constitution, which came into force in October 1997.)

Between 1985 and 1997 twelve justices sat on the Constitutional Tribunal. Appointment remained with the *Sejm*. In the first Tribunal six judges were appointed for four years and six for eight, so that the composition was altered by 50 per cent after four years. Thus, in December 1989 six justices were due to be replaced, including the chair. By December 1993 no justice remained from the original Tribunal of 1985. In December 1997 those appointed in 1989 completed their terms.

In November 1989 the 'contract *Sejm*' elected six new justices. All but one were academics of professorial status. Four were closely associated with Solidarity. Andrzej Zoll had participated in the Round Table on the Solidarity side. Five were joint cross-party nominees, with two nominated by the communist party. Candidates were voted upon individually, not *en bloc* as was previous (and later) practice. The five joint candidates came top of the vote, albeit with minimal parliamentary debate (this lack of scrutiny was criticized and later provided the basis for reform proposals aimed at greater transparency).[4] Although most deputies voted a 'straight' ticket, about eighty (of 460) split their votes between the two major camps, including some communist deputies who voted for Janina Zakrzewska, the only woman.[5]

This court – evenly divided between new and inherited appointees – remained in place until after the 1993 elections, when the terms of the original six justices expired. Despite the different backgrounds of its members, the TK reflected a strong consensus and a willingness to deal with controversial issues.[6] Most judgments were unanimous. This was also true of the early verdicts in the sphere of transitional justice. All justices confirmed the narrowness of the remit of the abolition law in 1990, expunging sentences for offences committed during strikes and protests between 1980 and 1989 but excluding acts of brutality. Similarly, all rejected the concept of 'Stalinist crimes' in the 1991 law on the IPN as imprecise and incompatible with the principle of the 'definability' of a prohibited act. That year the TK also invalidated the law permitting the removal of judges 'who had compromised judicial independence': it was too broad, and the threat of 'extraordinary dismissal' could be used to pressure judges facing politically unpopular decisions (the judges dismissed were not reinstated, however). In June 1992 the Constitutional Tribunal vindicated critics of the 'exceptionally obscure' lustration resolution, declaring it incompatible with the Constitution's commitment to democratic principles and human rights. Only one judge dissented; he argued that the TK had exceeded its powers.

The 1993 elections gave the new SLD–PSL government control of the *Sejm* and, effectively, of recruitment to the Tribunal. During the period of SLD government (1993–7) the Court was roughly evenly balanced: five of the twelve justices had links to the SLD and five to the Solidarity opposition. No contentious issues emerged in the sphere of transitional justice. There was no dissent in 1994, when the TK argued that the combatants' law could not exclude communist functionaries who had worked in sections of the security apparatus not engaged in repression (none of the presiding judges had links to the communist party).

Up to the passage of the new Constitution in 1997 the TK built up a body of case law and binding interpretations. Lech Garlicki, a justice from 1993 to 2000 who subsequently served on the European Court of Human Rights, looked back positively on the first years: the TK established a rich body of judgment, 'filling many gaps and clarifying doubts arising from the absence of a modern constitution', and it gained considerable authority among both political elites and the legal profession.[7]

## The TK after the new Constitution

The Constitution of 1997, promulgated under the SLD government on the basis of wide parliamentary consensus and a popular referendum, nevertheless remained controversial for some time. The Solidarity trade union and many of the small right-wing parties excluded from the 1993–7 *Sejm* continued to oppose it. However, there was widespread support for the strengthening of the Constitutional Tribunal in the new Constitution and in the new law on the Constitutional Tribunal of September 1997. The size of the TK was increased to fifteen, with a tenure of nine years. The Tribunal was now the final arbiter of the constitutionality of law and the conformity of domestic law with international treaties, with no override by the *Sejm*. All courts could now submit questions to the TK regarding the constitutionality of a law or treaty, while individual citizens could submit a 'constitutional complaint'. The TK could rule on conflicts between organs of state of central and local government.

The area of 'preventive control' was also made more precise in cases where the TK decided – at the request of the president – that certain provisions of a law passed by parliament but not yet signed by the president were unconstitutional. Now the president could sign such a law into force minus the unconstitutional provisions, so long as these were not 'inextricably linked to the law in its entirety'. The TK continued the practice of issuing 'interpretive judgments' specifying that a certain statutory provision was constitutional only if given a specific interpretation.

### 1997–2001

The SLD lost power just before the new Constitution came into effect. Although it could have nominated candidates for the extra places on the Tribunal, it did not do so, leaving the matter until after parliamentary elections. When Solidarity Election Action (*Akcja Wyborcza Solidarność,* AWS) won the elections in September 1997, the increased size of the Tribunal provided the opportunity for the AWS–UW government to make six appointments. This rose to seven after SLD nominee Błażej Wierzbowski resigned following allegations of collaboration with the security services, and to eight a year later when Wojciech Sokolewicz resigned after similar allegations.[8]

Six of the eight new justices were AWS nominees and two were supported by the UW. All had been engaged in the Solidarity opposition in the 1980s. The political balance of the Constitutional Tribunal appeared to shift to the right. Academic credentials were no longer essential, and more nominees had political experience. During the period of AWS–UW government from 1997 to 2001 nine justices had a Solidarity pedigree and four had been appointed by the left. Did this matter? Political parties appeared to believe so. Increasingly, judges were divided into 'theirs' and 'ours'. Yet these political differences were of little import until Law and Justice raised the issue high on its political agenda.

The TK itself stressed continuity in its report to the *Sejm* in 1998, noting that the new Constitution had maintained the wording adopted in 1989 to define the key elements of the new system: 'The Republic of Poland is a democratic state based on the rule of law and realising the principles of social justice.' Judgments reached previously on the basis of this clause would still apply: 'Some principles and rules which have functioned up to now … because they were deduced from the general clause on the democratic law-based state have now gained support in the explicit wording of the new Constitution. Other principles and rules … are derived, as previously, from the general content of the democratic law-based state.'[9] These included legal security, trust of the individual in the state and the law, the defence of existing entitlements, the prohibition against retroactivity, a suitable *vacatio legis*, and the principles of proportionality and equality before the law.[10]

The following year the 'Tribunal continued its previous line in judgments relating to the basic elements of the democratic state.'[11] It cited the lustration law as an example of a judgment based on the 'broad principles of democracy': the Tribunal accepted the general principle of lustration, but provisions for the resumption of lustration proceedings against an individual at any time were unacceptable, since creating a 'state of permanent uncertainty' for a lustrated person constituted an unconstitutional restriction of individual freedom.[12] In its subsequent reports the TK noted continuity in the 'understanding of many constitutional principles, the rights and freedoms of individuals, and the institutions serving their protection.'[13]

Despite an appointments' process resting largely on political considerations, it is difficult to argue the politicization of the Constitutional Tribunal throughout the first post-communist decade. Justices of the TK played a political role through their interpretation of law, but there were few cases of division along partisan lines. The continuing preponderance of academics as distinct from practitioners appeared to favour a legal culture based on pragmatism and the acceptance of a measure of judicial creativity. It is also the case that there were few cases involving considerations of transitional justice – often among the most contentious and politically charged.

### The SLD Government of 2001–5

After the SLD's convincing election victory in September 2001 the high level of agreement continued. The Tribunal was briefly dominated by ten judges nominated by the previous AWS coalition. As the terms of the 1993 appointees came to an end, SLD nominees replaced them. By 2003 the court included six SLD-nominated justices, six nominated by AWS and two by the Freedom Union.

In 2002 the TK invalidated several provisions of laws compensating the dispossessed from beyond the Bug River, though it did not endorse the principle of 'full compensation' for property left behind. Payments by the Polish authorities were a surrogate of the right to property, provided chiefly as 'an ancillary social benefit to assist in resettlement'. No justice dissented from this creative approach to property rights. However, both the European Court of Human Rights and the Constitutional Tribunal[14] criticized the government's response in the law of 2003. The new limits for compensation were discriminatory and arbitrary.

The Constitutional Tribunal (TK) returned to lustration with its judgment of March 2003 when it dealt with the issue of employment in the security services. The TK noted that publishing the fact that someone worked or served in the security services (Annex A of the lustration form) did not specify whether they had been part of the repressive apparatus. The second part of the lustration form should be published, clarifying the individual's function and the duration of service.

In May 2003 the TK again reviewed the issue of collaboration. The Court agreed that excluding the intelligence services violated the constitutional principles of the democratic law-based state, equality before the law and the right of citizens to gain information about persons holding public office. Three of the four dissenters (all of whom had been nominated by the SLD) argued that since the lustration law had been deemed constitutional despite considerable imprecision, a law lessening its inherently repressive nature must also be constitutional, even if imprecise. The fourth, TK Chair Bohdan Zdziennicki touched the implicit ideological divide between those who saw the intelligence services as defending the security and integrity of the state, and those for whom the state itself was immoral and illegitimate. He argued that the law may not determine historical truth by imposing a 'single assessment of the past' with specific legal consequences. Whatever one's historical judgment, cooperating with intelligence services was a legal activity not criminalized in international law and thus not a reason for discrimination.

Less controversially that month the Tribunal also returned to the combatants' law, when it found that time limits for filing for combatant status denied equality before the law and violated citizens' confidence in the state. Definitions of combatants and repressed persons, however, were a matter solely for parliament.

## The Tribunal in 2005–7

The new parliament of 2005 was troubled and short-lived, without a stable majority. Law and Justice (PiS) was the largest party, and Lech Kaczyński won the presidency that year. The first minority PiS government was succeeded by a volatile coalition of PiS, the League of Polish Families (LPR) and Self-Defence (SO). This *Sejm* had the opportunity to appoint six new justices. These appointments marked the beginning of controversies that would erupt in the full-blown crisis of 2016. For the first time the press raised questions about the past activities, questionable calibre, partisan attitudes and lack of higher qualifications of certain candidates for the TK.

The *Sejm*'s Justice Commission questioned candidates, and there was a semblance of parliamentary debate.[15] Though it rarely prevented the coalition parties from securing their nominations, negative publicity was not without effect. Jerzy Majewski, nominated by Self-Defence, was the very first candidate not assessed positively by the Justice Commission. After press reports of alcoholism, unpaid damages and pending cases in the courts,[16] Self-Defence withdrew his nomination. The SLD withdrew Bogusław Moraczewski's candidacy after revelations that he had sentenced Solidarity activists during martial law.[17] PiS's nominee Bogdan Szlachta was the first candidate of a governing party to be rejected by the *Sejm*, ostensibly because his field was humanities, not law.

The leader of the League of Polish Families Marek Kotlinowski was also contentious.[18] As the LPR's candidate, he was elected to the TK despite misgivings about his lack of experience. Self-Defence candidate Lidia Bagińska was elected, but after strong criticism surrounding her business dealings,[19] she resigned before taking her place on the Tribunal. The other new members were PiS nominees but more in the previous mould: Professor Teresa Liszcz, Senator and three times deputy, had been associated with Jarosław Kaczvński since the early 1990s; Professor Zbigniew Cieślak was undersecretary in the Interior Ministry in 1997–8 and a member of the team negotiating Poland's accession to the European Union; Professor Maria Gintowt-Jankowicz was an expert in the reform of public administration; and Wojciech Hermeliński, a lawyer also associated with Kaczyński since 1990, was a member of the Helsinki Committee (2004–6). Following Bagińska's resignation Professor Mieczysław Granat, another LPR nominee, joined the Tribunal in April 2007.

Several important judgments issued from the TK in this period, many not to the liking of PiS and Jarosław Kaczyński. At the beginning of the new parliament the Constitutional Tribunal pronounced on the question of access to the files. In its judgment of October 2005 on the statute of the IPN the TK found that restricting file access to those 'harmed' (*pokrzywdzony*) breached the constitutional provision that persons must have the right of access to documents concerning them.

PiS's attacks on the Tribunal accelerated throughout 2006, escalating from January, when the TK declared unconstitutional the ban on a Pride march by Warsaw's president, Kaczyński's twin brother Lech.[20] Jarosław remarked, 'We cannot introduce certain laws because they would not get through the Constitutional Tribunal. The TK represents a specific political line – but that will change when its membership changes.'[21] He explained that

> in Poland a specific way of interpreting the law effectively means that nothing is permitted ....This *imposybilizm* ... is functional for the elite networks (*układ*) we want to change ....A huge number of specialists in public law are people closely – I emphasise closely – connected to the former system ... People who were members of the PZPR up to 1989 have their chosen pupils. This situation is an element of the petrification of the *układ*. We don't agree to that.[22]

In the *Sejm* Kaczyński, now prime minister, referred to the Tribunal's history of 'cowardice' and 'revolting opportunism'.[23] The following month the TK struck down the new media law, which had effectively suspended the National Broadcasting Council, a constitutional organ.[24] Kaczyński said that it was 'erroneous' to view the Tribunal as a 'collection of wise men' beyond criticism.[25] He continued to blame TK decisions on judges associated with the SLD.[26] President Lech Kaczyński (himself a lawyer) entered the fray, mooting a constitutional change that would challenge the separation of powers: 'Should a group of a dozen or so generally eminent lawyers have such enormous power? ....I find this highly doubtful.'[27]

The-then Chair of the Tribunal Marek Safjan called Kaczyński's speech to the *Sejm* 'astonishing' and a slanderous 'violation of the fundamental canons of culture and good behaviour'.[28] Successive TK decisions exacerbated relations with the government. The most important public confrontation concerned the Lustration Law in May 2007.[29]

The subject of this complex judgment, with nine out of eleven judges issuing dissenting opinions, had already been controversial. We saw how President Kaczyński submitted fundamental amendments even before the law came into force rather than referring the law to the TK. Former Chair of the Tribunal Andrzej Zoll observed that 'PiS's lustration bill was apparently written by those who have neither experience nor any concept of how lustration works'.[30] On 10 May Chair Jerzy Stępień removed Justices Grzybowski and Jamróz from the case after a PiS deputy claimed they had been 'operational contacts' of the security services (the IPN maintained that Jamróz had no case to answer, while Grzybowski was finally exonerated in 2013). Stępień too had earlier condemned the 'theatricalisation' of politics and suggested that attacks on the Tribunal represented a lowering of standards of public life.[31] Perhaps by excluding the two judges he hoped to strengthen the integrity of the TK in the eyes of the public.

Eleven justices assessed seventy-seven elements of the new law and set aside thirty-nine as unconstitutional. They noted inter alia that the provision on 'collaboration' did not incorporate previous TK judgments, namely it did not specify that collaboration be 'conscious and genuine'. PiS politicians reacted furiously. 'Instead of controlling the law, the Tribunal is increasingly creating it', said one senator.[32] PiS Deputy Artur Wołek described the TK as 'like a handcuff, an undemocratic institution controlling two democratic bodies, the *Sejm* and the *Senate*'.[33] The Ombudsman, PiS's ally Janusz Kochanowski, called the judgment 'one of the most inconsistent and internally contradictory in the history of the TK'.[34] In this context PiS's proposals for changes to the law on the Tribunal were not unexpected. They altered the tenure of the chair; increased the size of the Tribunal to eleven, all of whom would sit in each case; and required cases to be adjudicated in the order in which they were received (these proposals returned with PiS's return to office in 2016).[35]

Yet despite all, the TK maintained its high degree of consensus. It should be noted that a large number of dissenters, as in the lustration decision, did not indicate disagreement with the broad findings of the Tribunal. No justice wanted to uphold the law, but there were many disagreements on technical legal points. Moreover, of forty-seven judgments declaring legal provisions unconstitutional in 2006, only three saw dissenting opinions. It was the specific findings of the unconstitutionality of the lustration law (nine dissenting opinions) and the law relating to judicial immunity (six dissenters) that saw the most divided judegments.

In 2007 the TK rejected (among others) the requirement of the new law on the courts that the decision to waive a judge's immunity should be taken by a disciplinary court within twenty-four hours.[36] This case marked the beginning of a series of judgments reached without the agreement of (most) PiS nominees. Five of the six dissenters had been nominated by the PiS coalition after 2006: Cieślak, Granat, Liszcz, Hermeliński and Gintowt-Jankowicz. They were joined by Niemcewicz, nominated earlier by the Freedom Union – but not by Jerzy Stępień nor Marek Kotlinowski. Their radically dissenting judgments reflected different political and philosophical views, but they were effectively limited to cases involving transitional justice and the communist past. The proportion of cases in which dissent was registered remained low. This was to change markedly over subsequent years.

## The TK under Civic Platform 2008–15

Following the victory of Civic Platform (PO) in the 2007 elections and its re-election in 2011, political tensions surrounding the Constitutional Tribunal subsided. This was the first prolonged period of government stability since 1989. After President Kaczyński perished in the plane crash at Smoleńsk in 2010, Civic Platform also gained the presidency with the election of Bronisław Komorowski in July. By the end of PO's tenure in 2015, the picture looked rather different. Komorowski unexpectedly lost the presidential election of May 2015 to PiS's candidate Andrzej Duda. At the same time PO introduced changes to the TK that set the stage for the constitutional drama of 2016.

With a secure governing majority, PO had numerous opportunities to affect the composition of the TK. Its candidate Professor Andrzej Rzepliński joined the Tribunal in December 2007 (he became chair in 2010). As successive judges saw out their terms, PO replaced them with its own nominees. By the middle of 2011 only one remaining judge had been nominated by the SLD, six by PiS or its coalition partners and six by Civic Platform.

Important judgments in the sphere of transitional justice continued in this period. In 2008 the Tribunal accepted extensions to the statute of limitations. In 2009 it accepted limiting heirs' right to compensation as 'unusual but reasonable'. In 2011 it found that the compensation for families for the death of a 'repressed person' was too narrow, excluding compensation for damage to health. The Court struck down proposed limits on compensation for repression and differential treatment of those repressed before or after 1956. Although the Tribunal was reluctant to intervene in the issue of Church restitution, in 2011 it paved the way for *gminas* affected by the decisions of the Property Commission to gain compensation. In 2012 it upheld residency requirements for compensation for acts committed by Soviet authorities on former Polish territory. The most important verdict during this period was undoubtedly that declaring martial law illegal in March 2011. All thirteen justices concurred in this complex and (in my view) deeply unconvincing judgment (see Chapter 4). Above all, the Court ignored its own strictures, failing to apply the prohibition on retroactivity to its own deliberations. Its historical analysis was simplistic and unnecessary.

It was the new law on the Constitutional Tribunal of June 2015[37] that proved the first shot in the battle for control of the Constitutional Court. Prepared on the initiative of a working group which included former and current justices of the Tribunal and proposed by President Komorowski, it aimed to improve the efficiency and quality of the TK. PiS spokespersons queried a number of provisions and questioned the increase in the TK's powers. They categorized the TK's right to issue interpretive judgements and to bridge legal lacunae as unconstitutional 'para-legislative functions'.[38]

PiS's hostility to the Constitutional Tribunal had grown steadily. Kaczyński roundly condemned the TK's judgment in April 2015, when it concluded (Granat dissenting) that judges in lustration proceedings were entitled to the constitutional guarantees of judicial immunity.[39]

Meanwhile the judicial consensus had been eroding. The share of verdicts which were not unanimous increased, reaching a high of one-third in 2012.[40] The number of dissenting opinions per case also rose. PiS's appointments Teresa Liszcz and Wojciech Hermeliński were most at odds with their colleagues. Between 2008 and 2015 Liszcz dissented fifty-five times and Hermeliński forty-four times. By contrast, Andrzej Rzepliński was in the minority ten times. Those justices nominated by the PiS coalition – Liszcz, Hermeliński, Kotlinowski, Cieślak, Granat and Gintowt-Jankowicz – displayed greater propensity to dissent than did other judges of the TK.[41]

We should not imply that only judges from 'the right-wing bloc' voted together in dissent. In 2010 the five putative SLD-oriented judges issued dissenting opinions, along with Stanisław Biernat, in another case involving judicial immunity.[42] Interestingly, their dissent was procedural rather than substantive; all six rejected TK jurisdiction in a case involving the respective roles of the TK and the Supreme Court. That same year the Constitutional Tribunal upheld the 'deubekisation law' reducing pensions for former functionaries who had functioned in the 'totalitarian system' as 'political police'. The TK argued that although the reduction of pensions was considerable, it fell within the scope of legislative freedom. The law did not aim to deprive representatives of the former regime of the social minimum 'nor to humiliate them'.[43] The same five dissenting justices viewed the law as variously violating the principle of trust in the state or a retributive application of collective guilt. Ewa Łętowska noted that the preamble, laying out the motivation of the law, was largely incompatible with its content; moreover, an 'Ubek' was defined by place of work, not its nature – thus embracing cleaners, drivers and others unconnected with repression.

## Civic Platform's court-packing efforts

It was, however, a clause in the 'Komorowski law' of June 2015 that triggered a tsunami of consequences for the Tribunal and ultimately for democracy itself. This provided that when the term of a Tribunal judge was due to expire in 2015, the deadline for nominations was thirty days after the law came into force. Officially, Civic Platform feared that because parliamentary elections were close, it was possible that almost one-third of judges would complete their term between the end of the current parliamentary session and the start of the new, creating a 'blockage' which would be deepened if the new *Sejm*'s preoccupations with government formation and coalition building delayed the choice of judges.[44]

Making new appointments to the Tribunal might give Civic Platform greater opportunity to influence it; it would certainly deprive PiS, expected to win the election, of such opportunity. Despite criticism of the amendment to elect all five judges together,[45] at its last session on 8 October 2015 the *Sejm* chose five new judges. Three would replace those whose terms ended on 6 and 7 November: Roman Hauser, Krzysztof Ślebzak and Andrzej Jakubecki; and – the disputed element – two would replace those whose terms were due to end in December. President Duda refused to receive the oath of office from all five.

## Law and Justice in the ascendant

Law and Justice (PiS) won in October 2015, gaining an absolute majority of seats in both houses and forming the first single-party government since 1989. For the first time there was no left-wing presence in the *Sejm*, as the United Left, embracing the SLD, failed to cross the electoral threshold. Two new parties entered parliament, the right-wing Kukiz'15, a potential ally for PiS, and the liberal-minded Modern Party (*Nowoczesna*) of Ryszard Petru. Jarosław Kaczyński, remaining behind the scenes, chose Beata Szydło as prime minister.

PiS used a variety of methods to gain control of the Constitutional Tribunal, many of them blatantly unconstitutional.[46] Its secure parliamentary majority also gave it the capacity to revise laws again and again – as it did with the law on the TK. On 19 November 2015, the new *Sejm* amended the law on the tribunal.[47] The draft bill had been submitted to the *Sejm* three days earlier. It was signed by the president on the day after its acceptance by the Senate. The law introduced a three-year term of office for the chair of the Tribunal and terminated the tenure of the incumbent, Andrzej Rzepliński. It stipulated that a justice's term of office would start not with his/her election but with taking the oath before the president. Challenges to the law came from deputies, the Ombudsman, judges and the chief justice of the Supreme Court.

On 30 November the Constitutional Tribunal took 'preventive measures', requesting the *Sejm* to abstain from electing new judges until its verdict was delivered. Notwithstanding, the *Sejm* rescinded the elections held by its predecessor and elected five judges on 2 December based on provisions of the November law which was due to enter into force on 4 December. The president accepted the oaths of four of these judges on 3 December at 1.30 am (and the fifth on 8 December). Rzepliński, chair of the TK, refused to admit to judgment the three judges, Henryk Cioch, Lech Morawski and Mariusz Muszyński, elected to replace those three already legitimately elected by the previous *Sejm*. This was the start of full-blown crisis and the beginning of the end of the TK's role as guardian of the rule of law.

The TK found that the procedure governing the election of three judges with terms from 7 November was constitutional but that for the two whose term expired in December was not. The Tribunal also considered the resolutions invalidating the election of TK justices by the previous *Sejm*. The *Sejm* could not terminate a judge's appointment and nor could the president do so – failing to administer the oath did not terminate a judge's appointment.[48] The Tribunal requested the president not to accept the oaths of the five judges elected on 2 December (he had already done so).

This judgment meant that three of the five judges elected by the new *Sejm* were illegitimate replacements for those whose terms had expired on 6 November. The previous *Sejm*'s election of Hauser, Ślebzak and Jakubecki must stand. However, Piotr Pszczółkowski, a sitting PiS deputy elected on 2 December, was the legitimate replacement for Zygmunt Cieślak, whose term expired then, while on 8 December

Julia Przyłębska could replace Teresa Liszcz, whose term expired on that day. The prime minister refused to publish the judgment in the *Journal of Laws* because of its 'legal flaws' (the Constitution requires the prime minister to publish TK judgments in the *Journal of Laws*).

On 9 December the Tribunal found the provision regarding re-election of the TK's chair in violation of the principle of judicial independence. Indeed, the law could not regulate the terms of the chair and deputy chair, since these positions did not have terms of office.[49] The requirement that a justice take the oath before the president within thirty days of election constituted interference in the *Sejm*'s exclusive constitutional competence. Moreover, providing that a TK justice's term begins when the oath is taken also violated the principle of the irremovability of judges and the independence of the judiciary. Furthermore, it was the president's duty to administer the oath of an elected judge without delay. The judgment reaffirmed the principle that the filling of positions on the TK should occur in the 'linked' session of the *Sejm*.

Two weeks later on 22 December the law was revised again.[50] This law provided that in virtually all cases the TK must sit *en banc* (a quorum was now thirteen justices instead of nine), deal with cases in order of their submission (not in order of importance) and reach its verdicts with a two-thirds majority (no longer a simple majority). The General Assembly of the TK would prepare a request to the *Sejm* to end a judge's term 'in particularly egregious cases'. The president or the minister of justice could initiate disciplinary proceedings against a judge. There was no *vacatio legis*; the law came into force immediately. The TK reviewed it on 9 March 2016.

In January the TK had dismissed the complaint lodged against the *Sejm*'s resolutions on the election of five new judges, because resolutions did not fall within its jurisdiction.[51] The Tribunal's Chair Andrzej Rzepliński admitted to judgment Pszczółkowski and Przyłębska, but not the three PiS nominees who had been elected to fill the places of the legitimate PO-nominated justices. Cioch, Morawski and Muszyński were assigned offices and put on the payroll but not included on judging panels (Morawski died 12 July 2017, Cioch died 20 December 2017). These three were known as the 'doubles' or 'quasi-judges'[52] or 'anti-judges'.[53] President Duda still refused to swear in the three legitimate judges.

The Tribunal decided that because the December law concerned its own functioning, it would not apply it, even though it was already in force (lacking a *vacatio legis*). It would apply the Constitution directly. Indeed, if the Tribunal were to apply the new law, it would be unable to deliberate; with only twelve sitting judges it could not reach the now-required quorum of thirteen. The two newly elected judges dissented on the grounds that the amendments were in force and so had to be applied.

On 7 March the procurator advised the TK that judgments with 'essential flaws' or arising from an 'improperly constituted panel' would not be published until the faults had been rectified.[54] On 9 March the TK, with Przyłębska and Pszczółkowski dissenting, found the entire act unconstitutional because of numerous violations of legislative procedures in its enactment.[55] Most of the new provisions were also unconstitutional, violating the separation of powers, judicial independence and the longstanding convention of *vacatio legis*. The law would make the TK dysfunctional and deprive it of the ability to respond to 'situations of crisis'. The government refused to publish this judgment: because the TK had 'not followed the procedures specified' in the law, the decision was merely the 'view of certain justices'.

The Council of Europe's Venice Commission broadly endorsed the Tribunal's analysis, finding problematic new rules on the chronological sequence of judgment, the two-thirds quorum, the election of judges to the TK, the new disciplinary proceedings against judges and the role of the *Sejm* in removing judges. These provisions 'would have endangered not only the rule of law, but also the functioning of the democratic system'. It criticized the president for not receiving the oath of the 'October judges', the *Sejm* for the undue haste of the legislative process and the government for not publishing the TK's judgments.[56] Up to 27 May seven further judgments remained unpublished in the *Journal of Laws*.

## The law on the Constitutional Tribunal of July 2016

In April a stormy session of the *Sejm* elected Zbigniew Jędrzejewski to replace outgoing justice Granat.[57] Jarosław Kaczyński announced that he would 'unblock' the TK, which was 'making a mockery of the law' and was 'paralysed by the actions of its chair Andrzej Rzepliński'.[58] The Council of Europe asked the Venice Commission whether a new draft bill accommodated the Opinion of March 2016. On 15 July the *Sejm*'s own 'committee of experts' reported. The law was enacted on 22 July.[59]

The new law responded implicitly to some elements of the VC's first Opinion. It dropped the initiation of disciplinary proceedings by the president or the justice minister and the dismissal of justices by the *Sejm* at the request of the TK's General Assembly. The president would now choose the Tribunal's chair from among three, not two, candidates presented by the General Assembly. However, PiS also relied on the 'Expert Group', which criticized the VC for its philosophical 'assumption of the supremacy of the Constitution over the will of the people' [*sic*] and for its specific conclusions. The TK should have adjudicated on the basis of the law in force (of 22 December) because *vacatio legis* is not a 'constitutional principle'; there would have been a quorum but for the illegitimate refusal of the chair to admit the December judges to judgment; the TK was acting inappropriately as an element of the legislative process.

The expert group argued that the VC had made serious errors, 'ignoring or marginalising the deep cultural, political and historic sources of the problems of the Tribunal'. Its references to European standards were 'paternalistic and condescending'. While the VC regarded the participation of TK judges as experts in the original preparation of the 'Komorowski law' of June 2015 as sensible and proper, the expert group argued that 'an expert must be neutral and may not be personally involved' (a detailed elaboration of the role of TK judges in the drafting process formed a significant part of its report).[60]

Further condemnation of the VC came from Mariusz Muszyński, one of the judges not admitted to judgment and a member of the VC (not contributing to this Opinion). Muszyński agreed that the Opinion was 'rife with scandalous errors, unjustified simplifications and manipulation'. It was illegal because the VC had exceeded its brief, preparing an 'evaluation of the systemic functioning of the Constitutional Tribunal'.[61] It perpetrated 'preposterous nonsense', like claiming that the TK had confirmed the validity of the election of the three judges in October 2015: as a court of law, not of fact, the TK lacked the competence to assess the election of judges.

This criticism is wrong-headed. It was clear that the TK's judgment legitimized the election of the three judges whose term was due to expire, but not the two elected to replace those whose term ended in December. The TK found Article 137, changing the timing of the election of judges, unconstitutional in regard to the replacement of judges whose terms did not end on 6 November 2015 but constitutional 'in so far as it affects the judges whose term ended on 6 November'. The judgment concerned the constitutionality of Article 137, not the election of judges. In August 2016 the TK reiterated that its judgments of December 2015 'unambiguously mean that the three judges elected by the VII *Sejm* were properly elected'.

The law of 22 July also provided that the full bench would review complex cases and laws concerning the TK itself. At least eleven members would constitute a full bench (more than the nine in the June 2015 law, fewer than the thirteen stipulated in December). Judgments should be passed by a simple majority, but if a case were reviewed *en banc*, a group of four judges could object, postponing judgment for up to six months. Cases would be reviewed chronologically except for laws on the Constitutional Tribunal and laws questioned by the president before signing. The chair could also decide that cases necessary to protect civil rights, national security or the constitutional order be resolved out of order. The law also specified new procedures for electing the chair and deputy chair.

Within the two-week *vacatio legis* the TK heard submissions challenging the law. Its verdict of 11 August 2016 found nine provisions unconstitutional – with the three most recently appointed judges dissenting.[62] The judgment was (again) based on the principle of the separation of powers, the independence of judges, and the 'integrity and efficiency of the workings of public institutions'. The TK found *inter alia* that the requirement that a judge receiving the oath from the president must be admitted to judgment constituted unwarranted interference in the workings of the Tribunal. Requiring a full bench if three judges demanded it was also an unconstitutional interference in the affairs of the TK and a departure from the practice of requiring a full bench only in the most complex cases. Specifying the order in which cases were heard was a further breach of the separation of powers. Making hearings dependent on the presence of the Procurator General was unacceptable because non-attendance could mean indefinite delay. Not publishing the TK's judgments was not an option provided in the Constitution.

The European Union was becoming increasingly concerned, but the Polish government ignored the Commission's criticisms (see Chapter 10). The prime minister refused to publish this judgment in the *Journal of Laws* because the Tribunal did not apply the law of 22 December, which it had found unconstitutional in its (unpublished) judgment of 9 March 2016. Unusually, the newest judge, Zbigniew Jędrychowski, criticized the Tribunal's Chair by name, claiming that Rzepliński's 'negative approach' to the law created 'doubts as to whether an objective assessment was possible ....and undermined the independence of the Tribunal'.

When the new law came into force on 16 August, the government published twenty-one so-called illegally adopted judgments of the Tribunal pursuant to the new law – but not the judgments of 9 March or 11 August 2016. When the Venice Commission adopted its second Opinion, the Polish government declined to send a representative.

The Venice Commission did not alter its view. It found the Tribunal's arguments 'convincing'.[63] In particular, the legal force of a court judgment 'cannot be dependent on whether or not that decision is published by an actor other than the Court. Such control … would egregiously violate the independence of the court and the rule of law. In matters concerning the Constitutional Tribunal, this is a challenge to its authority as the final arbiter on constitutional issues'. Moreover, the provision declaring all rulings since 9 March 2015 to be in breach of the Law on the Tribunal could not stand. 'Declaring judgments of a Constitutional Court "illegal" through legislation contradicts … the Constitution.'

The Venice Commission regarded the government's defence as feeble. The government had not explained the legal basis of its actions. The Opinion concluded that neither the executive nor the legislature 'may pick and choose which judgments of a court are to be published'. The government had also failed to resolve the issue of the appointment of judges. Full respect of the Tribunal's judgments would have resulted in the integration of the October judges into the Tribunal. Yet in April 2016 the vacancy was not used to administer the oath to one of them but to elect a new candidate, from whom President Duda accepted the oath. The law of 22 July did not provide 'a solution in line with the principle of the rule of law'.

The government maintained that the VC had repeated previous errors; it tried to exert pressure on the government 'to affirm the illegal actions taken by the Constitutional Tribunal' [*sic*]. The Opinion was one-sided and riddled with errors. It exceeded its terms of reference. It showed that the experts who drafted it supported the opposition.[64] This obdurate response put paid to any chance of a reasonable outcome.

The battle over the Constitutional Tribunal continued. When a group of deputies challenged the new procedures for electing the chair of the Tribunal, Jędrychowski and Przyłębska boycotted the proceedings, Pszczółkowski was ill, and neither the Procurator General nor a representative of the *Sejm* attended. The chair ruled that in order for the TK to carry out its essential functions, the judgment would be heard by a panel of five judges regardless of the absence of the Procurator and the *Sejm*'s representative.[65]

According to the new procedure, the General Assembly (GA), made up of all justices of the Tribunal (with a quorum of ten), would choose three candidates each for chair and deputy chair to submit to the final choice of the president of Poland. Each judge had one vote for each position and the top three would go forward (previously there were two candidates, two votes per judge and successive rounds of voting to ensure majority support).

The TK found that the identification of three candidates was compatible with the Constitution, which empowers the lawgiver to regulate the 'organisation of the Constitutional Tribunal' and thus also its internal bodies, including the General Assembly. But the method of one-round voting might mean the GA could not fulfil its function of presenting candidates to the president. It could lead to a situation where (a) more than three candidates gained the same number of votes; (b) only two candidates gained the support of the judges; or (c) each judge voted for him/herself. Only candidates supported by a majority are 'candidates in the constitutional sense', since only they may be deemed 'supported by the General Assembly'. Therefore, the second sentence of Article 16 (7) – 'each judge participating in the election procedure has only one vote and may vote for a single candidate' – must be understood as not applying to a resolution identifying candidates to be submitted to the president.[66]

The matter of the Tribunal's chair was ever more pressing, as Rzepliński's term would expire on 19 December. When the GA convened on 8 November, Przyłębska and Jędrzejewski were absent again, and Pszczółkowski was still on sick leave. Rzepliński had not admitted the three 'December judges' to judgment. The nine judges present did not constitute the quorum established by the Law of 22 July. On 30 November Przyłębska, Pszczółkowski and Jędrzejewski informed the GA that they were ill. Given the statutory duty to present the president with candidates for chair of the TK, nine judges presented him with a resolution not 'of the General Assembly' but 'of the judges gathered for the General Assembly' submitting the candidacies of Marek Zubik, Stanisław Rymar and Piotr Tuleja.

That day the *Sejm* passed another law on the organization of the Constitutional Tribunal and another on the status of judges.[67] It established an age limit of seventy for judges of the TK and required them to make full financial disclosure. Restructuring the Tribunal meant that contracts with existing employees would cease on 31 December 2017. These laws invalidated the nomination of candidates adopted before the new law came into force – the 'October judges' – and provided that the General Assembly would comprise all judges who had taken the oath (so including the three 'December judges'). The GA would present all those securing at least five votes as candidates for chair of the TK to the president within a month of the day of vacancy with proceedings conducted by the newest judge of the TK (PiS had already announced the young Michał Warciński as its candidate for Rzepliński's vacancy). In order to avoid the risk of the 'old' judges rendering the process invalid, the quorum was suspended for the nomination meeting so long as two candidates were proposed and one secured at least five votes. The president would name the judge with the longest professional tenure as Acting Chair until a new one was elected. A very odd method of calculating tenure secured the role for Julia Przyłębska.

Former chairs of the TK – Andrzej Zoll, Marek Safjan, Jerzy Stępień and Bohdan Zdziennicki – urged the president to veto the bills under discussion in the *Sejm* and 'to accept the oath of office from the three constitutionally appointed judges (the October judges)'. They noted that 'actions aimed at undermining the role of the Constitutional Tribunal, lowering its authority in the eyes of society, and limiting or indeed paralysing its functioning – have resulted in a dramatic situation where the most fundamental mechanism for the protection of the rule of law will be annihilated'.[68]

President Duda signed the laws and duly appointed Julia Przyłębska as Acting Chair, despite protests that the Constitution did not recognize this position (Stanisław Biernat was the deputy chair). Przyłębska immediately recognized the disputed judges. With four hours' notice she convened the General Assembly, which nominated two judges including Przyłębska, whom President Duda duly confirmed as chair on

21 December. The protocol of the meeting, released by the Helsinki Foundation, raised serious doubts about the validity of the nomination process and thus the legitimacy of Przyłębska's appointment.[69] It showed that Przyłębska took the chair regardless of the dubious constitutionality of the post of Acting Chair, refused to summon Stanisław Rymar back from holiday to meet the requirement that all fifteen judges be present, rejected attempts to postpone the proceedings and held a vote of only six judges after the refusal of eight – Biernat, Kieres, Pszczółkowski, Pyziak-Szafnicka, Tuleja, Wronkowska-Jaśkiewicz, Wróbel and Zubik – to participate in an improperly constituted meeting (the 'old judges' plus Pszczółkowski, who severed his links with PiS). Moreover, there was no formal resolution (*uchwała*) submitting the nominees to the president.

In January 2017 Procurator General Zbigniew Ziobro requested the TK to analyse the constitutionality of the (previous) *Sejm*'s resolution electing Stanisław Rymar, Piotr Tuleja and Marek Zubik to the TK in 2010. Ziobro claimed that since they had not been elected 'individually' as the rules required, the three 'could not be regarded as judges'.[70] This was incorrect; each had received a different number of votes. However, the three were excluded from judgment while the case was pending (in practice until their terms expired in December 2019).

By the start of 2017 PiS had emerged victorious in its battle for the Tribunal. By 2019 PiS had nominated nine justices and three had been neutralized. After winning the 2019 election PiS could look forward to a Tribunal of members exclusively nominated by PiS. All nine had longstanding relations with PiS and had publicly declared themselves sympathetic to its aims. None were specialists in constitutional law, and all save Pszczółkowski proved compliant in PiS's attempts to control the TK. Przyłębska easily manipulated panels to bypass the 'old' judges. Even open discontent within the TK over her role[71] could not threaten PiS's ascendancy over the Tribunal, which became the dutiful servant of the executive.

# Conclusion

This chapter tells a sorry tale of the subversion of an institution conceived as a keystone of liberal democratic architecture. Like most of its European counterparts the Polish Constitutional Tribunal is charged with upholding the supremacy of the constitution, maintaining the rule of law, arbitrating jurisdictional conflicts, safeguarding minorities and protecting the citizen from the state. After 1989 the Tribunal gained in power and status, providing the legal stability, consensus and political independence needed to underpin the democracy-building project. For more than two decades justices of the Tribunal honed and applied a legal culture to become 'one of the most influential and successful European constitutional courts and living proof of 'the rule of law in action'.[72]

PiS's attack on the separation of powers, a basic principle of liberal constitutionalism, claimed the superior value of majoritarian democracy: since the majority reflected the will of the people, the representatives of the majority were not bound by constitutional limits.[73] However, it was not only the ruthless abuse of the powers of judicial appointment and the cavalier use of unconstitutional mechanisms that made possible the capture of the Constitutional Tribunal. It was also the ease with which PiS suborned its new appointees to the Tribunal to deny fundamental European and constitutional values, including judicial independence, the separation of powers and the rule of law itself.

# 10

# From transitional justice to social engineering

After Law and Justice returned to power in 2015 with a strong parliamentary majority, concerns for transitional justice were subsumed and subordinated to PiS's wider project of decommunization. Jarosław Kaczyński's view was that since PiS had won the election, it could effectively do as it pleased: the people (or the Nation) were sovereign. Winning again in 2019 merely confirmed that view.

PiS's electoral support increased in the European parliamentary elections of 2019, when it gained 45.4 per cent of the vote. In October PiS repeated this performance, with 43.6 per cent of the vote, retaining a majority of seats. PiS's majority was tempered by two factors. First was the ambition of members of several small parties on PiS's electoral lists like Zbigniew Ziobro's Solidarni and the new parliamentary presence of the far right, Korwin-Mikke's Confederation. Secondly, PiS failed to achieve overall control of the Senate. Neither of these factors were likely to impede PiS's plans for continuing 'reform' of the judiciary and the media (Senate agreement was necessary however to replace PiS's bugbear, Human Rights Ombudsman Adam Bodnar). Moreover, continuing pressure from the European Union (EU) and the forthcoming presidential election of 2020 could suggest a more cautious approach.

This chapter reviews the radical reforms of PiS's term in office 2015–19. In those years PiS continued to tinker with some elements of the classic transitional justice agenda. We have noted this in the chapters above. It was, however, concerned primarily with structural changes. The strategy pursued by the Law and Justice government after 2015 represented a multi-pronged attempt to provide a 'deep cleansing' of the existing system that would bring 'justice at last'. In this view the country was neither just nor democratic because the old networks continued to penetrate the structures of the state and its communications with society. The Constitution itself was 'a pure petrified post-communism' and the state structures were still 'a mutation of the communist apparatus'.[1]

Although lacking a constitutional majority, once PiS had control of the Constitutional Tribunal (see Chapter 9) Kaczyński now had the political capacity to carry out the multi-faceted programme of decommunization which he had advocated since the onset of the Polish transformation. It was necessary to change the structures because otherwise, according to Kaczyński's concept of 'impossibilism', serious reform was thwarted by the system of checks and balances and by the vested interests of liberal elites and foreigners intent on exploiting the country. PiS would also enable Poland 'to rise from its knees' in international relations, including relations with the EU.

The new PiS government introduced legislative and institutional changes, notably in the workings of the Constitutional Tribunal (TK) and the Institute of National Remembrance (IPN). Laws followed on the judiciary; criminal justice; the Human Rights Ombudsman; the procuracy; retirement provision for (*inter alia*) the police, security services, intelligence and counter-intelligence; and the 'decommunization of public space'. Drafts were often submitted by PiS deputies rather than the government, removing the need for public consultation, enabling rapid passage and a minimal *vacatio legis*. Retired TK justice Mirosław Wyrzykowski noted that 'although the constitution is still formally binding, in fact the constitutional order has been changed through ordinary legislation'.[2]

Control of the Constitutional Tribunal and judicial personnel altered the structures of government and removed some checks and balances derived from the classic separation of powers. PiS effectively colonized all state institutions: by 2019 it controlled the government, the presidency, Parliament, the public media, the constitutional court, the civil service and state-run companies. Only the Ombudsman remained out of reach. Challenges to the rule of law were not exclusive to Poland,[3] but in Poland they formed part of a wider package of political and social transformation. Despite pressure from the European Union, the EU proved a paper tiger. PiS's victory in 2019 gave a green light for further entrenching the project of social transformation.

## The Constitutional Tribunal

Kaczyński saw the Constitutional Tribunal as the greatest obstacle to change. It had been his *bête noir* since the coalition governments of 2005–7.[4] He echoed the sentiments of Deputy Kornel Morawiecki, who received a standing ovation when he said in the *Sejm*, 'The law is important, but it is not sacred. The good of the nation is above the law'.[5] We saw in Chapter 9 that after Julia Przyłębska's (dubious) instauration as chair of the Constitutional Tribunal, she admitted to judgment the disputed judges (or 'non-judges'), establishing a majority of PiS appointees after compelling the Deputy Chair of the TK, Stanisław Biernat, to take allegedly accrued holiday. She made several *ad hoc* modifications to the composition of ruling panels of judges or replaced rapporteurs to make sure that cases that were important to the government were adjudicated by certain judges and 'non-judges', most frequently Mariusz Muszyński. The rulings from 2016 that had been 'so bitterly opposed by the government' were removed from the Tribunal's website.[6]

Of the three individuals illegitimately elected by the *Sejm* in 2015, Lech Morawski and Henryk Cioch died in 2017. The third, Mariusz Muszyński, was subsequently appointed by President Duda to the post of Deputy Chair of the Tribunal. For many judges, lawyers and academics this appointment had no legal effect because only a legitimate justice of the Tribunal may be appointed vice chair, pursuant to the Constitution. The legitimacy of the two new individuals, Justyn Piskorski and Jarosław Wyrembak, elected to replace Cioch and Morawski was also questioned. These two were elected in addition to fifteen existing judges of the Tribunal, including the three judges properly elected by the *Sejm* of the previous term (Hauser, Ślebzak and Jakubecki) who had not taken the oath nor been admitted to judgment.

We reviewed the politicization of the Constitutional Tribunal in Chapter 9. All PiS-appointed judges had publicly declared themselves sympathetic to its aims. The late Lech Morawski was the most vocally political, long known as an ardent supporter of lustration[7] and a critic of the Constitutional Tribunal. In November 2016 at a seminar in Berlin Morawski declared that the TK was 'the defender of the richest and most influential in society' and that all elites were still dominated by the old *nomenklatura*.[8] At Oxford in the following May he noted that while the 'much criticised government' did not enjoy the support of the 'so-called enlightened elites', it was supported by the 'majority of ordinary people'. He called the government's reforms 'essential in a country riddled with all-embracing corruption', including the corruption of judges of the Supreme Court and the Constitutional Tribunal.[9]

The Tribunal reduced its activity, giving priority to cases filed by the governing majority.[10] Its rulings increasingly repeated the justifications of bills drafted by the government and the TK coordinated its actions closely with those of the government. Political scientist Jerzy Zajadło referred to 'the total degeneration of the Constitutional Tribunal'.[11] Because the composition of the Tribunal was disputed, some called into question all judgments taken since December 2016. This caused enormous confusion as some courts recognized the Tribunal's rulings but others did not.[12]

## Changes in the judiciary

The taming of the Constitutional Court opened the way to further changes in the judiciary. The minister of justice announced a series of proposals to 'refresh' the judiciary, restore its 'honesty and sense of service' and respond to public concerns. Ziobro had 'needed to wait until the problem of the Constitutional Tribunal was resolved'; otherwise, the Tribunal would have blocked the legislation, just as it had torpedoed earlier attempts.[13] His view was endorsed by right-wing academics. For example, Maria Los and Andrzej Zybertowicz, longstanding supporters of PiS, referred to the 'rule-of-law rhetoric and its glorification in public discourse' [*sic*] as a barrier to judicial reform. The lengthy time taken for trials suggested 'that the old networks ... (had) not lost their vitality'.[14] PiS's media campaign stressed the persistence of a communist ethos among judges, the lack of 'democratic control', and the malfunctioning and inefficiency of the judiciary. Since the media was the main source of views on the judiciary, it seemed to have an effect.[15] Tadeusz Koncewicz detected 'growing anti-judicial sentiment'.[16]

The newly malleable Constitutional Tribunal did not dissent from the government's position. Its vital judgment on the 2011 Law on the National Council of the Judiciary (*Krajowa Rada Sądownictwa*, KRS) agreed with Minister Ziobro that several provisions were unconstitutional; this paved the way for new legislation on the appointment, composition, tenure and functions of the KRS, which had hitherto played a key role in the appointment of judges.[17] Wojciech Sadurski called the decision a 'pseudo-judgment', issued by an unconstitutional panel (because two judges sat in the places of previously legitimately elected judges) and based on Ziobro's 'absurd' arguments.[18]

In June 2016 President Duda rejected ten of thirteen recommendations of the National Judicial Council (KRS), nine of which concerned promotions to appeal courts. The president did not justify his decision. In November the *Sejm* passed laws providing for the publication of judges' declarations of assets and criminal liability for their accuracy. It also extended the statute of limitations in disciplinary cases of judges from five to eight years and increased the period for inaugurating disciplinary proceedings against judges. Financial penalties were added to the list of punishments in disciplinary action.[19]

### The National Judicial Council

A series of key changes altered the rules governing the National Judicial Council (KRS), which selected judges and oversaw the operation of the courts. According to the Constitution the KRS is the guardian of the independence of the judiciary and the impartiality of judges. The Ministry of Justice first proposed that deputies would elect its judges from among candidates selected by the Marshal of the *Sejm*. A new Council would be formed and divided into two chambers, the 'political' and the 'judicial'. Both chambers would need to agree on a candidacy for judicial vacancy (Ziobro had halted the appointments process for 500 vacancies in November).

A wave of protests swept all major cities in July 2017[20] as the *Sejm* passed a law ending the terms of all members of the KRS. Thousands of Poles stood before courthouses with candles in their hands. The normally loyal President Duda gave 'public anxiety' as the reason for his veto and he offered a revised version: Groups of at least 200 citizens and groups of at least twenty-five judges could propose candidates; the *Sejm* would choose members of the KRS by a three-fifths majority. The KRS itself opposed these changes[21] and further protests followed. The *Sejm* passed the amended law on 8 December.[22] In the opinion of the Venice Commission, when taken in conjunction with other new legislation, the new arrangements for electing the KRS weakened the independence of the judiciary and risked the politicization of the appointments mechanism.[23]

Supreme Court President Małgorzata Gersdorf had resigned as chair of the KRS in March 2017 but in her role as head of the Supreme Court convened the KRS as required, although she saw the election of new members as 'a blatant and obvious violation of the legal order of the Republic'.[24] The parliamentary majority now enjoyed 'unmediated power of appointment to the body that appoints all Polish judges'.[25]

The overwhelming majority of Polish judges boycotted the appointments process – only eighteen candidates agreed to stand. Of the fifteen new members, nine were PiS nominees and six came from the right-wing Kukiz'15.[26] 'The meeting of 27 April 2018, when the new members assembled, would go down in history', argued Łukasz Bojarski, former member of the KRS.[27] This was the beginning of 'the direct destruction of the judicial system', said Ewa Siedlecka in *Polityka*.[28] Most new members of the KRS had links to Minister of Justice Ziobro. Their calibre was distinctly unimpressive. In September the General Council of the European Network of Councils for the Judiciary suspended the membership of the KRS because it no longer met the condition that institutions be independent of the executive and legislature.[29]

The 'old judges' of the TK continued to resist. In March 2019 seven justices wrote to Julia Przyłębska after a secret session of five judges had declared the constitutionality of the new KRS procedures. The seven demanded a reconsideration of the case by a full bench. They protested against Przyłębska's repeated failure to constitute panels by following alphabetical order as 'depriving the Tribunal of transparency and undermining its credibility'.[30] Przyłębska declared that TK judgments were final. In their Declaration of February 2020 twenty-two retired justices noted the 'profound decline in the significance and prestige of this constitutional organ and the practical impossibility of fulfilling the functions envisaged for it in the Constitution. Unfortunately, the widespread view that the Constitutional Tribunal has effectively been dismantled is correct'.[31]

## The tenure of Supreme Court judges

After the TK and the KRS came the turn of the Supreme Court. PiS clashed with Małgorzata Gersdorf after the Warsaw Court of Appeal asked the Supreme Court to rule on the validity of Julia Przyłębska's appointment as chair of the Tribunal. Then fifty PiS deputies filed a motion with the TK challenging Gersdorf's appointment as president of the Supreme Court. Przyłębska appointed herself to the panel for the deputies' motion. This created 'a bizarre situation' in which the president of the Constitutional Tribunal would assess whether the president of the Supreme Court 'was empowered to assess the powers of the president of the Constitutional Tribunal'.[32]

The next step was the lowering of the retirement age for Supreme Court judges from seventy to sixty-five. This proved a highly contentious way of trying to shape the Supreme Court. On 2 July 2018 the European Commission launched an infringement procedure centred on the retirement provisions and their impact on the independence of the Supreme Court. The new provisions came into effect at midnight on 4 July and affected twenty-seven of the Court's seventy-three members. Nine justices submitted formal documentation for extending their terms (the president could do this), four simply declared that they could not be dismissed and a further three cited the provisions of the Constitution regarding judicial tenure. Eleven Supreme Court justices did not seek an extension, including Małgorzata Gersdorf, who reported for work arguing that her six-year term of office, ending in 2020, was specified by the Constitution.

President Duda swamped the court by increasing the number of Supreme Court judges to 120, and he appointed 38 new judges proposed by the newly configured KRS. In June 2019 Duda further increased the number of Supreme Court judges and introduced the requirement that cases be assigned to judges in alphabetical order rather than by specialism.

In August a group of Polish judges requested a preliminary opinion from the European Court of Justice (ECJ). On 24 September 2018, the Commission referred the case to the ECJ. In December the Court imposed interim measures to stop the implementation of the law on the Supreme Court. Poland backed down and reinstated the ousted judges, and President Duda signed new legislation. On 24 June 2019 the ECJ confirmed that the law lowering the retirement age was contrary to EU law, breaching the principle of the irremovability of judges.

In March the ECJ held hearings relating to three pending cases on the rule of law in Poland and the situation of its judiciary. The spate of disciplinary hearings against judges for apparently political reasons[33] and the radically increased role of the justice minister in disciplinary proceedings led the European Commission to launch another in a series of infringement proceedings against the Polish government in April 2019, claiming that disciplinary procedures lacked the necessary guarantees to protect judges from political control. Meanwhile retired Constitutional Court Chair Jerzy Stępień was the first to face the TK's own disciplinary tribunal, charged with having violating the principle of judicial independence by public appearances, notably in the Freedom March of 6 June 2017 under the banner 'support for European values' [*sic*].[34]

The Commission worried that judges were subject to disciplinary investigations, procedures and sanctions because of their judicial decisions. Moreover, there were no guarantees of the independence and impartiality of the new Disciplinary Chamber of the Supreme Court, which reviewed decisions taken in disciplinary proceedings against judges. The chamber was composed solely of new judges selected by the KRS, itself now appointed by the *Sejm*. It had jurisdiction over disciplinary proceedings against judges (including Supreme Court judges), prosecutors, legal advisors and lawyers. The second new chamber, Extraordinary Control and Public Affairs, had jurisdiction over cases of extreme importance for the political system, such as certifying the validity of elections and referenda, and other cases under public law, reviewing electoral protests and complaints about unreasonable delays in trials before the courts.

In May 2019, the *Sejm* rushed through its ninth amendment to the law reforming the Supreme Court. This amendment removed the right of appeal from failed candidates for the Supreme Court. The government dropped two other contentious provisions, one on the appointment of the president, the second making it easier to strip judges of their immunity.

## The lower courts

The reform of the lower courts between 2016 and 2018 further increased executive control of the judiciary. After amendments to the law on the courts in July 2017[35] the minister of justice acquired far-reaching discretionary power to interfere with the staffing of the courts and indirectly influence judges and their careers. The minister controlled the appointment of court assessors and oversaw the training of future assessors and judges. The minister gained extensive authority to appoint court presidents, vice presidents and directors (previously, a negative ZRS opinion was binding on the minister). The law introduced two methods for dismissing court presidents and vice presidents. During a transition period, from August 2017 until February 2018, they were dismissed at the discretion of the minister of justice.

At the beginning of April 2018 the *Sejm* further amended the Law on the Common Court System. It vested the minister of justice 'with a far-reaching and often completely discretionary power to interfere with the staffing of common courts and to indirectly influence judges and control their careers'.[36] According to a report by the Helsinki Committee 'in practice the main purpose of the ... Law was not improving the work of the courts, but far-reaching replacements of personnel'.[37] Moreover, 'the process of appointing new presidents and vice presidents was conducted in a non-transparent way and based on irrelevant criteria ... (such as) private friendships'.[38]

Despite the 'reforms', the government continued its propaganda assault on the judiciary. The prime minister deemed Polish judges 'deeply corrupt' and compared the task of the reformers to those dealing with the aftermath of Vichy France. Judges reacted angrily to this 'shameful' comparison of Polish judges with fascist collaborators.[39] Not long afterwards the deputy minister of justice resigned after revelations that he had promoted an online trolling campaign against judges opposing PiS's changes, including the head of Iustitia, an association of Polish judges that was fiercely critical.[40] Onet published alleged communications via WhatsApp and Facebook Messenger with 'Emilia' @MalaEmiE and revealed the spread of scurrilous misinformation with the minister's connivance.[41] She was Emilia Szmydt, wife of judge Tomasz Szmydt, newly of the National Judicial Council (KRS).

## Capturing the media

PiS's election programme in 2015 had promised a reduction in foreign ownership of media businesses to a maximum of 25 per cent, and PiS spokespersons made much of 're-Polonizing' the media. Under the 'small media law' passed in November 2015, the job of hiring and firing senior TV and radio executives was removed from the Broadcasting Council (KRRiT) and switched to the direct control of the Treasury. The channels' management boards were dismissed and party loyalists installed in the editors' offices. Hundreds of journalists and broadcasters in the national public service broadcasting channels of Polish Television (TVP) and Radio Poland lost their jobs, either through dismissal or because they resigned in protest. There followed another hundred or so who also lost or left their jobs in the regional public service broadcasters.

The proposed 'big media law' included measures to turn public broadcasters into so-called national media required to transmit the views of the Polish parliament, government and president and to commission programmes to cultivate 'national traditions and patriotic values'. Following a negative assessment by the Council of Europe[42] the government put the 'big media law' on hold. Among others, the Council of Europe's experts identified provisions increasing government control and interference in editorial independence, as well as articles reflecting 'a deeply conservative and political agenda for content programming'. The summary dismissal of senior employees would lead to 'an atmosphere of fear' and the possibility of a 'chilling effect' on freedom of expression.[43] The government also promised to address concerns about the composition of the new National Media Council, with its so-called bridging law, passed almost immediately by the *Sejm*, providing for three members chosen by the *Sejm* and two by the president from nominations by the largest opposition parties.[44]

In fact, changes in personnel proved sufficient to ensure control of the public broadcasting media and the degradation of public debate. TVP became an effective propaganda weapon stressing the achievements of the government, lauding the person of Jarosław Kaczyński, endorsing his anti-immigrant and anti-Islamic themes, and castigating the opposition as treacherous and corrupt. A trenchant critic of government policy, castigated by the media, Professor Wojciech Sadurski found himself sued by both PiS and TVP for civil defamation and by TVP for criminal defamation.[45] State television became 'an instrument of brutal propaganda, spewing out hate speech and xenophobia on a daily basis'.[46] Discussions about the culpability of journalists in promoting hate speech increased after the assassination of the progressive mayor of Gdańsk Paweł Adamowicz in January 2019.[47]

Capture of the public media did not remove all aspects of media pluralism in Poland – it would have been difficult to write this otherwise – but harassment of the independent media increased steadily.[48] In December 2016, during a parliamentary crisis that had brought thousands onto the streets, PiS enacted a regulation restricting journalists' ability to cover parliamentary sessions. (In protest, the opposition blocked access to the main parliamentary chamber for several days. So PiS deputies gathered elsewhere to pass the 2017 budget.) Poland dropped to 59th in the rankings of the World Press Freedom Index in 2019.[49] There is no doubt that its control of the media had nothing to do with justice. It gave PiS a powerful instrument for propagating its 'reform' agenda.

Was there no barrier to the PiS takeover? Poland's history gave few opportunities to entrench the rule of law. Adam Czarnota argued that 'it is commonplace for sociologists of law to argue that the operation or functioning of specific norms and legal institutions depends on the institutional and cultural context. That context in the Polish case, and probably in any other post-communist country, is rather fragile as far as democratic institutional infrastructure and legal culture are concerned.'[50] The social mobilization after 2015 spearheaded by the Committee for the Defence of Democracy (KOD) made little impression. In theory, the EU should have acted.

## Poland and the European Union

Poland demonstrated the wholesale inadequacy of EU mechanisms designed to maintain and ensure EU values. Because the mechanisms are predicated on good will and dialogue, they fail in the absence of good will and a refusal to engage in any meaningful dialogue, as was the case in Poland. The Commission adopted a three-phase mechanism for addressing systemic threats to the rule of law in a Member State in March 2014. The Commission would initiate a dialogue by noting its concerns in a Rule of Law Opinion. Then, if the concerns were not addressed satisfactorily, the Commission would issue a Rule of Law Recommendation. It would identify the problems and recommend that the Member State resolve them within a fixed time limit. In the third phase the Commission monitors the follow-up by the Member State to the Recommendation. Lack of satisfactory response may trigger formal resort to the procedure under Article 7, which is launched when there is 'a clear risk' of breach of the EU's fundamental values, including human dignity, freedom, democracy, equality, the rule of law and respect for human rights, including minority rights. Article 7.1 allows the European Council to give a formal warning. Article 7.2 imposes sanctions and suspends voting rights.

The European Commission opened a dialogue with the Polish Government in January 2016 under the Rule of Law Framework ('the pre-Article 7 procedure'), requesting information on the situation concerning the Constitutional Tribunal and changes in the law on public service broadcasters. With no effective response the European Commission adopted its first 'Rule of Law Opinion' on 1 June 2016 and invited the Polish government to reply. With the new Law on the Constitutional Tribunal enacted on 22 July 2016 (repeating elements criticized by the Venice Commission and challenged by the TK itself in August), the Commission moved to the second stage of its pre-Article 7 procedure; on 27 July it issued a strongly worded Recommendation on the Rule of Law, adopted because of the 'systemic threat to the rule of law in Poland'. It argued that 'the fact that the Constitutional Tribunal is prevented from fully ensuring an effective constitutional review adversely affects its integrity, stability and proper functioning, which is one of the essential safeguards of the rule of law in Poland'.[51] Poland should, as a matter of urgency, fully implement the Tribunal's judgments of December 2015 such that the three judges lawfully nominated by the previous *Sejm* take their places on the Tribunal, while the three judges nominated without a valid legal basis should not. All judgments must be published and implemented fully, with mechanisms introduced to ensure that publication is automatic. Furthermore, reform of the Law on the TK must respect its judgments, and the Polish government must screen the July law for compliance with the Opinion of the Venice Commission.

The European Commission gave Poland three months to comply with its recommendations. The Polish government replied within the time limit on 27 October. In a further Recommendation in December the Commission noted that the government had disagreed with all points raised but offered no 'new measures to alleviate the rule of law concerns addressed by the Commission'.[52] The Commission criticized the legislation recently introduced and reiterated the criticisms made earlier by the Venice Commission and the Constitutional Tribunal itself. It also noted the irregularity of the appointment of Julia Przyłębska as chair of the TK and her incorporation of the problematic justices (see Chapter 9). It found continuing evidence of a 'systemic threat to the rule of law in Poland' and ordered the completion of a long list of 'must dos' within two months. The government failed on all counts and the Third Rule of Law Recommendation followed on 26 July 2017.

After several fruitless debates and three hearings later, on 20 December 2017 the Commission triggered the Article 7(1) TEU procedure for the very first time (it was invoked a year later against Hungary) because of a clear risk of a 'serious breach of the rule of law' by Poland: the Polish government had failed to respond to earlier concerns and new laws meant that the situation had seriously deteriorated.[53] PiS ignored demands for the repeal of unconstitutional laws and the proper constitution of the Constitutional Tribunal. The EU's emphasis on continuing dialogue proved to be a dialogue of the deaf, with each side maintaining its original stance.

The White Paper offered by the Polish government in March 2018 did nothing to alter the situation. It attributed the need for judicial reform to low public confidence, excessively lengthy proceedings, and the **lack of a practical method to hold to account judges who were directly and shamefully involved with the communist system**.[54] Since judicial appointments remained in the hands of judges themselves, violating the principle of the separation and balance of powers [*sic*], the system had no way of ridding itself of the bad apples. The Polish Supreme Court assessed the White Paper as methodologically inconsistent, with false, contradictory and mutually exclusive claims. The alleged failings would not be addressed by the changes made. 'The problem is not that the current government is changing the functioning of the Polish judicial system; the problem is that it evidently does so in conflict with the Constitution.'[55]

In May 2018 the Polish government offered some half-hearted concessions, but the foreign minister warned that Warsaw would not abandon fundamental elements of its reforms.[56] The European Commission challenged the new retirement ages for judges in the European Court of Justice. In October the ECJ required the immediate suspension of the provisions. The government complied, and in December the *Sejm* passed legislation providing for the reinstatement of judges forced into early retirement. The ECJ confirmed its preliminary finding in June 2019.

That same month three Polish judges went to the ECJ questioning the independence of the new disciplinary chamber of the Supreme Court. The advocate general agreed that the new chamber 'does not satisfy the requirements of judicial independence established by EU law'. Justice Minister Ziobro claimed that the opinion was contradictory and effectively defended the 'pathology of the Polish judiciary'.[57]

In 19 July 2019 the European Commission set yet another deadline for Warsaw to act before the arrival of its new President Ursula von der Leyen on 1 November. Things did not bode well for any substantive modification of the recalcitrance and obduracy of the Polish government. It was hard to find a scholar, journalist or general observer with a good word to say for the European Commission's handling of Poland's defiance (and, we should note in passing, Hungary's). Tadeusz Koncewicz saw the EU reduced to 'an idle bystander, extending deadlines and assurances of a dialogue … while Polish authoritarians laughed in the EU's face and … marched on.'[58] Laurent Pech and Kim Lane Scheppele condemned the European Commission's 'abdication'[59] and its reluctance 'to confront the reality of a belligerent government bent on violating the rule of law in plain sight.'[60] Bojan Bugarič observed that 'the EU's interest is in maintaining stability, and EU institutions and elites seem to lack the enthusiasm and political will for protecting fundamental values such as democracy and the rule of law'.[61]

One problem was that the Rule of Law Framework and Article 7 TEU allowed the EU only to issue recommendations and to suspend voting rights in the Council, with no steps in between. Given that Hungary and Poland had a mutual support arrangement, with so many major decisions requiring unanimity, the problem became acute. Yet 'inaction helps the political elites in the backsliding Member States to consolidate their assault on the values of democracy and the Rule of Law even further, entrenching the breach of EU values'.[62] Ursula von der Leyen's appointment as president of the Commission gave no cause for optimism.[63]

## New roles for the IPN

Alongside attempts to purge state institutions of putative corruption and continuing communist influence, PiS sought to gain the hearts and minds of the population. The government introduced changes to the law on the IPN in April 2016[64] and again in

January[65] and June 2018,[66] reversing PO's attempts to 'depoliticize' it and adding new tasks to its remit.

The new departments marked a shift in the IPN's functions in favour of greater emphasis on memory-making: the Bureau for Commemorating Struggles and Martyrdom was to commemorate events, places and figures 'in the history of the struggle and martyrdom of Poles at home and abroad and of other nations on the territory of Poland'. The Bureau of Search and Identification took over the exhumation, begun in 2011, of bodies from cemeteries, prisons and other burial sites of anonymous victims of the communists.[67] In 2016 the scope of the IPN's investigations was backdated to cover the period from 8 November 1917 to 31 July 1990 to facilitate the search for graves and burial sites 'of those who perished as a result of the struggle against the totalitarian system or totalitarian repression or ethnic cleansing'.

## History and memory

Law and Justice worked to make collective memory an instrument of domestic politics and partisan polarization. It was widely observed that the identity of the Third Republic remained 'inadequately defined and ambiguous'.[68] Halas notes that not even the Gdańsk Agreement merited a new public holiday. Poland had a 'fractured and fragmented memory regime'.[69]

Greater focus on memory included a renewed stress on the promotion of patriotism, especially among the young. It sought an end to the 'pedagogy of shame' and an emphasis on valour and sacrifice. Jarosław Kaczyński maintained his view that the 'dissident' wing of Solidarity had allied with former communists not only to entrench them in society but to undermine the very idea of the nation and to destroy national pride.[70]

Old arguments were reopened, not least the controversy over the small town of Jedwabne. The IPN had devoted much attention to Polish–Jewish relations in the twentieth century, work stimulated by the controversy surrounding the publication in 2000 of Jan Gross's book *Neighbours* on the murder of some 1,600 Jews of Jedwabne in 1941.[71] Although he found Gross's estimation of the number of deaths to be inflated, IPN prosecutor Radosław Ignatiew effectively confirmed Gross's conclusions that '(despite German inspiration) the perpetrators of the crime, in the strict sense, were Polish residents of Jedwabne and nearby'.[72] Later the IPN published an impressive two-volume study.[73]

*Neighbours'* tale of Jews being corralled into a barn and burned alive caused a 'narrative shock' that 'shook Polish national identity to its core'.[74] The Jedwabne debate was 'probably the most profound on any historical issue in Poland since 1989 ....(It) can be viewed as a battle over memory ... a battle in which the "counter-memory" of the Holocaust ... confronted the Polish orthodoxy in the most confident and sharpest way'.[75] The Jedwabne debate 'also raised questions concerning collective responsibility, historical memory, collective identity and patriotism of the Polish people, then and now'.[76] *Sans doute*, in the case of Jedwabne truth was necessary to historical justice.

The image of Poles as the main victims of Nazism was deeply rooted. Broadly there were two reactions to the notion that Poles could have been both perpetrators and victims: for some it was a 'national catharsis', for others it 'served to strengthen the need to construct a defensive fortress of Polishness in the face of external enemies'.[77] At the July 2001 ceremony of commemoration at Jedwabne, a heartfelt public apology by President Kwaśniewski 'marked the zenith of the ceremony but not the end of the discourse'.[78]

Serious study continued with a new Center for Holocaust Research at the Polish Academy of Sciences, examining Polish anti-Semitism and the Polish realities of the Holocaust. Yet in popular and political parlance the 'defensive fortress' remained. In 'radical apologetic' circles the massacre was understood from the start as a crime committed by the Germans and not by the Poles.[79] If the perpetrators were Poles they were, as local PiS deputy Michał Kamiński put it, 'a few tramps, bums and outcasts'.[80] This position retained widespread support among right-wing politicians and conservative elements of the Polish Catholic Church. Stress on Jewish suffering was viewed as a means of devaluing Polish suffering.[81] The narrative depicting Poland as the 'unblemished victim of both Nazi and Soviet aggression' was sustained by '(d)emonstrating the Jews' culpability in their own slaughter and providing the pseudohistorical basis for Polish anti-Semitism'.[82] The Canadian historian Jan Grabowski called the IPN a form of state-funded 'history police' guarding the state-approved myth of Polish national innocence.[83]

Indeed, the 'new patriotism' endorsed by PiS did not seek to incorporate the 'dark past' into collective memory but to ignore it. The 'new patriotism' fostered the heroic tradition by stressing those Poles who had hidden and protected Jews during the Nazi occupation – many of whom were later named 'righteous among the nations'. Questioning the Jedwabne research findings became commonplace. Education Minister Anna Zalewska refused to admit Poles' complicity, saying that Jedwabne was a 'historical fact which has often been misunderstood, with many very biased opinions ....The dramatic situation which took place ... is controversial. Many historians, distinguished professors, paint a completely different picture'.[84] Anti-Semitism was explicit in many right-wing publications and popular blogs which flatly denied the IPN findings.[85]

After becoming chair of the IPN in 2016 Jarosław Szarek dismissed Krzysztof Persak, co-author of the IPN's study of Jedwabne. Szarek backtracked from his claim that the Germans were responsible for the atrocity, but he maintained that responsibility lay with 'the German totalitarian system which somehow forced or inspired Poles to commit this crime'.[86] Szarek had surely not read the IPN study.

Nor was Jedwabne the only source of Polish–Jewish contention. In September 2017 it transpired that the Polish publisher of holocaust-denier David Irving was the new deputy director of IPN Publishing. Then the head of the IPN's Bureau of National Education in Lublin Tomasz Panfil created a storm by claiming that the situation of Polish Jews following the Nazi invasion 'was not really so bad'.[87] The Jewish Historical Institute commented that 'the creation of Jewish administrative bodies in the ghettos should not be seen as a privilege', as Panfil suggested, 'but as the first step in the direction of extermination'.[88] Although the *Times of Israel* noted that the IPN had distanced itself from Panfil's comments,[89] Minister Zalewska awarded Panfil a medal for 'services to education and nurture'. Then in January 2018 the government presented its most controversial amendments to the Law on the IPN.

## The Law on the Holocaust

The 2018 law on the IPN became known as the Law on the Holocaust. Jarosław Kaczyński had long been incensed at offensive and inaccurate shorthand references, especially in the foreign media, to Nazi concentration camps in German-occupied Poland as 'Polish death camps'. The first incarnation of the law provided that 'whoever accuses, publicly and against the facts, the Polish nation, or the Polish state, of being responsible or complicit in Nazi crimes committed by the Third German Reich … shall be subject to a fine or a penalty of imprisonment of up to three years'.

This was a classic 'memory law' in the strict sense. It did not simply declare one version of history to be correct but characterized other views as inadmissible. The government was surprised by the widespread outrage the law caused, not just from the Opposition, historians[90] and the Ombudsman,[91] but from two key Polish allies, Israel and the United States, which saw it as an attempt to deny historical truth and muzzle research. President Duda put the law on hold by referring it to the Constitutional Tribunal.

The government moved quickly to assuage the damage to Poland's international relations, with parliament backing new amendments in an emergency session. The final version in June removed the criminal penalties.[92] When Kaczyński met the Israeli prime minister, he claimed success: the strong reaction was because 'Poland is a much more important country now'. The prime minister agrees that 'our view of the Holocaust is correct; it was one hundred per cent the Germans'.[93]

The law remained contentious and problematic for the freedom of scholarly research. It was also seen as 'dangerous' for Polish–Ukrainian relations. The law attached penalties to denying the crimes of Ukrainian nationalists between 1925 and 1950 or those of Ukrainian formations which collaborated with the Third Reich. Leaving these provisions intact, argued Krzysztof Burnetko, meant 'that the Polish state continues to treat Ukrainian nationalism as the equivalent of communism and Nazism; this is not only a historical falsehood. It also conceives the Ukrainians … as one of the main enemies of Poles and Poland'.[94]

## Patriotic education

After 2016 the Bureau of Education was divided into the Bureau of National Education and the Bureau of Historical Research. The educational functions of the IPN included evaluating the 'most important events for the Polish Nation'; promoting knowledge of the participation of Poles on the field of battle; and countering historical untruths, defaming or damaging Poland and the Poles. The Institute acquired a nationwide educational mission to educate the country's youth in the 'correct and patriotic' fashion and to support social organizations aiming to stimulate patriotism and strengthen national identity. It would also submit proposals regarding the teaching of history. The historian Andrzej Friszke noted that identity politics had been joined by 'identity historiography'.[95] 'Right' or 'real' or 'truthful' history emphasized the evil of the communists and the heroism of the opposition.

We see this clearly in the IPN's short film of 2017 *The Unconquered*,[96] a slick, animated survey of fifty years of Polish resistance showing 'the fight of Poles for freedom, from the first day of World War II to the fall of communism in 1989' as part of 'an international education campaign to present the Polish historical perspective'. To call it a revisionist view is something of an understatement; the film managed to avoid all mention of Solidarity, the Gdańsk Agreement or Lech Wałęsa.

### Museums as bearers of memory

Museums became another focus of patriotic education. The Museum of the Warsaw Uprising, opened in 2004, was enthusiastically supported by then-president of Warsaw Lech Kaczyński. In December 2015 Minister Piotr Gliński announced the creation of a new Museum on the site of the Battle of Westerplatte, often treated as the start of the Second World War and a symbolic date in the struggle for independence. Almost immediately he announced the 'cost effective' merger of this new non-existent Westerplatte Museum with the Museum of the Second World War.

The Director of the Second World War Museum Paweł Machcewicz lost his battle against the merger in the courts. Machcewicz lost his job after the museum opened amid allegations of incompetence and murmurings about corruption alongside criticisms of substance about the strategy of the museum. The layout of the exhibitions was said to focus too much on the sufferings of the civilian population and too little on the 'positive' aspects of war such as heroism and sacrifice. (After police investigation Machcewicz was later fully exonerated of all charges of wrongdoing.)

Even the proposed Museum of the Warsaw Ghetto (2023) proved controversial. Its senior historian, Professor Daniel Blatman of the University of Jerusalem, promised an accurate and thought-provoking examination of the Ghetto. His opponents feared that Blatman was the political instrument of PiS, overseeing a project offering a distorted view of the Holocaust and glossing over instances of collaboration.[97] The IPN supported Blatman and condemned his critics.

# The Institute of Solidarity and Valour

In November 2017 the *Sejm* established the Institute of Solidarity and Valour (*Solidarność i Męstwo*), devoted to the memory of foreign citizens helping Poles during wartime. This was another element of PiS's 'historical politics'. Its aim was to remember and honour 'persons living, dead, or murdered, distinguished in their service to the Polish Nation, both at home and abroad, in the nurturing of memory or bringing aid to the Polish nationality or Polish citizens of other nationality who were victims' of Soviet or Nazi crimes, crimes arising from nationalist sentiments, war crimes or crimes against peace or humanity between 1917 and 1990.[98] A Council of Memory would advise and support the Director of the Institute and would help identify candidates for recognition.

The rationale for the new Institute remained unclear. Several functions seemed to overlap with those of the IPN: the conduct of scholarly research, gathering data, creating databases and archives, popularizing and disseminating knowledge about persons who had served the Polish Nation. The minister of culture declared in the *Sejm*: 'Yes, Poland needs a serious history policy and serious research. For years there has been no research into very important ... periods of Polish history. We have to make up for lost time ....a responsible history policy is the duty of government.'[99] Civic Platform's Stefan Niesiołowski called the Institute 'harmful, absurd, unnecessary, and costly'. He accused PiS of historical illiteracy, fostering 'anti-Polish history', stressing Polish victimhood, favouring the accursed soldiers over the Home Army, equating the Holocaust with anti-Polishness and undermining relations with Israel and the Ukraine. 'This institute smacks of Orwell and the Ministry of Truth.'[100]

## Naming places

The IPN's historians were also given a role in implementing a new memory law, that is a law which enshrines 'state-approved interpretations of historical events'.[101] This was the so-called decommunization law, the law of 1 April 2016 on 'prohibiting the propagation of communism or other totalitarian system in the names of buildings, objects and installations of public utility'.[102] It required the changing of names of buildings, roads, squares and bridges which commemorated persons, organizations, events or dates symbolizing 'the repressive, authoritarian and dependent (*niesuwerenny*) system of authority in Poland 1944–1989'. (Later, statues and the names of institutions were added to the list and the rules were made more precise.[103]) Local governments were given one year to apply to change names, while decisions to remove statues would lie with the provincial governor (*wojewoda*). One source of local resistance was overcome when the law provided that identity documents would not have to be changed; nor would changes in administrative documents, property registers and the like incur costs.

The IPN's role was to initiate changes and to confirm their validity, as well as providing guidance on some names 'which in the communist period were falsely interpreted', such as Pioneers' Street or the Street of the Defenders of Peace. These could be kept so long as the local council issued a new 'justification' for the name. 'Yuri Gagarin Street' was acceptable, but councils could change it if they wished. Radom renamed Adam Rapacki Street, named after the highly respected former Polish foreign minister; it became Adam Rapacki Street, after the musician, director and composer.

Other changes were more overtly reflective of the current political divide. The rehabilitation of the 'accursed soldiers', the anti-Soviet nationalists who had fought against the communist takeover of Poland, was a deep source of pride for the visceral anti-communists of the Right but a bitter wound for those who claimed the complicity of the anti-communist movement in a series of atrocities. New streets 'of the Accursed Soldiers' aroused strong emotions.

Many decisions were contentious. In Płock, for example, the local council proposed to change the Street of the People's Guard (*Gwardia Ludowa*, GL) to the Street of the 11th Operational Group of the National Armed Forces (*11. Grupy Operacyjnej*

*Narodowych Sił Zbrojnych*, NSZ). This was provocative to say the least. The GL was the communist wartime resistance movement. The NSZ was a nationalist anti-Nazi and anti-communist resistance force – they were the 'accursed soldiers'. The internet overflows with vitriol and lists of atrocities committed by both the communist GL ('thieves, rapists and murderers'; 'a malign cancer')[104] and the nationalist NSZ ('collaborators and bandits').[105] This is not neutral territory in a society still so divided over its past.

The IPN noted that local inaction entrenched the social indoctrination of the communist period and was a 'shameful belittling of the memory of the victims of national socialism and communism and contempt for the legacy of the struggle for civic freedom and independence ... '.[106] The IPN also prepared biographical leaflets of potential suitable candidates under its project, 'Patrons of our streets'.[107] The IPN could not contemplate the view of Soviet soldiers as liberators or understand the continuing importance for many of the hundreds of 'monuments of gratitude' erected for the 600,000 Soviet soldiers estimated to have died fighting the Nazis on Polish territory.[108]

# Conclusion

The supremacy of the rule of law is the foundation of the liberal democratic order. Citizens and government alike are subject to 'the government of laws, not of men'. No one stands above the law; all are equal before it. Law and Justice rejected this fundamental premise, offering instead a view of democracy as the unconstrained ability to act on behalf of a putative majority in accordance with the 'will of the nation'. Kaczyński lacked a constitutional majority enabling him to change the constitution. Instead, he and his allies violated the constitution – for example, by refusing to publish decisions of the Constitutional Tribunal in the *Journal of Laws*. They ignored its unwritten customs – for example, the election of judges by judges, removed in the new law on the KRS. They changed the law frequently, as with the Law on the Constitutional Tribunal itself. They used provisions in ways for which they were not designed. Under this veneer of legality there was no aversion to corrupt practices either, as we saw in attempts to discredit judges by planting false rumours about their private lives. Their monolithic view of history turned notions of historical justice into historical injustice. It is difficult not to agree that 'a façade of "normal" democracy' hid 'a set of interconnecting arrangements converging into an overall pattern of authoritarianism ..., radically contrary to democratic values'.[109] Notions of justice went missing along the way.

# Conclusion: Some reflections on the justice of transitional justice

Poland's record in dealing with the wrongs of the past was erratic and not always consistent. In the first years following the fall of communism a reconciliatory, collaborative approach dominated. Between 1989 and 1991 ex-communists cooperated effectively with the new liberal elites, with consensus on the need to redress the communist regime's most blatant human rights' violations. The provision of welfare entitlements for veterans, the restoration of trade union rights, the reinstatement of those who had lost jobs because of political activity, the expunging of political offences in the 'abolition law' of 1989, laws providing for the restitution of Church property – all signalled the good faith of the ex-communists and their acceptance of democratic principles.

However, diametrically opposed perceptions of the past remained a fundamental element of Polish politics as control swung from right to left and back again. The social democrats eschewed radical policies. Centre–right liberals remained sensitive to individual rights. When the conservative right took control, with AWS in 1997 and PiS in 2005, policies became harsher, more vengeful and more divisive. Then after PiS's election victory in 2015 Jarosław Kaczyński's recipe for dealing with the past required wholesale structural reform to eliminate vestiges of the past from the 'deep structures' of the state.

In January 1991 the 'contract' *Sejm* overwhelmingly passed the first law on veterans' privileges, embracing Poland's national struggles, the whole of the anti-Nazi resistance, victims of Soviet and Nazi occupation, as well as political opponents of the communist regime up to 1956. One month later it passed the law on the invalidity of convictions of persons repressed for actions in support of the independent Polish state. Subsequently, debates over who was entitled to combatant status and which putative crimes should be forgiven were perennial sources of political conflict. The views of the anti-communists were irreconcilable with those who had welcomed Soviet soldiers as liberators and who viewed the new regime positively. Later they clashed over martial law – on the one hand an atrocity against the citizenry, on the other the appropriate self-defence of the system.

In all areas of transitional justice there were deeply problematic elements. Despite determined attempts to prosecute communist leaders, there were few successes. The difficulties of gaining convictions were in part objective – the length of time that had passed, the deaths and infirmities of witnesses and the accused, the statute of limitations. The inexperience of the courts also told: arguments over jurisdiction, procedural irregularities, large numbers of retrials ordered on appeal. However, many prosecutions were ideologically motivated and the charges ill conceived.

Anti-communist fervour and desire for revenge reached their peak with the martial law trials, postulating martial law as the product of 'an armed criminal conspiracy' led by the country's senior politicians. This was the work of the Institute of National Remembrance supported by the politicians of Law and Justice. This was elite-led vengeance; there was no baying for blood on the part of the population. It is still difficult to understand some of the decisions reached. After Kiszczak had been found to be physically ill and seriously mentally impaired, the appellate court in spring 2015 did not dismiss proceedings: Kiszczak's health would make it difficult but 'not impossible' to continue. What was to be gained, one wonders.

The sphere of restitution was also complex, and the long-promised reprivatization never materialized. There was little dispute over the restoration of Solidarity property confiscated during martial law. Restoring property to the Catholic Church proved more contentious, with an institutional bias and an ideological predilection favouring the Church at the expense of other claimants such as local government authorities. The Church was the big winner in the restitution stakes, and persistent corruption allegations about the process did nothing to stem the tide.

Lustration was the most complex area of all, the most political and the most emotionally charged. Although much has been made of Poland's 'late lustration', with the first lustration law in 1997,[1] this is explained by many contingent factors – communists in government after the Round Table election; the uncertain international context; the fragmented nature of the first democratic parliament. In the scale of things lustration was not really 'late'. Although Aleks Szczerbiak conceived lustration primarily as a 'truth-revelation' procedure,[2] it was far from clear that 'truth' could be revealed through lustration – or even the nature of that 'truth', given the chaotic, unreliable, partial nature of the files.

Our sympathies lie with Adam Czarnota, who lamented the 'unwillingness to adopt a strategy of public debate' over the moral compromises inherent in living under the communist system.[3] Retired Constitutional Tribunal justice Marek Safjan also proved sensitive to the shades of grey involved in cooperation with the system – with strong differentiation 'by motives and degrees of culpability'. It is possible, said Safjan, that one can never 'uncover the truth about the role and conduct of persons qualified as "TW" (secret collaborators) in the past'.[4] I once heard Jacek Kuroń say that the only way to deal with the complicity of all citizens with the communist system was to 'give everyone a rope with which to hang himself'. Lustration remained rife with moral ambiguities, but not for PiS or the IPN.

Dealing with the past led to the establishment of some new institutions, such as the Social Claims Commission dealing with trades union claims for return of property. The Supreme Administrative Court (1991[5]) and the Constitutional Tribunal (1992)[6] also affirmed the distinctive status of the Property Commission (*Komisja Majątkowa*, KM), dealing with claims by the Catholic Church. It was neither a judicial nor an administrative body of the state but rather a 'type of mediating institution'. In effect it was a quasi-mediating body specific to the cause of transitional justice and itself 'transitional'. The unparalleled success of the Church's claims for restoration suggests that there was little 'mediation'. The strength of the Roman Catholic Church, the Catholic sympathies of politicians and the organization and structure of the KM explain why the Church was the main beneficiary in the sphere of restitution. However, the corrupt nature of the restoration process made it hard to argue that the KM served the cause of justice.

By the end of the 1990s the Institute of National Remembrance (IPN) had become the main instrument of transitional justice. Its prosecutors pursued the perpetrators of 'communist crimes'. It provided documentation needed for the rehabilitation and compensation of individuals, for example, by confirming their record of political opposition to the old regime. Later it was the body charged with identifying 'suspicious' lustration affidavits for further investigation and referral to the courts. The extension of lustration to new categories increased the investigative role of the IPN.

Responsible for securing, conserving and analysing the archives, the IPN became a centre for historical research. It controlled access to communist files – granting the status of victim (*pokrzywdzony*) which was needed for individuals to gain access to their own files. It was not until 2010 that all citizens could gain access.

The IPN was given a key role in PiS's project of 'historical politics' and the 'correction' of the historical record, charged with restoring social memory and historical justice by eliminating communism's 'historical lies'. It gained responsibility for the naming of places to ensure the removal of the communist taint. In short, it became an ideological arm of the Law and Justice Party.

If the IPN was the key instrument, the Constitutional Tribunal was the main adjudicator of transitional justice, overseeing the processes and policies for dealing with the past through the processes of judicial review. The TK developed the criteria of the law-based state and the rule of law with reference to classic formulations of legal doctrine, such as the ban on retroactivity, the principle of proportionality, 'no crime without law' and the clear definition of a prohibited act. It resisted attempts to introduce new categories of crime such as 'Stalinist crimes'.

In some cases the Tribunal had to decide the balance of conflicting rights. It argued, for example, that veterans' privileges were a permitted departure from the principle of equality because the Constitution ascribed 'exceptional value to the struggle for independence'. In other cases the 'transitional nature' of measures was made clear. The sphere of restitution provides some important examples of distinctive adaptation to the needs of transitional justice.

In one important restitution case the journalists' organization the SDPRP, which had gained property during martial law, challenged its return, arguing that property relations between trades unions and social organizations were not administrative matters and should not be settled through administrative processes. In an unusual reference to the requirements of transitional justice, the TK argued that the restoration was lawful because 'the extraordinary nature of the institution of the return of property to social organizations … justified the adoption of various extraordinary legal means)'.[7] (The Supreme Court also made occasional reference to 'special circumstances'.)

The case of the people dispossessed from beyond the Bug River when Poland's eastern boundary shifted westward was also distinctive. Their property could not be 'restored' because it was now in a foreign country. They were entitled to redress for their losses – not just as compensation but chiefly as a 'social benefit to assist in resettlement'. Their rights were 'a specific surrogate of the right to property' which nevertheless enjoyed the constitutional protection of property rights and the equal protection of the law. The law specifying which heirs had rights to compensation of a deceased repressed person was also reasonable, if unusual. These were not normal testamentary or property rights but – in effect – measures of transitional justice.

The TK occasionally departed from strict legal positivism with its 'openness to active and creative interpretation'.[8] Some justices like Ewa Łętowska explicitly accepted the 'Radbruch principle', which argued that an unjust law need not be obeyed; the courts could not be bound solely by the strictures of the positive law.[9] This enabled the courts occasionally to violate their own precepts. In 2007 in a lustration case the Constitutional Tribunal argued that although the law may not enact retrospective penalties, it can punish persons 'for actions which were not deemed crimes when committed but were regarded as offences when judged by the principles acknowledged by civilized countries'. A similar example comes from the Supreme Court, which rejected a lower court's application of the statute of limitations because of 'special circumstances': 'Disregarding the legitimate claims of a person injured by the unjust sentencing and repression of the martial law period violates the interests of the Polish Republic'.[10]

However, the Constitutional Tribunal rarely claimed the necessity of special transitional measures. It claimed by and large to be applying the legal principles of the time when the crimes were committed, but the application of legal rules to a system not governed by the rule of law often made this difficult. The most egregious case was certainly that of martial law, where the Tribunal over-stretched its own jurisdiction, first in regard to the Supreme Court and second by failing to apply the prohibition against retroactivity to its own deliberations and ignoring the political realities of the communist regime (see Chapter 4).

If we return to the questions posed in Chapter 1, the answers emerging from our investigation are clear in some respects, murky in others. Firstly, was there a particular, distinctive quality of justice in measures taken to 'deal with the past'? No, broadly speaking, there was not. We have noted a few examples of institutional and procedural adaptations designed to secure justice through the redress of grievances. We have also noted some instances of protracted legal processes and absence of transparency. These were exceptions, however.

Secondly, how far did the measures taken reflected a coherent, consistent policy to deal with past wrongs? Not very far. Too often, ideology got in the way of justice. Certainly, the victims of previous injustices were now brought centre stage, exonerated and compensated. In other areas, however, the burden of history was great. The visceral anti-communism of the Polish right and the sense of moral outrage conjured by the old regime offered a picture in stark black and white. Although PiS will not endure, its views paved the way for an enduring legacy. Dealing with the past was not only about the past. It was also about the future.

What of PiS's transformation project? It is hard to give credence to the view that the Round Table was a betrayal, still less that after thirty years communists, ex-communists or communist sympathizers continued to penetrate and control the structures of the state. We are forced to conclude that the project was not about justice. It was about political power and the removal of obstacles to a PiS hegemony by subverting the judiciary and undermining the rule of law. This was a tragic trajectory for a country which throughout the 1990s served as a beacon of successful democratization.

# Notes

## Chapter 1

1   Laurel Fletcher and Harvey Weinstein, 'Writing Transitional Justice: An Empirical Evaluation of Transitional Justice Scholarship in Academic Journals', *Journal of Human Rights Practice* 7, no. 2 (2015): 177–98.

2   Claus Offe, 'Capitalism by Democratic Design? Democratic Theory Facing the Triple Transition in East Central Europe', *Social Research* 58, no. 4 (1991): 865–92.

3   Leszek Koczanowicz, *Politics of Time. Dynamics of Identity in Post-Communist Poland* (no place: Berghahn Books, 2008), 21–2.

4   See for example M. N. Kaminski and Monika Nalepa, 'Judging Transitional Justice: A New Criterion for Evaluating Truth Revelation Procedures', *The Journal of Conflict Resolution* 50, no. 3 (2006): 384.

5   Tim Snyder and M. Vachudova, 'Are Transitions Transitory? Two Types of Political Change in Eastern Europe since 1989', *East European Politics and Societies* 11, no. 1 (1997): 1–35; Thomas Carrothers, 'The End of the Transition Paradigm', *Journal of Democracy* 13 (2002): 5–21.

6   Harold Berman, *Justice in the USSR* (New York: Vintage, 1963), 31.

7   See Peter H. Solomon, Jr., *Soviet Criminal Justice under Stalin* (Cambridge: Cambridge University Press, 1996).

8   Ruti Teitel, *Transitional Justice* (Oxford: Oxford University Press, 2003), 69.

9   Neil J. Kritz, ed., *Transitional Justice: How Emerging Democracies Reckon with Former Regimes* (Washington, DC: United States Institute of Peace Press, 1995), 3 vols.

10  Jamal Benomar, 'Confronting the Past. Justice after Transitions', *Journal of Democracy* 4, no. 1 (1993): 13; see also Luc Huyse, 'Justice after Transition: On the Choices Successor Elites Make in Dealing with the Past', *Law and Social Inquiry* 20 (1995): 54–5.

11  Claus Offe and Ulrike Poppe, 'Transitional Justice in the GDR and in Unified Germany' in *Retribution and Reparation in the Transition to Democracy*, ed. Jon Elster (Cambridge: Cambridge University Press, 2006), 239; also Noel Calhoun, *Dilemmas of Justice in Eastern Europe's Democratic Transition* (London: Palgrave Macmillan, 2004), 36–7.

12  Eric Posner and Adrian Vermeule, 'Transitional Justice as Ordinary Justice', *Harvard Law Review* 117, no. 3 (2004): 761–825.

13  W. Sadurski, '"Decommunisation," "Lustration" and Constitutional Continuity: Dilemmas of Traditional Justice in Central Europe', EU Working Papers, LW No 2003/15 (Badia Fiesolana, San Dominico: European University Institute, 2003), 2.

14  In 2010 the Transitional Justice Bibliography contained 2,497 entries of scholarly work; https://sites.google.com/site/transitionaljusticedatabase/transitional-justice-bibliography

15  K. Crossley-Frolick, 'The European Union and Transitional Justice: Human Rights and Post-Conflict Reconciliation in Europe and Beyond', *Contemporary Readings in*

*Law and Social Justice* 3, no. 1 (2011): 33–4; Rosemary Nagy, 'Transitional Justice as Global Project: Critical Reflections', *Third World Quarterly* 29, no. 2 (2008): 275–89.

16  C. Bell, C. Campbell and F. Ni Aoláin, 'Justice Discourses in Transition', *Social and Legal Studies* 13, no. 3 (2004): 305.

17  Louis Bickford, 'Transitional Justice' in *Encyclopedia of Genocide and Crimes against Humanity*, ed. Dinah Shelton (Farmington Hills, MI: Thomson Gale, c2005), vol. 3, 1045.

18  International Center for Transitional Justice, 'What Is Transitional Justice?' from http://www.ictj.org/sites/default/files/ICTJ-Global-Transitional-Justice-2009-English.pdf

19  Paige Arthur, 'How Transitions Reshaped Human Rights: A Conceptual History of Transitional Justice', *Human Rights Quarterly* 31 (2009): 358.

20  S. Buckley-Zistel and R. Stanley, eds, *Gender in Transitional Justice* (London: Palgrave Macmillan, 2012).

21  http://www.justice-data.com/pcj-dataset

22  Bell, Campbell, and Ni Aoláin, 'Justice Discourses', 306.

23  See for example Victor Peskin, *International Justice in Rwanda and the Balkans: Virtual Trials and the Struggle for State Cooperation* (New York: Cambridge University Press, 2008).

24  T. O. Hansen, 'Transitional Justice: Toward a Differentiated Theory', *Oregon Review of International Law* 13, no. 1 (2011): 3.

25  Huyse, 'Justice after Transition', 54–5; Arthur, 'How Transitions Reshaped Human Rights', 353–5.

26  Tina Rosenberg, 'Latin America' in *Dealing with the Past: Truth and Reconciliation in South Africa*, eds. A. Boraine, J. Levy and R. Scheffer (Cape Town: IDASA, 1994), 95.

27  Guillermo O'Donnell, 'Challenges to Democratization in Brazil', *World Policy Journal* 5, no. 2 (1988): 283.

28  Vernon Bogdanor, 'Founding Elections and Regime Change', *Electoral Studies* 9, no. 4 (1990): 288–94.

29  Aurora Voiculescu, *Human Rights and Political Justice in Post-Communist Eastern Europe: Prosecuting History* (Lewiston, NY: Edwin Mellen Press, 2000), 24.

30  B. A. Leebaw, 'The Irreconcilable Goals of Transitional Justice', *Human Rights Quarterly* 30 (2008): 95–6.

31  Alexandra Barahona de Brito, Carmen Gonzaléz-Enríquez and Paloma Aguilar, 'Introduction' in *The Politics of Memory. Transitional Justice in Democratizing Societies*, eds. Alexandra Barahona de Brito, Carmen Gonzaléz-Enríquez and Paloma Aguilar (Oxford: Oxford University Press, 2001), 1.

32  Stanley Cohen, 'Crimes of the State. Accountability, Lustration and the Policing of the Past', *Law and Social Inquiry* 20, no. 1 (1995): 34.

33  Adam Michnik and Václav Havel, 'Justice or Revenge?', *Journal of Democracy* 4, no. 1 (1993): 26.

34  Leebaw, 'The Irreconcilable Goals', 118.

35  Ibid., 102.

36  Cohen, 'Crimes of the State', 37.

37  Calhoun, *Dilemmas of Justice*, 47.

38  Peter Digeser, *Political Forgiveness* (Ithaca: Cornell University Press, 2001), 166; cf. Cohen, 'Crimes of the State', 31.

39  Steven Ratner and Jason Adams, *Accountability for Human Rights Violations in International Law. Beyond the Nuremberg Legacy* (Oxford: Oxford University Press, 2001), 158.

40   Cohen, 'Crimes of the State', 12.

41   Calhoun, *Dilemmas of Justice*, 9.

42   Cohen, 'Crimes of the State', 18.

43   Offe and Poppe, 'Transitional Justice in the GDR', 247.

44   Andrzej Walicki, 'The Three Traditions in Polish Patriotism' in *Polish Paradoxes*, eds. Stanisław Gomułka and Antony Polonsky (London: Routledge, 1990), 21.

45   Koczanowicz, *Politics of Time*, 20.

46   Barahona de Brito et al., 'Introduction', 26.

47   Cohen, 'Crimes of the State', 10.

48   Ibid., 20.

49   Ibid., 33–4.

50   Ibid., 12.

51   Istvan Pogany, *Righting Wrongs in Eastern Europe* (Manchester: Manchester University Press, 1997), 215.

52   Neil Kritz, ed., *Transitional Justice. How Emerging Democracies Reckon with Former Regimes* (Washington, DC: United States Institute of Peace Press, 1995), vol. 1.

53   Samuel Huntington, *The Third Wave: Democratization in the Late Twentieth Century* (London: University of Oklahoma Press, 1991), 213.

54   Eva Jaskovska and John P. Moran, 'Justice or Politics? Criminal, Civil and Political Adjudication in the Newly Independent Baltic States', *Journal of Communist Studies and Transition Politics* 22, no. 4 (2006):493

55   Cohen, 'Crimes of the State', 23.

56   Calhoun, *Dilemmas of Justice,* 8.

57   Raluca Grosescu, 'Judging Communist Crimes in Romania: Transnational and Global Influences', *International Journal of Transitional Justice* 11, no. 3 (2017): 505–24.

58   Cohen, 'Crimes of the State', 38.

59   Lavinia Stan, *Transitional Justice in Post-Communist Romania: The Politics of Memory* (Cambridge: Cambridge University Press, 2012), 166.

60   Quoted in Pogany, Righting Wrongs in Eastern Europe, 146.

61   V. Cepl, 'A Note on the Restitution of Property in Post-Communist Czechoslovakia', *Journal of Communist Studies* 7, no. 3 (1991): 367–75.

62   Vojtech Cepl and Mark Gillis, 'Making Amends after Communism', *Journal of Democracy* 7, no. 4 (1996): 120.

63   Leebaw, 'The Irreconcilable Goals', 99.

64   Roman David, *Lustration and Transitional Justice: Personnel Systems in the Czech Republic, Hungary and Poland* (Philadelphia: University of Pennsylvania, 2011).

65   M. Los 'Lustration and Truth Claims: Unfinished Revolutions in Central Europe', *Law and Social Inquiry* 20 (1995): 147. Or – one might say – 'virtue is its own reward'.

66   Monika Nalepa, *Skeletons in the Closet. Transitional Justice in Post-Communist Europe* (Cambridge: Cambridge University Press, 2010), 3.

67   Bulgaria, the Czech Republic, Germany, Hungary, Poland, Romania, and Slovakia Cooperate in The European Network of Official Authorities in Charge of the Secret-Police Files; see http://eureconciliation.wordpress.com/national-institutions-responsible-for-the-investigation-and-archival-of-communist-crimes/

68   Jaskovska and Moran, 'Justice or Politics?', 489.

69   Lavinia Stan, 'Vigilante Justice in Post-Communist Europe', *Communist and Post-Communist Studies* 44, no. 4 (2011): 319.

70   Ibid., 320–1.
71   Offe and Poppe, 'Transitional Justice in the GDR', 251; Nalepa, *Skeletons in the Closet*.
72   John P. Moran, 'The Communist Torturers of Eastern Europe: Prosecute and Punish or Forgive and Forget?', *Communist and Post-Communist Studies* 27, no. 1 (1994): 95–109.
73   Aleks Szczerbiak, *Politicising the Communist Past: The Politics of Truth Revelation in Post-Communist Poland* (London: Taylor and Francis, 2018).
74   Huntington, *The Third Wave*, 228.
75   Ibid.
76   Moran, 'The Communist Torturers …', 95.
77   Nadya Nedelsky, 'Divergent Responses to a Common Past? Transitional Justice in the Czech Republic and Slovakia', *Theory and Society* 33, no. 1 (2004): 66.
78   Ibid., 81.
79   See for example David Doellinger, 'Prayers, pilgrimages and petitions: The secret church and the growth of civil society in Slovakia', *Nationalities Papers* 30, no. 2 (2002): 215–40.
80   Jaskovska, and Moran, 'Justice or Politics?', 501.
81   Carmen Gonzaléz-Enríquez, 'De-communization and Political Justice in Central and Eastern Europe' in *The Politics of Memory. Transitional Justice in Democratizing Societies*, eds. Alexandra Barahona de Brito, Carmen Gonzaléz-Enríquez and Paloma Aguilar (Oxford: Oxford University Press, 2001), 219–21.
82   Elazar Barkan, *The Guilt of Nations: Restitution and Negotiating Historical Injustices* (New York: Norton, 2000), 115.
83   Helga Welsh, 'Dealing with the Communist Past: Central and East European Experiences after 1990', *Europe-Asia Studies* 48, no. 3 (1996), 419, 422.
84   Calhoun, *Dilemmas of Justice*, 15–16.
85   Welsh, 'Dealing with the Communist Past', 425.
86   Kieran Williams, Brigid Fowler and Aleks Szczerbiak, 'Explaining Lustration in Central Europe: A "Post-Communist Politics" Approach', *Democratization* 12, no. 1 (2005): 34.
87   Kieran Williams, 'Lustration as the Securitization of Democracy in Czechoslovakia and the Czech Republic', *Journal of Communist Studies and Transition Politics* 19, no 4 (2003): 1–24.
88   Aleks Szczerbiak, 'Dealing with the Communist Past or the Politics of the Present? Lustration in Post-Communist Poland', *Europe-Asia Studies* 54, no. 4 (2002): 562.
89   See Stan, ed., *Transitional Justice in Eastern Europe*; also the summary in Lavinia Stan and Nadya Nedelsky, 'Post-Communist Transitional Justice Predictors', SciTopics, 9 February 2009, from http://www.scitopics.com/Post_Communist_Transitional_Justice_Predictors.html
90   Nalepa, *Skeletons*, 2.
91   Andrzej Friske, 'Okrągły Stol, Geneza i przebieg' in *Polska 1986–1989: koniec systemu*, eds. Antoni Dudek and Andrzej Friszke Materiały międzynarodowej konferencji. Miedzeszyn, 21–23 października 1999 (Warsaw: Wydawnictwo Trio, 2002), vol. 1, referaty, 117.
92   Wiktor Osiatyński, 'Poland' in *Dealing with the Past. Truth and Reconciliation in South Africa*, eds. Alex Boraine, Janet Levy and Ronel Scheffer (Capetown: IDASA, 1997), 2nd ed, 61.
93   The document cited is a report from a Central Committee member to the ambassador to Czechoslovakia. The Politburo meeting on 20 June 1989 discussed

a report on 'the opposition following the elections', laying out several variants: the most likely outcome was 'political impasse leading to pressure for the dissolution of parliament and fresh elections'; 'Wyciąg z opracowania Komisji Analiz i Prognoz Społecznego-Politycznych na temat konsekewncji sukcesu wyborczego opozycji przedstawiony członkom Biura Politycznego 20 czerwca 1989 r' in *Polska 1986–1989: koniec systemu*, eds. Antoni Dudek and Andrzej Friszke (Warsaw: Wydawnictwo Trio, 2002), vol. 3, Dokument 50: 281–4; see also 314–15.

94   Nalepa, *Skeletons*, 12.
95   Ibid., 83.
96   Ibid., 16.
97   Ibid., 19.
98   Lavinia Stan, 'Introduction: Post-Communist Transition, Justice, and Transitional Justice' in *Transitional Justice in Eastern Europe and the former Soviet Union*, ed. Lavinia Stan (London: Routledge, 2010), 4.

# Chapter 2

1   Jan Widacki, Mazowiecki's deputy minister of the interior, quoted numerous documents and intelligence reports to show the parallel strategy of disinformation, infiltration and provocation against the opposition, including the Church. See J. Widacki, *Czego nie powiedział Generał Kiszczak* (Warsaw: BGW, 1992).
2   Bronisław Geremek and Jacek Żakowski, *Rok 1989. Bronisław Geremek Opowiada. Jacek Żakowski Pyta* (Warsaw: Plejada, 1990), 18.
3   A. Kemp-Welch, *Poland under Communism. A Cold War History* (Cambridge: Cambridge University Press, 2008), 361–90.
4   Wiktor Osiatyński, 'The Roundtable Talks in Poland' in *The Roundtable Talks and the Breakdown of Communism*, ed. Jon Elster (Chicago: University of Chicago Press, 1996), 53.
5   Krzysztof Dubiński, *Magdalenka. Transakcja epochu* (Warsaw: Sylwa, 1990), 20.
6   Osiatyński, 'The Roundtable', 46.
7   'Ustawa o przebaczeniu i puszczeniu w niepamięć niektórych przestępstw i wykroczeń', *Dziennik Ustaw*, 1989, poz. 179, from http://www.dziennikustaw.gov.pl/ DU/1989/179/1. The law was revoked in 1997.
8   Jacqueline Hayden, *The Collapse of Communist Power in Poland: Strategic Misperceptions and Unanticipated Outcomes* (London: Routledge Curzon, 2006); also Frances Millard, *The Anatomy of the New Poland* (Aldershot: Edward Elgar, 1994).
9   'Memorandum on the Economic Reform Programme in Poland', *East European Reporter* 4, no. 1 (1989/90): 66–9 (English text).
10  Mazowiecki's speech is reproduced in Z. Domarańczyk, *100 dni Mazowieckiego* (Warsaw: Andrzej Bonarski, 1990), 106–8.
11  'Rząd, który utworzę, nie ponosi odpowiedzialności za hipotekę, którą dziedziczy. Ma ona jednak wpływ na okoliczności, w których przychodzi nam działać. Przeszłość odkreślamy grubą linią. Odpowiadać będziemy jedynie za to, co uczyniliśmy, by wydobyć Polskę z obecnego stanu załamania … Przejście jest trudne ale nie musi powodować wstrząsów. Przeciwnie – będzie drogą do normalności. Zasadę walki, która prędzej czy później prowadzi do wyeliminowania przeciwnika, musi zastąpić zasada partnerstwa. Nie przejdziemy inaczej od systemu totalitarnego do demokratycznego …'.

12  Osiatyński, 'The Roundtable', 40; Kaczyński himself claimed to have advocated the criminalizing of the PZPR and the immediate trials of communist leaders in 1990; Jarosław Kaczyński, *Czas na zmiany* (Warsaw: Editions Spotkania, *c.* 1993), 26, 110.

13  Jarosław Kaczyński, *Odwrotna strona medalu* (Warsaw: Most, 1991), 37–8; Geremek and Żakowski, *Rok 1989*, 244.

14  Kaczyński, *Odwrotna strona*, 50.

15  'Jarosław Kaczyński' in *My*, ed. Teresa Torańska (Warsaw: Most, 1994), 100.

16  Noel Calhoun, *Dilemmas of Justice in Eastern Europe's Democratic Transition* (London: Palgrave Macmillan, 2004), 15.

17  Lavinia Stan, 'Poland' in *Transitional Justice in Eastern Europe and the Former Soviet Union*, ed. Lavinia Stan (London: Routledge, 2010), 79.

18  Stan, 'Poland', 76. Spain's unwritten pact, the 'pact of forgetting', stayed in place until 2000. Teitel saw Spain's amnesty policy as 'paradigmatic of amnesty's potential in political transition'; Ruti Teitel, *Transitional Justice* (Oxford: Oxford University Press, 2003), 53.

19  Calhoun, *Dilemmas of Justice*, 99.

20  Monika Nalepa, *Skeletons in the Closet. Transitional Justice in Post-Communist Europe* (Cambridge: Cambridge University Press, 2010), 16.

21  M. Los, 'Lustration and Truth Claims: Unfinished Revolutions in Central Europe', *Law and Social Inquiry* 20 (1995): 123.

22  Andrzej Walicki, 'Transitional Justice and the Political Struggles of Post-Communist Poland' in *Transitional Justice and the Rule of Law in New Democracies*, ed. A. J. McAdams (Notre Dame, IN: University of Notre Dame Press, 1997), 189.

23  Formally the Extraordinary Commission for Investigating the Activities of the Interior Ministry (*Sejmowa Komisja Nadzwyczajna do Zbadania Działalności MSW*).

24  See for example Peter Solomon, ed., *Reforming Justice in Russia, 1864–1996: Power, Culture, and the Limits of Legal Order* (Armonk, NY: M.E. Sharpe, c1997).

25  *Raport Rokity. Sprawozdanie Sejmowej Komisji Nadzwyczajnej do Zbadania Działalności MSW* (Kraków: Arcana, 2005), 176–7.

26  Cited in Calhoun, *Dilemmas of Justice*, 112.

27  *Raport Rokity*, 179–80.

28  Andrzej Ajnikiel, cited in Skaner, 'Komisja Michnika', *Wprost*, 20 February 2005; Jerzy Holzer, 'Byłem naiwny', *Gazeta Wyborcza*, 15 June 2005.

29  Geremek and Żakowski, *Rok 1989*, 316.

30  Maria Los and Andrzej Zybertowicz, *Privatizing the Police-State. The Case of Poland* (Basingstoke: Macmillan Press, 2000), 66–8.

31  Andrew Michta, *The Red Eagle: The Army in Polish Politics, 1944–1988* (Stanford: Hoover Institution Press, c.1990), 189.

32  Krzysztof Kozłowski, 'Rewolucja po polsku', *Przegląd Bezpieczeństwa Wewnętrznego*, Special Edition, 2010: 14, from http://www.abw.gov.pl/portal/pl/336/764/Przeglad_ Bezpieczenstwa_Wewnetrznego__WYDANIE_SPECJALNE_z_okazji_80_rocznicy_ uro.html

33  'Uchwała nr 69 Rady Ministrów z dnia 21 maja 1990 r. w sprawie trybu i warunków przyjmowania byłych funkcjonariuszy Służby Bezpieczeństwa do służby w Urzędzie Ochrony Państwa i w innych jednostkach organizacyjnych podległych Ministrowi Spraw Wewnętrznych oraz zatrudniania ich w Ministerstwie Spraw Wewnętrznych', *Monitor Polski*, 1990, no. 20, poz. 159, http://www.monitorpolski.gov.pl/ MP/1990/159/1

34  Widacki, *Czego nie powiedział*, 26–8.

35    Kozłowski, 'Rewolucja po polsku', 14.
36    Cited in Calhoun, *Dilemmas of Justice*, 106.
37    'Ustawa z dnia 16 października 1991 r. o zmianie ustaw – Prawo o ustroju sądów
      powszechnych, o Sądzie Najwyższym, o prokuraturze, o wynagrodzeniu osób
      zajmujących kierownicze stanowiska państwowe', *Dziennik Ustaw*, 1991, poz. 443,
      http://www.dziennikustaw.gov.pl/DU/1991/443/1
38    Trybunał Konstytucyjny, 'Orzeczenie z dnia 9 listopada 1993 r', Sygn. akt K. 11/93,
      http://otkzu.trybunal.gov.pl/1993
39    *Rzeczpospolita*, 11 September 1990.
40    'Ustawa z dnia 24 stycznia 1991r. o kombatantach oraz niektórych osobach będących
      ofiarami represji wojennych i okresu powojennego', *Dziennik Ustaw* 1991, poz. 75,
      http://www.dziennikustaw.gov.pl/DU/1991/75/1
41    'Ustawa z dnia 23 lutego 1991 r. o uznaniu za nieważne orzeczeń wydanych wobec
      osób represjonowanych za działalność na rzecz niepodległego bytu Państwa
      Polskiego', *Dziennik Ustaw*, 1991, poz. 149, http://www.dziennikustaw.gov.pl/
      DU/1991/149/1
42    'Ustawa z dnia 17 maja 1989 r. o stosunku Państwa do Kościoła Katolickiego
      w Polskiej Rzeczypospolitej Ludowej', *Dziennik Ustaw*, 1989, poz. 154, http://
      www.dziennikustaw.gov.pl/DU/1989/154/1. Its implementing regulations were
      'Zarządzenie Ministra - Kierownika Urzędu Rady Ministrów z dnia 8 lutego 1990
      r. w sprawie szczegółowego trybu postępowania regulacyjnego w przedmiocie
      przywrócenia osobom prawnym Kościoła Katolickiego własności nieruchomości
      lub ich części', *Monitor Polski* 1990, poz. 39, http://www.monitorpolski.gov.pl/
      MP/1990/39/1
43    He maintained this position throughout his life; see for example his interviews with
      Janina Paradowska, *Polityka*, 9 November 1999 and Ewa Milewicz, *Gazeta Wyborcza*,
      9 November 1999.
44    Roman David, *Lustration and Transitional Justice: Personnel Systems in the Czech
      Republic, Hungary, and Poland* (Philadelphia: Pennsylvania University Press, 2011).
45    On the presidential election, see Frances Millard, *Polish Politics and Society* (London:
      Routledge, 1999), 82–3.
46    On the election see Frances Millard, *Democratic Elections in Poland* (London:
      Routledge, 2010), 36–55.
47    'Uchwała w sprawie uznania decyzji o wprowadzeniu stanu wojennego za nielegalną
      oraz powołania Komisji Nadzwyczajnej', *Monitor Polski*,1992 no. 5 poz. 23, http://
      www.monitorpolski.gov.pl/MP/1992/23/1
48    The record of the debate of 1 February is 'Sprawozdanie stenograficzne Sejmu',
      1 kadencja, 7 posiedzenie, 3 dzień, http://orka2.sejm.gov.pl/Debata1.nsf/
      main/49286D56
49    'Uchwała Sejmu Rzeczypospolitej Polskiej z dnia 28 maja 1992 r', *Monitor Polski*,
      1992 no. 16 poz.116, http://www.monitorpolski.gov.pl/MP/1992/116/1
50    *Rzeczpospolita*, 4–5 July 1992; *Zycie Warszawy*, 4–5 July 1992, *Gazeta Wyborcza*, 4–5
      July 1992.
51    *Rzeczpospolita*, 5 June 1992.
52    *Rzeczpospolita*, 11 June 1992.
53    See Antoni Dudek, *Pierwsze lata III Rzeczpospolitej 1989–2001* (Krakow: Arcana
      Historii, 2005), 275–88.
54    Aleksander Kwaśniewski in the *Sejm* on 9 November 1993; http://orka2.sejm.gov.pl/
      Debata2.nsf/9a905bcb5531f478c125745f0037938e/cb37146b870db3d7c12574e4003f5
      209?OpenDocument

55  See for example Janina Paradowska and Jerzy Baczyński, 'Cudze błędy' (Interview with Lech Wałęsa), *Polityka*, 14 January 1995.
56  'Orzeczenie Trybunału Konstytucyjnego z 1994–02-15', sygn. K 15/93', https://ipo. trybunal.gov.pl/ipo/view/sprawa.xhtml?sprawa=3162&dokument=57
57  'Ustawa z dnia 24 kwietnia 1997 r. o zmianie ustawy o kombatantach oraz niektórych osobach będących ofiarami represji wojennych i okresu powojennego', *Dziennik Ustaw*, 1997, poz. 405, http://www.dziennikustaw.gov.pl/DU/1997/405/1
58  Milczanowski's and Oleksy's speeches to parliament were published in *Rzeczpospolita*, 11 December 1995.
59  'Ustawa z dnia 11 kwietnia 1997 r. o ujawnieniu pracy, służby w organach bezpieczeństwa państwa lub współpracy z nimi w latach 1944–1990', *Dzienik Ustaw* 1997 nr 70 poz. 443, http://www.dziennikustaw.gov.pl/DU/1997/443/1
60  Roman David, 'From Prague to Baghdad: Lustration Systems and Their Political Effects', *Government and Opposition* 41, no. 3 (2006): 360.
61  Monika Nalepa, 'To Punish the Guilty and Protect the Innocent: Comparing Truth Revelation Procedures', *Journal of Theoretical Politics* 2, no. 2 (2008): 241.
62  The Commission's arguments were elucidated in the *Sejm*, Kadencja 2, 90th sitting, day three (11 October 1996), http://orka2.sejm.gov.pl/Debata2.nsf/main/40B59F55
63  'Ustawa z dnia 18 czerwca 1998 r. o zmianie ustawy o ujawnieniu pracy lub służby w organach bezpieczeństwa państwa lub współpracy z nimi w latach 1944–1990 osób pełniących funkcje publiczne oraz o zmianie niektórych innych ustaw', *Dziennik Ustaw* 1998, poz. 860, http://www.dziennikustaw.gov.pl/DU/1998/860/1
64  'Ustawa z dnia 18 grudnia 1998 r. o Instytucie Pamięci Narodowej – Komisji Ścigania Zbrodni przeciwko Narodowi Polskiemu', *Dziennik Ustaw*, 1998, poz. 1016, http:// dziennikustaw.gov.pl/DU/1998/1016/1
65  *Rzeczpospolita*, 5 March 1999.
66  'Ustawa z dnia 14 grudnia 2001 r. o zmianie ustawy o kombatantach oraz niektórych osobach będących ofiarami represji i okresu powojennego', *Dziennik Ustaw* 2001, poz. 1788, http://www.dziennikustaw.gov.pl/DU/2001/1788/1
67  'Wyrok Trybunału Konstytucyjnego z dnia 9 marca 2004 r.', sygn. akt K 12/02, https:// ipo.trybunal.gov.pl/ipo/Sprawa?cid=1&dokument=2&sprawa=3603
68  'Ustawa z dnia 13 września 2002 r. o zmianie ustawy o ujawnieniu pracy lub służby w organach bezpieczeństwa państwa lub współpracy z nimi w latach 1944–1990 osób pełniących funkcje publiczne', *Dziennik Ustaw*, 2002, poz. 1434, http://www. dziennikustaw.gov.pl/DU/2002/s/175/1434/1
69  *Rzeczpospolita*, 21 April 2005.
70  Jarosław Kaczyński, 'Wprowadzenie', IV RZECZPOSPOLITA Sprawiedliwość dla Wszystkich', Prawo i Sprawiedliwość Program 2005, 7–13, http://old.pis.org.pl/ dokumenty.php?s=partia&iddoc=3
71  'Ustawa z dnia 18 października 2006 r. o ujawnianiu informacji o dokumentach organów bezpieczeństwa państwa z lat 1944–1990 oraz treści tych dokumentów', *Dziennik Ustaw* 2006, poz 1592, http://www.dziennikustaw.gov.pl/ DU/2006/s/218/1592/1
72  'Ustawa z dnia 7 września 2007 r. o zmianie ustawy o ujawnianiu informacji o dokumentach organów bezpieczeństwa państwa z lat 1944–1990 oraz treści tych dokumentów', *Dziennik Ustaw* 2007, poz. 1171, http://www.dziennikustaw.gov.pl/ DU/2007/1171/1
73  Quoted in *Gazeta Wyborcza*, 25 April 2007.
74  Piotr Semka, 'Kto się schowa za plecami Ewy Milewicz?', *Rzeczpospolita*, 9 March 2007.

75 'Wyrok z dnia 11 maja 2007 r., Sygn. akt K 2/07, http://ipo.trybunal.gov.pl/ipo/Spraw a?cid=1&dokument=444&sprawa=4291

76 'Ustawa z dnia 19 września 2007 r. o zmianie ustawy o uznaniu za nieważne orzeczeń wydanych wobec osob represjonowanych za działalność na rzecz niepodległego bytu Państwa Polskiego', *Dziennik Ustaw* 2007, poz. 1372, http://dziennikustaw.gov.pl/ DU/2007/s/191/1372/1

77 'Klub PO złożył w czwartek w Sejmie projekt zmian w ustawie o IPN', Polish Press Agency, 3 December 2009, http://www.tvs.pl/informacje/klub-po-zlozyl-w-sejmie-projekt-zmian-w-ustawie-o-ipn-2009-12-03

78 'Ustawa z dnia 18 marca 2010 r.o zmianie ustawy o Instytucie Pamięci Narodowej – Komisji Ścigania Zbrodni przeciwko Narodowi Polskiemu oraz ustawy o ujawnianiu informacji o dokumentach organów bezpieczeństwa państwa z lat 1944–1990 oraz treści tych dokumentów', *Dziennik Ustaw* 2010, poz. 522, http://www.dziennikustaw. gov.pl/DU/2010/522/1

79 'Ustawa z dnia 7 maja 2009 r. o zadośćuczynieniu rodzinom ofiar zbiorowych wystąpień wolnościowych w latach 1956–1989', *Dziennik Ustaw* 2009, poz. 741, http://dziennikustaw.gov.pl/DU/2009/741/1

80 'Ustawa z dnia 9 lipca 2015 r. o zmianie ustawy o uznaniu za nieważne orzeczeń wydanych wobec osób represjonowanych za działalność na rzecz niepodległego bytu Państwa Polskiego', *Dziennik Ustaw* 2015, poz 1188, http://dziennikustaw.gov.pl/ du/2015/1188/1

# Chapter 3

1 Czechoslovakia cancelled virtually all sentences from the Stalinist period in Law 119/1990. In 1991 the 'Large Restitution' (Law 87/1991) rehabilitated those convicted of crimes against the state in 1948–89; John Borneman, *Settling Accounts. Violence, Justice, and Accountability in Postsocialist Europe* (Princeton: Princeton University Press, 1997), 153. In 2011 Czech Law 262/2011 awarded documented participants in the 'anti-communist resistance' a one-off payment of 100,000 crowns. In Romania action was late and ineffective; Monica Ciobanu, 'Recent Restorative Justice Measures in Romania (2006–2010)', *Problems of Post Communism* 60, no. 5 (2013): 45–57.

2 Wiktor Osiatyński, 'The Roundtable Talks in Poland' in *The Roundtable Talks and the Breakdown of Communism*, ed. Jon Elster (Chicago: University of Chicago Press, 1996), 46, 55.

3 'Ustawa z dnia 24 maja 1989 r. o szczególnych uprawnieniach niektórych osób do ponownego nawiązania stosunku pracy', *Dziennik Ustaw*, 1989, poz. 112, http:// dziennikustaw.gov.pl/DU/1989/s/32/172/1

4 'Ustawa z dnia 7 grudnia 1989 r. o zmianie ustawy o szczególnych uprawnieniach niektórych osób do ponownego nawiązania stosunku pracy', *Dziennik Ustaw* 1989, poz. 391, http://dziennikustaw.gov.pl/1989/s/64/D1989064000001.pdf

5 'Uchwała składu 7 sędziów SN z dnia 10 kwietnia 1992 r., sygn. I PZP 9/92, *Orzecznictwo Sądu Najwyższego Cywilne i Pracy*, 1992, nr. 12, poz. 210 (not available online).

6 'Wyrok z dnia 28 marca 1996 r., sygn. I PRN 1/96, http://dokumenty.e-prawnik.pl/ orzecznictwo/sad-najwyzszy/izba-pracy/3iprn961.html

7 'Wyrok SN', I PRN 105/95, 5 March 1996, http://prawo.money.pl/orzecznictwo/sad-najwyzszy/wyrok;sn;izba;pracy;ubezpieczen;spolecznych;i;spraw;publicznych,ia,i,prn,105,95,925,orzeczenie.html

8     'Postanowienie Trybunału Konstytucyjnego z dnia 10 marca 1998 r.', Sygn. K. 31/97,
      https://ipo.trybunal.gov.pl/ipo/Sprawa?cid=1&dokument=482&sprawa=3068
9     Blanka Stefańska, 'Zatarcie skazania z mocy prawa', *Prokurator i Prawo*, no. 2 (2008):
      62–86.
10    'Ustawa o przebaczeniu i puszczeniu w niepamięć niektórych przestępstw i
      wykroczeń', *Dziennik Ustaw* 1989, poz. 179, http://www.dziennikustaw.gov.pl/
      DU/1989/179/1
11    'Uchwała Trybunału Konstytucyjnego z dnia 2 maja 1990 r ...', Syg. W2/89, *Dziennik
      Ustaw* 1990, poz 189, http://www.dziennikustaw.gov.pl/DU/1990/189/1
12    'Ustawa z dnia 4 kwietnia 1991 r. o zmianie ustawy o Głównej Komisji Badania
      Zbrodni Hitlerowskich w Polsce – Instytucie Pamięci Narodowej', *Dziennik Ustaw*
      1991, poz. 195, http://www.dziennikustaw.gov.pl/DU/1991/195/1
13    'Wyrok z dnia 16 Września 1991 r.', WRN 81/91.
14    Wanda Fałkowska, 'Przebaczenie nie będzie', *Gazeta Wyborcza*, 5 June 1991 (this
      verdict was unpublished).
15    Postanowienie o 'przebaczeniu i puszczeniu w niepamięć przestępstwa',
      http://13grudnia81.pl/sip/index.php?opt=1&n=P&idS=1776&p=1&sG=1435&spra
      wa=6594
16    https://13grudnia81.pl/
17    *Rzeczpospolita*, 11 September 1990.
18    Reported in the *Sejm*, 23 February 1991, http://orka2.sejm.gov.pl/StenogramyX.nsf/0
      /6708C2DA34014432C1257D20002CC72B/$file/052_000007049.pdf
19    http://ipn.gov.pl/__data/assets/pdf_file/0004/145957/30.06.2005-Sprawa-
      pozbawienia-zycia-79-osob-mieszkancow-pow.-Bielsk-Podlaski,-w-tym-30-tzw.-
      furmanow,-w-lesie-kolo-Puchal-Starych-S-28-02-Zi.pdf; see Timothy Snyder,
      'To Resolve the Ukrainian Question Once and for All: The Ethnic Cleansing of
      Ukrainians in Poland, 1943–1947', *Journal of Cold War Studies* 1, no. 2 (1999):
      98–9; Tadeusz Piotrowski, ed., *Genocide and Rescue in Wolyn: Recollections of the
      Ukrainian Nationalist Ethnic Cleansing Campaign against the Poles during World
      War II* (Jefferson, NC: McFarland & Company, 2000).
20    Macej Jasiak, 'Overcoming Ukrainian Resistance. The Deportations of Ukrainians
      within Poland in 1947' in *Redrawing Nations: Ethnic Cleansing in East-Central
      Europe, 1944–1948*, eds. Philipp Ther and Ana Siljak (Lanham, MD: Rowman &
      Littlefield, 2001), 174.
21    Igor Hałagida, *Ukraińcy na zachodnich i północnych ziemiach Polski 1947–1957*
      (Warsaw: Instytut Pamięci Narodowej, 2002), 25.
22    Berling's Army was formed in the USSR in 1944 from the Polish I Corps, recruited
      from Polish soldiers taken prisoner during the 1939 Soviet invasion and those
      deported from Soviet-occupied Poland in 1939–41.
23    Anthony Polonsky and Bolesław Drukier, eds, *The Beginnings of Communist Rule in
      Poland, December 1943–June 1945* (London: Routledge & Kegan Paul, 1980), 30–1.
24    Polonsky and Drukier, *The Beginnings*, 108.
25    Snyder, 'To Resolve ...', 107–14.
26    'Postanowienie o umorzeniu śledztwa', Katowice, Sygn. akt S 71/12/Zk, 28 October
      2013, http://ipn.gov.pl/__data/assets/pdf_file/0008/138077/28.10.2013-Likwidacja-
      czlonkow-zgromadzenia-NSZ-pod-dow.-Henryka-Flamego-ps.-Bartek-S-71-12-
      Zk.pdf Apologetic sites litter the web, for example https://obserwatorpolityczny.
      pl/?p=8306

27  Polonsky and Drukier, *The Beginnings*, 146; Rafał Wnuk et al., eds, *Atlas polskiego podziemia niepodległościowego 1944–1956* (Warsaw: IPN, 2007); R. Sierchuła, 'Wizja Polski w koncepcjach ideologów Organizacji Polskiej w latach 1944–1945' in *Narodowcy. Myśl polityczna i społeczna obozu narodowego w Polsce w latach 1944–1947*, eds. L. Kulińska et al. (Warsaw: PWN, 2001), 134–40; Paweł Machcewicz, quoted in Adam Leszczyński, 'Pamięć historyczna bez polityków', *Gazeta Wyborcza*, 29 March 2012.

28  Tadeusz Piotrowski, *Poland's Holocaust: Ethnic Strife, Collaboration with Occupying Forces, and Genocide in the Second Republic, 1918–1947* (Jefferson: McFarland & Company, 1990), 97; Adam Michnik with Agnieszka Marczyk, 'Introduction: Poland and Anti-Semitism' in *Against Anti-Semitism: An Anthology of Twentieth Century Polish Writings*, eds. Adam Michnik and Agnieszka Marczyk (Oxford: Oxford University Press, 2017).

29  Emanuel Ringelblum, *Polish-Jewish Relations during the Second World War* (Evanston: Northwestern University Press, 1992), 311–12. Compare Żebrowski, who judges the NSZ a victim of vicious propaganda, denies charges of anti-Semitism and describes the NSZ as 'the most anti-German element of the Polish independence movement'; Leszek Żebrowski, *Narodowe Siły Zbrojne. Dokumenty. Struktury. Personalia* (Warsaw: Burchard Edition, 1994), 9.

30  'Informacja o ustaleniach końcowych śledztwa S 28/02/Zi w sprawie pozbawienia życia 79 osób – mieszkańców powiatu Bielsk Podlaski, w tym 30 osób tzw. furmanów, w lesie koło Puchał Starych, dokonanego w okresie od dnia 29 stycznia 1946 r. do dnia 2 lutego 1946 r', http://ipn.gov.pl/__data/assets/pdf_file/0004/145957/30.06.2005-Sprawa-pozbawienia-zycia-79-osob-mieszkancow-pow.-Bielsk-Podlaski,-w-tym-30-tzw.-furmanow,-w-lesie-kolo-Puchal-Starych-S-28-02-Zi.pdf

31  For example, https://obserwatorpolityczny.pl/?p=8306 and https://historiamniejznanaizapomniana.wordpress.com/2016/01/29/70-rocznica-pacyfikacji-bialoruskich-wsi-przez-oddzial-nzw-burego/

32  http://parezja.pl/wplyw-postaw-losow-i-walk-zolnierzy-wykletych-na-stosunek-spoleczenstwa-polskiego-wobec-wladz-prl/ or http://wpolityce.pl/polityka/139702-leszek-zebrowski-narodowe-sily-zbrojne-wobec-dwoch-okupantow or http://tropemwilczym.pl/

33  Both sides are represented in the comments at http://wiadomosci.onet.pl/tablica/zolnierze-wykleci-czy-zwyczajni-bandyci,1666,270154,134583232,watek.html

34  *Sejm*, Debate of 22–23 November 1990, http://orka2.sejm.gov.pl/StenogramyX.nsf/0/C962506510FE8E1FC1257D20002CC723/$file/044_000007433.pdf

35  *Sejm*, Debate of 29–30 November 1990, http://orka2.sejm.gov.pl/StenogramyX.nsf/0/AD079EEC0A59D207C1257D20002CC724/$file/045_000006909.pdf

36  'Ustawa z dnia 24 stycznia 1991r. o kombatantach oraz niektórych osobach będących ofiarami represji wojennych i okresu powojennego', *Dziennik Ustaw* 1991, poz. 75, http://dziennikustaw.gov.pl/DU/1991/75/1

37  'Ustawa z dnia 23 lutego 1991 r. o uznaniu za nieważne orzeczeń wydanych wobec osób represjonowanych za działalność na rzecz niepodległego bytu Państwa Polskiego', *Dziennik Ustaw* 1991, poz. 149, http://dziennikustaw.gov.pl/DU/1991/s/34/149/1

38  *Sejm*, Debate of 23 February 1991, http://orka2.sejm.gov.pl/StenogramyX.nsf/0/6708C2DA34014432C1257D20002CC72B/$file/052_000007049.pdf

39  'Wyrok NSA z 1993–10–19', Syg. V SA 250/93 from http://www.orzeczenia-nsa.
    pl/wyrok/v-sa-250-93/sprawy_kombatantow_swiadczenia_z_tytulu_pracy_
    przymusowej_kombatanci/4bd4dd.html
40  This was not published; see http://orka2.sejm.gov.pl/Debata2.nsf/main/5425A08E
41  'Ustawa z dnia 20 lutego 1993 r. zmieniająca ustawę o uznaniu za nieważne orzeczeń
    wydanych wobec osób represjonowanych …', *Dziennik Ustaw* 1993, poz. 159, http://
    dziennikustaw.gov.pl/DU/1993/s/36/159/1
42  'Orzeczenie w imieniu Rzeczypospolitej Polskiej z dnia 15 lutego 1994 r.', Sygn. K.
    15/93, https://ipo.trybunal.gov.pl/ipo/Sprawa?cid=3&dokument=57&sprawa=3162
43  'Ustawa z dnia 24 stycznia 1997 r. o zmianie ustawy o kombatantach …', *Dziennik
    Ustaw* 1997, poz. 83, http://dziennikustaw.gov.pl/DU/1997/83/1
44  'Ustawa z dnia 24 kwietnia 1997 r. o zmianie ustawy o kombatantach …', *Dziennik
    Ustaw*, 1997, poz. 405, http://dziennikustaw.gov.pl/DU/1997/405/1
45  'Ustawa z dnia 25 kwietnia 1997 o zmianie ustawy o kombatantach …', *Dziennik
    Ustaw* 1997, poz. 436, http://dziennikustaw.gov.pl/DU/1997/436/1
46  Tomasz Balbus, 'Polskie "Istriebitielne Bataliony" NKWD w latach 1944–1945',
    *Biuletyn Instytutu Pamięci Narodowej*, no. 6 (2002): 71–5.
47  The full text of the judgment (sygn. akt 293/95, 4 June 1996) is not available. The
    quotations here are taken from available summaries, http://solidarni2010.pl/29253-
    posel-sld-e-czykwin-chce-zeby-ipn-zablokowalo-powstanie-ronda-zolnierzy-
    wykletych-w-bialymstoku.html?PHPSESSID=7e5dad5f1c48a316e30ef96db331fc34
    and http://www.przegladprawoslawny.pl/articles.php?id_n=3206&id=2
48  http://ipn.gov.pl/__data/assets/pdf_file/0004/145957/30.06.2005-Sprawa-
    pozbawienia-zycia-79-osob-mieszkancow-pow.-Bielsk-Podlaski,-w-tym-30-tzw.-
    furmanow,-w-lesie-kolo-Puchal-Starych-S-28-02-Zi.pdf
49  'Ustawa z dnia 6 lutego 1998 r. o zmianie ustawy o kombatantach …', *Dziennik Ustaw*
    1998, poz. 204, http://dziennikustaw.gov.pl/du/1998/s/37/204
50  'Ustawa z dnia 4 marca 1999 r. o zmianie ustawy o kombatantach …', *Dziennik Ustaw*
    1999, poz. 862, http://www.dziennikustaw.gov.pl/DU/1999/s/77/862/1
51  'Wyrok z 15 IX 1999 r.', sygn. K 11/99, https://ipo.trybunal.gov.pl/ipo/Sprawa?cid=2&
    dokument=201&sprawa=2812
52  'Ustawa z dnia 9 kwietnia 1999 r. o zmianie ustawy o Instytucie Pamięci Narodowej
    …', *Dziennik Ustaw* 1999, poz. 360, http://dziennikustaw.gov.pl/DU/1999/s/38/360
53  Marek Henzler, 'Ciągle w boju', *Polityka*, 12 May 2001; Paweł Dybicz, 'Prawo
    kombatanta', *Tygodnik Przegląd*, 9 May 2004 (Interview with Jan Turski).
54  Dybicz, 'Prawo kombatanta'.
55  'Ustawa z dnia 14 grudnia 2001 r. o zmianie ustawy o kombatantach …', *Dziennik
    Ustaw* 2001, poz. 1788, from http://www.dziennikustaw.gov.pl/DU/2001/1788/1
56  'Wyrok z dnia 9 marca 2004 r.', sygn. akt K 12/02, http://ipo.trybunal.gov.pl/ipo/Spra
    wa?cid=1&dokument=2&sprawa=3603
57  Dybicz, 'Prawo kombatanta'.
58  *Druk* 3437, 20 October 2004, from http://orka.sejm.gov.pl/Druki4ka.
    nsf/($vAllByUnid)/EB72003291FE79E3C1256F4F002EB711/$file/3437.pdf
59  *Druk* 4056, 29 April 2005, http://orka.sejm.gov.pl/Druki4ka.nsf/$vAllByUnid/5D8A
    A7ED5E0B8BD2C125700A004468CC/$file/4056.pdf
60  *Druk* 3526, 23 November 2004, http://orka.sejm.gov.pl/Druki4ka.nsf/($vAllByUnid)/
    CBAF1CA0B5588CA3C1256F5F003A94D7/$file/3526.pdf

61 Urząd do Spraw Kombatantów i Osób Represjonowanych, 'Założenia nowelizacji (reformy) prawa kombatanckiego', Warsaw, 30 November 2006, http://radalegislacyjna.gov.pl/sites/default/files/dokumenty/projekt_ustawy_56.pdf

62 'Projekt ustawy o uprawnieniach kombatantów, uczestników walki cywilnej lat 1914–1945, działaczy opozycji wobec dyktatury komunistycznej oraz niektórych ofiar represji systemów totalitarnych', http://orka.sejm.gov.pl/proc6.nsf/0/164C25FC4 F46E8FFC12577BA004A74AE?OpenDocument

63 Biuro Analiz, 'Opinia Prawna dotyczącą projektu ustawy – o uprawnieniach kombatantów, uczestników walki cywilnej lat 1914–1945, działaczy opozycji wobec dyktatury komunistycznej oraz niektórych ofiar represji systemów totalitarnych', Warsaw, 16 October 2008, http://orka.sejm.gov.pl/rexdomk6.nsf/ Opdodr?OpenPage&nr=818

64 'Projekt Ustawy o zmianie ustawy o kombatantach oraz niektórych osobach będących ofiarami represji wojennych i okresu powojennego', *Druk* 813, 29 May 2008, http://orka.sejm.gov.pl/Druki6ka.nsf/0/68544C3F25F77B98C125749000318ED B/$file/813.pdf

65 *Druk* 180, 28 December 2011, http://orka.sejm.gov.pl/Druki7ka.nsf/0/3F727C97AB3 E50C8C125799F0035BE99/%24File/180.pdf

66 See his moving speech to the Committee, 19 June 2013, http://www.sejm.gov.pl/ Sejm7.nsf/biuletyn.xsp?documentId=4A638D947EF6D9E3C1257B950063A44A

67 'Ustawa z dnia 3 lutego 2011 r. o ustanowieniu Narodowego Dnia Pamięci "Żołnierzy Wyklętych"', *Dziennik Ustaw* 2011, poz. 160, http://dziennikustaw.gov.pl/ DU/2011/160/1

68 'Ustawa z dnia 14 marca 2014 r. o zmianie ustawy o kombatantach ...', *Dziennik Ustaw* 2014, poz. 496, http://dziennikustaw.gov.pl/DU/2014/496/1

69 'Ustawa z dnia 26 stycznia 2017 r. o zmianie ustawy o kombatantach ...', *Dziennik Ustaw*, 2017, poz. 456, http://dziennikustaw.gov.pl/DU/2017/456/1

70 The limit was between 17 September 1939 and 5 February 1946, when Poland's new boundaries were ratified.

71 'Ustawa z dnia 19 września 2007 r. o zmianie ustawy o uznaniu za nieważne orzeczeń wydanych wobec osob represjonowanych za działalność na rzecz niepodległego bytu Państwa Polskiego', *Dziennik Ustaw* 2007, poz. 1372, http://dziennikustaw.gov.pl/ DU/2007/s/191/1372/1

72 'Ustawa z dnia 9 lipca 2015 r. o zmianie ustawy o uznaniu za nieważne orzeczeń wydanych wobec osób represjonowanych za działalność na rzecz niepodległego bytu Państwa Polskiego', *Dziennik Ustaw* 2015, poz. 1188, from http://dziennikustaw.gov. pl/du/2015/1188/1

73 'Ustawa z 2 września 1994 r. o dodatku i uprawnieniach przysługujących żołnierzom zastępczej służby wojskowej przymusowo zatrudnianym w kopalniach węgla, kamieniołomach i zakładach wydobywania rud uranu', *Dziennik Ustaw* 1994, poz. 537, http://dziennikustaw.gov.pl/DU/1994/537/1

74 'Ustawa z dnia 31 maja 1996 r. o świadczeniu pieniężnym przysługującym osobom deportowanym do pracy przymusowej oraz osadzonym w obozach pracy przez III Rzeszę i Związek Socjalistycznych Republik Radzieckich', *Dziennik Ustaw* 1996, poz. 395, http://www.dziennikustaw.gov.pl/DU/1996/s/87/395/1

75 'Ustawa z dnia 7 maja 2009 r. o zadośćuczynieniu rodzinom ofiar zbiorowych wystąpień wolnościowych w latach 1956–1989', *Dziennik Ustaw* 2009, poz. 741, http://dziennikustaw.gov.pl/DU/2009/741/1

76 'Ustawa z dnia 20 marca 2015 r. o działaczach opozycji antykomunistycznej oraz osobach represjonowanych z powodów politycznych', *Dziennik Ustaw* 2015, poz. 693, http://dziennikustaw.gov.pl/DU/2015/693/1

77 In the *Sejm*, 18 March 2015, http://orka2.sejm.gov.pl/StenoInter7.nsf/0/A38BBC87C 2AAAF73C1257E0D00088104/%24File/89_a_ksiazka_bis.pdf

78 'Poselski projekt ustawy o uznaniu za nieważne orzeczeń wydanych wobec byłych posłów na Sejm Rzeczypospolitej Polskiej skazanych w procesie brzeskim za działalność na rzecz demokratycznego Państwa Polskiego', *Druk* 232, 20 January 2016, http://orka.sejm.gov.pl/Druki8ka.nsf/0/F3DB16210A042C53C1257F54003877 7C/%24File/232.pdf

79 Norman Davies, *Heart of Europe: The Past in Poland's Present* (Oxford: Oxford University Press, 2001), 132.

80 'Odpowiedź zastępcy prokuratora generalnego - z upoważnienia ministra – na interpelację nr 5297', http://orka2.sejm.gov.pl/IZ6.nsf/2df80fe4116b3f62c12573be003 cb40d/3a4315196139cff5c1257512003b9c8f?OpenDocument

81 'Obwieszczenie Presa Trybunału Konstytucyjnego z dnia 9 września 1994 r. o utracie mocy obowiązującej art. 21 ust. 2 pkt 4 a) ustawy o kombatantach oraz niektórych osobach będących ofiarami represji wojennych i okresu powojenego', *Dziennik Ustaw* 1994, 99 poz 482, http://www.dziennikustaw.gov.pl/DU/1994/482/1

82 'Wyrok z dnia 15 kwietnia 2003 r.', Sygn. Akt SK4/02, https://ipo.trybunal.gov.pl/ipo/ Sprawa?cid=1&dokument=1302&sprawa=3279

83 'Wyrok Trybunału Konstytucyjnego z dnia 16 czerwca 2009 r', Syg. SK 42/08, 85/6/A/2009, https://ipo.trybunal.gov.pl/ipo/Sprawa?cid=2&dokument=1252&spra wa=4718

84 'Wyrok Trybunału Konstytucyjnego z dnia 26 lipca 2012 r', sygn. akt P 8/11, http:// otkzu.trybunal.gov.pl/2012/7A/84

85 Trybunał Konstytucyjny, 'Ograniczenie możliwości dochodzenia odszkodowania i zadośćuczynienia przez osoby represjonowane', Wyrok w imieniu Rzeczypospolitej Polskiej', Sygn. akt P 21/09, 1 March 2011, https://ipo.trybunal.gov.pl/ipo/Sprawa?cid =7&dokument=6362&sprawa=5197

86 'Wyrok w imieniu Rzeczypospolitej Polskiej', Sygn. akt K 35/08, Warsaw 16 March 2011, from https://ipo.trybunal.gov.pl/ipo/Sprawa?cid=1&dokument=6583&spra wa=4934

87 'Postanowienie Trybunału Konstytucyjnego z dnia 2 grudnia 2014 r.', sygn. akt SK7/14, http://otkzu.trybunal.gov.pl/2014/11A/123

88 It took until 2013 for the daughter of AK fighter Stanisław Rożek to receive compensation for his eight-year imprisonment and torture; http://www.polskieradio. pl/39/1240/Artykul/810855,Corka-zolnierza-AK-dostanie-200-tys-zl-odszkodowania

89 See Tomasz Kozłowski, 'Solidarność w sądzie', Pamięć.pl, http://testowyserwis. axiomcomputing.pl/pdf/solidarnosc-w-sadzie,1395.pdf

90 A. Grabowski and B. Naleziński, 'Kłopoty z obowiązywaniem prawa. Uwagi na tle orzecznictwa Trybunału Konstytucyjnego', in *Studia z filozofii prawa*, ed. J. Stelmach (Kraków, 2001), 227. T. Kozłowski and J. Olaszek, 'Internowani w stanie wojennym. Dane statystyczne', *Pamięć i Sprawiedliwość* 2 (2010): 505–10, http://ipn.gov.pl/__ data/assets/pdf_file/0007/107962/PIS_16.pdf

91 These figures come from Grzegorz Majchrzak, 'Obóz władzy w stanie wojennym', http://ipn.gov.pl/archiwalia/13-grudnia-1981-wprowadzenie-stanu-wojennego/ grzegorz-majchrzak-oboz-wladzy-w-stanie-wojennym

92 They are listed in Article 21 of the decree on procedures for offences committed during martial law.

93 Cited in Zenon Baranowski, 'Sądy blokują odszkodowania', *Nasz Dziennik*, 10 March 2014; also Cezary Łazarewicz and Mariusz Janicki, 'Zbrodnia, Kara, Odszkodowania', *Polityka*, 7 December 2011.

94 Ministerstwo Sprawiedliwości, 'Decyzja Ministra Sprawiedliwości: kolejne wnioski o unieważnienie orzeczeń wydanych wobec osób represjonowanych w PRL z powodów politycznych', 3 November 2011, http://ms.gov.pl/pl/archiwum-informacji/news,3623,10,decyzja-ministra-sprawiedliwosci-kolejne-wnioski.html; Archiwum informacji Ministerstwa Sprawiedliwości, 10 November 2011, http://ms.gov.pl/pl/archiwum-informacji/news,3645,10,wspolpraca-na-rzecz-odnalezienia-nieznanych-dotad.html

95 IPN, 'Instytut Pamięci Narodowej – Komisja Ścigania Zbrodni przeciwko Narodowi Polskiemu. Informacje o działalności 1 stycznia 2016 r. - 31 grudnia 2016.r', *Druk* 1573, 10 May 2017, http://orka.sejm.gov.pl/Druki8ka.nsf/0/FD860616136E9E33C125812A003E6142/%24File/1573.pdf

96 'Internowano go w stanie wojennym – dostał odszkodowanie', *Wprost*, 7 August 2012.

97 'Walczył o 2 miliony złotych za represje. Były opozycjonista dostał cztery tysiące', 24 September 2014, tvn24 Wrocław, http://www.tvn24.pl/wroclaw,44/walczyl-o-2-miliony-zlotych-za-represje-byly-opozycjonista-dostal-cztery-tysiace,471251.html

98 'Romaszewski dostał 240 tys. za więzienie w PRL. Lech Wałęsa: Jak senator może się domagać pieniędzy za opozycję?', NaTemat.pl, 15 January 2013, http://natemat.pl/47045,romaszewski-dostal-240-tys-za-wiezienie-w-prl-lech-walesa-jak-senator-moze-sie-domagac-pieniedzy-za-opozycje

# Chapter 4

1 Samuel Huntington, *The Third Wave: Democratization in the Late Twentieth Century* (London: University of Oklahoma Press, 1991), 228.

2 John Moran, 'The Communist Torturers of Eastern Europe: Prosecute and Punish or Forgive and Forget?' *Communist and Post-Communist Studies* 27, no. 1 (1994): 95.

3 CBOS, 'Opinia społeczna o wyborze Wojciecha Jaruzelskiego na prezydenta PRL', BD/175/34/89, Warsaw, August 1989.

4 CBOS, 'Wojciech Jaruzelski w opinii publicznej', BS/101/2009, Warsaw, July 2009.

5 'Uchwała w sprawie uznania decyzji o wprowadzeniu stanu wojennego za nielegalną oraz powołania Komisji Nadzwyczajnej', *Monitor Polski*, 1992, poz. 23, http://monitorpolski.gov.pl/MP/1992/23/1

6 Wojciech Sadurski, '"Decommunisation," "Lustration" and Constitutional Continuity: Dilemmas of Transitional Justice in Central Europe', European University Institute, 2003, Badia Fiesolana, San Dominico, Italy from http://cadmus.eui.eu/dspace/bitstream/1814/1869/2/law03-15.pdf; Lavinia Stan, *Transitional Justice in Post-Communist Romania: The Politics of Memory* (Cambridge: Cambridge University Press, 2013), 34–5.

7 'Ustawa z dnia 4 kwietnia 1991 r. o zmianie ustawy o Głównej Komisji Badania Zbrodni Hitlerowskich w Polsce – Instytucie Pamięci Narodowej', *Dziennik Ustaw* 1991, poz. 195, http://www.dziennikustaw.gov.pl/DU/1991/195/1

8 'Postanowienie z dnia 25 września 1991 r', Sygn S. 6/91, 25 September 1991, https://ipo.trybunal.gov.pl/ipo/view/sprawa.xhtml?sprawa=5777&dokument=908

9   'Ustawa z dnia 6 czerwca 1997 r., Kodeks karny', *Dziennik Ustaw* 1997, poz. 553, http://www.dziennikustaw.gov.pl/DU/1997/553/1

10  'Ustawa z dnia 18 grudnia 1998 r. o Instytucie Pamięci Narodowej – Komisji Ścigania Zbrodni przeciwko Narodowi Polskiemu', *Dziennik Ustaw*, 1998, poz. 1016, http://www.dziennikustaw.gov.pl/DU1998155101601.pdf

11  'Ustawa z dnia 3 czerwca 2005 r. o zmianie ustawy – Kodeks karny', *Dziennik Ustaw* 2005, poz 1109, http://www.dziennikustaw.gov.pl/DU/2005/1109/1

12  The unified version of the Law on the IPN is 'Ustawa z dnia 18 grudnia 1998 r. o Instytucie Pamięci Narodowej – Komisji Ścigania Zbrodni przeciwko Narodowi Polskiemu', *Dziennik Ustaw* 2007, poz. 424, Załącznik, http://dziennikustaw.gov.pl/DU/2007/424/1

13  'Wyrok z dnia 15 października 2008 r.', Sygn. akt P 32/06, 138/8/A/2008, http://ipo.trybunal.gov.pl/ipo/Sprawa?cid=5&dokument=863&sprawa=4115

14  Sąd Narodowy, 'Uchwała z dnia 25 Maja 2010 r.', I KZP 5/10, http://www.sn.pl/sites/orzecznictwo/Orzeczenia1/I%20KZP%205-10.pdf

15  http://ipn.gov.pl/kszpnp/akty-oskarzenia/216.-akt-oskarzenia-przeciwko-bogdanowi-m.html

16  IPN, 'Informacja o działalności Instytutu Pamięci Narodowej – Komisja Ścigania Zbrodni przeciwko Narodowi Polskiemu w okresie 1 stycznia 2010 r. – 31 grudnia 2010 r.', *Druk Sejmowy* 66, http://www.sejm.gov.pl/Sejm7.nsf/PrzebiegProc.xsp?nr=66

17  For the time line see Wiesława Kwiatkowska, 'Grudzień '70 – kalendarium śledztwa i procesu', *Biuletyn Pamięci Narodowej*, no. 11–12 (2006): 21–6.

18  (1) Wojciech Jaruzelski, d. 2014; (2) Kazimierz Świtała, d 2011; (3) Stanisław Kociołek, d 2015; (4) Tadeusz Tuczapski, d 2009; (5) Józef Kamiński, d.2015; (6) Stanisław Kruczek, d. 2013; (7) Edward Łańcucki; (8) Mirosław Wiekiera; (9) Wiesław Gop; (10) Władysław Łomot, d. before 2012; (11) Bolesław Fałdasz; (12) Karol Kubalica, d. 2001.

19  Article 16 defines preparation as occurring only 'when the perpetrator with the aim of carrying out a prohibited action undertakes actions to create the conditions for undertaking it … in particular when the perpetrator enters an understanding with another person, gaining or facilitating information, collects information or lays out a plan of action'.

20  The charges are available at http://grudzien70.solidarnosc.gda.pl/grudzien70/Grudzien70_09.htm

21  Kociołek, Tuczapski, Kruczek, Wiekiera, Gop, Łomot, and Fałdasz.

22  'Postanowieniem z dnia 8 listopada 1999 r.', sygn. III Ko 106/99, https://www.saos.org.pl/judgments/96859. According to Article 34 § 2 of the Code of Criminal Procedure if a crime involves several closely connected persons, their cases should be conducted together.

23  Bogdan Szegda, 'Nie zgadzam się z wyrokiem ws. Grudnia'70', *Dziennik Bałtycki*, 20 April 2013, from http://www.dziennikbaltycki.pl/artykul/873857,nie-zgadzam-sie-z-wyrokiem-ws-grudnia70,id,t.html

24  'Z przemówienia gen. Wojciecha Jaruzelskiego', Stenogram VIII Plenum KC 6–7 II 1971 r., Dokument 21, *Tajne dokumenty Biura Politycznego, Grudzień 1970*, ed. Paweł Domański (London: Aneks, 1991), 183.

25  This is a theme of Zbigniew Branach, *Oskarżony Jaruzelski i inni …* (Torun: AR Cetera, 2002).

26  'Sprawozdanie komisji powołanej przez Biuro Polityczne KC PZPR dla zbadania niektórych kwestii szczegółowych związanych z wydarzeniami grudniowymi 1970 r.',

Dokument 47, *Tajne dokumenty Biura Politycznego, Grudzień 1970*, ed. Paweł Domański (London: Aneks, 1991), 438.

27   Wojciech Jaruzelski, *Wyjaśniam. Wyjaśnienie złożone przed Sądem Okręgowym w Warszawie w dniach 18.10 i 08.11. 2001* (Torun: Mado, 2001).

28   See the testimony of party, state, and military officials in Branach, *Oskarżony Jaruzelski*; and in *Tajne dokumenty Biura Politycznego, Grudzień 1970*, ed. Paweł Domański (London: Aneks, 1991).

29   http://dzieje.pl/aktualnosci/sad-decyzja-o-uzyciu-broni-w-grudniu-1970-r-byla-bezprawna-i-przestepcza (italics mine).

30   'Wyrok w imieniu Rzeczypospolitej Polskiej', Sygn. akt K 35/08, 16 March 2011, from http://otk.trybunal.gov.pl/orzeczenia/teksty/OTKZU/2011/2011A_02.pdf

31   Michal Brzezinski, *Stany naszwyczajne w polskich konstytucjach* (Warsaw: Wydawnictwo Sejmowe, 2007), 128–9.

32   'Uchwała Rada Państwa z dnia 12 grudnia 1981 r. w sprawie wprowadzenia stany wojennego ze względu na bezpieczeństwa państwa', *Dziennik Ustaw* 1981, poz. 155, http://dziennikustaw.gov.pl/DU/1981/155/1

33   'Dekret Rady Państwa z dnia 12 grudnia 1981 r. o stanie wojennym', *Dziennik Ustaw* 1981, poz. 154, http://dziennikustaw.gov.pl/DU/1981/156/1

34   'Dekret z dnia 12 grudnia 1981 r. o postępowaniach szczególnych w sprawach o przestępstwa i wykroczenia w czasie obowiązywania stanu wojennego', *Dziennik Ustaw* 1981, poz. 156, http://dziennikustaw.gov.pl/DU/1981/s/29/156/1

35   'Dekret z dnia 12 grudnia 1981 r. o przekazaniu do właściwości sądów wojskowych spraw o niektóre przestępstwa oraz o zmianie ustroju sądów wojskowych i wojskowych jednostek organizacyjnych Prokuratury Polskiej Rzeczypospolitej Ludowej w czasie obowiązywania stanu wojennego', *Dziennik Ustaw* 1981, poz. 157, http://dziennikustaw.gov.pl/DU/1981/157/1

36   Ewa Milewicz and Mikołaj Lizut, 'Co zbóje, z którymi się spotkałem (Interview with Alojzy Orszulik)', *Gazeta Wyborcza*, 2 March 1999.

37   Lech Mażewski, *Problem legalności stanu wojennego z 12–13 grudnia 1981 r.* (Warsaw: Wydawnictwo von Borowiecky, 2012), 45, n. 21.

38   'Ustawa z dnia 25 stycznia 1982 r. o szczególnej regulacji prawnej w okresie stanu wojennego', *Dziennik Ustaw* 1982, poz. 18, http://isap.sejm.gov.pl/DetailsServlet?id=WDU19820030018

39   See Mażewski, 'Problem legalności', 57–63.

40   See for example Jerzy Holzer, 'Martial Law Evaluated by Historians and Generals at Jachranka. Are They Going In? They Did Not', http://www.wilsoncenter.org/sites/default/files/Martial%20Law%20Evaluated%20by%20Historians%20and%20Generals%20at%20Jachranka.pdf

41   'Dekret z dnia 12 grudnia o stanie wojennym', *Dziennik Ustaw* 1981, poz. 154, http://dziennikustaw.gov.pl/DU/1981/154/1

42   Vojtech Mastny, 'The Soviet Non-Invasion of Poland in 1980/81 and the End of the Cold War', Working Paper No. 23, Woodrow Wilson Center, Cold War International History Project, September 1998: 14, from http://www.wilsoncenter.org/sites/default/files/ACFB35.PDF

43   Matthew Ouimet, *The Rise and Fall of the Brezhnev Doctrine in Soviet Foreign Policy* (Chapel Hill: The University of North Carolina Press, 2003), 172.

44   Mark Kramer, 'Jaruzelski, the Soviet Union, and the Imposition of Martial Law in Poland: New Light on the Mystery of December 1981', *Cold War International History Project Bulletin*, Issue 11 (1998): 5 from http://www.wilsoncenter.org/publication/bulletin-no-11-winter-1998

45   Ouimet, *The Rise and Fall*, 172.
46   Ouimet; also Wilfried Loth, *Overcoming the Cold War: A History of Détente, 1950–1991* (Basingstoke: Palgrave, 2002), 230.
47   Mark Kramer, 'Jaruzelski, the Soviet Union, and the Imposition of Martial Law in Poland'.
48   Wojciech Jaruzelski, 'Commentary', *Cold War International History Project Bulletin*, Issue 11 (1998), from http://www.wilsoncenter.org/publication/bulletin-no-11-winter-1998
49   'Uchwała Sądu Najwyższego (Izba Karna) z dnia 20 grudnia 2007 r.', I KZP 37/07, http://sn.pl/Sites/orzecznictwo/Orzeczenia1/I%20KZP%2037-07.pdfMSN - I
50   'Akt oskarzenia przeciwko Wojciechowi Jaruzelskiemu (y innym)', sygn. akt S101/04/Zk, Katowice, 16 April 2007, from http://ipn.gov.pl/__data/assets/pdf_file/0018/128223/akt-oskarzenia-S-101-04-Zk_2.pdf
51   'Ustawa z dnia 27 lipca 2001 r. Prawo o ustroju sądów powszechnych', *Dziennik Ustaw* 2001, poz. 1070, http://dziennikustaw.gov.pl/DU/2001/1070/1
52   'Wyrok z dnia 27 października 2010 r.', Sygn. akt K 10/08, https://ipo.trybunal.gov.pl/ipo/Sprawa?cid=2&dokument=173&sprawa=4635
53   Stanisław Biernat, Adam Jamróz, Ewa Łętowska, Marek Mazurkiewicz, Bohdan Zdziennicki and Mirosław Wyrzykowski dissented. Their minority views are included in the Wyrok (see n. 52).
54   Ewa Łosińska, 'IPN rozliczy za stan wojenny', *Rzeczpospolita*, 6 November 2010.
55   'Wniosek Rzecznika Praw Obywatelskich', RPO-604624-1/08/MK/MZ, Warsaw, 12 December 2008, http://www.rpo.gov.pl/pliki/12290801120.pdf
56   'Wyrok w imieniu Rzeczypospolitej Polskiej', Sygn. akt K 35/08, Warsaw, 16 March 2011, https://ipo.trybunal.gov.pl/ipo/Sprawa?cid=3&dokument=6583&sprawa=4934 The documents pertaining to this case are available at http://trybunal.gov.pl/s/k-3508/under Dokumenty w sprawie (IPO).
57   'Ustawa z dnia 1 sierpnia 1997 r. o Trybunale Konstytucyjnym', *Dziennik Ustaw* 1997, poz. 643, http://dziennikustaw.gov.pl/DU/1997/643/1
58   Bohdan Zdziennicki, 'Badanie konstytucyjności stanu wojennego. Uwagi na tle wyroku Trybunału Konstytucyjnego z dnia 16 marca 2011 r.', *Przegląd Prawa Konstytucyjnego*, no. 3 (2012), http://www.marszalek.com.pl/przegladprawakonstytucyjnego/ppk11/07.pdf
59   'Wyrok z uzasadnieniem Sąd Okręgowy w Warszawie z 2012–01–12', VIII K 24/08, http://orzeczenia.ms.gov.pl/content/$N/154505000002406_VIII_K_000024_2008_Uz_2012-01-12_001; Judge Ewa Jethon's oral justification of the verdict was published in full by *Wprost*, 12 January 2012, http://www.wprost.pl/ar/287868/Wyrok-w-sprawie-stanu-wojennego-sprawdz-co-oglosil-sad/
60   It was provided for in Article 23 of the Criminal Code of 1969, in force at the time of martial law; it was retained in the 1997 Criminal Code (Art. 26).
61   Maria Los and Andrzej Zybertowicz, *Privatizing the Police-State. The Case of Poland* (Basingstoke: Macmillan, 2000), 187.
62   Ibid.

# Chapter 5

1   Csonger Kuti, *Post-Communist Restitution and the Rule of Law* (Budapest: Central European University Press, 2009), 65, 92. Kuti offers a sound comparative analysis of the region.

2   The United Nations Basic Principles (2005) describe five categories of reparation: restitution, compensation, rehabilitation, satisfaction and guarantees of non-repetition. See http://www.ohchr.org/EN/ProfessionalInterest/Pages/ RemedyAndReparation.aspx This categorization differs somewhat from the Polish approach, but we retain Polish terminology.

3   'Ustawa z dnia 25 października 1990 r. o zwrocie majątku utraconego przez związki zawodowe i organizacje społeczne w wyniku wprowadzenia stanu wojennego', *Dziennik Ustaw*, poz. 17, 1991, http://www.dziennikustaw.gov.pl/D1991004001701. pdf

4   For the unified text, see http://www.isap.sejm.gov.pl/Download?id=WDU19961430661

5   'Orzeczenie Trybunału Konstytucyjnego z dnia 25 lutego 1992 r', Sygn. akt K. 4/91, https://www.saos.org.pl/judgments/205506

6   See for example the Supreme Court; Sąd Najwyższy, 'Uchwała z dnia 7 marca 1996 r', III AZP 30/95, http://sn.pl/Sites/orzecznictwo/Orzeczenia1/III%20AZP%2030-95.pdf

7   'Wyrok Naczelnego Sądu Administracyjnego z dnia 13 stycznia 1992 r', I SA 1140/91, https://sip.lex.pl/orzeczenia-i-pisma-urzedowe/orzeczenia-sadow/ii-sa-1140-91-wyrok-naczelnego-sadu-administracyjnego-520103993

8   'Wyrok Naczelnego Sądu Administracyjnego z dnia 16 lipca 1992 r', I SA 642/92, http://orzeczenia.nsa.gov.pl/doc/0227F02B9F

9   According to AWS Deputy Stanisław Szwed in the *Sejm*, 2 December 1998, http:// orka2.sejm.gov.pl/Debata3.nsf/9a905bcb5531f478c125745f0037938e/eec821b61d4fb 11ac125749b003a417e?OpenDocument

10  SLD Deputy Bogdan Lewandowski in the *Sejm*: 'Interpelacja nr 6811', 2 July 2011, http://orka2.sejm.gov.pl/IZ3.nsf/main/33907061

11  See for example 'Wyrok Wojewódzkiwgo Sądu Administracyjnego w Warszawie', II SA 3705/03, 7 May 2004, http://orzeczenia.nsa.gov.pl/doc/0E1AC1633C

12  'Wyrok z dnia 14 listopada 2006 r', Sygn. akt SK 41/04, https://ipo.trybunal.gov.pl/ ipo/Sprawa?cid=1&dokument=1240&sprawa=3694

13  Marian Mazgaj, *Church and State in Communist Poland: A History, 1944–1989* (Jefferson, NC: McFarland, 2010), 57.

14  'Ustawa z dnia 17 maja 1989 r. o stosunku Państwa do Kościoła Katolickiego w Polskiej Rzeczypospolitej Ludowej', *Dziennik Ustaw* 1989, poz. 154, http://www. dziennikustaw.gov.pl/DU/1989/154/1

15  Elazar Barkan, *The Guilt of Nations: Restitution and Negotiating Historical Injustices* (New York: Norton, 2000), 123.

16  'Ustawa z dnia 11 października 1991 r. o zmianie ustawy o stosunku Państwa do Kościoła Katolickiego …', *Dziennik Ustaw* 1991, poz. 459, http://dziennikustaw.gov. pl/DU/1991/459/1

17  'Ustawa z dnia 16 grudnia 2010 r. o zmianie ustawy o stosunku Państwa do Kościoła Katolickiego …', *Dziennik Ustaw* 2011, poz. 89, http://www.dziennikustaw.gov.pl/ DU/2011/89/1

18  Paweł Borecki, 'Likwidacja Funduszu Kościelnego', http://www.radgoszcz.diecezja. tarnow.pl/index.php?option=com_content&view=article&id=650:likwidacja-funduszu-kocielnego&catid=15&Itemid=239

19  Czesław Ryszka, 'Rekompensata za kościelny majątek', *Niedziela*, no. 25 (2008), http:// www.niedziela.pl/artykul/85832/nd/Rekompensata-za-koscielny-majatek

20  Komisja Majątkowa, 'Sprawozdanie z działalności Komisji Majątkowej w latach 1989–2011', Warsaw, 24 February 2011, www.propertyrestitution.pl/ komisja_majatkowa__ds_kościoła_rzymsko-katolickiego_raport_02_2012.pdf.

Some journalists reported higher figures: 76,000 hectares granted to the Church from the Agricultural Land Agency and 4,000 from the Forestry Commission; 'Komisja Majątkowa zgubiła 16 tys. hektarów', https://polskieradio24.pl/5/115/Artykul/264523,Komisja-Majatkowa-zgubila-16-tys-ha

21  Narodowy Sąd Administracyjny, 'Postawienie', 26 September 1991, sygn. I SA 768/1991, http://orzeczenia.nsa.gov.pl/doc/0FE9CA982B

22  'Uchwała Trybunału Konstytucyjnego z dnia 24 czerwca 1992 r. w sprawie wykładni art. 61 ustawy z dnia 17 maja 1989 r. o stosunku Państwa do Kościoła Katolickiego w Rzeczypospolitej Polskiej', *Dziennik Ustaw*, 1992, poz. 250, http://otk.trybunal.gov.pl/orzeczenia/teksty/otkpdf/1992/W_11_91.pdf

23  The Uniates were Eastern Catholics, who retained their own liturgy and certain customs while remaining loyal to the Roman Catholic Church. They had suffered many forms of persecution, including forcible conversion to Orthodoxy.

24  For example, 'Poselski projekt ustawy o zmianie ustawy o stosunku Państwa do Kościoła Katolickiego ...', *Druk Sejmowy* 1106, 25 May 1995, http://orka.sejm.gov.pl/proc2.nsf/0/FBA2425AA28C2821C125745800218D09?OpenDocument; and 'Poselski projekt ustawy o zmianie ustawy o stosunku Państwa do Kościoła Katolickiego ...', *Druk Sejmowy* 1671, 26 March 1996, http://orka.sejm.gov.pl/proc2.nsf/0/6128CAF0DEEA1982C1257458002194D9?OpenDocument; and the report of the *Sejm*'s debate of 29 March 1996, http://orka2.sejm.gov.pl/Debata2.nsf

25  'Uchwała Sądu Najwyższego – Izba Cywilna z dnia 27 września 1996 r', III CZP 96/96, http://www.lexlege.pl/orzeczenie/11896/iii-czp-96-96-uchwala-sadu-najwyzszego-izba-cywilna/

26  Związek Nauczycielstwa Polskiego v. Poland, Application no. 42049/98, Strasbourg, 21 September 2004, http://hudoc.echr.coe.int/sites/eng/pages/search.aspx?i=001-66638

27  'Postanowienie Sądu Najwyższego – Izba Cywilna z dnia 12 kwietnia 2007 r', III CSK 427/06, http://www.sn.pl/sites/orzecznictwo/orzeczenia1/iii%20csk%20427-06-1.pdf

28  Wojciech Czuchnowski and Magdalena Kursa, 'Bezkarna Komisja Majątkowa', *Gazeta Wyborcza*, 1 March 2011.

29  Joanna Jałowiec, 'Ziemia dla jezuitów? Nie od razu', *Gazeta Wyborcza*, 8 November 2008.

30  Odpowiedź sekretarza stanu w Ministerstwie Spraw Wewnętrznych i Administracji – z upoważnienia ministra – na interpelację nr 11590, http://orka2.sejm.gov.pl/IZ6.nsf/main/099E35C5

31  'Wyrok w imieniu Rzeczypospolitej Polskiej z dnia 8 czerwca 2011 r', Syg. Akt K 3/09, http://otkzu.trybunal.gov.pl/2011/5A/39

32  Ewa Łętowska, 'Uprawienia gmin w swietle skutków orzeczenia TK o Kościelnej Komisji Majątkowej', *Państwo i Prawo* LVI, no. 9 (2011): 6.

33  Marcin Pietraszewski, 'Komisja majątkowa – skrywany raport rządu: Kościołowi ile się da', *Gazeta Wyborcza*, 17 February 2012.

34  'Śledztwo w sprawie działek Elżbietanek umorzone', Polskie Radio, 30 June 2011, http://www.polskieradio.pl/5/3/Artykul/394408,Sledztwo-w-sprawie-dzialek-Elzbietanek-umorzone

35  Marcin Przeciszewski, 'Sąd gani abstrakcję w prokuraturze. Postępowanie ws. 47 ha dla zakonu elżbietanek zacznie się od nowa', *Gazeta Wyborcza*, 5 September 2014.

36  Marta Paluch, 'Kraków. Wiceszef Komisji Majątkowej i były esbek zostali oskarżeni', *Gazeta Krakowska*, 8 January 2015.

37 'Nieprawidłowości w Komisji Majątkowej: Marek P. nie przyznaje się do winy', TVN24, 26 June 2013, from http://www.tvn24.pl/krakow,50/nieprawidlowosci-w-komisji-majatkowej-marek-p-nie-przyznaje-sie-do-winy,335660.html

38 Marcin Przeciszewski, 'Pełen emocji częściowy zwrot majątków Kościelnych', 18 November 2011, http://ekai.pl/wydarzenia/temat_dnia/x48307/pelen-emocji-czesciowy-zwrot-majatkow-koscielnych/?print=1

39 'Sześć osób z zarzutami w związku z działaniem Komisji Majątkowej 12 czerwca 2014', http://www.tvn24.pl/krakow,50/szesc-osob-z-zarzutami-w-zwiazku-z-dzialaniem-komisji-majatkowej,438831.html

40 Marcin Pietraszewski, 'Rodzina śląskiego miliardera uniewinniona', *Gazeta Wyborcza*, 15 May 2015.

41 '143 mln zł dla Kościoła', *Rzeczpospolita*, 2 March 2011.

42 'Zakon elżbietanek domaga się 13 mln zł od państwa. Prokuratoria: Oddalić pozew', *Gazeta Wyborcza*, 6 November 2014.

43 As in Kłodzko, where local government sought compensation to build a clinic to replace that occupying the plot allocated to the Missionaries of the Holy Family because it had not been a party to the proceedings; http://www.polskieradio.pl/5/3/Artykul/1045541,Sad-nie-przyznal-odszkodowania-za-zamek-oddany-Kosciolowi

44 Mika Ewelina, 'RPO ws. odwoływania się do sądu ws. orzeczeń Komisji Majątkowej', *Temidium*, 4 May 2015, http://www.temidium.pl/artykul/rpo_ws_odwolywania_sie_do_sadu_ws_orzeczen_komisji_majatkowej-1716.html

45 These figures come from the Property Restitution website: http://propertyrestitution.pl/Dane,i,mapy,13.html

46 'Wyrok z dnia 2 kwietnia 2003 r', Sygn. akt K 13/02, http://otkzu.trybunal.gov.pl/2003/4A/28

47 'Uzasadnienie. Stan dotychczasowy oraz potrzeba wprowadzenia zmian', http://bip.kprm.gov.pl/download.php?s=75&id=12597

48 'Ustawa o uregulowaniu stanu prawnego niektórych nieruchomości pozostających we władaniu Polskiego Autokefalicznego Kościoła Prawosławnego', *Dziennik Ustaw* 2010, poz. 43, http://dziennikustaw.gov.pl/DU/2010/43/1

49 'DÉCISION Requête no 31994/03 présentée par L'Église Orthodoxe Autocephale de Pologne contre la Pologne', http://hudoc.echr.coe.int/eng?i=001-98644

50 'Ustawa z dnia 20 lutego 1997 r. o stosunku Państwa do gmin wyznaniowych żydowskich ...', *Dziennik Ustaw* 1997, poz. 251, http://dziennikustaw.gov.pl/du/1997/s/41/251

51 Barkan, *The Guilt of Nations*,146.

52 Ibid., 147.

53 Bureau of European and Eurasian Affairs, *Property Restitution in Central and Eastern Europe* (Washington, DC: United States State Department, October 3, 2007), http://2001-2009.state.gov/p/eur/rls/or/93062.htm

54 Grazyna Skapska, 'Paying for past Injustices and Creating New Ones: On Property Rights Restoration in Poland as an element of the Unfinished Transformation' in *Legal Institutions and Collective Memories*, ed. Susanne Karstedt (Oxford: Hart Publishing, 2009), 276.

55 Pietraszewski, 'Komisja majątkowa'.

56 Paweł Borecki, 'Reprywatyzacja nieruchomości na rzecz gmin wyznaniowych żydowskich', *Państwo i Prawo* 66, no. 9 (2011): 72.

57 Pietraszewski, 'Komisja majątkowa'.

58 Istvan Pogany, *Righting Wrongs in Eastern Europe* (Manchester: Manchester University Press, 1997), 146.
59 Stanisław Tyszka, 'Restytucja mienia i pamięć zbiorowa w Polsce i w Czechach po 1989 roku' in *Normy, Dewiacje i Kontrola Społeczna*, ed. Joanna Zamecka (University of Warsaw, 2012) (no. 13), 217–36.
60 CBOS, 'Opinia publiczna o reprywatyzacji', Komunikat z badań BS/418/109/92. Warsaw: December 1992.
61 CBOS, 'Polacy o Reprywatyzacji', Komunikat z badań BS/87/2008, Warsaw: June 2008.
62 Skapska, 'Paying', 277–9.
63 http://propertyrestitution.pl/Databases,and,maps,21.html
64 Skapska, 'Paying', 263.
65 Monika Krawczyk, 'Restytucja mienia gmin żydowskich w Polsce – stan rzeczy z perspektywy (prawie) 10 lat', http://fodz.pl/doc/1.pdf
66 Monika Krawczyk, 'Restitution of Jewish Assets in Poland – Legal Aspects', *Justice*, no. 28 (2001): 24–8; http://www.intjewishlawyers.org/main/files/Justice%20No.28%20Summer%202001.pdf
67 http://polishrestitution.com/
68 On the complexities of calculating the value of assets lost long ago in another country, see Agnieszka Grzesiok, 'The "Right of Offset" of the Value of Property Left Behind the Present Polish Borders', *Organizacja i Zarządzania* 4, no. 8 (2009): 35–54.
69 'Wyrok Trybunału Konstytucyjnego z 19 grudnia 2002 r.', sygn. akt K 33/02, https://ipo.trybunal.gov.pl/ipo/Sprawa?cid=1&dokument=500&sprawa=2713
70 Their validity and hence the reasoning of the Tribunal have been questioned; see Anna Młynarska-Sobaczewska, 'Odpowiedzialność państwa polskiego za mienie zabużańskie', *Państwo i Prawo* 65, no. 2 (2010): 63–4.
71 'Ustawa o zaliczaniu na poczet ceny sprzedaży albo opłat z tytułu użytkowania wieczystego nieruchomości Skarbu Państwa wartości nieruchomości pozostawionych poza obecnymi granicami Państwa Polskiego', *Dziennik Ustaw* 2004, poz. 39, http://dziennikustaw.gov.pl/DU/2004/39/1
72 'Case of Broniowski v. Poland', Application no. 31443/96, Judgment, Strasbourg, 22 June 2004, http://hudoc.echr.coe.int/eng?i=001-61828#{'itemid':['001-61828']}
73 'Wyrok Trybunału Konstytucyjnego z dnia 15 grudnia 2004 r.', sygn. Akt K2/04, https://ipo.trybunal.gov.pl/ipo/Sprawa?cid=1&dokument=441&sprawa=3597
74 'Ustawa z dnia 8 lipca 2005 r. o realizacji prawa do rekompensaty z tytułu pozostawienia nieruchomości poza obecnymi granicami Rzeczypospolitej Polskiej', *Dziennik Ustaw* 2005, poz. 1418, http://dziennikustaw.gov.pl/DU/2005/s/169/1418/1. In 2006 and 2008 some technical amendments were passed; they did not alter the fundamentals of the law.
75 'Wyrok z dnia 23 października 2012 r.', Sygn. akt SK 11/12, https://ipo.trybunal.gov.pl/ipo/Sprawa?cid=1&dokument=8341&sprawa=8732
76 'Ustawa z dnia 12 grudnia 2013 r. o zmianie ustawy o realizacji prawa do rekompensaty z tytułu pozostawienia nieruchomości poza obecnymi granicami Rzeczypospolitej Polskiej', *Dziennik Ustaw*, 2014, poz. 195, http://dziennikustaw.gov.pl/DU/2014/195/1
77 'Ustawa z 25 czerwca 2015 r. o zmianie ustawy o gospodarce nieruchomościami', *Dziennik Ustaw* 2016, poz. 1271, http://www.dziennikustaw.gov.pl/DU/2016/1271/1

78 Iwona Szpala and Małgorzata Zubik, 'Układ warszawski. Czy reprywatyzacja w stolicy zatrzęsie polską polityką?' *Gazeta Wyborcza*, 20 August 2016; Iwona Szpala and Małgorzata Zubik, 'Jak mecenas Robert Nowaczyk reprywatyzuje nieruchomości w Warszawie', *Gazeta Wyborcza*, 17 October 2016.

79 Małgorzata Zubik, 'Reprywatyzacja. Andrzej Waltz, mąż prezydent Warszawy, zeznaje w sprawie Noakowskiego 16', *Gazeta Wyborcza*, 5 December 2017; Isabela Kacprzak and Grażyna Zawadzka, 'Noakowskiego 16: kolejne kontrowersje', *Rzeczpospolita*, 28 December 2017.

80 Patryk Słowik, 'Pierwsza przegrana komisji weryfikacyjnej w sądzie', *Gazeta Prawna,pl*, 4 March 2019, https://prawo.gazetaprawna.pl/artykuly/1406310,komisja-weryfikacyjna-przegrala-w-sadzie.html

# Chapter 6

1 Roman David, *Lustration and Transitional Justice: Personnel Systems in the Czech Republic, Hungary, and Poland* (Philadelphia: Pennsylvania University Press, 2011).

2 Monika Nalepa and Jaroslaw Kurski, 'Prologue' to Andrzej Romanowski, *Roskosze lustracji, wybór publicystyki (1997–2007)* (Krakow: Universitas, 2007), xii.

3 Lavinia Stan and Nadya Nedelsky, 'Post-Communist Transitional Justice Predictors', SciTopics, 9 February 2009, http://www.scitopics.com/Post_Communist_Transitional_Justice_Predictors.html, 4.

4 Hilary Appel, 'Anti-Communist Justice and Founding the Post-Communist Order: Lustration and Restitution in Central Europe', *East European Politics and Societies* 19, no. 3 (2005): 379–405.

5 Cynthia Horne, 'Late Lustration Programmes in Romania and Poland: Supporting or Undermining Democratic Transitions?' *Democratization* 16, no. 2 (2009): 346.

6 Aleks Szczerbiak, 'Why Did Poland Adopt a Radical Lustration Law in 2006?' SEI Working Paper No 139, University of Sussex, 2016.

7 Monika Nalepa, 'Lustration as a Trust-Building Mechanism? Transitional Justice in Poland' in *After Oppression: Transitional Justice in Latin America and Eastern Europe*, eds. Monica Serrano and Vesselin Popovski (Washington, DC: Brookings Institute Press, 2012), 333.

8 Monika Nalepa, *Skeletons in the Closet. Transitional Justice in Post-Communist Europe* (Cambridge: Cambridge University Press, 2010); also Nalepa, 'Lustration as a Trust-Building Mechanism?', 344.

9 Nalepa, as a Trust-Building Mechanism?', 344.

10 Stefan Myszkiewicz-Niesiołowski in the *Sejm,* 10 May 1991, http://orka2.sejm.gov.pl/StenogramyX.nsf/0/6696E246859B8B83C1257D20002CC732/$file/059_000007425.pdf

11 Jan Widacki in ibid.

12 Jan Olszewski, 'Exposé', *Sejm*, 21 December 1991, http://orka2.sejm.gov.pl/Debata1.nsf/

13 'Wielkie Łowy MSW', *Gazeta Wyborcza*, 1 June 1992.

14 Stenographic report of the *Sejm*'s debate, 13 February 1992, http://orka2.sejm.gov.pl/Debata1.nsf

15 Stenographic report of the *Sejm*'s debate, 28 May 1992, http://orka2.sejm.gov.pl/Debata1.nsf

16 Ibid.
17 'Oświadczenie Jacka Taylora', ibid.
18 Jacek Kurski, *Nocna zmiana*, Production Jacek-FILM 1994, You Tube at https://www.youtube.com/watch?v=KgJw2PIgBzk (accessed 6 April 2020); also quoted in *Rzeczpospolita* 127, 30–31 May 1992.
19 Piotr Grzelak, *Wojna o lustrację* (Warszaw: Wydawnictwo Trio, 2005), 62.
20 Katarzyna Ostrowska and Mariusz Żuławnik, 'Niszczenie kartotek Biura "C" MSW w latach 1989–1990', *Przegląd Archiwalny Instytutu Pamięci Narodowej* 4 (2011): 235–50, http://bazhum.muzhp.pl/media//files/Przeglad_Archiwalny_Instytutu_Pamieci_Narodowej/Przeglad_Archiwalny_Instytutu_Pamieci_Narodowej-r2011-t4/Przeglad_Archiwalny_Instytutu_Pamieci_Narodowej-r2011-t4-s235-250/Przeglad_Archiwalny_Instytutu_Pamieci_Narodowej-r2011-t4-s235-250.pdf
21 This was deleted from the Stenogram of the *Sejm*; see Grzelak, *Wojna*, 67.
22 *Rzeczpospolita*, 5 June 1992.
23 'Orzeczenie Trybunału Konstytucyjnego z dnia 19 czerwca', sygn. Akt U 6/92, OTK 1992, poz. 13, from http://otkzu.trybunal.gov.pl/otk.xhtml?rok=1992&pozycja=13
24 Both appeared in *Rzeczpospolita*, 6 October 1992.
25 'Ustawa z dnia 28 maja 1993 r. – Ordynacja wyborcza do Sejmu Rzeczypospolitej Polskiej', *Dziennik Ustaw* 1993, poz. 205, http://dziennikustaw.gov.pl/DU/1993/s/45/205/1
26 The chair of the Supreme Court asked the Constitutional Tribunal whether submitting a false declaration amounted to a criminal offence – for if so, the Court would be required in effect to act as an organ of lustration. The finding is 'Uchwała Trybunału Konstytucyjnego z dnia 14 lipca 1993 r. dotycząca ustalenia powszechnie obowiązującej wykładni przepisów art. 124 ust. 1 ustawy z dnia 28 maja 1993 r. – Ordynacja wyborcza do Sejmu Rzeczypospolitej Polskiej oraz art. 81 ust. 5 pkt 4 tejże ustawy w związku z art. 189 k.k.', Sygn. akt W. 5/93, http://otk.trybunal.gov.pl/orzeczenia/teksty/otkpdf/1993/W_05_93.pdf
27 'Poselski projekt ustawy o trybie sprawdzania i ujawniania okoliczności dotyczących współpracy z organami Urzędu Bezpieczeństwa Publicznego i Służby Bezpieczeństwa oraz z innymi służbami specjalnymi osób pełniących lub ubiegających się o pełnienie publicznych funkcji państwowych', *Druk Sejmowy* no. 399, 24 July 1992 (not available on-line).
28 'Poselski projekt ustawy o warunkach wstępnych zajmowania niektórych stanowisk w Rzeczypospolitej Polskiej', *Druk Sejmowy* no. 423, 31 July 1992 (not available on-line).
29 Michał Krotoszyński, *Lustracja w Polsce w świetle modeli sprawiedliwości okresu tranzycji* (Warsaw: Helsińska Fundacja Praw Człowieka, 2014), 71, http://www.hfhr.pl/wp-content/uploads/2014/06/Lustracja-w-Polsce-w-s%CC%81wietle-modeli-sprawiedliwos%CC%81ci-okresu-tranzycji_Micha%C5%82-Krotoszyn%CC%81ski.pdf
30 I cannot agree with Zolkos that pro-lustration views stemmed from a 'civic-republican' retributive ethos, while people hostile to lustration were liberal seekers of 'reconciliatory' justice; Magdalena Zolkos, 'The Conceptual Nexus of Human Rights and Democracy in the Polish Lustration Debates 1989–97', *Journal of Communist Studies and Transition Politics* 22, no. 2 (2006): 244.
31 Jarosław Kaczyński was the leading critic of the Round Table, but his views found wide echo in the right-wing press as well as in his own party, the PC. See for example

Jan Walc, 'Z dziejów infamii w Polsce', *Wokanda*, 17 Feburary 1991; Jakub Karpiński, 'Wielka fikcja', *Tygodnik Powszechny*, 8 January 1995.

32  All quotations in this section come from the stenographic report of the *Sejm*'s debate, 5 September 1992, http://orka2.sejm.gov.pl/Debata1.nsf

33  OBOP data from *Zycie Warszawy*, 8 June 1992; CBOS, 'Oczekiwanie i Obawy związane z lustracją', Komunikat z badań BS/38/29/93, Warsaw, March 1993.

34  Kazimierz Gróblewski, 'Lustracja źle obecna' (Interview with Bronisław Geremek), *Rzeczpospolita*, 4 June 1993.

35  Grzelak, Wojna, 96–7.

36  'Poselski projekt ustawy o warunkach wstępnych zajmowania niektórych stanowisk państwowych w Rzeczypospolitej Polskiej', *Druk Sejmowy* 499, 23 June 1994 (not available on line). Although this was not strictly a lustration proposal, it was referred to the Extraordinary Parliamentary Commission on Lustration.

37  The final resolution is available at http://assembly.coe.int/nw/xml/XRef/Xref-XML2HTML-en.asp?fileid=16507&lang=en; the Guidelines form part of the draft resolution, Document Doc. 7568, 3 June 1996, available at http://assembly.coe.int/nw/xml/xref/x2h-xref-viewhtml.asp?fileid=7506&lang=en

38  These are reviewed in Krotoszyński, 'Lustracja w Polsce', 77–8.

39  The record of meetings is the *Biuletyn Komisji Sejmowych* at http://orka.sejm.gov.pl/Biuletyn.nsf, record of meetings of the Komisja Nadzwyczajna do rozpatrzenia projektów ustaw lustracyjnych: 3328/II, 3306/II, 3280/II, 3272/II, 3258/II, 3252/II, 3233/II, 3222/II, 3194/II, 3174/II. 3172/II

40  Sprawozdanie stenograficzne Sejmu, 2nd term, session 104, day 4, 11 April 1997, http://orka2.sejm.gov.pl/Debata2.nsf

41  Janusz Niemcewicz, in the *Sejm* debate of 7 July 1994, 'Sprawozdanie stenograficzne Sejmu', http://orka2.sejm.gov.pl/Debata2.nsf

42  Marek Borowski in the *Sejm* debate of 11 April 1997, 'Sprawozdanie stenograficzne Sejmu', http://orka2.sejm.gov.pl/Debata2.nsf

43  The vote was 214 to 162, with 16 abstentions; 'Sprawozdanie stenograficzne *Sejmu*', 1 April 1997, http://orka2.sejm.gov.pl/Debata2.nsf

44  'Ustawa z dnia 11 kwietnia 1997 r. o ujawnieniu pracy lub służby w organach bezpieczeństwa państwa lub współpracy z nimi w latach 1944–1990 osób pełniących funkcje publiczne', *Dziennik Ustaw*, 1997, poz. 443, http://dziennikustaw.gov.pl/DU/1997/s/70/443/1

45  Wojciech Sadurski, '"Decommunisation," "Lustration" and Constitutional Continuity: Dilemmas of Transitional Justice in Central Europe', European University Institute, 2003, Badia Fiesolana, San Dominico, Italy, http://cadmus.eui.eu/dspace/bitstream/1814/1869/2/law03-15.pdf

46  Monika Nalepa, 'To Punish the Guilty and Protect the Innocent: Comparing Truth Revelation Procedures', *Journal of Theoretical Politics* 2, no. 2 (2008): 221–45.

47  Sadurski, 'Decommunisation', 27.

48  Krzysztof Kauba and Boleslaw Nizienski, 'Lustracja' in *Ius et Lux. Księga Jubileuszowa ku czci Profesora Adama Strzembosza*, eds. Antomi Dębinski et al. (Lublin: Wydawnictwo KUL, 2002), 324.

49  Stanisław Podemski, 'Lustracja zlustrowana', *Polityka*, 13 September 1997; Barbara Pietkiewicz, 'Sąd nad sędziami', *Polityka*, 17 January 1998.

50  'Ustawa z dnia 18 czerwca 1998 r. o zmianie ustawy o ujawnieniu pracy lub służby w organach bezpieczeństwa państwa lub współpracy z nimi w latach 1944–1990 osób pełniących funkcje publiczne oraz o zmianie niektórych innych ustaw', *Dziennik Ustaw* 1998, poz. 860, http://www.dziennikustaw.gov.pl/DU/1998/860/1

51 'Wyrok z dnia 21 października 1998 r'., Sygn. K. 24/98, 21 October 1998, http://otkzu.trybunal.gov.pl/1998/6/97; http://otkzu.trybunal.gov.pl/1998/6/99

52 'Ustawa z dnia 20 maja 1999 r. o zmianie ustawy o wyborze Prezydenta Rzeczypospolitej Polskiej oraz ustawy o ujawnieniu pracy lub służby w organach bezpieczeństwa państwa lub współpracy z nimi w latach 1944-1990 osób pełniących funkcje publiczne', *Dziennik Ustaw* 1999, poz. 681, http://dziennikustaw.gov.pl/DU/1999/681/1

53 'Wyrok z dnia 10 listopada 1998 r'., Sygn. K. 39/97, http://otkzu.trybunal.gov.pl/1998/6/99

54 Sławomir Cenckiewicz and Piotr Gontarczyk, *SB a Lech Wałęsa. Przyczynek do biografii* (Warsaw: IPN, 2008), 237-8.

55 'Ustawa z dnia 18 grudnia 1998 r. o Instytucie Pamięci Narodowej – Komisji Ścigania Zbrodni przeciwko Narodowi Polskiemu (unified text)', *Dziennik Ustaw* 1998, poz. 1016, http://orka.sejm.gov.pl/proc3.nsf/ustawy/31_u.htm

56 'Projekt ustawy o utworzeniu Archiwum Obywatelskiego oraz o powszechnym udostępnianiu dokumentacji wytworzonej w latach 1944-1990 przez organy bezpieczeństwa państwa', November 1997, *Druk Sejmowy* 31, from http://orka.sejm.gov.pl/SQL.nsf/projustkom3?OpenAgent&NAD

57 'Z góry na dół', *Polityka*, 3 June 2000.

58 'Przedstawiony przez Prezydenta Rzeczypospolitej Polskiej projekt ustawy o zmianie ustawy o ujawnieniu pracy lub służby w organach bezpieczeństwa państwa lub współpracy z nimi w latach 1944-1990 osób pełniących funkcje publiczne', *Druk Sejmowy* 13, 22 October 2001, http://orka.sejm.gov.pl/Druki4ka.nsf/$vAllByUnid/C194DAA200C7CE89C1256AF00022092D/$file/13.pdf

59 Bogdan Klich in the *Sejm* debate of 7 November 2001, http://orka2.sejm.gov.pl/Debata4.nsf

60 Joint proceedings of the Administration Commission and the Justice Commission are recorded in *Biuletyn* 135/IV, http://orka.sejm.gov.pl/Biuletyn.nsf/0/330692E8261BE764C1256B7200438D14?OpenDocument

61 Sprawozdanie stenograficzne Sejmu, 9 January 2002, http://orka2.sejm.gov.pl/Debata4.nsf

62 'Ustawa z dnia 15 lutego 2002 r. ozmianie ustawy o ujawnieniu pracy lub służby worganach bezpieczeństwa państwa lub współpracy znimi wlatach 1944 – 1990 osób pełniących funkcje publiczne oraz ustawy – Ordynacja wyborcza do Sejmu Rzeczypospolitej Polskiej i do Senatu Rzeczypospolitej Polskiej', *Dziennik Ustaw* 2002, poz 128, http://dziennikustaw.gov.pl/DU/2002/128/1

63 'Wyrok Trybunału Konstytucyjnego z dnia 19 czerwca 2002 r'., Sygn. akt K 11/02, 19 June 2002, http://otkzu.trybunal.gov.pl/2002/4A/43

64 'Senacki projekt ustawy o zmianie ustawy o ujawnieniu pracy lub służby w organach bezpieczeństwa państwa lub współpracy z nimi w latach 1944-1990 osób pełniących funkcje publiczne', *Druk Sejmowy* nr 765, 19 July 2002, http://orka.sejm.gov.pl/Druki4ka.nsf/$vAllByUnid/4290C962757BD8A3C1256C0200307227/$file/765.pdf/orka.sejm.gov.pl/Druki4ka.nsf/$vAllByUnid/4290C962757BD8A3C1256C0200307227/$file/765.pdf

65 'Ustawa z dnia 13 września 2002 r. o zmianie ustawy o ujawnieniu pracy lub służby w organach bezpieczeństwa państwa lub współpracy z nimi w latach 1944-1990 osób pełniących funkcje publiczne', *Dziennik Ustaw* 2002, poz. 1434, http://dziennikustaw.gov.pl/DU/2002/1434/1

66 'Ustawa z dnia 30 sierpnia 2002 r. – Przepisy wprowadzające ustawę – Prawo o ustroju sądów administracyjnych i ustawę – Prawo o postępowaniu przed sądami administracyjnymi', *Dziennik Ustaw* 2002, poz. 1271, http://dziennikustaw.gov.pl/DU/2002/1271/1

67 'Ustawy z dnia 23 stycznia 2004 r. – Ordynacja wyborcza do Parlamentu Europejskiego, art. 9 (2), art. 70(1) i art. 178', *Dziennik Ustaw* 2004, poz. 219, http://dziennikustaw.gov.pl/DU/2004/219/1

68 'Wyrok Trybunału Konstytucyjnego z dnia 5 marca 2003 r.', Syg. Aktu K 7/01, 5 March 2003, http://otkzu.trybunal.gov.pl/2003/3A/19

69 ' Wyrok z dnia 28 maja 2003 r.', Sygn. akt K 44/02, 28 May 2003, http://otkzu.trybunal.gov.pl/2003/5A/44

70 'Ustawa z dnia 27 lipca 2005 r. Prawo o szkolnictwie wyższym', *Dziennik Ustaw,* 2005, poz. 1365, http://www.dziennikustaw.gov.pl/DU/2005/1365/1

71 The list was on line at http://lista.atspace.org/and http://lista-wildsteina.n8.pl/but these links are now inactive. On 8 April 2020, http://www.ny.pl/Lista_Wildsteina/ was still functioning.

72 Bronisław Wildstein, 'Cały ten antylustracyjny zgiełk', *Rzeczpospolita*, 14 January 2005.

73 Marek Henzler, 'Wielki Lustrator', *Polityka*, 8 January 2005.

74 Jerzy Morawski, '"Monika" cenna dla służb', *Rzeczpospolita*, 23 March 2005. The journal *Wprost* defended Wildstein and supported the lustration of journalists. Attacks on Wildstein featured in *Rzeczpospolita*, *Gazeta Wyborcza* and *Polityka*.

75 'Ustawa z dnia 4 marca 2005 r. o zmianie ustawy o Instytucie Pamięci Narodowej – Komisji Ścigania Zbrodni przeciwko Narodowi Polskiemu', *Dziennik Ustaw* 2005, poz. 567, http://dziennikustaw.gov.pl/DU/2005/s/64/567/1

76 Cited in Luiza Zalewska, 'Świadkowie zadowoleni z zeznań', *Rzeczpospolita*, 17 January 2005.

77 *Rzeczpospolita*, 11–12 June 2005.

# Chapter 7

1 See Aleks Szczerbiak, 'An Anti-Establishment Backlash That Shook up the Party System? The October 2015 Polish Parliamentary Election', *European Politics and Society* 18, no. 4 (2017): 404–27.

2 'Wyrok Trybunału Konstytucyjnego z dnia 26 października 2005 r.', Sygn. akt K 31/04, 26 October 2005, http://otkzu.trybunal.gov.pl/2005/9A/103

3 'Poselski projekt ustawy o zmianie ustawy o Instytucie Pamięci Narodowej', *Druk Sejmowy* nr. 359, 23 February 2006, http://orka.sejm.gov.pl/Druki5ka.nsf/wgdruku/359

4 'Ustawa z 18.10.2006 r. o ujawnianiu informacji o dokumentach organów bezpieczeństwa państwa z lat 1944–1990', *Dziennik Ustaw* 2006, poz. 1592, http://dziennikustaw.gov.pl/DU/2006/s/218/1592/1

5 Michał Krotoszyński, 'Lustracja w Polsce w świetle modeli sprawiedliwości okresu tranzycji' (Warsaw: Helsińska Fundacja Praw Człowieka, 2014), 109 from http://www.hfhr.pl/wp-content/uploads/2014/06/Lustracja-w-Polsce-w-s%CC%81wietle-modeli-sprawiedliwos%CC%81ci-okresu-tranzycji_Micha%C5%82-Krotoszyn%CC%81ski.pdf

6 Krotoszyński, 'Lustracja', 111.

7 'Przedstawiony przez Prezydenta Rzeczypospolitej Polskiej projekt ustawy o zmianie ustawy o ujawnianiu informacji o dokumentach organów bezpieczeństwa państwa z lat 1944–1990 oraz treści tych dokumentów. Uzasadnienie', *Druk Sejmowy* nr 1258, from http://orka.sejm.gov.pl/Druki5ka.nsf/wgdruku/1585

8 'Ustawa z dnia 14 lutego 2007 r. o zmianie ustawy o ujawnianiu informacji o dokumentach organów bezpieczeństwa państwa z lat 1944–1990 oraz treści tych dokumentów i ustawy o Instytucie Pamięci Narodowej', *Dziennik Ustaw* 2007, poz. 162, http://dziennikustaw.gov.pl/DU/2007/s/25/162/1

9 Cited by Krotoszyński, 'Lustracja', 115. Nalepa's figure of 700,000 seems too high; see Monika Nalepa, 'Lustration as a Trust-Building Mechanism? Transitional Justice in Poland' in *After Oppression: Transitional Justice in Latin America and Eastern Europe*, eds. Monica Serrano and Vesselin Popovski (Washington, DC: Brookings Institute Press, 2012), 349.

10 'Wyrok z dnia 11 maja 2007 r.', Sygn. akt K 2/07, from http://ipo.trybunal.gov.pl/ipo/Sprawa?cid=1&dokument=444&sprawa=4291

11 Jan Woleński pointed out that he could not submit an affidavit on the day of his appointment (as a professor), since he had been appointed some fifteen years earlier; he posted an annotated affidavit on his office door at the university. Jan Woleński, *Lustracja jako zwierciadło* (Krakow: Universitas, 2007), 142–9.

12 In their dissenting judgments Jerzy Ciemniewski, Ewa Łętowska, Marek Mazurkiewicz and Mirosław Wyrzykowski expressed the view that the definition should simply have been labelled unconstitutional.

13 Krotoszyński, 'Lustracja', 124.

14 'Rzecznik Praw Obywatelskich dowiódł niespójnosci wyroku TK w sprawie lustracji' (Interview with Beata Michniewicz), Polskie Radio, 17 July 2007, from https://www.polskieradio.pl/9/301/Artykul/220453,Rzecznik-Praw-Obywatelskich-dowiodl-niespojnosci-wyroku-TK-w-sprawie-lustracji

15 Piotr Radziewicz, 'Opinie dotyczące skutków wyroku Trybunału Konstytucyjnego z 11 Maja 2007 r. (Sygn. Akt K 2/07) w sprawie niezgodności z Konstytucją RP przepisów lustracyjnych', *Przegląd Sejmowy* XV, no. 6 (2007): 143–66, http://orka.sejm.gov.pl/przeglad.nsf/0/0FC2C29875A51C80C12579370043F919/$file/ps83.pdf

16 'Ustawa z dnia 15 czerwca 2007 r. o Narodowym Centrum Badań i Rozwoju', *Dziennik Ustaw* 2007, poz. 789, http://dziennikustaw.gov.pl/DU/2007/789/1

17 'Ustawa z dnia 24 sierpnia 2007 r. o zmianie ustawy o służbie wojskowej żołnierzy zawodowych oraz o zmianie niektórych innych ustaw', *Dziennik Ustaw* 2007, poz. 1242, http://dziennikustaw.gov.pl/DU/2007/1242/1

18 'Ustawa z dnia 29 czerwca 2007 r. o zmianie ustawy o Instytucie Pamięci Narodowej ...', *Dziennik Ustaw* 2007, poz. 983, http://dziennikustaw.gov.pl/DU/2007/983/1

19 'Ustawa z dnia 7 września 2007 r. o zmianie ustawy o ujawnianiu informacji o dokumentach organów bezpieczeństwa państwa z lat 1944—1990 ...', *Dziennik Ustaw* 2007, poz. 1171, http://dziennikustaw.gov.pl/DU/2007/s/165/1171/1

20 Tomasz Terlikowski and Odwaga prawdy, *Spór o lustrację w polskim Kościele* (Warsaw: Prószynski i S-ka, 2007), 40–1.

21 Peter Raina, *Anatomia lynczu. Sprawa Ojca Konrada Hejmo* (Warsaw: von Borowiecki, 2006).

22 'Memoriał Episkopatu Polski w sprawie współpracy niektórych duchownych z organami bezpieczeństwa w Polsce w latach 1944–1989', Jasna Góra, 25 August 2006, http://episkopat.pl/memorial-episkopatu-polski-w-sprawie-wspolpracy-niektorych-duchownych-z-organami-bezpieczenstwa-w-polsce-w-latach-1944-1989/

23 'Prałat Jankowski ujawnił nazwiska agentów SB', *Życie Warszawy*, 27 September 2006.

24 See for example 'Biskupi metropolii krakowskiej solidaryzują się z oświadczeniem ws. Nuncjusza Apostolskiego', 8 January 2009, eKai.pl, https://ekai.pl/wydarzenia/temat_dnia/x17434/biskupi-metropolii-krakowskiej-solidaryzuja-sie-z-oswiadczeniem-ws-nuncjusza-apostolskiego/

25 See for example Andrzej Luter, 'Ks. Zaleski-Isakowicz nie ustaje w lustracji Kościoła', *Gazeta Wyborcza*, 21 November 2008.

26 'Komunikat Kościelnej Komisji Historycznej', 5 January 2007, http://www.opoka.org.pl/biblioteka/W/WE/kep/komunikat_hist_05012007.html (accessed 2 June 2013).

27 'Wyrok z dnia 5 Października 2000 r.', II KKN 271/2000, http://www.sn.pl/orzecznictwo/SitePages/Baza_orzeczen.aspx?sygnatura=II%20KKN%20271/00

28 Tadeusz Isakowicz-Zaleski, *Księża wobec bezpieki na przykładzie archidiecezji krakowskiej* (Krakow: Znak, 2007).

29 Kościelna Komisja Historyczna, 'Komunikat po kwerendzie', Vatican Radio, http://pl.radiovaticana.va/storico/2007/06/27/ko%C5%9Bcielna_komisja_historyczna:_komunikat_po_kwerendzie/pol-141740

30 See the interview with Father Stanisław Małkowski, 'Lustracja hierarchów a komisja "Niepamięć i beztroska"' on the website Strona Mirosława Dakowskiego at http://dakowski.pl/index.php?option=com_content&task=view&id=4097&Itemid=46 ; also 'HIERARCHOWIE SZATANA czyli lista "UBeków" w Kościele katolickim' ('Hierarchs of Satan, List of Agents in the Catholic Church') at Lustracja.net from http://lustracja.net/index.php/duchowna-agentura/112-hierarchowie-szatana-czyli-lista-ubekow-w-kosciele-katolickim?showall=&limitstart.

31 Sławomir Cenckiewicz and Piotr Gontarczyk, *SB a Lech Wałęsa. Przyczynek do biografii* (Warsaw: IPN, 2008); also Ewa Ochman, *Post-Communist Poland – Contested Pasts and Future Identities* (London: Routledge, 2013).

32 Dariusz Stola, 'Poland's Institute of National Remembrance: A Ministry of Memory?' in *The Convolutions of Historical Politics*, eds. A. Miller and M. Lipman (Budapest: Central European University Press, 2012), 55.

33 'Oświadczenie w sprawie nowelizacji ustawy o Instytucie Pamięci Narodowej', Poznań, 2 May 2010, https://lustronauki.wordpress.com/2010/05/02/oswiadczenie-w-sprawie-nowelizacji-ustawy-o-instytucie-pamieci-narodowej/

34 See Joanna Niżyńska, 'The Politics of Mourning and the Crisis of Poland's Symbolic Language after April 10', *East European Politics and Societies* 24, no. 4 (2010): 467–79.

35 'Ustawa z dnia 29 kwietnia 2010 r. o zmianie ustawy o Instytucie Pamięci Narodowej … ', *Dziennik Ustaw* 2010, poz 602, http://dziennikustaw.gov.pl/DU/2010/602/1 There were minor changes in August dealing with nomintions for the chair of the IPN; Ustawa z dnia 5 sierpnia 2010 r. zmieniająca ustawę o zmianie ustawy o Instytucie Pamięci Narodowej …', *Dziennik Ustaw* 2010, poz 1087, http://dziennikustaw.gov.pl/DU/2010/1087/1

36 Paweł Kośmiński and Agnieszka Kublik, 'IPN publikuje listy do Kiszczaka. Zniesmaczeni autorzy: "Podano prywatny adres, gdzie żyje moja rodzina"', *Gazeta Wyborcza*, 25 February 2016.

37 'Łukasz Kamiński kandydatem na prezesa IPN', *Newsweek*, 31 May 2011.

38 IPN, 'Informacja o działalności Instytutu Pamięci Narodowej – Komisja Ścigania Zbrodni przeciwko Narodowi Polskiemu w okresie 1 stycznia 2010 r. – 31 grudnia 2010 r.', *Druk Sejmowy* no. 66, 13 December 2011, http://orka.sejm.gov.pl/Druki7ka.nsf/0/C37002F68A8FBD48C1257966002BAEF3/%24File/66.pdf

39    IPN, 'Informacja o działalności Instytutu Pamięci Narodowej – Komisji Ścigania
      Zbrodni przeciwko Narodowi Polskiemu w okresie 1 stycznia 2011 r. – 31 grudnia
      2011 r.', *Druk Sejmowy* 328, Warsaw, 5 April 2012, http://orka.sejm.gov.pl/Druki7ka.
      nsf/0/921A5A3541B067BFC12579E500383557/%24File/328.pdf
40    Cezary Gmyz, 'IPN utajnia agentów', *Do Rzeczy*, no. 26, 24 July 2013.
41    'Informacja o działalności Instytutu Pamięci Narodowej – Komisji Ścigania Zbrodni
      przeciwko Narodowi Polskiemu w okresie od 1 stycznia 2018 r. do 31 grudnia 2018 r.',
      324; *Druk Sejmowy* 3422, 25 April 2019, http://orka.sejm.gov.pl/Druki8ka.nsf/0/C29
      E58432C8FBFA0C12583F50032E809/%24File/3422.pdf
42    'Nizieński: sąd wierzy ebsekom, gdy oczyszczają lustrowanego', *Gazeta Wyborcza*,
      11 March 2001.
43    Maciej Gawlikowski and Mirosław Lewandowski, 'Sprawa Moczulskiego: Ostateczna
      klęska lustracji', *Rzeczpospolita*, 26 July 2018.
44    'IPN: Kłamcy lustracyjni są w parlamencie', *Dziennik*, 12 January 2009.
45    'Ustawa z dnia 18 marca 2010 r. o zmianie ustawy o Instytucie Pamięci Narodowej
      … oraz ustawy o ujawnianiu informacji o dokumentach organów bezpieczeństwa
      państwa z lat 1944–1990 oraz treści tych dokumentów', *Dziennik Ustaw* 2010, poz.
      522, http://dziennikustaw.gov.pl/DU/2010/522/1
46    'Poselski projekt ustawy o zmianie ustawy o Instytucie Pamięci Narodowej … oraz
      ustawy o ujawnianiu informacji o dokumentach organów bezpieczeństwa państwa z
      lat 1944–1990 oraz treści tych dokumentów', *Druk Sejmowy* 2625, 3 December 2009,
      http://orka.sejm.gov.pl/Druki6ka.nsf/wgdruku/2625
47    European Court of Human Rights Fourth Section, 'Case of Matyjek v. Poland, no.
      38184/03', Judgment, Strasbourg, 24 April 2007, Final, http://hudoc.echr.coe.int/
      eng?i=001-80219
48    See the comment on his lawyer's website at http://www.przezdziecki.eu/eng/?p=564
49    European Court of Human Rights, Fourth Section, 'Case of Luboch v. Poland
      (Application no. 37469/05) Judgment, Strasbourg, 15 January 2008, FINAL, 15
      April 2008 ', http://hudoc.echr.coe.int/eng#{'dmdocnumber':['827747'],"item
      id":['001-84373']}.
50    European Court of Human Rights, Fourth Section, Case of Rasmussen v Poland
      (Application no. 38886/05), Judgment, Strasbourg, 28 April 2009, https://hudoc.echr.
      coe.int/eng#{%22fulltext%22:[%22\%22CASE%20OF%20RASMUSSEN%20v.%20PO
      LAND\%22%22],%22documentcollectionid2%22:[%22GRANDCHAMBER%22,%22
      CHAMBER%22],%22itemid%22:[%22001-92429%22]}
51    European Court of Human Rights, Fourth Section, Case of Jałowiecki v Poland
      (Application no. 34030/07), Judgment, Strasbourg, 17 February 2009, https://hudoc.
      echr.coe.int/eng#{%22fulltext%22:[%22Ja%C5%82owiecki%20v%20Poland%22],%22
      documentcollectionid2%22:[%22GRANDCHAMBER%22,%22CHAMBER%22],%22
      itemid%22:[%22001-91290%22]}
52    European Court of Human Rights, Fourth Section, 'Case of Moczulski v. Poland
      (Application no. 49974/08)', Judgment, Strasbourg, 19 April 2011, Final 19 July 2011,
      http://hudoc.echr.coe.int/eng?i=001-104574
53    Norbert Nowotnik, 'Leszek Moczulski: przedłużanie mojej autolustracji odbieram
      jako odmawianie mi sprawiedliwości', Dzieje.pl, 16 August 2018, https://dzieje.pl/
      aktualnosci/leszek-moczulski-przedluzanie-mojej-autolustracji-odbieram-jako-
      odmawianie-mi

54 IPN, 'Informację ... 2014'.
55 Wojciech Czuchnowski, 'Sąd kończy proces lustracyjny: SB fałszowała kwity', *Gazeta Wyborcza*, 4 November 2015.
56 Piotr Pytlakowski, 'Zbrodnicza salowa', *Polityka*, 8 July 2015.
57 Joanna Sawicka, 'Nowelizacja ustawy o IPN weszła już w życie. Do Instytutu wkracza polityka', *Polityka*, 16 June 2016.
58 Joanna Podgórska, 'Policja historyczna' (Interview with Andrzej Duda), *Polityka*, 18 May 2016.
59 Wojciech Czuchnowski, 'IPN już nie zastrzega. Czas na "listy agentów"?', *Gazeta Wyborcza*, 24 January 2017.
60 'Gość Studia 3–17.09.2016 – Jarosław Gowin', *TVP Katowice*, 17 September 2016, http://www.katowice.tvp.pl/26984916/17092016-jaroslaw-gowin
61 Joanna Podgórska, 'Jak czytać te teczki (Interview with Andrzej Friszke)', *Polityka*, 1 March 2016.
62 'Wyszkowski: Wałęsa ma krew na rękach. W moim przekonaniu jego współpraca trwa do dzisiaj', *DoRzeczy*, 5 February 2017, from https://dorzeczy.pl/obserwator-mediow/21142/Wyszkowski-Walesa-ma-krew-na-rekach-W-moim-przekonaniu-jego-wspolpraca-trwa-do-dzisiaj.html
63 Michał Szułdrzyński, 'Polacy nie zmienili opinii na temat Lecha Wałęsy', *Rzeczpospolita*, 29 February 2016; Andrzej Stankiewicz, 'Wałęsa wciąż bohaterem', *Rzeczpospolita*, 28 February 2016.
64 CBOS, 'Społeczne oceny osobistości ostatniego stulecia', Komunikat z badan, Nr 101/2018.
65 Michał Michalak, 'Wildstein: Lustracja to już historia' (Interview with Bronisław Wildstein), *Interia Fakty*, 4 January 2016, http://fakty.interia.pl/tylko-u-nas/news-bronislaw-wildstein-lustracja-to-juz-historia,nId,1947745
66 Proceedings of the Senate, 'Stenogram Senatu' 23. posiedzenie Senatu RP IX kadencji, 2 dzień', 21 July 2016, from http://www.senat.gov.pl/prace/senat/posiedzenia/przebieg,467,2.html
67 Wojciech Czuchnowski and Radosław Leniarski, 'Czy wrotkarze byli w SB? PiS bierze się do lustracji w sporcie', *Gazeta Wyborcza*, 11 January 2017.
68 'Szykuje się lustracja w urzędach? „Solidarność" będzie wnioskować do Szydło', *Wprost*, 24 March 2017.
69 'Interpelacja nr 11101 do ministra środowiska w sprawie lustracji w Polskim Związku Łowieckim', from http://www.sejm.gov.pl/sejm8.nsf/interpelacjaTresc.xsp?documentId=F430680506FD6A5FC12580EC003EC5DB&view=1t
70 Agnieszka Kublik and Wojciech Czuchnowski, 'Wraca lustracja dziennikarzy. Uchwałę przygotowała Joanna Lichocka', *Gazeta Wyborcza*, 25 April 2017.
71 Quoted in ibid.
72 Jarosław Sellin, quoted in 'Projekt uchwały PiS o lustracji dziennikarzy z pozytywną oceną RMN', *Wprost*, 26 April 2017.
73 Kublik and Czuchnowski, 'Wraca lustracja dziennikarzy'.
74 Szymon Grela, 'PiS lustruje dziennikarzy w mediach publicznych. Uchwałę podjęto wbrew regulaminowi i trochę bez sensu', *Oko*, 26 April 2017 from https://oko.press/pis-lustruje-dziennikarzy-mediach-publicznych-uchwale-podjeto-wbrew-regulaminowi-troche-bez-sensu/
75 'Ustawa o zmianie ustawy o sporcie oraz ustawy o ujawnianiu informacji o dokumentach organów bezpieczeństwa państwa z lat 1944–1990 ...', *Dziennik Ustaw* 2017, poz 1600, from http://www.dziennikustaw.gov.pl/DU/2017/1600/1

76 'Rzecznik Praw Obywatelskich przedstawił stanowisko w sprawie projektu ustawy o jawności życia publicznego, który 25 października 2017 r. został przekazany do konsultacji publicznych i równolegle do uzgodnień międzyresortowych', 3 November 2017, https://www.rpo.gov.pl/pl/content/RPO-w-sprawie-projektu-tzw-ustawy-o-jawno%C5%9Bci

77 Andrzej Gajcy, 'Jawność nie dla wszystkich. Rząd utajni powszechną lustrację majątkową', Onet Wiadomości, from https://wiadomosci.onet.pl/tylko-w-onecie/jawnosc-nie-dla-wszystkich-rzad-utajni-powszechna-lustracje-majatkowa/dqj4pzb

78 'Wyrok z dnia 24 lutego 2010 r.', Sygn. akt K 6/09, http://otkzu.trybunal.gov.pl/2010/2A/15

79 'Ustawa z dnia 16 grudnia 2016 r. o zmianie ustawy o zaopatrzeniu emerytalnym funkcjonariuszy Policji, Agencji Bezpieczeństwa Wewnętrznego, Agencji Wywiadu, Służby Kontrwywiadu Wojskowego, Służby Wywiadu Wojskowego, Centralnego Biura Antykorupcyjnego, Straży Granicznej, Biura Ochrony Rządu, Państwowej Straży Pożarnej i Służby Więziennej oraz ich rodzin', *Dziennik Ustaw* 2016, poz. 2270, http://dziennikustaw.gov.pl/DU/2016/2270/1

80 Tomasz Zalasiński, 'Ślepa dezubekizacja i domniemanie winy', *Gazeta Prawna. pl*, 11 September 2019, https://serwisy.gazetaprawna.pl/emerytury-i-renty/artykuly/1429588,bledy-ustawy-dezubekizacyjnej.html

81 Szczerbiak, 'An anti-establishment backlash …', 422.

82 Aleks Szczerbiak, *Politicising the Communist Past. The Politics of Truth Revelation in Post-Communist Poland* (London: Routledge, 2018),181.

83 Ibid., 185.

# Chapter 8

1 'Ustawa z dnia 18 grudnia 1998 r. o Instytucie Pamięci Narodowej – Komisji Ścigania Zbrodni przeciwko Narodowi Polskiemu', *Dziennik Ustaw*, 1998 nr 155 poz. 1016, http://dziennikustaw.gov.pl/DU/1998/1016/1

2 James Mark, *The Unfinished Revolution. Making Sense of the Communist Past in Central-Eastern Europe* (New Haven: Yale University Press, 2010), 2.

3 Ibid., 6–7.

4 Paweł Machcewicz, *Poland's Way of Coming to Terms with the Legacy of Communism* (Warsaw: Institute of Political Studies, 2006), http://www.eurhistxx.de/spip.php%3Farticle40&lang=en.html

5 Dariusz Stola, 'Poland's Institute of National Remembrance: A Ministry of Memory?' in *The Convolutions of Historical Politics*, eds. A. Miller and M. Lipman (Budapest: Central European University Press, 2012), 47.

6 Sławomir Nowinowski, 'Dziesięć lat IPN. Historycy czy architekci politycznej wyobraźni?', *Gazeta Wyborcza*, 21 March 2011.

7 Trybunał Konstytucyjny, 'Wyrok z dnia 26 października 2005 r.', Sygn. akt K 31/04, 26 October 2005, from http://otkzu.trybunal.gov.pl/2005/9A/103

8 'Ustawa z dnia 14 lutego 2007 r. o zmianie ustawy o ujawnianiu informacji o dokumentach organów bezpieczeństwa państwa z lat 1944–1990 oraz treści tych dokumentów i ustawy o Instytucie Pamięci Narodowej – Komisji Ścigania Zbrodni przeciwko Narodowi Polskiemu', *Dziennik Ustaw* 2007, poz. 162, http://dziennikustaw.gov.pl/DU/2007/s/25/162/1

9   'Wyrok z dnia 11 maja 2007 r.', Sygn. akt K 2/07, https://ipo.trybunal.gov.pl/ipo/Spra wa?cid=2&dokument=444&sprawa=4291

10  'Ustawa z dnia 18 marca 2010 r. o zmianie ustawy o Instytucie Pamięci Narodowej – Komisji Ścigania Zbrodni przeciwko Narodowi Polskiemu oraz ustawy o ujawnianiu informacji o dokumentach organów bezpieczeństwa państwa z lat 1944–1990 oraz treści tych dokumentów', *Dziennik Ustaw* 2010, poz. 522, http://dziennikustaw.gov.pl/ DU/2010/522/1

11  Helsińska Fundacja, 'NSA oddalił skargę kasacyjną Prezesa IPN w sprawie dostępu do informacji publicznej', 10 December 2010, http://www.hfhrpol.waw.pl/przeszlosc-rozliczenia/aktualnosci/nsa-oddalil-skarge-kasacyjna-prezesa-ipn-w-sprawie-dostepu-do-informacji-publicznej.html

12  Krzysztof Krajewski, 'Prosecution and Prosecutors in Poland: In Quest of Independence', *Crime and Justice* 41, no. 1 (2012): 75–116.

13  Rzecznik Praw Obywatelskich, 'Wniosek do Trybunału Konstytucyjnego w sprawie przedawnienia zbrodni komunistycznych', 20 April 2016, https://www.rpo.gov.pl/ pl/content/wniosek-do-trybunalu-konstytucyjnego-ws-przedawnienia-zbrodni-komunistycznych

14  'Akt oskarzenia przeciwko Wojciechowi Jaruzelskiemu (y innym)', sygn. akt S101/04/Zk, Katowice, 16 April 2007, from http://ipn.gov.pl/__data/assets/pdf_file/0018/128223/akt-oskarzenia-S-101-04-Zk_2.pdf

15  'Prokuratura IPN: zabójstwo ks. Jerzego Popiełuszki w ramach śledztwa ws. związku zbrojnego w MSW', PAP, from Polskie Radio, 21 October 2016, http:// www.polskieradio.pl/5/3/Artykul/1683837,Prokuratura-IPN-zabojstwo-ks-Jerzego-Popieluszki-w-ramach-sledztwa-ws-zwiazku-zbrojnego-w-MSW

16  IPN, 'Dlaczego strzelano do papieża – nowe ustalenia w śledztwie prowadzonym przez katowicki IPN', Warsaw, 12 May 2017, http://ipn.gov.pl/pl/ aktualnosci/40021,Dlaczego-strzelano-do-papieza-nowe-ustalenia-w-sledztwie-prowadzonym-przez-katow.html

17  IPN, 'Zakończenie śledztwa w sprawie podrobienia przez funkcjonariuszy Służby Bezpieczeństwa dokumentów na szkodę Lecha Wałęsy', Komunikat, 28 June 2017, http://ipn.gov.pl/pl/dla-mediow/komunikaty/40776,Zakonczenie-sledztwa-w-sprawie-podrabiania-przez-funkcjonariuszy-Sluzby-Bezpiecz.html

18  IPN, 'IPN prowadzi postępowanie karne w sprawie fałszywych zeznań Lecha Wałęsy', Komunikat, 22 August 2017, http://ipn.gov.pl/pl/dla-mediow/ komunikaty/41376,IPN-prowadzi-postepowanie-karne-w-sprawie-falszywych-zeznan-Lecha-Walesy.html

19  IPN, 'Informacje o działalności Instytutu Pamięci Narodowej w okresie 1 stycznia 2016 r. – 31 grudnia 2016 r.', Warsaw 2017, https://ipn.gov.pl/pl/o-ipn/informacje-o-dzialalnos/39982,w-okresie-1-stycznia-2016-r-31-grudnia-2016-r.html#page

20  Andrzej Romanowski, *Rozkosze lustracji. Wybór publicystyki (1998–2007)* (Krakow: Universitas, 2007), 6.

21  Ibid., 9.

22  Andrzej Romanowski, 'IPN, dziwoląg ponad państwem', *Gazeta Wyborcza*, 11 September 2012.

23  IPN, 'Informacja o działalności Instytutu Pamięci Narodowej – Komisja Ścigania Zbrodni przeciwko Narodowi Polskiemu 1 Stycznia 2008 r. – 31 grudnia 2008 r.', *Druk Sejmowy* 1864, Warsaw, 30 March 2009, http://orka.sejm.gov.pl/Druki6ka.nsf/0 /1B18A69A193D9162C125758D003C7AFB/$file/1864.pdf

24 IPN, 'Informację o działalności Instytutu Pamięci Narodowej – Komisji Ścigania Zbrodni przeciwko Narodowi Polskiemu w okresie od 1 stycznia do 31 grudnia 2014 r.', *Druk Sejmowy* 2437, Warsaw, 15 May 2015, http://orka.sejm.gov.pl/Druki7ka.nsf/0 /105CAE3AFF4AD092C1257E5100421165/%24File/3437.pdf

25 Kamil Śmiechowski, "'Życzliwa krytyka, nie krytykanctwo" – Prof. Rafał Stobiecki o IPN-ie' (Interview with Rafał Stobiecki), 18 December 2010, HISTMAG.org., from https://histmag.org/Zyczliwa-krytyka-nie-krytykanctwo-Prof.-Rafal-Stobiecki-o-IPN-ie-4993

26 Nowinowski, 'Dziesięć lat IPN'.

27 A. Dudek, 'Dyskusja "Pamięć narodowa i jej strażnicy"', *Arcana* no. 2 (2001): 5.

28 See for example M. Pawłowski ed., *Spór o PRL* (Krakow: Znak, 1996). See also Andrzej Friszke on the positive contribution of many historians during the communist period and the limitations under which they worked: 'Spór o PRL w III Rzeczypospolitej (1989–2001)', *Pamięć i Sprawiedliwość* 1, no. 1 (2002), Warsaw: Instytut Pamięci Narodowej: 9–28.

29 See the quotations from (among others) Tomasz Strzembosz and Tomasz Wituch in Rafał Stobiecki, 'Historians Facing Politics of History. The Case of Poland' in *Past in the Making. Historical Revisionism in Central Europe after 1989*, ed. Michał Kopeč (Budapest: Central European University Press, 2008), 179–92, also at http://books. openedition.org/ceup/1600?lang=en

30 IPN, 'Informacja o działalności Instytutu Pamięci Narodowej – Komisja Ścigania Zbrodni przeciwko Narodowi Polskiemu w okresie 1 lipca 2001 r. – 30 czerwca 2002 r.', Warsaw, 19 November 2002, *Druk Sejmowy* no. 1117, http://orka.sejm.gov.pl/ Druki4ka.nsf/0/F2BF9B382E5A490FC1256C7C004C10A5/$file/1117.PDF

31 See the interviews noted in Mark, *The Unfinished Revolution*, 49–50.

32 Śmiechowski, 'Życzliwa krytyka'.

33 Stola, 'Poland's Institute of National Remembrance', 52.

34 Romanowski, 'IPN, dziwoląg ponad państwem'. This is a reference to Roman Graczyk, *Cena przetrwania? SB wobec Tygodnika Powszechnego* (Warsaw: Wydawnictwo Czerwone i Czarne, 2011).

35 Peter Raina, *Anatomia lynczu. Sprawa Ojca Konrada Hejmo* (Warsaw: von Borowiecki, 2006).

36 Sławomir Cenckiewicz and Piotr Gontarczyk, *SB a Lech Wałęsa. Przyczynek do biografii* (Warsaw: IPN, 2008).

37 Sławomir Cenckiewicz, *Wałęsa. Człowiek z teczki* (Poznań: Zysk i S-ka), 2013.

38 'Sławomir Cenckiewicz obala 14 mitów Wałęsy', *Niezależna*, 2 February 2017, http://niezalezna.pl/93236-tylko-u-nas-slawomir-cenckiewicz-obala-14-mitow-walesy

39 'Friszke rozbija w OKO.press 14 mitów Cenckiewicza o Wałęsie: to oszczerstwa, insynuacje i manipulacje', *Gazeta Wyborcza*, 8 February 2017. Cenckiewicz's defenders included Andrzej Zybertowicz, 'Strategie unieważniania prawdy: na przykładzie dyskusji wokół książki Sławomira Cenckiewicza i Piotra Gontarczyka o Lechu Wałęsie', *Oblicza Przeszłości*, Bydgoszcz 2011, 431–66, http://i.wp.pl/a/f/ pdf/36348/zybertowicz,_strategie_uniewazniania_prawdy.pdf

40 Dariusz Gowin and Paweł Kowal, 'Polska polityka historyczna' in *Polityka historyczna: historycy – politycy – prasa: konferencja pod honorowym patronatem Jana Nowaka-Jeziorańskiego, Pałac Raczyńskich w Warszawie, 15 grudnia 2004*, ed. Agnieszka Panecka (Warsaw: Muzeum Powstania Warszawskiego, 2005): 11–15,

available from http://www.teologiapolityczna.pl/polska-polityka-historyczna-tekst-dariusza-gawina-i-pawla-kowala-2/. See also Marek A. Cichocki, *Władza i Pamięć* (Krakow: Ośrodek Myśli Politycznej, 2005).

41  Krzysztof Pilawski, 'Historia mitów i łupów', *Przegląd*, 1 February 2009, from https://www.tygodnikprzeglad.pl/historia-mitow-lupow/

42  Robert Traba, 'Polityka wobec historii: kontrowersje i perspektywy', *Teksty Drugie* 1–2, 2010, Instytut Badań Literackich, Centrum Humanistyki Cyfrowej, 300–19, available from http://rcin.org.pl/Content/48995/WA248_66069_P-I-2524_traba-polityka.pdf

43  Anna Wolff-Powęska, 'Polityka historyczna. Polskie spory o historię i pamięć', Paper presented at the Conference Czym jest mała ojczyzna, Collegium Polonicum, 18–19 November 2006, from http://www.transodra-online.net/pl/node/1256

44  Eugeniusz Ponczek, 'Polityka wobec pamięci versus polityka historyczna: aspekty semantyczny, aksjologiczny i merytoryczny w narracji polskiej', Łódź, 2013, from http://przeglad.amu.edu.pl/wp-content/uploads/2013/09/pp-2013-2-007-022.pdf

45  Marek Jurek in the Discussion, 'Polska polityka historyczna', *Biuletyn Instytutu Pamięci Narodowej*, no. 5, May 2006, https://ipn.gov.pl/pl/publikacje/biuletyn-ipn/9627,nr-52006.html

46  Andrzej Nowak in the Discussion, 'Polska polityka historyczna', *Biuletyn Instytutu Pamięci Narodowej*, no. 5, May 2006, https://ipn.gov.pl/pl/publikacje/biuletyn-ipn/9627,nr-52006.html

47  Zdzisław Krasnodębski, 'Zwycięzcy i pokonani' in *Pamięc i Odpowiedzialność*, ed. Dariusz Gawin et al. (Krakow: Ośrodek Myśli Politycznej, Centrum Konserwatywne, nd), 55–70.

48  Filip Musiał, 'Polityka historyczna czy historyczna świadomość? Działalność Instytutu Pamięci Narodowej', *Horyzonty Polityki* 3 (2011): 154.

49  Dariusz Gawin, 'Co to jest polityka historyczna?' (Interview with Dariusz Gawin by Ireneusz Wywiał), Rozmowy Wiadomości Historycznych, *Wiadomości Historyczne*, no. 5, 2006.

50  See for example Wojciech Roszkowski, 'O potrzebie polskiej polityki historycznej' in *Pamięc i Odpowiedzialność*, ed. Dariusz Gowin et al. (Kraków: Ośrodek Myśli Konserwatywnej, 2005), 125.

51  Joanna Sanecka, 'Polityka historyczna partii Prawo i Sprawiedliwość: założenia i realizacja', *Athenaeum. Polskie Studia Politologiczne* 19 (2008): 56, http://www.athenaeum.umk.pl/numery/19.pdf

52  Filip Musiał, 'Polityka historyczna czy historyczna świadomość? Działalność Instytutu Pamięci Narodowej', *Horyzonty Polityki* 03 (2011): 165; Eugeniusz Ponczek, 'Polityka wobec pamięci versus polityka historyczna: aspekty semantyczny, aksjologiczny i merytoryczny w narracji polskiej', Łódź, 2013, http://przeglad.amu.edu.pl/wp-content/uploads/2013/09/pp-2013-2-007-022.pdf

53  Andrzej Friszke, 'Jak hartował się radykalizm Kurtyki', *Gazeta Wyborcza*, 7 April 2009.

54  Stola, 'Poland's Institute of National Remembrance', 56.

55  Andrzej Romanowski, 'Historia, kłamstwo i banał', *Gazeta Wyborcza*, 15 July 2006.

56  Wiesław Władyka, 'Czym była PRL – niedokończona debata', *Polityka*, 15 July 2014.

57  Bogdan Zdrojewski, 'Dajmy Polakom być dumnymi ze swojej historii', *Gazeta Wyborcza*, 4 November 2008.

58  Sanecka, 'Polityka historyczna partii Prawo i Sprawiedliwość', 59.

59  Dorota Szeligowska explores the links between historical policy and PiD's fostering of 'the patriotism of tomorrow'; Dorota Szeligowska, 'The Dynamics of Polish

Patriotism after 1989: Concepts, Debates, Identities', PhD thesis, Central European University, Budapest 2014, http://www.etd.ceu.hu/2014/szeligowska_dorota.pdf

60   Jan Kubik and Amy Linch, 'The Original Sin of Poland's Third Republic: Discounting "Solidarity" and Its Consequences for Political Reconciliation', *Polish Sociological Review* no. 153 (2006): 9–38.

61   Michael Bernhard and Jan Kubik, 'Roundtable Discord. The Contested Legacy of 1989 in Poland' in *Twenty Years after Communism*, eds. Michael Bernhard and Jan Kubik (Oxford: Oxford University Press, 2014), 61.

62   Robert Brier, 'The Roots of the "Fourth Republic." Solidarity's Cultural Legacy to Polish Politics', *East European Politics and Societies* 23, no 1 (2009): 77.

63   Bernhard and Kubik, 'Roundtable Discord', 80.

64   Mark, *The Unfinished Revolution*, 15–16.

65   Martina Klosova, 'Social Performance, Cultural Trauma, and the Polish Tragedy in Smolensk', nd from https://is.muni.cz/do/fss/ SOCIOLOGIE/57823/26143701/26503523/Klosova_Cultural_Sociology_Paper. txt?so=nx

66   Geneviève Zubrzycki, 'Polish Mythology and the Traps of Messianic Martyrology' in *National Myths: Constructed Pasts, Contested Presents*, ed. Gérard Bouchard (London: Routledge, 2013), 110–32.

67   Ewa Ochman, *Communist Poland – Contested Pasts and Future Identities* (London: Routledge, 2013), 6.

68   P. Szubarczyk, 'Pora oczyścić dom ze śmieci', reprinted from *Nasz Dziennik*, 14–15 April 2007 at http://archiwum.dlapolski.pl/informacje/Czytaj-art-1921.html

69   Quoted in Inga Domurat, 'Prezes IPN apeluje do władz Połczyna: – Zmieńcie nazwy ulic', *Głos Koszaliński*, 3 November 2008, from http://www.gk24.pl/wiadomosci/ swidwin/art/4293343,prezes-ipn-apeluje-do-wladz-polczyna-zmiencie-nazwy-ulic,id,t.html

70   CBOS, 'Opinia Społeczna o nazwach ulic', Komunikat z Badań BS/38/2007, Warsaw, March 2007.

71   'Projekt ustawy o miejscach pamięci narodowej', *Druk Sejmowy* 745, 13 December 2007, http://orka.sejm.gov.pl/Druki6ka.nsf/0/AA56F61E11E91DE3C1257482005811 B5/$file/745.pdf

72   'Ustawa z dnia 29 kwietnia 2016 r. o zmianie ustawy o Instytucie Pamięci Narodowej – Komisji Ścigania Zbrodni przeciwko Narodowi Polskiemu oraz niektórych innych ustaw', *Dziennik Ustaw*, 2016, poz. 749, http://dziennikustaw.gov. pl/DU/2016/749/1

73   Anna Kondek-Dyoniziak, 'Zmiany, które budzą zaniepokojenie. Łukasz Kamiński o projekcie noweli o IPN' (Interview with Łukasz Kamiński), *Polish Radio*, 20 March 2016, http://www.polskieradio.pl/5/3/Artykul/1596978,Zmiany-ktore-budza-zaniepokojenie-Lukasz-Kaminski-o-projekcie-noweli-o-IPN

74   Mira Suchodolska, 'Gangsterski skok na IPN. Prezes będzie figurantem', *Gazeta Prawna*, 10 July 2016.

75   Witold Bagieński, Sławomir Cenckiewicz and Piotr Woyciechowski, *Konfidenci* (Warsaw: Editions Spotkanie, 2015).

76   See for example 'Teczka Wałęsy. Cenckiewicz ujawnia NIESAMOWITY dokument. Spiskowa teoria', *Super express*, 9 August 2016, from http://www.se.pl/wiadomosci/ polityka/teczka-walesy-cenckiewicz-ujawnia-niesamowity-dokument-spiskowa-teoria_876926.html. For an unflattering picture of Cenckiewicz see Piotr Pytlakowski, 'Rycerz jednej prawdy', *Polityka*, 13 April 2016.

77  Cenckiewicz and Gontarczyk, *SB a Lech Wałęsa*, 237–8.
78  Jan Darasz, 'The History Men' in *Poland's Memory Wars*, ed. Jo Harper (Budapest: CEU Press), 2018, 131.

# Chapter 9

1   Lech Garlicki, 'Pierwsze orzeczenie Trybunału Konstytucyjnego (Refleksje w 15 lat później)' (Warsaw: Trybunału Konstytucyjny, 2000), http://trybunal.gov.pl/ fileadmin/content/dokumenty/pierwsza-rozprawa/Leszek_Garlicki_Pierwsza_ rozprawa.pdf.
2   'Ustawa z dnia 1 grudnia 1989 r. o zmianie ustawy o Trybunale Konstytucyjnym', *Dziennik Ustaw* 1989, poz. 16, http://www.dziennikustaw.gov.pl/DU/1990/s/3/16/1; it merely altered the oath of office; 'Ustawa z dnia 20 grudnia 1989 r. o zmianie ustaw – Prawo o ustroju sądów powszechnych, o Sądzie Najwyższym, o Naczelnym Sądzie Administracyjnym, o Trybunale Konstytucyjnym, o ustroju sądów wojskowych i Prawo o notariacie', *Dziennik Ustaw* 1989, poz. 73, http://www.dziennikustaw.gov.pl/ DU/1989/436/1.
3   'Ustawa z dnia 29 maja 1989 r. o przekazaniu dotychczasowych kompetencji Rady Państwa Prezydentowi Polskiej Rzeczypospolitej Ludowej i innym organom państwowym', *Dziennik Ustaw* 1989, poz. 178, http://www.dziennikustaw.gov.pl/ DU/1989/178/1.
4   See Łukasz Bokarski with Monika Szulecka, 'Wybory sędziów do Trybunału Konstytucyjnego' (Warsaw: Instytut Prawa i Społeczeństwa, 2010), http://www.inpris. pl/fileadmin/user_upload/documents/raport_wybory_sedziow_TK.pdf.
5   With each deputy having up to five votes, Tomasz Dybowski gained 238 votes, Antoni Filcek 250, Wojciech Łączkowski and Andrzej Zoll 233, and Janina Zakrzewska 201. See the proceedings of the *Sejm*, 17 November 1989, http://orka2. sejm.gov.pl/StenogramyX.nsf/0/EEE4AFE0B578F693C1257D20002CC703/$fi le/012_000006935.pdf.
6   Ryszard Cholewiński, 'The Protection of Human Rights in the New Polish Constitution'. *Fordham International Law Journal* 1, no. 2 (1998): 283.
7   Garlicki, 'Pierwsze orzecenie'.
8   Similar allegations were made about Czeszejko-Sochacki, Rymarz, Garlicki and Maczynski; see Sławomir Cenckiewicz and Piotr Gontarczyk, *SB a Lech Wałęsa. Przyczynek do biografii* (Warsaw: IPN, 2008), 238–9; also https://lustronauki. wordpress.com/2008/12/08/blazej-wierzbowski/; http://polonus.forumoteka.pl/ temat,2101,quotwaclawquot-czyli-agent-ubsb-sokolewicz.html; https://lustronauki. wordpress.com/2009/06/10/zdzislaw-czeszejko-sochacki/
9   Trybunał Konstytucyjny, 'Informacja przedstawiona Sejmowi Rzeczypospolitej Polskiej przez Prezesa Trybunału Konstytucyjnego na 50 posiedzeniu Sejmu RP 3 lipca 1998 roku' (Warsaw: Trybunał Konstytucyjny, 1998), http://trybunal.gov.pl/ publikacje/informacje-o-problemach-wynikajacych-z-dzialalnosci-i-orzecznictwa- tk/1997/
10  On the development of these principles, see Jerzy Oniszczuk, *Orzecznictwo Trybunału Konstytucyjnego w latach 1989–1996* (Warsaw: Wydawnictwo Sejmowe, 1998), 127–95.

11  Trybunał Konstytucyjny, 'Informacja o istotnych problemach wynikających z działalności i orzecznictwa Trybunału Konstytucyjnego w 1998 roku' (Warsaw: Trybunał Konstytucyjny, March 1999), http://trybunal.gov.pl/publikacje/informacje-o-problemach-wynikajacych-z-dzialalnosci-i-orzecznictwa-tk/1998/

12  Ibid. The judgment in question was 'Wyrok z dnia 10 listopada 1998 r.', Sygn. K. 39/97, http://otkzu.trybunal.gov.pl/1998/6/99

13  Trybunał Konstytucyjny, 'Informacja o istotnych problemach wynikających z działalności i orzecznictwa Trybunału Konstytucyjnego w 2000 r.' (Warsaw: Trybunał Konstytucyjny, March 2001), http://trybunal.gov.pl/publikacje/informacje-o-problemach-wynikajacych-z-dzialalnosci-i-orzecznictwa-tk/2000/

14  'Case of Broniowski v. Poland', Application no. 31443/96, Judgment, Strasbourg, 22 June 2004, http://hudoc.echr.coe.int/eng?i=001-61828#{'item id':['001-61828']}; 'Wyrok Trybunału Konstytucyjnego z dnia 15 grudnia 2004 r.', sygn. Akt K2/04, https://ipo.trybunal.gov.pl/ipo/Sprawa?cid=1&dokument=441&sprawa=3597

15  '27. posiedzenie Sejmu w dniu 27 października 2006 r.', http://orka.sejm.gov.pl/StenoInter5.nsf/0/B03406CD394EE0D9C1257214006E71EB/$file/27_c_ksiazka.pdf; '29. posiedzenie Sejmu w dniu 8 grudnia 2006 r.', http://orka.sejm.gov.pl/StenoInter5.nsf/0/B59B23336D123725C125723E006082A3/$file/29_d_ksiazka.pdf

16  Marcin Kącki, 'Kandydat Samoobrony do TK ma sprawę w sądzie', *Gazeta Wyborcza*, 8 November 2006.

17  'Kandydat do Trybunału sądził opozycjonistów', *Wprost*, 27 October 2006.

18  Marcin Kowalski and Marcin Kącki with Szymon Jadczak, 'Marek Kotlinowski pomógł naciągaczowi?' *Gazeta Wyborcza*, 24 October 2006.

19  Mariusz Jałoszewski, 'Czerwona kartka dla Bagińskiej', *Rzeczpospolita*, 8 February 2007.

20  'Wyrok z dnia 18 stycznia 2006 r.', Sygn. akt K 21/05, http://otkzu.trybunal.gov.pl/2006/1A/4

21  Quoted in Ewa Siedlecka, 'Prawo Kulą u nogi Prawa i Sprawiedliwości', *Gazeta Wyborcza*, 21 January 2006.

22  Janina Paradowska, 'Może być pięknie (Interview with Jarosław Kaczyński)', *Polityka*, 14 January 2006.

23  Jarosław Kaczyński, 'Informacja prezesa Rady Ministrów o działalności rządu w okresie 100 dni jego funkcjonowania', Sprawozdanie stenograficzne Sejmu, 10. posiedzenie Sejmu w dniu 17 lutego 2006 r., http://orka.sejm.gov.pl/StenoInter5.nsf/0/124DF224F5085F73C125711B0031F0BD/$file/10_c_ksiazka.pdf

24  'Wyrok z 23 marca 2006', Sygn. K 4/06, http://otkzu.trybunal.gov.pl/2006/3A/32 (six of these judges had some association with the SLD; nine did not).

25  Quoted in 'Grzechy główne ustawy', *Rzeczpospolita*, 24 March 2006.

26  Agnieszka Kublik and Monika Olejnik, 'Jarosław Kaczyński: We mnie jest czyste dobro' (Interview with Jarosław Kaczyński)', *Gazeta Wyborcza*, 2 February 2006.

27  'Prezydent: Konstytucja wymaga zmian', *Wiadomości*, 2 May 2007, http://wiadomosci.wp.pl/wid,8845896,wiadomosc.html?T%5Bpage%5D=5&ticaid=118689

28  Marek Safjan, 'Oświadczenie Prezesa Trybunału', http://trybunal.gov.pl/fileadmin/content/dokumenty/wystapienia/1998_2006/oswiadczenie20060221.pdf

29  'Wyrok z dnia 11 maja 2007 r.', Sygn. akt K 2/07, https://ipo.trybunal.gov.pl/ipo/Sprawa?cid=2&dokument=444&sprawa=4291

30 Jolanta Kroner and Katarzyna Sadłowska, 'Trzeba będzie posprzątać po IV RP' (Interview with Andrzej Zoll), *Rzeczpospolita*, 23 February 2006.

31 Małgorzata Subotić, 'Nie biorę pod uwagę konsekewncji politycznych (Interview with Jerzy Stępień)', *Rzeczpospolita* 31 March–1 April 2007.

32 Quoted in Eliza Olczyk and Bernadeta Waszkielewicz, 'Ostry spór polityków o rolę Trybunału', *Rzeczpospolita*, 14 May 2007.

33 Quoted in ibid.

34 Janusz Kochanowski, 'Trybunał wywołał zamęt', *Rzeczpospolita*, 25 July 2007.

35 Aleksandra Gardynik and Bernadeta Waszkielewicz, 'PiS chce zmian w Trybunale', *Rzeczpospolita*, 29 June 2007.

36 'Wyrok z dnia 28 listopada 2007 r.', Sygn. akt K 39/07, http://otkzu.trybunal.gov.pl/2007/10A/129

37 'Ustawa z dnia 25 czerwca 2015 r. o Trybunale Konstytucyjnym, *Dziennik Ustaw* 2015, poz. 1064', http://dziennikustaw.gov.pl/du/2015/1064/1. See Maria Kruk, 'Nowa ustawa o Trybunale Konstytucyjnym z 25 czerwca 2015', *Przegląd Sejmowy*, no. 5, 2015: 9–28.

38 In the *Sejm*, 26 May 2015, http://orka2.sejm.gov.pl/StenoInter7.nsf/0/5DE6FDF11053 9359C1257E51007BED49/%24File/93_a_ksiazka.pdf

39 'Wyrok z dnia 2 kwietnia 2015 r.' sygn. akt P 31/12, http://otkzu.trybunal.gov.pl/2015/4A/44

40 Trybunał Konstytucyjny, 'Przedstawiona przez Prezesa Trybunału Konstytucyjnego Informacja o istotnych problemach wynikających z działalności i orzecznictwa Trybunału Konstytucyjnego w 2015 r.', *Druk Sejmowy* 470, 27 April 2016, from http://orka.sejm.gov.pl/Druki8ka.nsf/0/733563C2E4108F15C1257FA4002FF70B/%24Fi le/470.pdf

41 Calculated from the annual reports, 'Informacja o istotnych problemach wynikających z działalności i orzecznictwa Trybunału Konstytucyjnego' 2008–15.

42 'Wyrok z dnia 27 października 2010 r.', Sygn. akt K 10/08, http://otkzu.trybunal.gov.pl/2010/8A/81

43 'Wyrok z dnia 24 lutego 2010 r.', Sygn. akt K 6/09, http://otkzu.trybunal.gov.pl/2010/2A/15

44 Robert Kropiwnicki in the *Sejm*, 26 May 2015, http://orka2.sejm.gov.pl/StenoInter7.nsf/0/5DE6FDF110539359C1257E51007BED49/%24File/93_a_ksiazka.pdf

45 See especially Małgorzata Szuleka, Marcin Wolny and Marcin Szwed, 'The Constitutional Crisis in Poland 2015–2016' (Warsaw: Helsinki Foundation for Human Rights, August 2016), http://www.hfhr.pl/wp-content/uploads/2016/09/HFHR_The-constitutional-crisis-in-Poland-2015-2016.pdf

46 Dariusz Mazur and Waldemar Żurek, 'So called "Good Change" in the Polish System of the Administration of Justice', https://ruleoflaw.pl/so-called-good-change-in-the-polish-system-of-the-administration-of-justice/

47 'Ustawa z dnia 19 listopada 2015 r. o zmianie ustawy o Trybunale Konstytucyjnym', *Dziennik Ustaw* 2015, poz. 1928, http://www.dziennikustaw.gov.pl/DU/2015/1928/1

48 'Wyrok z dnia 3 grudnia 2015 r.', Sygn. akt K 34/15, http://otkzu.trybunal.gov.pl/2015/11A/185

49 'Wyrok z dnia 9 grudnia 2015 r.', Sygn. akt K 35/15, http://otkzu.trybunal.gov.pl/2015/11A/186

50 'Ustawa z dnia 22 grudnia 2015 r. o zmianie ustawy o Trybunale Konstytucyjnym', *Dziennik Ustaw* 2015, poz. 2217, http://www.dziennikustaw.gov.pl/DU/2015/2217/1

51 'Komunikat prasowy w sprawie U 8/15', http://trybunal.gov.pl/uploads/media/ Komunikat_prasowy_w_sprawie_U_8_15_12012016.pdf

52 Wojciech Sadurski, *Poland's Constitutional Breakdown* (Oxford: Oxford University Press, 2019), 64ff.

53 Marcin Matczak, 'An Eye for an Eye: Law as an Instrument of Revenge in Poland', Verfassungsblog, 8 March 2017, https://verfassungsblog.de/an-eye-for-an-eye-law-as-an-instrument-of-revenge-in-poland/

54 Polskie Radio, 7 March 2016, http://www.polskieradio.pl/5/3/ Artykul/1592022,Zbigniew-Ziobro-pisze-do-Trybunalu-Konstytucyjnego

55 'Wyrok z dnia 9 marca 2016 r.', Sygn. akt K 47/15, https://ipo.trybunal.gov.pl/ipo/ view/sprawa.xhtml?&pokaz=dokumenty&sygnatura=K%2047/15

56 European Commission for Democracy through Law, 'Opinion on Amendments to the Act of 25 June 2015 on the Constitutional Tribunal of Poland', Opinion no. 833/2015, Venice, 11 March 2016, http://www.venice.coe.int/webforms/documents/ default.aspx?pdffile=CDL-AD(2016)001-e

57 Andrzej Stankiewicz, 'Wybór sędziego Trybunału Konstytucyjnego: Awantura w Sejmie', *Rzeczpospolita*, 14 April 2016.

58 'Jarosław Kaczyński: Do końca kadencji Rzeplińskiego na opamiętanie nie ma co liczyć', *Dziennik.pl*, 24 May 2016, http://wiadomosci.dziennik.pl/polityka/ artykuly/521593,jaroslaw-kaczynski-do-konca-kadencji-rzeplinskiego-na-opamietanie-nie-ma-co-liczyc.html

59 'Ustawa z dnia 22 lipca 2016 r. o Trybunale Konstytucyjnym', *Dziennik Ustaw* 2016, poz. 1157, http://www.dziennikustaw.gov.pl/DU/2016/1157/1

60 'Raport Zespołu Ekspertów do spraw Problematyki Trybunału Konstytucyjnego z dnia 15 lipca 2016 r.', http://www.sejm.gov.pl/media8.nsf/files/ASEA-ADRKBW/%24File/Raport%20Zespo%C5%82u%20Ekspert%C3%B3w%20do%20 spraw%20Problematyki%20Trybuna%C5%82u%20Konstytucyjnego.pdf

61 Mariusz Muszyński, 'Krótka analiza opinii Komisji Weneckiej z 11 marca 2016 r, dotyczącej Trybunału Konstytucyjnego dla Pana Andrzeja Rzeplińskiego, Prezesa TK', Warsaw, 27 May 2016, http://wpolityce.pl/polityka/295429-nasz-news-prof-mariusz-muszynski-sedzia-tk-i-przedstawiciel-polski-w-komisji-weneckiej-miazdzy-jej-opinie.

62 'Wyrok z dnia 11 sierpnia 2016 r.', Sygn. akt K 39/16, http://otkzu.trybunal.gov. pl/2016/A/71

63 European Commission for Democracy through Law, 'Poland. Opinion on the Act on the Constitutional Tribunal Adopted by the Venice Commission at its 108th Plenary Session', Opinion 860/2016, Venice, 14–15 October 2016, http://www.venice.coe.int/ webforms/documents/default.aspx?pdffile=CDL-AD(2016)026-e

64 The Polish government's response is 'Position regarding draft Opinion of the Venice Commission on the Act on the Constitutional Tribunal of 22 July 2016. Overall assessment of the draft Opinion', no author, no date, http://www.venice.coe.int/ webforms/documents/default.aspx?pdffile=CDL-REF(2016)060-e

65 'Stenogram rozprawy z dnia 7 listopada 2016 r. w sprawie o sygn. K 44/16', http://ipo. trybunal.gov.pl/ipo/Sprawa?&pokaz=dokumenty&sygnatura=K%2044/16

66 'Wrok z dnia 7 listopada 2016 r.', Sygn. akt K 44/16, http://otkzu.trybunal.gov. pl/2016/A/86

67 'Ustawa z dnia 30 listopada 2016 r. o organizacji i trybie postępowania przed Trybunałem Konstytucyjnym', *Dziennik Ustaw* 2016, poz. 2072, http://www. dziennikustaw.gov.pl/DU/2016/2072/1; 'Ustawa z dnia 30 listopada 2016 r. o statusie

sędziów Trybunału Konstytucyjnego', *Dziennik Ustaw* 2016, poz. 2073, http://www.dziennikustaw.gov.pl/DU/2016/2073/1

68  Maximilian Steinbeis, 'Statement by the Former Presidents of the Constitutional Tribunal: Marek Safjan, Jerzy Stępień, Bohdan Zdziennicki and Andrzej Zoll' (English translation), 30 November 2016, https://verfassungsblog.de/statement-by-the-former-presidents-of-the-constitutional-tribunal-marek-safjan-jerzy-stepien-bohdan-zdziennicki-and-andrzej-zoll/

69  'Protokól z Obrad Zgromadzenia Ogólnego Sędziów Trybunału Konstytucyjnego w dniu 20 grudnia 2016 r.', http://www.hfhr.pl/wp-content/uploads/2017/01/protokol-obrad-Zgromadzenia-Ogolnego-STK-w-dniu-20-XII-2016-r.pdf; Załącznik do Protokołu Zgromadzenia Sędziów Trybunału Konstytucyjnego z dnia 20 grudnia 2016 r.', http://www.hfhr.pl/wp-content/uploads/2017/01/Za%C5%82acznik-do-protoko%C5%82u-ZO-Sedzi%C3%B3w-TK.pdf; Piotr Pszczółkowski, 'Załącznik do Protokołu Zgromadzenia Sędziów Trybunału Konstytucyjnego z 20 grudnia 2016 r.', http://www.hfhr.pl/wp-content/uploads/2017/01/Za%C5%82acznik-do-protoko%C5%82u-obrad-ZO-sedzia-Piotr-Pszczolkowski.pdf; also Krzysztof Burnetko, 'Kim jest Julia Przyłębska – czy rzeczywiście prezesem Trybunału Konstytucyjnego?' *Polityka*, 11 February 2017.

70  'Ziobro: Rymar, Tuleja i Zubik nie mogą być uznani za sędziów TK', 13 January 2017, http://www.pap.pl/aktualnosci/news,769084,ziobro-rymar-tuleja-i-zubik-nie-moga-byc-uznani-za-sedziow-tk.html

71  Andrzej Stankiewicz, 'Sędzia z PiS zarzuca Julii Przyłębskiej łamanie prawa', onenet.pl, 16 October 2019, https://wiadomosci.onet.pl/tylko-w-onecie/sedzia-jaroslaw-wyrembak-zada-dymisji-prezes-tk-julii-przylebskiej/ddnn9yg

72  Tadeusz Koncewicz, 'The Capture of the Polish Constitutional Tribunal and Beyond: Of Institution(s), Fidelities and the Rule of Law in Flux', *Review of Central and East European Law* 43, no. 2 (2018): 118.

73  PiS had won 37.6 per cent of the vote in the 2015 elections on a 50.92 per cent turnout. In 2019 it won 43.6 per cent on a 61.7 per cent turnout.

# Chapter 10

1  Andrzej Stankiewicz et al., 'Biznes często to przystań ludzi PRL (Interview with Jarosław Kaczyński)', *Rzeczpospolita*, 4 September 2013.

2  Anna Wójcik, 'Prof. Mirosław Wyrzykowski: Pozakonstytucyjna zmiana ustroju staje się faktem. O tym trzeba debatować, panie Prezydencie' (Interview), OKO.press, 26 August 2017, https://oko.press/prof-miroslaw-wyrzykowski-pozakonstytucyjna-zmiana-ustroju-staje-sie-faktem-o-tym-trzeba-debatowac-panie-prezydencie/

3  Bojan Bugarič and Tom Ginsburg, 'The Assault on Postcommunist Courts', *Journal of Democracy* 27, no. 3 (2016): 69–82. Hungary under Victor Orban was the most significant analogue; Kriszta Kovács, 'Hungary's Orbánistan: A Complete Arsenal of Emergency Powers', *VerfBlog*, 6 April, 2020, https://verfassungsblog.de/hungarys-orbanistan-a-complete-arsenal-of-emergency-powers/

4  Ben Stanley, 'Confrontation by Default and Confrontation by Design: Strategic and Institutional Responses to Poland's Populist Coalition Government', *Democratization* 23, no. 2 (2016): 263–82.

5  M. Morawiecki, Speech of 15 November 2015, https://www.youtube.com/watch?v=OK4maOASQIs. Morawiecki is the father of the current prime minister (2020).

6    Christian Davies, *Hostile Takeover: How Law and Justice Captured Poland's Courts*,
     Nations in Transit Brief, Freedom House, May 2018: 4, https://freedomhouse.org/
     report/special-reports/hostile-takeover-how-law-and-justice-captured-poland-s-
     courts
7    Wojciech Czuchnowski and Tomasz Ciechoński, 'Trybunał Konstytucyjny. Sylwetka
     Lecha Morawskiego – kandydata PiS na sędziego TK', *Gazeta Wyborcza*, 2 December
     2015; also Lech Morawski, 'Wspólnotowość jako wartość konstytucyjna – 31.03.2012.
     mp4', at https://www.youtube.com/watch?v=yKCRrayPK-I
8    'Kryzys Trybunału Konstytucyjnego RP', https://www.youtube.com/
     watch?v=VgoKX2NHbz0
9    'Oxford Symposium on the Polish Constitutional Crisis and Institutional Self-
     Defence', the second panel, 9 May 2017, on line at THE SECOND PANEL OF THE
     SYMPOSIUM: PROFESSOR TOMASZ GIZBERT-STUDNICKI, PROFESSOR
     TIMOTHY ENDICOTT, AND PROFESSOR LECH MORAWSKI https://www.law.
     ox.ac.uk/news/2017-05-11-oxford-symposium-polish-constitutional-crisis-sparks-
     public-debate
10   Stefan Batory Foundation Legal Expert Group, 'Report of the Stefan Batory
     Foundation Legal Expert Group on the Impact of the Judiciary Reform in Poland
     in 2015–2018', 16; http://www.batory.org.pl/upload/files/Programy%20operacyjne/
     Odpowiedzialne%20Panstwo/Batory%20Foundation_Report%20on%20the%20
     judiciary%20reform%20in%20Poland.pdf
11   Jerzy Zajadło, 'Fałszywość hasła " demokracja, a nie sędziokracja" – analiza
     filozoficzno-prawna', Konstytucyjny.pl, https://konstytucyjny.pl/falszywosc-hasla-
     demokracja-a-nie-sedziokracja-analiza-filozoficzno-prawna-jerzy-zajadlo/
12   Davies, *Hostile Takeover*, 8.
13   Quoted in 'Zbigniew Ziobro: są propozycje reformy wymiaru sądownictwa,
     ale problemem jest TK', *WP Wiadomości*, http://wiadomosci.wp.pl/
     kat,1342,title,Zbigniew-Ziobro-sa-propozycje-reformy-wymiaru-sadownictwa-ale-
     problemem-jest-TK,wid,18500270,wiadomosc.html?&ticaid=1189ea
14   Maria Los and Andrzej Zybertowicz, *Privatizing the Police-State, The Case of Poland*
     (Basingstoke: Macmillan Press, 2000), 136, 69.
15   CBOS, 'Społeczne oceny wymiaru sprawiedliwości', Komunikat z Badań NR 31/2017,
     Warsaw, March 2017.
16   Tadeusz Koncewicz, 'On the Separation of Powers and Judicial Self-Defence at Times
     of Unconstitutional Capture', VerfassungBlog, 4 June 2017, https://verfassungsblog.
     de/on-the-separation-of-powers-and-the-judicial-self-defence-at-times-of-
     unconstitutional-capture/
17   'Wyrok z dnia 20 czerwca 2017 r.', sygn. akt K 5/17, https://ipo.trybunal.gov.pl/ipo/Sp
     rawa?cid=1&dokument=15759&sprawa=19036
18   Quoted in 'Prof. Sadurski: Pseudowyrok Trybunału w sprawie KRS to prymitywna
     ustawka', *Gazeta Wyborcza*, 20 June 2017.
19   'Ustawa z dnia 4 listopada 2016 r. o zmianie ustawy – Prawo o ustroju sądów
     powszechnych oraz niektórych innych ustaw', *Dziennik Ustaw* 2016, poz. 2103, http://
     dziennikustaw.gov.pl/DU/2016/2103/1
20   Piotr Pytlakowski, 'Społeczny opór na ulicach polskich miast', *Polityka*, 26 July 2017.
21   'Nie ma zgody na niszczenie niezależnych sądów', http://krs.gov.pl/pl/aktualnosci/
     d,2017,11/5095,nie-ma-zgody-na-niszczenie-niezaleznych-sadow
22   'Ustawa z dnia 8 grudnia 2017 r. o zmianie ustawy o Krajowej Radzie Sądownictwa',
     *Dziennik Ustaw*, 2018, poz. 3, http://dziennikustaw.gov.pl/DU/2018/3/1

23 European Commission for Democracy through Law (Venice Commission), Opinion No. 904/2017, 11 December 2017, https://www.venice.coe.int/webforms/documents/?pdf=CDL-AD(2017)031-e#

24 'Gersdorf: Nie mogłam postąpić wbrew przepisowi ustawy', *Gazeta prawna.pl*, 27 April 2018, from https://prawo.gazetaprawna.pl/artykuly/1120441,gersdorf-o-zmianie-w-krs.html

25 Davies, *Hostile Takeover*, 5.

26 'Kim są nowi sędziowie wybrani do KRS?', *Polityka*, 6 March 2018.

27 Łukasz Bojarski, 'Bez żadnego trybu', *Dziennik Gazeta Prawna*, 14 May 2018.

28 Ewa Siedlecka, 'W nowej KRS prawo znów ustąpiło przed siłą', *Polityka*, 27 April 2018.

29 Michael Cross, 'Poland Suspended from Judicial Council', *The Law Society Gazette*, 18 September 2018, https://www.lawgazette.co.uk/news/poland-suspended-from-judicial-council/5067594.article

30 'Siedmioro sędziów TK wydało oświadczenie', 27 March 2019, https://www.polsatnews.pl/wiadomosc/2019-03-27/siedmioro-sedziow-trybunal-konstytucyjnego-wydalo-oswiadczenie/

31 The Declaration was reproduced in full by OKO Press: https://oko.press/22-sedziow-tk-w-oswiadczeniu-bez-precedensu-pawlowicz-i-piotrowicz-w-skladzie-orzekajacym-to-naruszenie-prawa/.

32 Marcin Matczak, 'An Eye for an Eye: Law as an Instrument of Revenge in Poland', Verfassungsblog, 8 March 2017, https://verfassungsblog.de/an-eye-for-an-eye-law-as-an-instrument-of-revenge-in-poland/

33 Małgorzata Szulecka and Maciej Kalisz, 'Disciplinary Proceedings against Judges and Prosecutors', Warsaw, Helsinki Foundation for Human Rights, February 2019, http://www.hfhr.pl/wp-content/uploads/2019/02/HFHR_Disciplinary-proceedings-against-judges-and-prosecutors.pdf; Zamira Djabarova and Brittany Benowitz, 'A Back Door to Controlling Judges: Poland's Ruling Party Tries Another Ploy', *Just Security*, 27 March 2019, from https://www.justsecurity.org/63381/a-back-door-to-controlling-judges-polands-ruling-party-tries-another-ploy/

34 Ewa Siedlecka, 'Dyscyplinowanie sędziego Stępnia', *Polityka*, 11 May 2018.

35 'Ustawa z dnia 12 lipca 2017 r. o zmianie ustawy – Prawo o ustroju sądów powszechnych', *Dziennik Ustaw* 2017, poz. 1452, http://dziennikustaw.gov.pl/DU/2017/1452/1

36 'Report of the Stefan Batory Foundation Legal Expert Group'.

37 Barbara Grabowska-Moroz and Małgorzata Szuleka, 'It Starts with the Personnel. Replacement of Common Court Presidents and Vice Presidents from August 2017 to February 2018', Warsaw: Helsinki Foundation for Human Rights, April 2018: 21, http://www.hfhr.pl/wp-content/uploads/2018/04/It-starts-with-the-personnel.pdf

38 Ibid., 27.

39 'Sędziowie piszą do premiera. "Porównanie do faszystowskich kolaborantów jest haniebne"', https://www.tvn24.pl/wiadomosci-z-kraju,3/morawiecki-mowil-w-usa-o-sedziach-kolaborantach-list-sedziow-do-premiera,929663.html

40 Gałczyńska, Małgorzata, 'Śledztwo Onetu. Farma trolli w Ministerstwie Sprawiedliwości, czyli "za czynienie dobra nie wsadzamy"', Onet Wiadomości, 19 August 2019, https://wiadomosci.onet.pl/tylko-w-onecie/sledztwo-onetu-farma-trolli-w-ministerstwie-sprawiedliwosci-czyli-za-czynienie-dobra/j6hwp7f?utm_source=wiadomosci.onet.pl_viasg_wiadomosci&utm_medium=referal&utm_campaign=leo_automatic&srcc=ucs&utm_v=2

41  Wojciech Czuchnowski and Agnieszka Kublik, 'Afera u Ziobry. Jak "Emi" przeprowadziła atak na sędziów, którzy opowiadali o Polsce w Brukseli', *Gazeta Wyborcza*, 26 August 2019.

42  Aleksandra Eriksson, 'Poland Postpones Overhaul of Public Media', *EU Observer*, 9 June 2016, https://euobserver.com/political/133761

43  'Opinion of Council of Europe Experts Mr. Jean-François Furnément and Dr. Eve Salomon on Three Draft Acts Regarding Polish Public Service Media', Council of Europe DGI(2016)13, Strasbourg, 6 June 2016, https://rm.coe.int/CoERMPublicCommonSearchServices/DisplayDCTMContent?documentId=090000 168065e9eb

44  'Ustawa z dnia 22 czerwca 2016 r. o Radzie Mediów Narodowych', *Dziennik Ustaw*, 2016, poz. 929, from http://dziennikustaw.gov.pl/DU/2016/929/1

45  Wojciech Sadurski, 'I Criticized Poland's Government. Now It's Trying to Ruin Me', *The Washington Post*, 21 May 2019, https://www.washingtonpost.com/opinions/2019/05/21/i-criticized-polands-government-now-its-trying-ruin-me/?utm_term=.66fd78291c33

46  Piotr Buras, 'The Killing of Gdańsk's Mayor Is the Tragic Result of Hate Speech', *The Guardian*, 17 January 2019.

47  Onenet, 'Czy TVP przesadziło? Jacek Kurski zostanie odwołany?', https://www.youtube.com/watch?v=ZwBABc8_9BA

48  Freedom House, 'Pluralism under Attack: The Assault on Press Freedom in Poland', https://freedomhouse.org/sites/default/files/FH_Poland_Report_Final_2017.pdf

49  Reporters without Borders, 2019 Press Freedom Index, https://rsf.org/en/ranking

50  Adam Czarnota, 'The Politics of the Lustration Law in Poland, 1989–2006' in *Justice as Prevention. Vetting Public Employees in Transitional Societies*, eds. A. Mayer-Rieckh and P. de Greiff (New York: Social Science Research Council, 2007), 244.

51  European Commission, 'Commission Recommendation of 27.7.2016 Regarding the Rule of Law in Poland', Brussels, 27 July 2016, http://ec.europa.eu/justice/effective-justice/files/recommendation-rule-of-law-poland-20160727_en.pdf

52  'Commission Recommendation (EU) 2017/146 of 21 December 2016 Regarding the Rule of Law in Poland Complementary to Recommendation (EU) 2016/1374', https://eur-lex.europa.eu/legal-content/EN/TXT/?qid=1555064086018&uri=CELEX%3A32 017H0146

53  Commission Recommendation (EU) 2018/103 of 20 December 2017 Regarding the Rule of Law in Poland Complementary to Recommendations (EU) 2016/1374, (EU) 2017/146 and (EU) 2017/1520, https://eur-lex.europa.eu/legal-content/EN/TXT/?qid =1555061792039&uri=CELEX%3A32018H0103

54  Chancellery of the Prime Minister, 'White Paper on the Reform of the Polish Judiciary', Warsaw, 7 March 2018:13 (bold original), https://www.premier.gov.pl/files/files/white_paper_en_full.pdf

55  Supreme Court of the Republic of Poland, 'Opinion on the White Paper on the Reform of the Polish Judiciary', Warsaw, 16 March 2018, http://www.sn.pl/aktualnosci/SiteAssets/Lists/Wydarzenia/EditForm/Supreme%20Court%20-%20 Opinion%20on%20the%20white%20paper%20on%20the%20Reform%20of%20 the%20Polish%20Judiciary.pdf

56  'Poland Offers Fresh Concession to EU over Legal Reforms', *Financial Times*, 3 May 2018.

57  James Shotter, 'Disciplinary Chamber for Polish Judges Not Independent, Says ECJ's Top', *Financial Times*, 27 June 2019.

58 Tadeusz Koncewicz, 'The Capture of the Polish Constitutional Tribunal and Beyond: Of Institution(s), Fidelities and the Rule of Law in Flux', *Review of Central and East European Law* 43, no. 2 (2018): 132.

59 Laurent Pech and Kim Lane Scheppele, 'Poland and the European Commission, Part II: Hearing the Siren Song of the Rule of Law', 6 January 2017, https://verfassungsblog.de/poland-and-the-european-commission-part-ii-hearing-the-siren-song-of-the-rule-of-law/

60 Laurent Pech and Kim Lane Scheppele, 'Poland and the European Commission, Part III: Requiem for the Rule of Law', 3 March 2017, http://verfassungsblog.de/poland-and-the-european-commission-part-iii-requiem-for-the-rule-of-law/

61 Bojan Bugarič, 'The Right to Democracy in a Populist Era', *AJIL Unbound*, vol. 112, 2018: 82, https://www.researchgate.net/publication/325290711_The_Right_to_Democracy_in_a_Populist_Era

62 Dimitry Kochenov, 'Busting the Myths Nuclear: A Commentary on Article 7 TEU', European University Institute Department of Law, EUI Working Paper LAW 2017/10, San Domenico di Fiesole, 2017, https://cadmus.eui.eu/bitstream/handle/1814/46345/LAW_2017_10.pdf?sequence=1

63 R. Daniel Kelemen, 'Professor R. Daniel Kelemen: New Leaders and Old Problems – Brexit and the Rule of Law Crisis', *Scottish Legal News*, 31 July 2019, https://www.scottishlegal.com/article/professor-r-daniel-kelemen-new-leaders-and-old-problems-brexit-and-the-rule-of-law-crisis

64 'Ustawa z dnia 29 kwietnia 2016 r. o zmianie ustawy o Instytucie Pamięci Narodowej … ', *Dziennik Ustaw*, 2016, poz. 749, http://dziennikustaw.gov.pl/DU/2016/749/1

65 'Ustawa z dnia 26 stycznia 2018 r. o zmianie ustawy o Instytucie Pamięci Narodowej …, ustawy o grobach i cmentarzach wojennych, ustawy o muzeach oraz ustawy o odpowiedzialności podmiotów zbiorowych za czyny zabronione pod groźbą kary', *Dziennik Ustaw* 2018, poz. 369, http://dziennikustaw.gov.pl/DU/2018/369/1

66 'Ustawa z dnia 27 czerwca 2018 r. o zmianie ustawy o Instytucie Pamięci Narodowej … ' and 'Ustawa o odpowiedzialności podmiotów zbiorowych za czyny zabronione pod groźbą kary', *Dziennik Ustaw* 2018, poz. 1277, http://www.dziennikustaw.gov.pl/DU/2018/1277/1

67 Łukasz Szleszkowski et al., 'The Possibility of Establishing Causes of Death on the Basis of the Exhumed Remains of Prisoners Executed during the Communist Regime in Poland: The Exhumations at Powązki Military Cemetery in Warsaw', *International Journal of Legal Medicine* 129, no. 4 (2015): 801–6.

68 Elżbieta Halas, 'Symbolic Politics of Public Time and Collective Memory. The Polish Case', *European Review* 10, no. 1 (2002): 127.

69 Michael Bernhard and Jan Kubik, 'Roundtable Discord. The Contested Legacy of 1989 in Poland' in *Twenty Years after Communism. The Politics of Memory and Commemoration*, eds. Michael Bernhard and Jan Kubik (Oxford: Oxford University Press, 2014), 77.

70 Jarosław Kaczyński, 'Oblicza manipulacji – źródła i skutki', Toruń: Wyższą Szkołę Kultury Społecznej i Medialnej, Lecture, 23 January 2016, https://www.youtube.com/watch?v=5r-Myxg6s_o

71 Jan Gross, *Sąsiedzi. Historia zagłady żydowskiego miasteczka* (Sejny: Pogranicze, 2000).

72 'Postanowienie o umorzeniu śledztwa', S 1/00/Zn, Białystok, 30 June 2003: 200.

73 P. Machcewicz and K. Persak, eds, *Wokół Jedwabnego* (Warsaw: IPN, 2002), 2 vols.

74  Geneviève Zubrzycki, 'Polish Mythology and the Traps of Messianic Martyrology' in *National Myths: Constructed Pasts, Contested Presents*, ed. Gérard Bouchard (London: Routledge, 2013), 126.

75  Antony Polonsky and Joanna Michlic, 'Introduction' in *The Neighbors Respond: The Controversy over the Jedwabne Massacre in Poland*, eds. Antony Polonsky and Joanna Michlic (Princeton: Princeton University Press, 2003), 30.

76  Dorota Szeligowska, 'The Dynamics of Polish Patriotism after 1989: Concepts, Debates, Identities', PhD thesis, Central European University, Budapest 2014, 170, from http://www.etd.ceu.hu/2014/szeligowska_dorota.pdf

77  Robert Traba, 'Polityka wobec historii: kontrowersje i perspektywy', *Teksty Drugie* 1–2, 2010, Instytut Badań Literackich, Centrum Humanistyki Cyfrowej, 309.

78  Annamaria Orla-Bukowska, 'New Threads on an Old Loom. National Memory and Social Identity in PostWar and PostCommunist Poland' in *The Politics of Memory in Postwar Europe*, eds. Richard Ned Lebow et al. (Durham, NC: Duke University Press, 2006), 197.

79  'Introduction', Polonsky and Michlic, 36.

80  Quoted in 'Is Michał Kamiński Fit to Lead the Tories in Europe?', *The Observer*, 11 October 2009.

81  'Introduction', Polonsky and Michlic, 36.

82  Jonathan Brent, 'The War between Polish Nationalism and Holocaust History', *Tablet*, 12 April 2019, https://www.tabletmag.com/jewish-news-and-politics/283216/polish-nationalism-and-holocaust-history

83  Jan Grabowski, 'Opinion Poland's Militant Nationalists Are Targeting Holocaust Scholars, with Help from an Israeli Historian', Haaretz, 19 May 2019, https://www.haaretz.com/world-news/.premium-the-israeli-historian-helping-poland-s-nationalists-target-scholars-of-the-holocaust-1.7255798

84  See the video and report from Tvn.24, 13 July 2016, at http://www.tvn24.pl/wiadomosci-z-kraju,3/anna-zalewska-w-kropce-nad-i-o-jedwabnem-i-pogromie-kieleckim,660799.html

85  'To nie jest stalinowska Polska, dlaczego więc nadal nie znamy prawdy?', 18 October 2016, http://www.sdp.pl/wywiady/13382,to-nie-jest-stalinowska-polska-dlaczego-wiec-nadal-nie-znamy-prawdy-,1476777429; 'Jedwabne to lewackie kłamstwo', Salon 24, https://www.salon24.pl/u/konfederat1000/730602,jedwabne-to-lewackie-klamstwo-rozmowa-z-dr-ewa-kurek

86  'Odpowiedzialność za zbrodnie na terenie okupowanym ponosi okupant – mówił na antenie TVP Info nowy szef Instytutu Pamięci Narodowej Jarosław Szarek', *Wprost*, 24 July 2016, https://www.wprost.pl/kraj/10016330/Nowy-szef-IPN-o-Jedwabnem-Tej-zbrodni-dokonala-garstka-Polakow.html

87  Tomasz Panfil, 'Świat patrzy i milczy. Sprzeciw Polaków wobec zła', *Gazeta Polska*, 27 September 2017.

88  'Oświadczenie ŻIH w sprawie wypowiedzi historyka lubelskiego IPN dr hab. Tomasza Panfila', Żydowski Instytut Historyczny, 9 October 2017, http://www.jhi.pl/blog/2017-10-09-oswiadczenie

89  'Polish Institute Rebuffs Historian Who Said Nazi Invasion Not That Bad for Jews', *The Times of Israel*, 14 November 2017, https://www.timesofisrael.com/polish-institute-rebuffs-historian-who-said-nazi-invasion-not-that-bad-for-jews/

90  Jan Grabowski, 'The Danger in Poland's Frontal Attack on Its Holocaust History', MacCleans, 20 September 2016, https://www.macleans.ca/news/world/as-poland-re-writes-its-holocaust-history-historians-face-prison/

91   See https://www.rpo.gov.pl/pl/content/rpo-ustawa-o-ipn-narusza-wolnosc-slowa-i-
     moze-rodzic-skutek-mrozacy
92   'Ustawa z dnia 27 czerwca 2018 r. o zmianie ustawy o Instytucie Pamięci Narodowej',
     Dziennik Ustaw 2018, poz. 1277, http://dziennikustaw.gov.pl/DU/2018/1277/1
93   'Prezes PiS: Stuprocentową odpowiedzialność za Holokaust ponoszą Niemcy', TVP
     Info, 29 June 2018, https://www.tvp.info/37865894/prezes-pis-stuprocentowa-
     odpowiedzialnosc-za-holokaust-ponosza-niemcy
94   Krzysztof Burnetko, 'Ustawa o IPN zmieniona, ale Ukraińcy dalej be', Polityka,
     28 June 2018.
95   Andrzej Friszke, 'Pamiec w centrum uwagi' in Pamiec i pytania o tozsamosci. Polska.
     Ukraina, eds. Tomasz Horbowski and Piotr Kosiewski (Warsaw: Fundacja Batorego,
     2013), 65–70.
96   The English version, narrated by Sean Bean, is on YouTube, https://www.youtube.
     com/watch?v=Q88AkN1hNYM
97   Shaun Walker, 'Holocaust historians divided over Warsaw ghetto museum', The
     Observer, 22 June 2019; Grabowski, 'Poland's Militant Nationalists'.
98   'Ustawa z dnia 9 listopada 2017 r. o Instytucie Solidarności i Męstwa', Dziennik Ustaw
     2017, poz. 2303, http://www.dziennikustaw.gov.pl/DU/2017/2303/1
99   Piotr Gliński, 'Wypowiedzi na posiedzeniach Sejmu Posiedzenie nr 51', 9 November
     2017, http://www.sejm.gov.pl/Sejm8.nsf/wypowiedz.xsp?posiedzenie=51&dzien=2&
     wyp=193&view=1
100  Stefan Niesiołowski, 'Wypowiedzi na posiedzeniach Sejmu. Posiedzenie nr 67', 18
     July 2018, http://www.sejm.gov.pl/Sejm8.nsf/wypowiedz.xsp?posiedzenie=67&dzien
     =1&wyp=136&view=1
101  Uladzislau Belavusau and Aleksandra Gliszczyńska-Grabias, 'Introduction: Memory
     Laws: Mapping a New Subject in Comparative Law and Transitional Justice' in Law
     and Memory: Towards Legal Governance of History, eds. Uladzislau Belavusau and
     Aleksandra Gliszczyńska-Grabias (Cambridge: Cambridge University Press, 2017), 1.
102  'Ustawa z dnia 1 kwietnia 2016 r. o zakazie propagowania komunizmu lub innego
     ustroju totalitarnego przez nazwy budowli, obiektów i urządzeń użyteczności
     publicznej', Dziennik Ustaw 2016, poz. 744, http://dziennikustaw.gov.pl/
     DU/2016/744/1
103  'Ustawa z dnia 22 czerwca 2017 r. o zmianie ustawy o zakazie propagowania
     komunizmu lub innego ustroju totalitarnego przez nazwy budowli, obiektów
     i urządzeń użyteczności publicznej', Dziennik Ustaw 2017, poz. 1389, http://
     dziennikustaw.gov.pl/DU/2017/1389/1
104  Patryk Frydel, 'Armia Ludowa – złodzieje, gwałciciele i mordercy', 9 April 2014,
     https://parezja.pl/armia-ludowa-zlodzieje-gwalciciele-mordercy/; 'Piotr Gontarczyk:
     Gwardia Ludowa to szkodliwy nowotwór, a nie bohaterska formacja', https://histmag.
     org/Piotr-Gontarczyk-Gwardia-Ludowa-to-szkodliwy-nowotwor-a-nie-bohaterska-
     formacja-6523
105  Piotr Szumlewicz, Facebook, 24 September 2017, https://www.facebook.com/
     PiotrSzumlewicz/posts/890818717739895; 'Zbrodnie Narodowych Sił Zbrojnych
     dokonane na ludności cywilnej, schwytanych do niewoli oraz rannych dokonane w
     latach 1942–1948', https://zolnierzeprzekleci.wordpress.com/zbrodnie/
106  IPN, 'Informacja o działaniach IPN w sprawie nazw ulic przed 2016 r.', Warsaw,
     2017, https://ipn.gov.pl/pl/aktualnosci/polityka/zmiany-nazw-ulic/informacja-o-
     dzialaniac/37963,Informacja-o-dzialaniach-IPN-w-sprawie-nazw-ulic-przed-2016-r.
     html

107  Its web page is at http://pamiec.pl/pa/edukacja/projekty-edukacyjne/ogolnopolskie/patroni-naszych-ulic/12930,Patroni-naszych-ulic-projekt-edukacyjny.html

108  Matthew Luxmoore, 'Poles Apart: The Bitter Conflict over a Nation's Communist History', *The Guardian*, 13 July 2018.

109  Wojciech Sadurski, *Poland's Constitutional Breakdown* (Oxford: Oxford University Press, 2018), 251.

# Conclusion

1  Aleks Szczerbiak, *Politicising the Communist Past: The Politics of Truth Revelation in Post-Communist Poland* (London: Taylor and Francis, 2018); Cynthia Horne, 'Late Lustration Programmes in Romania and Poland: Supporting or Undermining Democratic Transitions?', *Democratization* 16, no. 2 (2009): 344–76.

2  Szczerbiak, *Politicising the Communist Past*.

3  A. Czarnota, 'Between Nemesis and Justitia. Dealing with the Past as a Constitutional Process' in *Rethinking the Rule of Law after Communism*, ed. A. Czarnota et al. (Budapest: Central European University Press, 2005), 128.

4  Marek Safjan, 'Transitional Justice: The Polish Example, the Case of Lustration', *European Journal of Legal Studies* 1, no. 2 (2007): 240–1.

5  Narodowy Sąd Administracyjny, 'Postawienie', 26 September 1991, sygn. I SA 768/1991, http://orzeczenia.nsa.gov.pl/doc/0FE9CA982B

6  'Uchwała Trybunału Konstytucyjnego z dnia 24 czerwca 1992 r. w sprawie wykładni art. 61 ustawy z dnia 17 maja 1989 r. o stosunku Państwa do Kościoła Katolickiego w Rzeczypospolitej Polskiej', *Dziennik Ustaw*, 1992 52 poz. 250, http://prawo.sejm.gov.pl/isap.nsf/DocDetails.xsp?id=WDU19920520250

7  'Wyrok z dnia 14 listopada 2006 r.', Sygn. akt SK 41/04, https://ipo.trybunal.gov.pl/ipo/Sprawa?cid=1&dokument=1240&sprawa=3694

8  Ibid.

9  F. Saliger, 'Content and Practical Significance of Radbruch's Formula', Проблеми філософії права 2 (2004), http://dspace.nbuv.gov.ua/bitstream/handle/123456789/9658/07-Saliger.pdf?sequence=1

10  'Wyrok SN', I PRN 105/95, 5 March 1996, http://prawo.money.pl/orzecznictwo/sad-najwyzszy/wyrok;sn;izba;pracy;ubezpieczen;spolecznych;i;spraw;publicznych,ia,i,prn,105,95,925,orzeczenie.html

# Bibliography

Appel, Hilary. 'Anti-Communist Justice and Founding the Post-Communist Order: Lustration and Restitution in Central Europe'. *East European Politics and Societies* 19, no. 3 (2005): 379–405.

Arthur, Paige. 'How Transitions Reshaped Human Rights: A Conceptual History of Transitional Justice'. *Human Rights Quarterly* 31, no. 2 (2009): 321–67.

Bagieński, Witold, Cenckiewicz, Sławomir and Woyciechowski, Piotr. *Konfidenci*. Warsaw: Editions Spotkanie, 2015.

Balbus, Tomasz. 'Polskie "Istriebitielne Bataliony" NKWD w latach 1944–1945'. *Biuletyn Instytutu Pamięci Narodowej* no. 6 (2002): 71–5.

Barahona de Brito, Alexandra, Gonzaléz-Enríquez, Carmen and Aguilar, Paloma. 'Introduction'. In *The Politics of Memory. Transitional Justice in Democratizing Societies*, edited by Alexandra Barahona de Brito, Carmen Gonzaléz-Enríquez and Paloma Aguilar, 1–39. Oxford: Oxford University Press, 2001.

Baranowski, Zenon. 'Sądy blokują odszkodowania'. *Nasz Dziennik*, 10 March 2014.

Barkan, Elazar. *The Guilt of Nations. Restitution and Negotiating Historical Injustices*. New York: Norton, 2000.

Behr, Valentin. 'La production du recit historique a l'Institut de la memoire nationale. Une etude des usages politiques du passe en Pologne'. MA dissertation, University of Strasbourg, Strasbourg, 2010, http://scd-theses.u-strasbg.fr/2008/01/BEHR_Valentin_2010.pdf.

Belavusau, Uladzislau and Gliszczyńska-Grabias, Aleksandra. 'Introduction: Memory Laws: Mapping a New Subject in Comparative Law and Transitional Justice'. In *Law and Memory: Towards Legal Governance of History*, edited by Uladzislau Belavusau and Aleksandra Gliszczyńska-Grabias, 1–26. Cambridge: Cambridge University Press, 2017.

Bell, C., Campbell, C. and Ni Aoláin, F. 'Justice Discourses in Transition'. *Social and Legal Studies* 13, no. 3 (2004): 305–28.

Benomar, Jamal. 'Confronting the Past. Justice after Transitions'. *Journal of Democracy* 4, no. 1 (1993): 3–14.

Berman, Harold. *Justice in the USSR*. New York: Vintage, 1963.

Bernhard, Michael and Kubik, Jan. 'Roundtable Discord. The Contested Legacy of 1989 in Poland'. In *Twenty Years after Communism. The Politics of Memory and Commemoration*, edited by Michael Bernhard and Jan Kubik, 60–84. Oxford: Oxford University Press, 2014.

Bertschi, Charles. 'Lustration and the Transition to Democracy. The Cases of Poland and Bulgaria'. *East European Quarterly* 2, no. 4 (1995): 435–51.

Bickford, Louis. 'Transitional Justice'. In *Encyclopedia of Genocide and Crimes against Humanity*, edited by Dinah L. Shelton, 1045–7. Farmington Hills, MI: Thomson Gale, 2005, vol. 3.

'Biskupi metropolii krakowskiej solidaryzują się z oświadczeniem ws. Nuncjusza Apostolskiego', 8 January 2009, eKai.pl, https://ekai.pl/wydarzenia/temat_dnia/x17434/

biskupi-metropolii-krakowskiej-solidaryzuja-sie-z-oswiadczeniem-ws-nuncjusza-apostolskiego/.

Boed, Roman. 'An Evaluation of the Legality and Efficacy of Lustration as a Tool of Transitional Justice'. *Columbia Journal of Transnational Law* 37, no. 2 (1998): 357–402.

Bogdanor, Vernon. 'Founding Elections and Regime Change'. *Electoral Studies* 9, no. 4 (1990): 288–94.

Bojarski, Łukasz. 'Bez żadnego trybu', *Dziennik Gazeta Prawna*, 14 May 2018.

Bojarski, Łukasz with Monika Szulecka. *Wybory sędziów do TrybunałuKonstytucyjnego.* Warsaw: INPRIS – Instytut Prawa i Społeczeństwa, 2010.

Borecki, Paweł. 'Reprywatyzacja nieruchomości na rzecz gmin wyznaniowych żydowskich'. *Państwo i Prawo*, no. 9 (2011): 61–73.

Borneman, John. *Settling Accounts. Violence, Justice, and Accountability in Postsocialist Europe.* Princeton: Princeton University Press, 1997.

Branach, Zbigniew. *Oskarżony Jaruzelski i inni ....* Torun: AR Cetera, 2002.

Brent, Jonathan. 'The War between Polish Nationalism and Holocaust History'. *Tablet*, 12 April 2019, https://www.tabletmag.com/jewish-news-and-politics/283216/polish-nationalism-and-holocaust-history.

Brier, Robert. 'The Roots of the "Fourth Republic." Solidarity's Cultural Legacy to Polish Politics'. *East European Politics and Societies* 23, no. 1 (2009): 63–85.

Brzezinski, Michal. *Stany naszwyczajne w polskich konstytucjach.* Warsaw: Wydawnictwo Sejmowe, 2007.

Buckley-Zistel, S. and Stanley, R. eds. *Gender in Transitional Justice.* London: Palgrave Macmillan, 2012.

Bugarič, Bojan. 'The Right to Democracy in a Populist Era'. *AJIL Unbound* 112 (2018): 79–83.

Bugarič, Bojan and Ginsburg, Tom. 'The Assault on Postcommunist Courts', *Journal of Democracy* 27, no. 3 (2016): 69–82.

Buras, Piotr. 'The Killing of Gdańsk's Mayor Is the Tragic Result of Hate Speech'. *Guardian*, 17 January 2019.

Bureau of European and Eurasian Affairs. 'Property Restitution in Central and Eastern Europe'. Washington, DC, October 3, 2007, http://2001-2009.state.gov/p/eur/rls/or/93062.htm.

Burnetko, Krzysztof. 'Ustawa o IPN zmieniona, ale Ukraińcy dalej be'. *Polityka*, 28 June 2018.

Burnetko, Krzysztof. 'Kim jest Julia Przyłębska – czy rzeczywiście prezesem Trybunału Konstytucyjnego?' *Polityka*, 11 February 2017.

Calhoun, Noel. *Dilemmas of Justice in Eastern Europe's Democratic Transition.* London: Palgrave Macmillan, 2004.

Carrothers, Thomas. 'The End of the Transition Paradigm'. *Journal of Democracy* 13, no. 1 (2002): 5–21.

CBOS. 'Społeczne oceny wymiaru sprawiedliwości'. Komunikat z Badań NR 31/2017, Warsaw, March 2017.

CBOS. 'Polacy o Wojciechu Jaruzelskim'. Nr. 92/2014, Warsaw, June 2014.

CBOS. 'Wybory czerwcowe w 1989 r. i rząd Tadeusz Mazowieckiego z perspektywy ćwierćwiecza'. Nr. 74/2014, Warsaw, May 2014.

CBOS. 'Trzydziesta rocznica wprowadzenia stanu wojennego'. Komunikat z Badań BS/154/2011, Warsaw, 13 January 2011.

CBOS. 'Wojciech Jaruzelski w opinii publicznej'. Komunikat z Badań BS/101/2009, Warsaw, July 2009.

CBOS. 'Polacy o Reprywatyzacji'. Komunikat z badań BS/87/2008, Warsaw, June 2008.

CBOS. 'Opinia Społeczna o nazwach ulic'. Komunikat z Badań BS/38/2007, Warsaw, March 2007.

CBOS. 'Dwadziecia lat po wprowadzeniu stanu wojennego'. Komunikat z Badań BS/171/2001, Warsaw, December 2001.

CBOS. '15 lat po 13 grudnia'. Komunikat z Badań BS/188/186/96, Warsaw, December 1996.

CBOS. 'Aktualne problemy i wydarzenia'. Komunikat nr 1531A, Warsaw, 14 February 1996.

CBOS. 'Polacy o Lustracji'. Komunikat z Badań BS/139/124/94, Warsaw, 12 August 1994.

CBOS. '13 lat po 13 grudnia'. Komunikat BS 216//189/94, Warsaw, December 1994.

CBOS. 'Opinia publiczna o reprywatyzacji'. Komunikat z badań BS/418/109/92, Warsaw, December 1992.

CBOS. 'Opinia społeczna o wyborze Wojciecha Jaruzelskiego na prezydenta PRL'. Komunikat z badań, BD/175/34/89, Warsaw, August 1989.

Cenckiewicz, Sławomir. 'Sławomir Cenckiewicz obala 14 mitów Wałęsy'. *Niezależna*, 2 February 2017, http://niezalezna.pl/93236-tylko-u-nas-slawomir-cenckiewicz-obala-14-mitow-walesy.

Cenckiewicz, Sławomir. *Wałęsa. Człowiek z teczki*. Poznań: Zysk i S-ka, 2013.

Cenckiewicz, Sławomir and Gontarczyk, Piotr. *SB a Lech Wałęsa. Przyczynek do biografii*, Warsaw, IPN, 2008.

Cepl, V. 'Lustration in the CSFR: Ritual Sacrifices'. *East European Constitutional Review* 1 (1993): 24–6.

Cepl, V. 'A Note on the Restitution of Property in Post-communist Czechoslovakia'. *Journal of Communist Studies* 7, no. 3 (1991): 367–75.

Cepl, Vojtech and Gillis, Mark. 'Making Amends after Communism'. *Journal of Democracy* 7, no. 4 (1996): 118–24.

Chancellery of the Prime Minister. 'White Paper on the Reform of the Polish Judiciary'. Warsaw, 7 March 2018, https://www.premier.gov.pl/files/files/white_paper_en_full.pdf.

Cholewiński, Ryszard. 'The Protection of Human Rights in the New Polish Constitution'. *Fordham International Law Journal* 1, no. 2 (1998): 236–91.

Cichocki, Marek A. *Władza i Pamięć*. Krakow: Ośrodek Myśli Politycznej, 2005.

Ciobanu, Monica. 'Recent Restorative Justice Measures in Romania (2006-2010)'. *Problems of Post Communism* 60, no. 5 (2013): 45–57.

Cohen, Stanley. 'State Crimes of Previous Regimes: Knowledge, Accountability, and the Policing of the Past'. *Law and Social Inquiry* 20, no. 1 (1995): 7–50.

Council of Europe. 'Opinion of Council of Europe Experts Mr. Jean-François Furnément and Dr. Eve Salomon on Three Draft Acts Regarding Polish Public Service Media', Council of Europe DGI(2016)13, Strasbourg, 6 June 2016, https://rm.coe.int/CoERMPublicCommonSearchServices/DisplayDCTMContent?documentId=0900001 68065e9eb.

Cross, Michael. 'Poland Suspended from Judicial Council'. *The Law Society Gazette*, 18 September 2018, from https://www.lawgazette.co.uk/news/poland-suspended-from-judicial-council/5067594.article.

Crossley-Frolick K. 'The European Union and Transitional Justice: Human Rights and Post-Conflict Reconciliation in Europe and Beyond'. *Contemporary Readings in Law and Social Justice* 3, no. 1 (2011): 33–57.

Crossley-Frolick K. 'Scales of Justice: The Vetting of Former East German Police and Teachers in Saxony 1990-1993'. *German Studies Review* 30, no. 1 (2007): 141–62.

Czarnota, Adam. 'The Politics of the Lustration Law in Poland, 1989–2006'. In *Justice as Prevention. Vetting Public Employees in Transitional Societies*, edited by A. Mayer-Rieckh and P. de Greiff, 222–59. New York: Social Science Research Council, 2007.

Czuchnowski, Wojciech. 'IPN już nie zastrzega. Czas na "listy agentów"?' *Gazeta Wyborcza*, 24 January 2017.

Czuchnowski, Wojciech. 'Sąd kończy proces lustracyjny: SB fałszowała kwity', *Gazeta Wyborcza*, 4 November 2015.

Czuchnowski, Wojciech and Ciechoński, Tomasz. 'Trybunał Konstytucyjny. Sylwetka Lecha Morawskiego - kandydata PiS na sędziego TK'. *Gazeta Wyborcza*, 2 December 2015.

Czuchnowski, Wojciech and Leniarski, Radosław. 'Czy wrotkarze byli w SB? PiS bierze się do lustracji w sporcie'. *Gazeta Wyborcza*, 11 January 2017.

Czuchnowski, Wojciech and Kursa, Magdalena. 'Bezkarna Komisja Majątkowa'. *Gazeta Wyborcza*, 1 March 2011.

David, Roman. *Lustration and Transitional Justice: Personnel Systems in the Czech Republic, Hungary, and Poland*. Philadelphia, PA, USA: Pennsylvania University Press, 2011.

David, Roman. 'From Prague to Baghdad: Lustration Systems and their Political Effects'. *Government and Opposition* 41, no. 3 (2006): 347–72.

Davies, Christian. *Hostile Takeover: How Law and Justice Captured Poland's Courts*. Nations in Transit Brief, Washington, DC: Freedom House, May 2018, https:// freedomhouse.org/report/special-reports/hostile-takeover-how-law-and-justice-captured-poland-s-courts.

Davies, Norman. *Rising '44. The Battle for Warsaw*. London: Macmillan, 2003.

Davies, Norman. *Heart of Europe: The Past in Poland's Present*. Oxford: Oxford University Press, 2001.

Digeser, Peter. *Political Forgiveness*. Ithaca: Cornell University Press, 2001.

Djabarova, Zamira and Benowitz, Brittany. 'A Back Door to Controlling Judges: Poland's Ruling Party Tries Another Ploy'. Just Security, 27 March 2019, https://www. justsecurity.org/63381/a-back-door-to-controlling-judges-polands-ruling-party-tries-another-ploy/.

Doellinger, David. 'Prayers, Pilgrimages and Petitions: The Secret Church and the Growth of Civil Society in Slovakia'. *Nationalities Papers* 30, no. 2 (2002): 215–40.

Domański, Paweł ed. *Tajne dokumenty Biura Politycznego, Grudzień 1970*. London: Aneks, 1991.

Domarańczyk, Z. *100 dni Mazowieckiego*. Warsaw: Andrzej Bonarski, 1990.

Domurat, Inga. 'Prezes IPN apeluje do władz Połczyna: – Zmieńcie nazwy ulic'. *Głos Koszaliński*, 3 November 2008, http://www.gk24.pl/wiadomosci/swidwin/ art/4293343,prezes-ipn-apeluje-do-wladz-polczyna-zmiencie-nazwy-ulic,id,t.html.

Dubiński, Krzysztof. *Magdalenka. Transakcja epochu*. Warsaw: Sylwa, 1990.

Dudek, Antoni. *Pierwsze lata III Rzeczpospolitej 1989–2001*. Krakow: Arcana Historii, 2005.

Dudek, Antoni. 'Dyskusja "Pamięć narodowa i jej strażnicy"', *Arcana* no. 2 (2001): 5.

Dudek, Antoni and Andrzej Friszke eds. *Polska 1986–1989: koniec systemu*. Warsaw: Wydawnictwo Trio. Instytut Studiow Politycznych Polskiej Akademii Nauk, 2002, 3 vols.

Dybicz, Paweł. 'Prawo kombatanta' (Interview with Jan Turski). *Tygodnik Przegląd*, 9 May 2004, http://www.tygodnikprzeglad.pl/prawa-kombatanta/.

Ellis, M. 'Purging the Past: The Current State of Lustration Laws in the Former Communist Bloc'. *Law and Contemporary Problems* 59, no. 4 (1996): 181–96.

Elster, Jon. *Closing the Books. Transitional Justice in Historical Perspective*. Cambridge: Cambridge University Press, 2009.

Eriksson, Aleksandra. 'Poland Postpones Overhaul of Public Media'. EU Observer, 9 June 2016, https://euobserver.com/political/133761

European Commission. 'Commission Recommendation (EU) 2018/103 of 20 December 2017 Regarding the Rule of Law in Poland Complementary to Recommendations (EU) 2016/1374, (EU) 2017/146 and (EU) 2017/1520', https://eur-lex.europa.eu/legal-content/EN/TXT/?qid=1555061792039&uri=CELEX%3A32018H0103.

European Commission. 'Commission Recommendation (EU) 2017/146 of 21 December 2016 Regarding the Rule of Law in Poland Complementary to Recommendation (EU) 2016/1374', https://eur-lex.europa.eu/legal-content/EN/TXT/?qid=1555064086018&uri=CELEX%3A32017H0146.

European Commission. 'Commission Recommendation of 27.7.2016 Regarding the Rule of Law in Poland'. Brussels, 27 July 2016, http://ec.europa.eu/justice/effective-justice/files/recommendation-rule-of-law-poland-20160727_en.pdf

European Commission for Democracy through Law (Venice Commission). Opinion No. 904/2017, 11 December 2017, https://www.venice.coe.int/webforms/documents/?pdf=CDL-AD2017031-e#.

European Commission for Democracy through Law (Venice Commission). 'Opinion on Amendments to the Act of 25 June 2015 on the Constitutional Tribunal of Poland'. Opinion no. 833/2015, Venice, 11 March 2016, http://www.venice.coe.int/webforms/documents/default.aspx?pdffile=CDL-AD2016001-e.

European Court of Human Rights. 'The Case of Broniowski v Poland'. Judgment, Strasbourg, 22 June 2004, from http://hudoc.echr.coe.int/eng?i=001-70326

European Court of Human Rights, Fourth Section. 'CASE OF MOCZULSKI v. POLAND (Application no. 49974/08)', JUDGMENT, STRASBOURG, 19 April 2011, FINAL 19 July 2011', http://hudoc.echr.coe.int/eng?i=001-104574.

European Court of Human Rights, Fourth Section. 'CASE OF LUBOCH v. POLAND (Application no. 37469/05) JUDGMENT', Strasbourg, 15 January 2008, FINAL, 15 April 2008', http://hudoc.echr.coe.int/eng?i=001-84373

European Court of Human Rights, Fourth Section. Case of Matyjek v. Poland, no. 38184/03, Judgment, Strasbourg, 24 April 2007, Final, http://hudoc.echr.coe.int/eng?i=001-80219.

European Shoah Legacy Institute. 'Overview of Immovable Property Restitution/Compensation Regime - Poland', 2017, https://archive.jpr.org.uk/object-pol71

Ewelina, Mika. 'RPO ws. odwoływania się do sądu ws. orzeczeń Komisji Majątkowej'. *Temidium*, 4 May 2015, http://www.temidium.pl/artykul/rpo_ws_odwolywania_sie_do_sadu_ws_orzeczen_komisji_majatkowej-1716.html.

Fałkowska, Wanda. 'Przebaczenie nie będzie'. *Gazeta Wyborcza*, 5 June 1991.

Fletcher, Laurel E. and Weinstein, Harvey M. 'Writing Transitional Justice: An Empirical Evaluation of Transitional Justice Scholarship in Academic Journals'. *Journal of Human Rights Practice* 7, no. 2 (2015): 177–98.

Freedom House. 'Pluralism under Attack: The Assault on Press Freedom in Poland'. https://freedomhouse.org/sites/default/files/FH_Poland_Report_Final_2017.pdf.

Friske, Andrzej. 'Pamięć w centrum uwagi'. In *Pamięć i pytania o tożsamości. Polska. Ukraina*, edited by Tomasz Horbowski and Piotr Kosiewski, 65–70. Warsaw: Fundacja Batorego, 2013.

Friszke, Andrzej. 'Jak hartował się radykalizm Kurtyki'. *Gazeta Wyborcza*, 7 April 2009.

Friske, Andrzej. 'Okrągły Stol, Geneza i przebieg'. In *Polska 1986–1989: koniec systemu*. Materiały międzynarodowej konferencji. Miedzeszyn, 21–23 October 1999, edited by Antoni Dudek and Andrzej Friszke, 74–117. Warsaw: Wydawnictwo Trio. Instytut Studiow Politycznych Polskiej Akademii Nauk, 2002, vol. 1: referaty.

Friszke, Andrzej. 'Spór o PRL w III Rzeczypospolitej (1989–2001)'. *Pamięć i Sprawiedliwość* 1, no. 1 (2002): 9–28.

Frydel, Patryk. 'Armia Ludowa – złodzieje, gwałciciele i mordercy', 9 April 2014, https://parezja.pl/armia-ludowa-zlodzieje-gwalciciele-mordercy/.

Gajcy, Andrzej. 'Jawność nie dla wszystkich. Rząd utajni powszechną lustrację majątkową'. *Onet Wiadomości*, 22 February 2018, https://wiadomosci.onet.pl/tylko-w-onecie/jawnosc-nie-dla-wszystkich-rzad-utajni-powszechna-lustracje-majatkowa/dqj4pzb.

Gałczyńska, Małgorzata. 'Śledztwo Onetu. Farma trolli w Ministerstwie Sprawiedliwości, czyli "za czynienie dobra nie wsadzamy"'. *Onet Wiadomości*, 19 August 2019, https://wiadomosci.onet.pl/tylko-w-onecie/sledztwo-onetu-farma-trolli-w-ministerstwie-sprawiedliwosci-czyli-za-czynienie-dobra/j6hwp7f?utm_source=wiadomosci.onet.pl_viasg_wiadomosci&utm_medium=referal&utm_campaign=leo_automatic&srcc=ucs&utm_v=2.

Gardynik, Aleksandra and Waszkielewicz, Bernadeta. 'PiS chce zmian w Trybunale'. *Rzeczpospolita*, 29 June 2007.

Garlicki, Lech. 'Pierwsze orzecenie Trybunału Konstytucyjnego (Refleksje w 15 lat później)'. Warsaw: Trybunał Konstytucyjny, 2000, http://trybunal.gov.pl/fileadmin/content/dokumenty/pierwsza-rozprawa/Leszek_Garlicki_Pierwsza_rozprawa.pdf.

Garton Ash, Timothy. 'Trials, Purges and History Lessons: Treating a Difficult Past in Post-Communist Europe'. In *Memory and Power in Post-War Europe, Studies in the Presence of the Past*, edited by Jan-Werner Müller, 265–82. Cambridge: Cambridge University Press, 2002.

Gawin, Dariusz. 'Co to jest polityka historyczna?' (Interview with Dariusz Gawin by Ireneusz Wywiał), Rozmowy Wiadomości Historycznych, *Wiadomości Historyczne*, no. 5, 2006.

Gawin, Dariusz and Kowal, Paweł. 'Polska polityka historyczna'. In *Polityka historyczna: historycy - politycy - prasa: konferencja pod honorowym patronatem Jana Nowaka-Jeziorańskiego, Pałac Raczyńskich w Warszawie, 15 grudnia 2004*, edited by Agnieszka Panecka, 11–15. Warsaw: Muzeum Powstania Warszawskiego, 2005.

Gawin, Dariusz, Karłowicz, Dariusz, Kostro, Robert, Krasnodębski, Zdzisław, Merta, Tomasz, Mikalski, Łukasz, Roszkowski, Wojciech, Skibiński, Pawel, Ujazdowski, Kazimierz Michal and Wróbel, Jan. *Pamięc i Odpowiedzialność*, Krakow: Ośrodek Myśli Politycznej, Centrum Konserwatywne, nd.

Geremek, Bronisław and Żakowski, Jacek. *Bronisław Geremek Opowiada. Jacek Żakowski Pyta. Rok 1989*. Warsaw: Plejada, 1990.

Gmyz, Cezary. 'IPN utajnia agentow'. *Do Rzeczy* no. 26, 24 July 2013.

Gonzalez-Enriquez, Carmen. 'De-communization and Political Justice in Central and Eastern Europe'. In *The Politics of Memory. Transitional Justice in Democratizing Societies*, edited by Alexandra Barahona de Brito, Carmen Gonzalez-Enriquez and Paloma Aguilar, 218–47. Oxford: Oxford University Press, 2001.

Grabowska-Moroz, Barbara and Szuleka, Małgorzata. 'It Starts with the Personnel. Replacement of Common Court Presidents and Vice Presidents from August 2017 to February 2018'. Warsaw: Helsinki Foundation for Human Rights, April 2018, http://www.hfhr.pl/wp-content/uploads/2018/04/It-starts-with-the-personnel.pdf.

Grabowski, A. and Naleziński, B. 'Kłopoty z obowiązywaniem prawa. Uwagi na tle orzecznictwa Trybunału Konstytucyjnego'. In *Studia z filozofii prawa*, edited by J. Stelmach, 219–57. Kraków: Uniwersytet Jagielloński, 2001.

Grabowski, Jan. 'Poland's Militant Nationalists Are Targeting Holocaust Scholars, with Help from an Israeli Historian', *Haaretz*, 19 May 2019, https://www.haaretz.com/world-news/.premium-the-israeli-historian-helping-poland-s-nationalists-target-scholars-of-the-holocaust-1.7255798.

Grabowski, Jan. 'The Danger in Poland's Frontal Attack on Its Holocaust History'. *MacCleans*, 20 September 2016, https://www.macleans.ca/news/world/as-poland-re-writes-its-holocaust-history-historians-face-prison/.

Gray, D. C. 'Extraordinary Justice'. *Alabama Law Review* 62, 1 (2010): 55–110.

Grela, Szymon. 'PiS lustruje dziennikarzy w mediach publicznych. Uchwałę podjęto wbrew regulaminowi i trochę bez sensu', *Oko*, 26 April 2017, https://oko.press/pis-lustruje-dziennikarzy-mediach-publicznych-uchwale-podjeto-wbrew-regulaminowi-troche-bez-sensu

Grosescu, Raluca. 'Judging Communist Crimes in Romania: Transnational and Global Influences'. *International Journal of Transitional Justice*, 11, no. 3 (2017): 505–24.

Gross, Jan T. *Sąsiedzi. Historia zagłady żydowskiego miasteczka*. Sejny: Pogranicze, 2000.

Grzelak, Piotr. *Wojna o lustrację*. Warsaw: Wydawnictwo Trio, 2005.

Grzesiok, Agnieszka. 'The "Right of Offset" of the Value of Property Left behind the Present Polish Borders'. *Organizacja i Zarządzania* 4, no. 8 (2009): 35–54, https://www.polsl.pl/Wydzialy/ROZ/Documents/Kwartalnik_naukowy/KN8.pdf.

Hałagida, Igor. *Ukraińcy na zachodnich i północnych ziemiach Polski 1947–1957*. Warsaw: Instytut Pamięci Narodowej, 2002.

Halas, Elżbieta. 'Symbolic Politics of Public Time and Collective Memory. The Polish Case'. *European Review* 10, no. 1 (2002): 115–29.

Hansen, T. O. 'Transitional Justice: Toward a Differentiated Theory'. *Oregon Review of International Law* 13, no. 1 (2011): 1–46.

Hayden, Jacqueline. *The Collapse of Communist Power in Poland: Strategic Misperceptions and Unanticipated Outcomes*. London: Routledge Curzon, 2006.

Helsińska Fundacja. 'NSA oddalił skargę kasacyjną Prezesa IPN w sprawie dostępu do informacji publicznej', 10 December 2010, http://www.hfhrpol.waw.pl/przeszlosc-rozliczenia/aktualnosci/nsa-oddalil-skarge-kasacyjna-prezesa-ipn-w-sprawie-dostepu-do-informacji-publicznej.html.

Henzler, Marek. 'Wielki Lustrator'. *Polityka*, 8 January 2005.

Henzler, Marek. 'Ciągle w boju'. *Polityka*, 12 May 2001.

Holzer, Jerzy. 'Byłem naiwny'. *Gazeta Wyborcza*, 15 June 2005.

Holzer, Jerzy. 'Martial Law Evaluated by Historians and Generals at Jachranka. Are They Going In? They Did Not'. http://www.wilsoncenter.org/sites/default/files/Martial%20Law%20Evaluated%20by%20Historians%20and%20Generals%20at%20Jachranka.pdf.

Horne, Cynthia. 'Late Lustration Programmes in Romania and Poland: Supporting or Undermining Democratic Transitions?' *Democratization* 16, no. 2 (2009): 344–76.

Huntington, Samuel. *The Third Wave: Democratization in the Late Twentieth Century*. London: University of Oklahoma Press, 1991.

Huyse, Luc. 'Justice after Transition: On the Choices Successor Elites Make in Dealing with the Past'. *Law and Social Inquiry* 20, no. 1 (1995): 51–78.

International Center for Transitional Justice. 'What Is Transitional Justice?', http://www.ictj.org/sites/default/files/ICTJ-Global-Transitional-Justice-2009-English.pdf.

IPN. 'IPN prowadzi postępowanie karne w sprawie fałszywych zeznań Lecha Wałęsy', Komunikat, 22 August 2017, http://ipn.gov.pl/pl/dla-mediow/komunikaty/41376,IPN-prowadzi-postepowanie-karne-w-sprawie-falszywych-zeznan-Lecha-Walesy.html.

IPN. 'Zakończenie śledztwa w sprawie podrobienia przez funkcjonariuszy Służby Bezpieczeństwa dokumentów na szkodę Lecha Wałęsy'. Komunikat, 28 June 2017, http://ipn.gov.pl/pl/dla-mediow/komunikaty/40776,Zakonczenie-sledztwa-w-sprawie-podrabiania-przez-funkcjonariuszy-Sluzby-Bezpiecz.html.

IPN. 'Informacja o działaniach IPN w sprawie nazw ulic przed 2016 r', Warsaw, 2017, https://ipn.gov.pl/pl/aktualnosci/polityka/zmiany-nazw-ulic/informacja-o-dzialaniac/37963,Informacja-o-dzialaniach-IPN-w-sprawie-nazw-ulic-przed-2016-r.html.

IPN. 'Informacja o działalności Instytutu Pamięci Narodowej – Komisja Ścigania Zbrodni przeciwko Narodowi Polskiemu 1 Stycznia 2013 r. – 31 grudnia 2013 r', Warsaw, 2014, *Druk Sejmowy* 2348, http://orka.sejm.gov.pl/Druki7ka.nsf/0/86E4CB1905DE75DCC12 57CC5002C40C3/%24File/2348.pdf.

IPN. 'Informacja o działalności Instytutu Pamięci Narodowej – Komisja Ścigania Zbrodni przeciwko Narodowi Polskiemu 1 Stycznia 2008 r. – 31 grudnia 2008 r', Warsaw, 2009, *Druk Sejmowy* 1864, http://orka.sejm.gov.pl/Druki6ka.nsf/0/1B18A69A193D9162C12 5758D003C7AFB/$file/1864.pdf.

IPN. 'Informacja o działalności Instytutu Pamięci Narodowej – Komisja Ścigania Zbrodni przeciwko Narodowi Polskiemu 1 Stycznia 2007 r. – 31 grudnia 2007 r', Warsaw, 2008, *Druk Sejmowy* no. 379, http://orka.sejm.gov.pl/Druki6ka.nsf/0/BD142516EA0A0365C 125742600369687/$file/379.pdf.

IPN. 'Informacja o działalności Instytutu Pamięci Narodowej – Komisja Ścigania Zbrodni przeciwko Narodowi Polskiemu w okresie 1 stycznia 2006. R – 31 grudnia 2006 r', Warsaw, February 2007, *Druk Sejmowy* 1608, http://orka.sejm.gov.pl/Druki5ka.nsf/0/8 97EBC77043D4589C12572BB002C0696/$file/1608.pdf.

IPN. 'Informacja o działalności Instytutu Pamięci Narodowej – Komisja Ścigania Zbrodni przeciwko Narodowi Polskiemu w okresie 1 lipca 2004 r. – 31 grudnia 2005 r', Warsaw, February 2006, *Druk Sejmowy* 451, http://orka.sejm.gov.pl/Druki5ka.nsf/0/9FCDF31F DDC0FE88C125713B0043749F/$file/451.pdf.

IPN. 'Informacja o działalności Instytutu Pamięci Narodowej – Komisja Ścigania Zbrodni przeciwko Narodowi Polskiemu w okresie 1 lipca 2003 r. – 30 czerwca 2004 r', Warsaw, January 2005, *Druk Sejmowy* 3771, http://orka.sejm.gov.pl/Druki4ka.nsf/$vAllByUnid/99DEA9E4A9E1072DC1256FB8004CFBA6/$file/3771.pdf.

IPN. 'Informacja o działalności Instytutu Pamięci Narodowej – Komisja Ścigania Zbrodni przeciwko Narodowi Polskiemu w okresie 1 lipca 2002 r. – 30 czerwca 2003 r', Warsaw, November 2003, *Druk Sejmowy* no. 2515, http://orka.sejm.gov.pl/Druki4ka.nsf/0/F8A9 4418F0E6328FC1256E4A0050BD85/$file/2515.pdf.

IPN. 'Informacja o działalności Instytutu Pamięci Narodowej – Komisja Ścigania Zbrodni przeciwko Narodowi Polskiemu w okresie 1 lipca 2001 r. – 30 czerwca 2002 r', Warsaw, 19 November 2002, *Druk Sejmowy* no. 1117, http://orka.sejm.gov.pl/Druki4ka.nsf/0/F2 BF9B382E5A490FC1256C7C004C10A5/$file/1117.PDF.

Isakowicz-Zaleski, Tadeusz. *Księża wobec bezpieki na przykładzie archidiecezji krakowskiej.* Krakow: Znak, 2007.

Jałoszewski, Mariusz. 'Czerwona kartka dla Bagińskiej'. *Rzeczpospolita*, 8 February 2007.

Jałowiec, Joanna. 'Ziemia dla jezuitów? Nie od razu'. *Gazeta Wyborcza*, 8 November 2008.

Jaruzelski, Wojciech. *Wyjaśniam. Wyjaśnienie złożone przed Sądem Okręgowym w Warszawie w dniach 18.10 i 08.11. 2001.* Torun: Mado, 2001.

Jaruzelski, Wojciech. 'Commentary'. *Cold War International History Project Bulletin*, Issue 11, 1998, http://www.wilsoncenter.org/publication/bulletin-no-11-winter-1998.

Jasiak, Macej. 'Overcoming Ukrainian Resistance. The Deportations of Ukrainians within Poland in 1947'. In *Redrawing Nations: Ethnic Cleansing in East-Central Europe, 1944–1948*, edited by Philipp Ther and Ana Siljak, 173–95. Lanham, MD: Rowman & Littlefield, 2001.

Jaskovska, Eva and Moran, John P. 'Justice or Politics? Criminal, Civil and Political Adjudication in the Newly Independent Baltic States'. *Journal of Communist Studies and Transition Politics* 22 no. 4 (2006): 485–506.

Kącki, Marcin. 'Kandydat Samoobrony do TK ma sprawę w sądzie'. *Gazeta Wyborcza*, 8 November 2006.

Kaczyński, Jarosław. 'Oblicza manipulacji - źródła i skutki'. Lecture. Toruń: Wyższą Szkołę Kultury Społecznej i Medialnej, 23 January 2016, https://www.youtube.com/watch?v=5r-Myxg6s_o.

Kaczyński, Jarosław. 'Wprowadzenie'. IV RZECZPOSPOLITA Sprawiedliwość dla Wszystkich', Prawo i Sprawiedliwość Program 2005, 7–13, http://old.pis.org.pl/dokumenty.php?s=partia&iddoc=3.

Kaczyński, Jarosław. *Czas na zmiany*. Warsaw: Editions Spotkania, 1993.

Kaczyński, Jarosław. *Odwrotna strona medalu*. Warsaw: Most, 1991.

Kaminski, M. N. and Nalepa, M. 'Judging Transitional Justice: A New Criterion for Evaluating Truth Revelation Procedures'. *The Journal of Conflict Resolution* 50, no. 3 (2006): 383–408.

Karpiński, Jakub. 'Wielka fikcja'. *Tygodnik Powszechny*, 8 January 1995.

Karpinski, J. 'Agenci i lustracja - politycy i przeszłość'. *Rzeczpospolita*, 15 July 1992.

Kauba, Krzysztof and Nizieński, Bolesław. 'Lustracja'. In *Ius et Lux. Księga Jubileuszowa ku czci Profesora Adama Strzembosza*, edited by Antomi Dębinski, Alicja Grześkowiak and Krzysztof Wiak, 339–51. Lublin: Wydawnictwo KUL, 2002.

Kelemen, R. Daniel. 'Professor R. Daniel Kelemen: New Leaders and Old Problems – Brexit and the Rule of Law Crisis'. *Scottish Legal News*, 31 July 2019, https://www.scottishlegal.com/article/professor-r-daniel-kelemen-new-leaders-and-old-problems-brexit-and-the-rule-of-law-crisis.

Kemp-Welch, A. *Poland under Communism. A Cold War History*. Cambridge: Cambridge University Press, 2008.

'Kim są nowi sędziowie wybrani do KRS?', *Polityka*, 6 March 2018.

Klosova, Martina. 'Social Performance, Cultural Trauma, and the Polish Tragedy in Smolensk'. nd, https://is.muni.cz/do/fss/SOCIOLOGIE/57823/26143701/26503523/Klosova_Cultural_Sociology_Paper.txt?so=nx.

Kochanowski, Janusz. 'Trybunał wywołał zamęt'. *Rzeczpospolita*, 25 July 2007.

Koczanowicz, Leszek. *Politics of Time. Dynamics of Identity in Post-Communist Poland*. Berghahn Books (n.p.), 2008.

Kochenov, Dimitry. 'Busting the Myths Nuclear: A Commentary on Article 7 TEU'. European University Institute Department of Law, EUI Working Paper LAW 2017/10, San Domenico di Fiesole, 2017, https://cadmus.eui.eu/bitstream/handle/1814/46345/LAW_2017_10.pdf?sequence=1.

Komisja Majątkowa. 'Sprawozdanie z działalności Komisji Majątkowej w latach 1989-2011'. Warsaw, 24 February 2011, www.propertyrestitution.pl/komisja_majatkowa__ds_kościoła_rzymsko-katolickiego_raport_02_2012.pdf.

Koncewicz, Tadeusz. 'The Capture of the Polish Constitutional Tribunal and beyond: Of Institution(s), Fidelities and the Rule of Law in Flux'. *Review of Central and East European Law* 43, no. 2 (2018): 116–73.

Koncewicz, Tadeusz. 'On the Separation of Powers and Judicial Self-Defence at Times of Unconstitutional Capture'. VerfassungBlog, 4 June 2017, https://verfassungsblog.de/on-the-separation-of-powers-and-the-judicial-self-defence-at-times-of-unconstitutional-capture/.

Kondek-Dyoniziak, Anna. 'Zmiany, ktore budzą zaniepokojenie. Łukasz Kamiński o projekcie noweli o IPN' (Interview with Łukasz Kamiński). *Polish Radio*, 20 March 2016, http://www.polskieradio.pl/5/3/Artykul/1596978,Zmiany-ktore-budza-zaniepokojenie-Lukasz-Kaminski-o-projekcie-noweli-o-IPN

Kościelna Komisja Historyczna. 'Kościelna Komisja Historyczna: komunikat po kwerendzie'. Radio Watykańskie, 27 June 2007, http://pl.radiovaticana.va/storico/2007/06/27/ko%C5%9Bcielna_komisja_historyczna:_komunikat_po_kwerendzie/pol-141740.

Kościelna Komisja Historyczna. 'Komunikat Kościelnej Komisji Historycznej', 5 January 2007, http://www.opoka.org.pl/biblioteka/W/WE/kep/komunikat_hist_05012007.html.

Kośmiński, Paweł and Kublik, Agnieszka. 'IPN publikuje listy do Kiszczaka. Zniesmaczeni autorzy: "Podano prywatny adres, gdzie żyje moja rodzina." "To świadectwo trwogi"'. *Gazeta Wyborcza*, 25 February 2016.

Kotar, T. 'Slovenia'. In *Transitional Justice in Eastern Europe and the Former Soviet Union: Reckoning with the Communist Past*, edited by Lavinia Stan, 200–21. London: Routledge, 2009.

Kowalski, Marcin and Kącki, Marcin with Szymon Jadczak. 'Marek Kotlinowski pomógł naciągaczowi?'. *Gazeta Wyborcza*, Krakow, 24 October 2006.

Kozłowski, Krzysztof. 'Rewolucja po polsku'. *Przegląd Bezpieczeństwa Wewnętrznego*, 13–17. Special Edition, 2010, http://www.abw.gov.pl/portal/pl/336/764/Przeglad_Bezpieczenstwa_Wewnetrznego__WYDANIE_SPECJALNE_z_okazji_80_rocznicy_uro.html.

Kozłowski, Tomasz. 'Solidarność w sądzie'. *Pamięć.pl*, http://testowyserwis.axiomcomputing.pl/pdf/solidarnosc-w-sadzie,1395.pdf.

Kozłowski, T. and Olaszek, J. 'Internowani w stanie wojennym. Dane statystyczne'. *Pamięć i Sprawiedliwość* 2 (2010): 505–10, http://ipn.gov.pl/__data/assets/pdf_file/0007/107962/PIS_16.pdf.

Kroner, Jolanta and Sadłowska, Katarzyna. 'Trzeba będzie posprzątać po IV RP' (Interview with Andrzej Zoll). *Rzeczpospolita*, 23 February 2006.

Kubik, Jan and Linch, Amy. 'The Original Sin of Poland's Third Republic: Discounting "Solidarity" and Its Consequences for Political Reconciliation'. *Polish Sociological Review*, no. 153 (2006): 9–38.

Kublik, Agnieszka and Czuchnowski, Wojciech. 'Wraca lustracja dziennikarzy. Uchwałę przygotowała Joanna Lichocka'. *Gazeta Wyborcza*, 25 April 2017.

Kublik, Agnieszka and Olejnik, Monika. 'Jarosław Kaczyński: We mnie jest czyste dobro' (Interview with Jarosław Kaczyński). *Gazeta Wyborcza*, 2 February 2006.

Krajewski, Krzysztof. 'Prosecution and Prosecutors in Poland: In Quest of Independence'. *Crime and Justice* 41, no. 1 (2012): 75–116.

Kramer, Mark. 'Jaruzelski, the Soviet Union, and the Imposition of Martial Law in Poland: New Light on the Mystery of December 1981'. *Cold War International History Project Bulletin*, Issue 11 (1998): 5, http://www.wilsoncenter.org/publication/bulletin-no-11-winter-1998.

Krasnodębska, Sylwia. *Czy jeszcze warto rozmawiać. Jan Pospieszalski, Paweł Nowacki, Maciej Pawlicki odpowiadają na pytania Sylwii Krasnodębskiej*. Krakow: Wydawnictwo M, 2011.

Krasnodębski, Zdzisław. 'Zwycięzcy i pokonani'. In *Pamięc i Odpowiedzialność*, edited by Dariusz Gowin, Dariusz Karłowicz, Robert Kostro, Zdzisław Krasnodębski, Tomasz Merta, Łukasz Mikalski, Wojciech Roszkowski, Pawel Skibiński, Kazimierz Michal Ujazdowski and Jan Wróbel, 55–70. Krakow: Ośrodek Myśli Politycznej, Centrum Konserwatywne, nd. Krawczyk, Monika. 'Restytucja mienia gmin żydowskich w Polsce – stan rzeczy z perspektywy (prawie) 10 lat'. http://fodz.pl/doc/1.pdf.

Krawczyk, Monika. 'Restitution of Jewish Assets in Poland – Legal Aspects'. *Justice*, no. 28 (2001): 24–8, http://www.intjewishlawyers.org/main/files/Justice%20No.28%20Summer%202001.pdf.

Kritz, Neil J. ed. *Transitional Justice: How Emerging Democracies Reckon with Former Regimes*. Washington, DC: United States Institute of Peace Press, 1995, 3 vols.

Krotoszyński, Michał. 'Lustracja w Polsce w świetle modeli sprawiedliwości okresu tranzycji'. Warsaw: Helsińska Fundacja Praw Człowieka, 2014, http://www.hfhr. pl/wp-content/uploads/2014/06/Lustracja-w-Polsce-w-s%CC%81wietle-modeli-sprawiedliwos%CC%81ci-okresu-tranzycji_Micha%C5%82-Krotoszyn%CC%81ski. pdf.

Kruk, Maria. 'Nowa ustawa o Trybunale Konstytucyjnym z 25 czerwca 2015'. *Przegląd Sejmowy* 23, no. 5 (2015): 9–28.

Kublik, Agnieszka and Czuchnowski, Wojciech. 'Polskie Radio zwalnia dziennikarzy, którzy nie zlustrowali się w IPN'. *Gazeta Wyborcza*, 3 December 2007.

Kurski, Jacek. *Nocna zmiana*, Production Jacek-FILM 1994, available on You Tube at https://www.youtube.com/watch?v=KgJw2PIgBzk

Kuti, Csonger. *Post-Communist Restitution and the Rule of Law*. Budapest: Central European University Press, 2009.

Kwiatkowska, Wiesława. 'Grudzień '70 – kalendarium śledztwa i procesu'. *Biuletyn Pamięci Narodowej*, no. 11–12 (2006): 21–6.

Labuz, Marek. 'Likwidacja Funduszu Kościelnego'. Radgoszcz: Parafia św. Kazimierza, nd, http://www.radgoszcz.diecezja.tarnow.pl/index.php?option=com_content&view=articl e&id=650:likwidacja-funduszu-kocielnego&catid=15&Itemid=239.

Laplante, Lisa. 'The Plural Justice Aims of Reparations'. In *Transitional Justice Theories*, edited by Susanne Buckley-Zistel, Teresa Koloma-Beck, Christian Braun and Friederike Mieth, 66–84. Abingdon: Routledge, 2014.

Laplante, L. J. 'Transitional Justice and Peace Building: Diagnosing and Addressing the Socioeconomic Roots of Violence through a Human Rights Framework'. *International Journal of Transitional Justice* 2, no. 3 (2008): 331–55.

Leebaw, B. A. 'The Irreconcilable Goals of Transitional Justice'. *Human Rights Quarterly* 30 (2008): 95–118.

Leszczyński, Adam. 'Pamięć historyczna bez polityków' (Interview with Professor Paweł Machcewicz). *Gazeta Wyborcza*, 29 March 2012.

Los, M. 'Lustration and Truth Claims: Unfinished Revolutions in Central Europe'. *Law and Social Inquiry* 20 (1995): 117–62.

Los, Maria and Zybertowicz, Andrzej. *Privatizing the Police-State. The Case of Poland*. Basingstoke: Macmillan Press, 2000.

Los, Maria and Zybertowicz, Andrzej. 'Is Revolution a Solution?' In *The Rule of Law after Communism*, edited by Martin Krygier and Adam Czarnota, 261–307. Abingdon: Routledge, 1999.

Loth, Wilfried. *Overcoming the Cold War: A History of Détente, 1950–1991*. Basingstoke: Palgrave, 2002.

Luter, Andrzej. 'Ks. Zaleski-Isakowicz nie ustaje w lustracji Kościoła'. *Gazeta Wyborcza*, 21 November 2008.

Luxmoore, Matthew. 'Poles Apart: The Bitter Conflict over a Nation's Communist History'. *The Guardian*, 13 July 2018.

Łazarewicz, Cezary and Janicki, Mariusz. 'Zbrodnia, Kara, Odszkodowania'. *Polityka*, 7 December 2011.

Łętowska, Ewa. 'Uprawienia gmin w swietle skutków orzeczenia TK o Kościelnej Komisji Majątkowej'. *Państwo i Prawo* LVI, no. 9 (2011): 3–19.

Łosińska, Ewa. 'IPN rozliczy za stan wojenny'. *Rzeczpospolita*, 6 November 2010.

McAdams, A. J. ed. *Transitional Justice and the Rule of Law in New Democracies*, Notre Dame, IN: University of Notre Dame Press, 1997.

Machcewicz, Paweł. 'Poland's Way of Coming to Terms with the Legacy of Communism'. Warsaw: Institute of Political Studies, *c*. 2006, http://www.eurhistxx.de/spip. php%3Farticle40&lang=en.html.

Machcewicz, Paweł and Persak, Krzysztof eds. *Wokół Jedwabnego*, Warsaw: IPN, 2002, 2 vols.

Majchrzak, Grzegorz. 'Obóz władzy w stanie wojennym', http://ipn.gov.pl/archiwalia/13-grudnia-1981-wprowadzenie-stanu-wojennego/grzegorz-majchrzak-oboz-wladzy-w-stanie-wojennym.

Mark, James. *The Unfinished Revolution. Making Sense of the Communist Past in Central-Eastern Europe*. New Haven: Yale University Press, 2010.

Markowski, Radosław. 'The Polish Parliamentary Election of 2015: A Free and Fair Election That Results in Unfair Political Consequences'. *West European Politics* 39, no. 6 (2016): 1311–22.

Mastny, Vojtech. 'The Soviet Non-Invasion of Poland in 1980/81 and the End of the Cold War', Working Paper No. 23, Woodrow Wilson Center, Cold War International History Project, September 1998, http://www.wilsoncenter.org/sites/default/files/ACFB35.PDF.

Matczak, Marcin. 'The Rule of Law in Poland: A Sorry Spectacle', VerfBlog, 1 March 2018, https://verfassungsblog.de/the-rule-of-law-in-poland-a-sorry-spectacle/.

Matczak, Marcin. 'An Eye for an Eye: Law as an Instrument of Revenge in Poland'. Verfassungsblog, 8 March 2017, https://verfassungsblog.de/an-eye-for-an-eye-law-as-an-instrument-of-revenge-in-poland/.

Mayer-Rieckh, A. and De Greiff, P. eds. *Justice as Prevention: Vetting Public Employees in Transitional Societies*. New York: Social Science Research Council, 2007.

Mażewski, Lech. *Problem legalności stanu wojennego z 12-13 grudnia 1981 r. Studium z historii prawa polskiego*. Warsaw: Wydawnictwo von Borowiecky, 2012.

Mazgaj, Marian. *Church and State in Communist Poland: A History, 1944–1989*. Jefferson, NC: McFarland, 2010.

Mazur, Dariusz and Żurek, Waldemar. 'So Called "Good Change" in the Polish System of the Administration of Justice', https://ruleoflaw.pl/so-called-good-change-in-the-polish-system-of-the-administration-of-justice/.

Michalak, Michał. 'Wildstein: Lustracja to już historia' (Interview with Bronisław Wildstein). *Interia Fakty*, 4 January 2016, http://fakty.interia.pl/tylko-u-nas/news-bronislaw-wildstein-lustracja-to-juz-historia,nId,1947745.

Michnik, Adam and Havel, Vaclav. 'Justice or Revenge?' *Journal of Democracy* 4, no. 1 (1993): 20–7.

Michnik, Adam and Marczyk, Agnieszka eds. *Against Anti-Semitism: An Anthology of Twentieth Century Polish Writings*. Oxford: Oxford University Press, 2017.

Michta, Andrew. *The Red Eagle: The Army in Polish* Politics, *1944–1988*. Stanford: Hoover Institution Press, c. 1990.

Milewicz, Ewa and Lizut, Mikołaj. 'Co zbóje, z którymi się spotkałem' (Interview with Alojzy Orszulik), *Gazeta Wyborcza*, 2 March 1999.

Millard, Frances. *Democratic Elections in Poland*. London: Routledge, 2010.

Millard, Frances. *Polish Politics and Society*. London: Routledge, 1999.

Millard, Frances. *The Anatomy of the New Poland*. Aldershot: Edward Elgar, 1994.

Miller, Zinaida. 'Effects of Invisibility: In Search of the "Economic" in Transitional Justice'. *International Journal of Transitional Justice* 2, no. 3 (2008): 266–91.

Misztal, Barbara. 'How Not to Deal with the Past: Lustration in Poland'. *Archives Europeennes De Sociologie* 40, no. 1 (1999): 31–55.

Młynarska-Sobaczewska, Anna. 'Odpowiedzialność państwa polskiego za mienie zabużańskie'. *Państwo i Prawo* 65, no. 2 (2010): 57–69.

Moran, John Paul. 'The Communist Torturers of Eastern Europe: Prosecute and Punish or Forgive and Forget?'. *Communist and Post-Communist Studies* 27, no. 1 (1994): 95–109.

Morawski, Jerzy. '"Monika" cenna dla służb'. *Rzeczpospolita*, 23 March 2005.

Morawski, Lech. 'Wspólnotowość jako wartość konstytucyjna – 31.03.2012.mp4'. https://www.youtube.com/watch?v=yKCRrayPK-I.

Müller, Jan-Werner ed. *Memory and Power in Post-War Europe, Studies in the Presence of the Past*. Cambridge: Cambridge University Press, 2002.

Musiał, Filip. 'Polityka historyczna czy historyczna świadomość? Działalność Instytutu Pamięci Narodowej'. *Horyzonty Polityki* 03 (2011): 149–70.

Muszyński, Mariusz. 'Krótka analiza opinii Komisji Weneckiej z 11 marca 2016 r, dotyczącej Trybunału Konstytucyjnego dla Pana Andrzeja Rzeplińskiego, Prezesa TK', Warsaw, 27 May 2016, http://wpolityce.pl/polityka/295429-nasz-news-prof-mariusz-muszynski-sedzia-tk-i-przedstawiciel-polski-w-komisji-weneckiej-miazdzy-jej-opinie.

Nagy, Rosemary. 'Transitional Justice as Global Project: Critical Reflections'. *Third World Quarterly* 29, no 2 (2008): 275–89.

Nalepa, Monika. 'Lustration as a Trust-Building Mechanism? Transitional Justice in Poland'. In *After Oppression: Transitional Justice in Latin America and Eastern Europe*, edited by Monica Serrano and Vesselin Popovski, 333–62. Washington, DC: Brookings Institute Press, 2012.

Nalepa, Monika. *Skeletons in the Closet. Transitional Justice in Post-Communist Europe*. Cambridge: Cambridge University Press, 2010.

Nalepa, Monika. 'To Punish the Guilty and Protect the Innocent: Comparing Truth Revelation Procedures'. *Journal of Theoretical Politics* 2, no. 2 (2008): 221–45.

Nalepa, Monika and Kurski, Jaroslaw. 'Prologue' to Andrzej Romanowski, *Roskosze lustracji, wybór publicystyki (1997–2007)*, Krakow: Universitas, 2007.

Nedelsky, Nadya. 'Divergent Responses to a Common Past? Transitional Justice in the Czech Republic and Slovakia'. *Theory and Society* 33 (2004): 65–115.

Ni Aoláin, F. 'Political Violence and Gender during Times of Transition'. *Columbia Journal of Gender and Law* 15, no. 3 (2006): 829–49.

Niżyńska, Joanna. 'The Politics of Mourning and the Crisis of Poland's Symbolic Language after April 10'. *East European Politics and Societies* 24, no. 4 (2010): 467–79.

Nowak, Andrzej. 'Dyskusja'. In *Pamięć i pytania o tożsamości. Polska. Ukraina*, edited by Tomasz Horbowski and Piotr Kosiewski, 71–4. Warsaw: Fundacja Batorego, 2013.

Nowinowski, Sławomir. 'Dziesięć lat IPN. Historycy czy architekci politycznej wyobraźni?' *Gazeta Wyborcza*, 21 March 2011.

Nowotnik, Norbert. 'Leszek Moczulski: przedłużanie mojej autolustracji odbieram jako odmawianie mi sprawiedliwości. Dzieje.pl', 16 August 2018, https://dzieje.pl/aktualnosci/leszek-moczulski-przedluzanie-mojej-autolustracji-odbieram-jako-odmawianie-mi.

Ochman, Ewa. *Post-Communist Poland – Contested Pasts and Future Identities*. London: Routledge, 2013.

O'Donnell, Guillermo. 'Challenges to Democratization in Brazil'. *World Policy Journal* 5, no. 2 (1988): 281–300.

Offe, Claus. 'Capitalism by Democratic Design? Democratic Theory Facing the Triple Transition in East Central Europe'. *Social Research* 58, no. 4 (1991): 865–92.

Offe, Claus and Poppe, Ulrike. 'Transitional Justice in the GDR and in Unified Germany'. In *Retribution and Reparation in the Transition to Democracy*, edited by Jon Elster, 239–75. Cambridge: Cambridge University Press, 2006.

Olczyk, Eliza and Waszkielewicz, Bernadeta. 'Ostry spór polityków o rolę Trybunału'. *Rzeczpospolita*, 14 May 2007.

Olszewski, Jan. *Przerywana Premiera*. Warsaw: BGW, 1992.

Oniszczuk, Jerzy. *Orzecznictwo Trybunału Konstytucyjnego w latach 1989–1996*. Warsaw: Wydawnictwo Sejmowe, 1998.

Orla-Bukowska, Annamaria. 'New Threads on an Old Loom. National Memory and Social Identity in PostWar and PostCommunist Poland'. In *The Politics of Memory in Postwar Europe*, edited by Richard Ned Lebow, Wulf Kansteiner and Claudio Fogu, 177–209. Durham, NC: Duke University Press, 2006.

Osiatyński, Wiktor. 'Poland'. In *Dealing with the Past. Truth and Reconciliation in South Africa*, edited by Alex Boraine, Janet Levy and Ronel Scheffer, 59–63. Cape Town, IDASA, 1997 (2nd ed).

Osiatyński, Wiktor. 'The Roundtable Talks in Poland'. In *The Roundtable Talks and the Breakdown of Communism*, edited by Jon Elster, 21–68. Chicago: University of Chicago Press, 1996.

Ostrowska, Katarzyna and Żuławnik, Mariusz. 'Niszczenie kartotek Biura "C" MSW w latach 1989-1990'. *Przegląd Archiwalny Instytutu Pamięci Narodowej* 4 (2011): 235–50.

Oświadczenie 22 Sędziów Trybunału Konstytucyjnego, 29 January 2020, https://oko.press/22-sedziow-tk-w-oswiadczeniu-bez-precedensu-pawlowicz-i-piotrowicz-w-skladzie-orzekajacym-to-naruszenie-prawa/.

Ouimet, Matthew. *The Rise and Fall of the Brezhnev Doctrine in Soviet Foreign Policy*. Chapel Hill: The University of North Carolina Press, 2003.

Paluch, Marta. 'Kraków. Wiceszef Komisji Majątkowej i były esbek zostali oskarżeni'. *Gazeta Krakowska*, 8 January 2015.

Panfil, Tomasz. 'Świat patrzy i milczy. Sprzeciw Polaków wobec zła'. *Gazeta Polska*, 27 September 2017.

Paradowska, Janina. 'Może być pięknie' (Interview with Jarosław Kaczyński). *Polityka*, 14 January 2006.

Paradowska, Janina and Baczyński, Jerzy. 'Cudze błędy' (Interview with Lech Wałęsa). *Polityka*, 14 January 1995.

Pawłowski, M. ed. *Spór o PRL*, Krakow: Znak, 1996.

Pech, Laurent and Scheppele, Kim Lane. 'Poland and the European Commission, Part III: Requiem for the Rule of Law', 3 March 2017, http://verfassungsblog.de/poland-and-the-european-commission-part-iii-requiem-for-the-rule-of-law/.

Pech, Laurent and Scheppele, Kim Lane. 'Poland and the European Commission, Part II: Hearing the Siren Song of the Rule of Law', 6 January 2017, https://verfassungsblog.de/poland-and-the-european-commission-part-ii-hearing-the-siren-song-of-the-rule-of-law/.

Pech, Laurent and Wachowiec, Patryk. '1095 Days Later: From Bad to Worse Regarding the Rule of Law in Poland (Part I)', 13 January 2019, https://verfassungsblog.de/1095-days-later-from-bad-to-worse-regarding-the-rule-of-law-in-poland-part-i/.

Peskin, Victor. *International Justice in Rwanda and the Balkans: Virtual Trials and the Struggle for State Cooperation.* New York: Cambridge University Press, 2008.

Pietkiewicz, Barbara. 'Sąd nad sędziami'. *Polityka*, 17 January 1998.

Pietraszewski, Marcin. 'Rodzina śląskiego miliardera uniewinniona. 'Nie prała brudnych pieniędzy'. *Gazeta Wyborcza*, 15 May 2015.

Pietraszewski, Marcin. 'Komisja majątkowa – skrywany raport rządu: Kościołowi ile się da'. *Gazeta Wyborcza*, 17 February 2012.

Pilawski, Krzysztof. 'Historia mitów i łupów'. *Przegląd*, 1 February 2009, from https://www.tygodnikprzeglad.pl/historia-mitow-lupow/.

Piotrowski, Tadeusz ed. *Genocide and Rescue in Wolyn: Recollections of the Ukrainian Nationalist Ethnic Cleansing Campaign Against the Poles During World War II.* Jefferson, NC: McFarland & Company, 2000.

Piotrowski, Tadeusz. *Poland's Holocaust: Ethnic Strife, Collaboration with Occupying Forces and Genocide in the Second Republic, 1918'1947.* Jefferson: McFarland & Company, 1990.

Podemski, Stanisław. 'Lustracja zlustrowana'. *Polityka*, 13 September 1997.

Podgórska, Joanna. 'Policja historyczna' (Interview with Andrzej Duda). *Polityka*, 18 May 2016.

Podgórska, Joanna. 'Jak czytać te teczki' (Interview with Andrzej Friszke). *Polityka*, 1 March 2016.

Pogany, Istvan. *Righting Wrongs in Eastern Europe.* Manchester: Manchester University Press, 1997.

Polonsky, Antony and Drukier, Bolesław eds. *The Beginnings of Communist Rule in Poland, December 1943–June 1945.* London: Routledge & Kegan Paul, 1980.

Polonsky, Antony and Michlic, Joanna B. eds. *The Neighbors Respond: The Controversy over the Jedwabne Massacre in Poland.* Princeton: Princeton University Press, 2003.

Ponczek, Eugeniusz. 'Polityka wobec pamięci versus polityka historyczna: aspekty semantyczny, aksjologiczny i merytoryczny w narracji polskiej', Łódź, 2013, http://przeglad.amu.edu.pl/wp-content/uploads/2013/09/pp-2013-2-007-022.pdf.

Posner, Eric and Vermeule, Adrian. 'Transitional Justice as Ordinary Justice'. *Harvard Law Review* 117, no. 3 (2004): 761–825.

Post-Conflict Justice (PCJ) Dataset. http://www.justice-data.com/pcj-dataset.

'Prałat Jankowski ujawnił nazwiska agentów SB'. *Życie Warszawy*, 27 September 2006.

'Prof. Sadurski: Pseudowyrok Trybunału w sprawie KRS to prymitywna ustawka'. *Gazeta Wyborcza*, 20 June 2017.

Przeciszewski, Marcin. 'Sąd gani abstrakcję w prokuraturze. Postępowanie ws. 47 ha dla zakonu elżbietanek zacznie się od nowa'. *Gazeta Wyborcza*, 5 September 2014.

Przeciszewski, Marcin. 'Komisja majątkowa – skrywany raport rządu: Kościołowi ile się da'. *Gazeta Wyborcza*, 17 February 2012.

Przeciszewski, Marcin. 'Pełen emocji częściowy zwrot majątków Kościelnych', 18 November 2011, http://ekai.pl/wydarzenia/temat_dnia/x48307/pelen-emocji-czesciowy-zwrot-majatkow-koscielnych/?print=1.

Pytlakowski, Piotr. 'Społeczny opór na ulicach polskich miast'. *Polityka*, 26 July 2017.

Pytlakowski, Piotr. 'Rycerz jednej prawdy'. *Polityka*, 13 April 2016.

Pytlakowski, Piotr. 'Zbrodnicza salowa'. *Polityka*, 8 July 2015.

Radziewicz, Piotr. 'Opinie dotyczące skutków wyroku Trybunału Konstytucyjnego z 11 Maja 2007 r. (Sygn. Akt K 2/07) w sprawie niezgodności z Konstytucją RP przepisów lustracyjnych'. *Przegląd Sejmowy* XV, no. 6 (2007): 143–66.

Raina, Peter. *Anatomia lynczu. Sprawa Ojca Konrada Hejmo.* Warsaw: von Borowiecki, 2006.

*Raport Rokity. Sprawozdanie Sejmowej Komisji Nadzwyczajnej do Zbadania Działalności MSW.* Kraków: Arcana, 2005.

'Raport Zespołu Ekspertów do spraw Problematyki Trybunału Konstytucyjnego z dnia 15 lipca 2016 r.', http://www.sejm.gov.pl/media8.nsf/files/ASEA-ADRKBW/%24File/Raport%20Zespo%C5%82u%20Ekspert%C3%B3w%20do%20spraw%20Problematyki%20Trybuna%C5%82u%20Konstytucyjnego.pdf.

Ratner, Steven and Adams, Jason. *Accountability for Human Rights Violations in International Law. Beyond the Nuremberg Legacy.* Oxford: Oxford University Press, 2001.

'Report of the Stefan Batory Foundation Legal Expert Group on the Impact of the Judiciary Reform in Poland in 2015–2018'. Warsaw: Batory Foundation, 5 March 2018, https://archiwumosiatynskiego.pl/wpis-w-debacie-en/attack-judiciary-in-poland-planned-and-successful-stefan-batory-foundation-legal-expert-group-reports/.

Reporters without Borders. *2019 Press Freedom Index*, https://rsf.org/en/ranking.

Ringelblum, Emanuel. *Polish–Jewish Relations during the Second World War.* Evanston: Northwestern University Press, 1992.

Rochowicz, Paweł. 'Emerytury dla byłych funkcjonariuszy SB nie będą wyższe'. *Rzeczpospolita*, 13 July 2016.

Romanowski, Andrzej. 'IPN, dziwoląg ponad państwem'. *Gazeta Wyborcza*, 11 September 2012.

Romanowski, Andrzej. *Roskosze lustracji, wybor publicystyki (1997-2007).* Krakow: Universitas, 2007.

Romanowski, Andrzej. 'Historia, kłamstwo i banał'. *Gazeta Wyborcza*, 15 July 2006.

Roszkowski, Wojciech. 'O potrzebie polskiej polityki historycznej'. In *Pamięc i Odpowiedzialność*, edited by Dariusz Gowin, Dariusz Karłowicz, Robert Kostro, Zdzisław Krasnodębski, Tomasz Merta, Łukasz Mikalski, Wojciech Roszkowski, Pawel Skibiński, Kazimierz Michal Ujazdowski and Jan Wróbel, 115–26. Krakow: Ośrodek Myśli Politycznej, Centrum Konserwatywne, nd.

Ryszka, Czesław. 'Rekompensata za kościelny majątek'. *Niedziela*, no. 25 (2008), http://www.niedziela.pl/artykul/85832/nd/Rekompensata-za-koscielny-majatek.

'Rzecznik Praw Obywatelskich dowiódł niespójnosci wyroku TK w sprawie lustracji' (Interview with Beata Michniewicz), Polskie Radio, 17 July 2007.

Sadurski, Wojciech. *Poland's Constitutional Breakdown.* Oxford: Oxford University Press, 2019.

Sadurski, Wojciech. 'I Criticized Poland's Government. Now It's Trying to Ruin Me'. *The Washington Post*, 21 May 2019, https://www.washingtonpost.com/opinions/2019/05/21/i-criticized-polands-government-now-its-trying-ruin-me/?utm_term=.66fd78291c33.

Sadurski, Wojciech. '"Decommunisation," "Lustration" and Constitutional Continuity: Dilemmas of Transitional Justice in Central Europe'. European University Institute, 2003, Badia Fiesolana, San Dominico, Italy, http://cadmus.eui.eu/dspace/bitstream/1814/1869/2/law03-15.pdf.

Safjan, Marek. 'Transitional Justice: The Polish Example, the Case of Lustration'. *European Journal of Legal Studies* 1, no. 2 (2007): 235-53.

Sanecka, Joanna. 'Polityka historyczna partii Prawo i Sprawiedliwość: założenia i realizacja'. *Athenaeum. Polskie Studia Politologiczne* 19 (2008): 54-66, http://www.athenaeum.umk.pl/numery/19.pdf.

Sawicka, Joanna. 'Nowelizacja ustawy o IPN weszła już w życie. Do Instytutu wkracza polityka'. *Polityka*, 16 June 2016.

Semka, Piotr. 'Kto się schowa za plecami Ewy Milewicz?'. *Rzeczpospolita*, 9 March 2007.

Siedlecka, Ewa. 'Dyscyplinowanie sędziego Stępnia'. *Polityka*, 11 May 2018.

Siedlecka, Ewa. 'W nowej KRS prawo znów ustąpiło przed siłą'. *Polityka*, 27 April 2018.

Siedlecka, Ewa. 'Trybunał na życzenie'. *Polityka*, 27 June 2017.

Siedlecka, Ewa. 'Sądy: być albo nie być'. *Polityka*, 8 February 2008.

Siedlecka, Ewa. 'Prawo kulą u nogi Prawa i Sprawiedliwości'. *Gazeta Wyborcza*, 21 January 2006.

Sierchuła, R. '"Wizja Polski w koncepcjach ideologów Organizacji Polskiej w latach 1944–1945'. In *Narodowcy. Myśl polityczna i społeczna obozu narodowego w Polsce w latach 1944-1947*, edited by L. Kulińska, M. Orłowski and R. Sierchuła, 134-40. Warsaw: Wydawnictwo Naukowe PWN, 2001.

Šipulová, Katarína and Hloušek, Vít. 'Different Paths of Transitional Justice in the Czech Republic, Slovakia and Poland'. *World Political Science Review* 9, no. 1 (2013): 31-69.

Skaner. 'Komisja Michnika'. *Wprost*, 20 February 2005.

Skapska, Grazyna. 'Paying for Past Injustices and Creating New Ones: On Property Rights Restoration in Poland as an Element of the Unfinished Transformation'. In *Legal Institutions and Collective Memories*, edited by Susanne Karsted, 260-80. Oxford and Portland, Oregon: Hart Publishing, 2009.

Śmiechowski, Kamil. '"Życzliwa krytyka, nie krytykanctwo" – Prof. Rafał Stobiecki o IPN-ie' (Interview with Rafał Stobiecki). 18 December 2010, HISTMAG.org., https://histmag.org/Zyczliwa-krytyka-nie-krytykanctwo-Prof.-Rafal-Stobiecki-o-IPN-ie-4993.

Snopkiewicz, Jacek. *Teczki, czyli widma bezpieki*. Warsaw: BGW, 1992.

Snyder, Timothy. 'Memory of Sovereignty and Sovereignty over Memory: Poland, Lithuania and Ukraine'. In *Memory and Power in Post-War Europe. Studies in the Presence of the Past*, edited by Jan-Werner Müller, 39-58. Cambridge: Cambridge University Press, 2002.

Snyder, Timothy. 'To Resolve the Ukrainian Question Once and for All: The Ethnic Cleansing of Ukrainians in Poland, 1943–1947'. *Journal of Cold War Studies* 1, no. 2 (1999): 86-120.

Snyder, Tim and Vachudova, M. 'Are Transitions Transitory? Two Types of Political Change in Eastern Europe since 1989'. *East European Politics and Societies* 11, no. 1 (1997): 1-35.

Solomon, Peter H., Jr. ed. *Reforming Justice in Russia, 1864-1996: Power, Culture, and the Limits of Legal Order*. Armonk, NY: M.E. Sharpe, 1997.

Solomon, Peter H., Jr. *Soviet Criminal Justice under Stalin*. Cambridge: Cambridge University Press, 1996.

Stan, Lavinia. *Transitional Justice in Post-Communist Romania: The Politics of Memory*. Cambridge: Cambridge University Press, 2013.

Stan, Lavinia. 'Vigilante Justice in Post-Communist Europe'. *Communist and Post-Communist Studies* 44, no 4 (2011): 319-27.

Stan, Lavinia. 'Poland'. In *Transitional Justice in Eastern Europe and the Former Soviet Union: Reckoning with the Communist Past*, edited by Lavinia Stan, 76-101. London: Routledge, 2010.

Stan, Lavinia and Nedelsky, Nadya. 'Post-Communist Transitional Justice Predictors', SciTopics, 9 February 2009, http://www.scitopics.com/Post_Communist_Transitional_ Justice_Predictors.html.

Stankiewicz, Andrzej. 'Sędzia z PiS zarzuca Julii Przyłębskiej łamanie prawa', onenet.pl, 16 October 2019, https://wiadomosci.onet.pl/tylko-w-onecie/sedzia-jaroslaw-wyrembak-zada-dymisji-prezes-tk-julii-przylebskiej/ddnn9yg.

Stankiewicz, Andrzej. 'Wałęsa wciąż bohaterem'. *Rzeczpospolita*, 28 February 2016.

Stankiewicz, Andrzej, Szułdrzyński, Michał and Jabłoński, Paweł. 'Biznes często to przystań ludzi PRL' (Interview with Jarosław Kaczyński). *Rzeczpospolita*, 4 September 2013.

Stanley, Ben. 'A New Populist Divide? Correspondences of Supply and Demand in the 2015 Polish Parliamentary Elections'. *East European Politics and Societies* 33, no. 1 (2019): 17–43.

Stanley, Ben. 'Confrontation by Default and Confrontation by Design: Strategic and Institutional Responses to Poland's Populist Coalition Government'. *Democratization* 23, no. 2 (2016): 263–82.

Stefańska, Blanka J. 'Zatarcie skazania z mocy prawa'. *Prokurator i Prawo*, no. 2 (2001): 62–86, http://www.pg.gov.pl/numer-2-748/numer-2-730.html.

Stinchcombe, Arthur L. 'Lustration as a Problem of the Social Basis of Constitutionalism'. *Law & Social Inquiry* 20, no. 1 (1995): 245–73.

Stobiecki, Rafał. 'Historians Facing Politics of History. The Case of Poland'. In *Past in the Making. Historical Revisionism in Central Europe after 1989*, edited by Michał Kopeč, 179–92. Budapest: Central European University Press, 2008.

Stola, Dariusz. 'Poland's Institute of National Remembrance: A Ministry of Memory?' In *The Convolutions of Historical Politics*, edited by A. Miller and M. Lipman, 45–58. Budapest: Central European University Press, 2012.

Subotić, Małgorzata. 'Nie biorę pod uwagę konsekewncji politycznych' (Interview with Jerzy Stępień). *Rzeczpospolita*, 31 March–1 April 2007.

Suchodolska, Mira. 'Gangsterski skok na IPN. Prezes będzie figurantem'. *Gazeta Prawna*, 10 July 2016.

Supreme Court of the Republic of Poland. 'Opinion on the White Paper on the Reform of the Polish Judiciary', Warsaw, 16 March 2018, http://www.sn.pl/aktualnosci/SiteAssets/ Lists/Wydarzenia/EditForm/Supreme%20Court%20-%20Opinion%20on%20the%20 white%20paper%20on%20the%20Reform%20of%20the%20Polish%20Judiciary.pdf.

Szczerbiak, Aleks. *Politicising the Communist Past: The Politics of Truth Revelation in Post-Communist Poland* (BASEES/Routledge Series on Russian and East European Studies). London: Taylor and Francis, 2018.

Szczerbiak, Aleks. 'Communist-Forgiving or Communist-Purging? Public Attitudes towards Transitional Justice and Truth Revelation in Post-1989 Poland'. *Europe-Asia Studies* 69, no. 2 (2017): 325–47.

Szczerbiak, Aleks. 'An Anti-Establishment Backlash That Shook Up the Party System? The October 2015 Polish Parliamentary Election'. *European Politics and Society* 18, no. 4 (2017): 404–27.

Szczerbiak, Aleks. 'Why Did Poland Adopt a Radical Lustration Law in 2006?', University of Sussex, SEI Working Paper No 139, 2016.

Szczerbiak, Aleks. 'Dealing with the Communist Past or the Politics of the Present? Lustration in Post-Communist Poland'. *Europe-Asia Studies* 54, no. 4 (2002): 553–72.

Szegda, Bogdan. 'Nie zgadzam się z wyrokiem ws. Grudnia'70'. *Dziennik Bałtycki*, 20 April 2013, http://www.dziennikbaltycki.pl/artykul/873857,nie-zgadzam-sie-z-wyrokiem-ws-grudnia70,id,t.html.

Szeligowska, Dorota. 'The Dynamics of Polish Patriotism after 1989: Concepts, Debates, Identities', PhD thesis, Central European University, Budapest 2014, http://www.etd. ceu.hu/2014/szeligowska_dorota.pdf.

Szleszkowski, Łukasz, Thannhäuser, Agata, Szwagrzyk, Krzysztof and Jurek, Tomasz. 'The Possibility of Establishing Causes of Death on the Basis of the Exhumed Remains of Prisoners Executed during the Communist Regime in Poland: The Exhumations at Powązki Military Cemetery in Warsaw'. *International Journal of Legal Medicine* 129, no. 4 (2015): 801–6.

Szpala, Iwona and Zubik, Małgorzata. 'Jak mecenas Robert Nowaczyk reprywatyzuje nieruchomości w Warszawie'. *Gazeta Wyborcza*, 17 October 2016.

Szpala, Iwona and Zubik, Małgorzata. 'Układ warszawski. Czy reprywatyzacja w stolicy zatrzęsie polską polityką?' *Gazeta Wyborcza*, 20 August 2016.

Szubarczyk, P. 'Pora oczyścić dom ze śmieci', reprinted from *Nasz Dziennik*, 14–15 April 2007, http://archiwum.dlapolski.pl/informacje/Czytaj-art-1921.html.

Szuleka, Małgorzata and Kalisz, Maciej. 'Disciplinary Proceedings against Judges and Prosecutors'. Warsaw: Helsinki Foundation for Human Rights, 2019, http://www.hfhr. pl/wp-content/uploads/2019/02/HFHR_Disciplinary-proceedings-against-judges-and-prosecutors.pdf.

Szuleka, Małgorzata, Wolny, Marcin, and Szwed, Marcin. 'The Constitutional Crisis in Poland 2015–2016'. Warsaw: Helsinki Foundation for Human Rights, August 2016, http://www.hfhr.pl/wp-content/uploads/2016/09/HFHR_The-constitutional-crisis-in-Poland-2015-2016.pdf.

Szułdrzyński, Michał. 'Polacy nie zmienili opinii na temat Lecha Wałęsy'. Rzeczpospolita, 29 February 2016.

'Szykuje się lustracja w urzędach? "Solidarność" będzie wnioskować do Szydło'. *Wprost*, 24 March 2017.

Teitel, Ruti. *Transitional Justice*. Oxford: Oxford University Press, 2003.

Terlikowski, Tomasz. *Odwaga prawdy. Spór o lustrację w polskim Kościele*. Warsaw: Prószynski i S-ka, 2007.

Torańska, Teresa. *My*. Warsaw: Most, 1994.

Traba, Robert. 'Polityka wobec historii: kontrowersje i perspektywy'. Teksty Drugie 1-2 (2010), Instytut Badań Literackich, Centrum Humanistyki Cyfrowej: 1-21, http://rcin. org.pl/Content/48995/WA248_66069_P-I-2524_traba-polityka.pdf.

Tucker, Aviezer. 'Rough Justice. Rectification in Post-Authoritarian and Post-Totalitarian Regimes'. In *Retribution and Reparation in the Transition to Democracy*, edited by Jon Elster, 276–98. Cambridge: Cambridge University Press, 2006.

Tyszka, Stanisław. 'Restytucja mienia i pamięć zbiorowa w Polsce i w Czechach po 1989 roku'. In *Normy, Dewiacje i Kontrola Społeczna*, edited by Joanna Zamecka, 217–36. Warsaw: University of Warsaw, 2012 (no. 13).

Urząd do Spraw Kombatantów i Osób Represjonowanych. 'Założenia nowelizacji (reformy) prawa kombatanckiego', Warsaw, 30 November 2006, http://radalegislacyjna. gov.pl/sites/default/files/dokumenty/projekt_ustawy_56.pdf.

Voiculescu, Aurora. *Human Rights and Political Justice in Post-Communist Eastern Europe*: *Prosecuting History*. Lewiston, NY and Queenston, ON: Edwin Mellen Press, 2000.

Walc, Jan. 'Z dziejów infamii w Polsce'. *Wokanda*, 17 February 1991.

Walicki, Andrzej. 'Transitional Justice and the Political Struggles of Post-Communist Poland'. In *Transitional Justice and the Rule of Law in New Democracies*, edited by A. J. McAdams, 185–237. Notre Dame, IN: University of Notre Dame Press, 1997.

Walicki, Andrzej. 'The Three Traditions in Polish Patriotism'. In *Polish Paradoxes*, edited by Stanisław Gomułka and Antony Polonsky, 21–39. London: Routledge, 1990.

Walker, Shaun. 'Holocaust Historians Divided over Warsaw Ghetto Museum', *The Observer*, 22 June 2019.

Welsh, Helga A. 'Dealing with the Communist Past. Central and East European Experiences after 1990'. *Europe-Asia Studies* 48, no. 3 (1996): 413–28.

Widacki, Jan. *Czego nie powiedział Generał Kiszczak*. Warsaw: BGW, 1992.

Wildstein, Bronisław. 'Cały ten antylustracyjny zgiełk', *Rzeczpospolita*, 14 January 2005.

Williams, Kieran. 'Lustration as the Securitization of Democracy in Czechoslovakia and the Czech Republic'. *Journal of Communist Studies and Transition Politics*, 19, no. 4 (2001): 1–24.

Williams, Kieran, Fowler, Brigid and Szczerbiak, Aleks. 'Explaining Lustration in Central Europe: A "Post-Communist Politics" Approach'. *Democratization* 12, no. 1 (2005): 22–43.

Władyka, Wiesław. 'Czym była PRL – niedokończona debata', *Polityka*, 15 July 2014.

Wnuk, Rafał, Poleszak, Sławomir, Jaczyńska, Agnieszka and Śladecka, Magdalena eds. *Atlas polskiego podziemia niepodległościowego 1944–1956*. Warsaw: IPN, 2007.

Wójcik, Anna. 'Prof. Mirosław Wyrzykowski: Pozakonstytucyjna zmiana ustroju staje się faktem. O tym trzeba debatować, panie Prezydencie' (Interview), OKO.press, 26 August 2017, https://oko.press/prof-miroslaw-wyrzykowski-pozakonstytucyjna-zmiana-ustroju-staje-sie-faktem-o-tym-trzeba-debatowac-panie-prezydencie/.

Woleński, Jan. *Lustracja jako zwierciadło*. Krakow: Universitas, 2007.

Wolff-Powęska, Anna. 'Polityka historyczna. Polskie spory o historię i pamięć'. Paper presented at the Conference Czym jest mała ojczyzna, Collegium Polonicum, 18–19 November 2006, from http://www.transodra-online.net/pl/node/1256.

'Wyciąg z opracowania Komisji Analiz i Prognoz Społeczno-Politycznych na temat konsekewncji sukcesu wyborczego opozycji przedstawiony członkom Biura Politycznego 20 czerwca 1989 r'. In *Polska 1986-1989: koniec systemu*, edited by Antoni Dudek and Andrzej Friszke, 281–4. Warsaw: Wydawnictwo Trio. Instytut Studiow Politycznych Polskiej Akademii Nauk, 2002, vol. 3, Dokument 50.

Zajadło, Jerzy. 'Fałszywość hasła "demokracja, a nie sędziokracja" – analiza filozoficzno-prawna'. Konstytucyjny.pl, https://konstytucyjny.pl/falszywosc-hasla-demokracja-a-nie-sedziokracja-analiza-filozoficzno-prawna-jerzy-zajadlo/.

Zalasiński, Tomasz. 'Ślepa dezubekizacja i domniemanie winy'. *Gazeta Prawna. pl*, 11 September 2019, https://serwisy.gazetaprawna.pl/emerytury-i-renty/artykuly/1429588,bledy-ustawy-dezubekizacyjnej.html.

Zalewska, Luiza. 'Świadkowie zadowoleni z zeznań'. *Rzeczpospolita*, 17 January 2005.

Zdrojewski, Bogdan. 'Dajmy Polakom być dumnymi ze swojej historii'. *Gazeta Wyborcza*, 4 November 2008.

Zdziennicki, Bohdan. 'Badanie konstytucyjności stanu wojennego. Uwagi na tle wyroku Trybunału Konstytucyjnego z dnia 16 marca 2011 r'. *Przegląd Prawa Konstytucyjnego*, 2012/Nr 3 (11), http://www.marszalek.com.pl/przegladprawakonstytucyjnego/ppk11/07.pdf.

Żebrowski, Leszek. *Narodowe Siły Zbrojne. Dokumenty. Struktury. Personalia*. Warsaw: Burchard Edition, 1994.

Ziobro, Zbigniew. 'Zbigniew Ziobro: są propozycje reformy wymiaru sądownictwa, ale problemem jest TK'. *WP Wiadomości*, http://wiadomosci.wp.pl/kat,1342,title,Zbigniew-Ziobro-sa-propozycje-reformy-wymiaru-sadownictwa-ale-problemem-jest-TK,wid,18500270,wiadomosc.html?&ticaid=1189ea.

Zolkos, Magdalena. 'The Conceptual Nexus of Human Rights and Democracy in the Polish Lustration Debates 1989-97'. *Journal of Communist Studies and Transition Politics* 22, no. 2 (June 2006): 228-48.

Zubik, Małgorzata. 'Reprywatyzacja. Andrzej Waltz, mąż prezydent Warszawy, zeznaje w sprawie Noakowskiego 16'. *Gazeta Wyborcza*, 5 December 2017.

Zubrzycki, Geneviève. 'Polish Mythology and the Traps of Messianic Martyrology'. In *National Myths: Constructed Pasts, Contested Presents*, edited by Gérard Bouchard, 110-32. London: Routledge, 2013.

Zybertowicz, Andrzej. *W Uścisku Tajnych Służb*. Komorow, Poland: Antyk, 1993.

Zybertowicz, Andrzej. 'Strategie unieważniania prawdy: na przykładzie dyskusji wokół książki Sławomira Cenckiewicza i Piotra Gontarczyka o Lechu Wałęsie'. *Oblicza Przeszłości*, Bydgoszcz 2011, 431-66, http://i.wp.pl/a/f/pdf/36348/zybertowicz,_strategie_uniewazniania_prawdy.pdf.

# Index

www.ingramcontent.com/pod-product-compliance
Lightning Source LLC
Chambersburg PA
CBHW050413280326
41932CB00013BA/1841